ROARING '20S FASHIONS

Jazz

Schiffer Publishing Ltd

4880 Lower Valley Road, Atglen, PA 19310 USA

SUSAN LANGLEY

WITH PHOTOGRAPHY BY JOHN DOWLING

Dedication

This book is dedicated to my grandchildren—Matt, Marysa, Grace, Dan, Sara, Joey, Peter, Michaela, John, Teresa, John Paul, and Billy.

Acknowledgments

Heartfelt thanks to my family and friends, fellow antique clothes lovers, and history buffs. To Steven Porterfield, Ken Weber, Janet Schwarz, Doris Butler, Amanda Bury, T.W. Conroy, and Margaret Brzostek for loan of their lovely items. Thanks to my husband, Joe, my walking history encyclopedia; to Lorenzo State Historic Site; to Decoeyes for their splendid job of mannequin restoration; to Emmanuel Voucher for French translations; and to Karl at Microtech for helping a computer illiterate.

And last, but not least, thanks to the original creators of the clothes—and the flapper owners who wore them with such panache!

Library of Congress Cataloging-in-Publication Data:

Langley, Susan.
  Roaring '20s fashions : jazz / Susan Langley ; with photography by John Dowling.
    p. cm.
  ISBN 0-7643-2319-9 (hardcover)
1. Clothing and dress—History—20th century. 2. Fashion—History—20th century. 3. Nineteen twenties. I. Title.

GT596.L36 2005
391'.009'04—dc22

2005013956

Designed by John P. Cheek
Cover Design by Bruce Waters
Type set in Bodoni Bd BT/Aldine 721 BT

ISBN: 0-7643-2319-9
Printed in China
1 2 3 4

Published by Schiffer Publishing Ltd.
4880 Lower Valley Road
Atglen, PA 19310
Phone: (610) 593-1777; Fax: (610) 593-2002
E-mail: Info@schifferbooks.com

For the largest selection of fine reference books on this and related subjects, please visit our web site at
www.schifferbooks.com
We are always looking for people to write books on new and related subjects. If you have an idea for a book please contact us at the above address.

This book may be purchased from the publisher.
Include $3.95 for shipping.
Please try your bookstore first.
You may write for a free catalog.

In Europe, Schiffer books are distributed by
Bushwood Books
6 Marksbury Ave.
Kew Gardens
Surrey TW9 4JF England
Phone: 44 (0) 20 8392-8585;
Fax: 44 (0) 20 8392-9876
E-mail: info@bushwoodbooks.co.uk
Free postage in the U.K., Europe; air mail at cost.

Contents

Introduction

On the wings of white doves of peace *THE TWENTIES* arrived…signaling an end to the terrors of World War I's trenches, and the equally deadly epidemic of Spanish influenza that came home with the soldiers. The world breathed a sigh of relief as this new decade of peace and prosperity arrived—it was a time for people to rejoice, to let their hair down, kick up their heels in an exuberant Charleston and *celebrate*! A new "modern" era had been born, with Art Deco its spirit and jazz its soul!

…On the wings of white doves of peace, THE TWENTIES arrives! Photograph, "All Decked Out for the Parade," ca. 1920-22.

Though Art Deco had begun with the new century, it took its name from the famous 1925 exhibit in Paris, the "*Exposition Internationale des Arts Decoratifs et Industriels Modernes.*" Art Deco had previously been known as *Art Moderne*. Though Art Deco is often referred to as a "Movement" today, it might be more accurately described as a feeling of modernism that captured the spirit of its age…and this new, modern feeling pervaded every aspect of life in the twenties—it was evident not only in art and architecture, but of course, in *FASHION*! It banished the ornate opulence of La Belle Epoch and replaced it with a streamlined, modern look that seemed to be always in motion as it speed towards the future. Art Deco has many facets; it's not one specific style, but encompasses futuristic visions as well as echoes of the past updated to the new century. New Cubist and Surrealist art coexists with the ancient art of the far east, Egypt, Africa, and Mexico—with art of the Renaissance and the Rococo periods thrown in for good measure!

This superb tapestry purse captures the essence of Art Deco with its wild and futuristic designs!

Music and Dancing—The Spice of Life!

The twenties was dubbed "The Jazz Age" by F. Scott Fitzgerald, whose bittersweet novels delineate the era. The Jazz Age is romanticized as a decade of frenetic FUN—with jazz an insatiable lust, and dancing a mania. Jazz, a child of ragtime, blues, and gospel, was a joyous, exciting new sound, a sound that celebrated life. Jazz originally meant "sex" in Creole, and it *was* sexy! Jazz originated in New Orleans in the late nineteenth century; played by musicians at parades and carnivals and in "houses of ill repute," it spread via river boats up the Mississippi to St. Louis, Chicago, and then to New York. Jazz traveled to Europe with the troops in 1917. Jazz proclaimed the soul of the twenties, not only with live bands but also as it blared from radios and phonographs—brash, confident, insouciant!

Since the new music set one's feet a-tapping, it was impossible not to get up and dance! Favorite dances of the first half of the decade include the comparatively sedate *fox trot*, the tempestuous *tango*, and the scandalous *"shimmy."*

The tango, a South American dance, originated in Argentina ("Tango" means *"to touch"* in Portuguese.) During the teens, it was popularized by the icons of dance, Vernon and Irene Castle. In 1912, the Castles danced the tango at an exhibition in Paris, where it created such a sensation that it became *"the dance"* of that decade. Though many thought the tango too seductive at the time, the Castles' version was mild compared to the tango of the twenties—in 1921, Rudolph Valentino shocked and titillated silent film fans as he danced

A young married couple tunes in their brand new radio to begin an evening of entertainment! (Snapshot, ca. 1925)

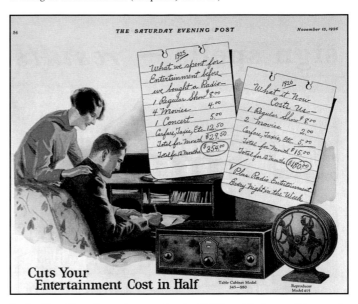

Radio "Cuts Your Entertainment Cost in Half," as this Stewart-Warner ad in *The Saturday Evening Post* proclaims. (November 13, 1926)

a torrid *apache* tango in the film that rocketed him to stardom, *The Four Horsemen of the Apocalypse*. Rudy's partner wore only a tantalizingly draped Spanish shawl, and every woman who saw the film immediately went out and bought one!

The shimmy, a dance said to have Haitian Voodoo origins, also became a favorite in the teens—it was a sexy dance that involved shaking the shoulders, hips, and whole body, so of course, it remained popular into the twenties. Ziegfeld star Gilda Gray was famous for her shimmy; in the 1922 Follies, Gilda shimmied so seductively that when a man from the audience called out, "What's that dance?", Gilda yelled back, "I'm shaking my chemise—or 'shimmy!'" Jazz great Fats Waller immortalized the shimmy in June 1923, with his recording of "I Wish I Could Shimmy Like My Sister Kate": "Oh, I wish I could shimmy like my sister Kate, she shimmies like jelly on a plate"! (written by Armand Piron, 1919). In addition, Irving Berlin wrote a priceless shimmy song that lamented the coming of Prohibition, "You Cannot Make Your Shimmy Shake on Tea!" (copyright 1919; Prohibition would become effective in January 1920).

"Gloria's out...she's dancing somewhere...She dances all afternoon and all night until I think she's going to wear herself to a shadow..." F. Scott Fitzgerald, *The Beautiful and the Damned*, 1922. As this charming Victrola ad illustrates, dancing was an insatiable craze. (July 1920 ad in *Vogue*)

"Cutting in" at dances was an accepted practice—guys constantly cut in to dance with the most popular girls. In his short story, "Bernice Bobs her Hair" (1920), F. Scott Fitzgerald explains cutting in: "No matter how beautiful or brilliant a girl may be, the reputation of not being frequently cut in on makes her position at a dance unfortunate ...youth in this jazz-nourished generation is temperamentally restless, and the idea of fox-trotting more than one full fox trot with the same girl is distasteful, not to say odious..."

This popular Irving Berlin tune was the hit of the Ziegfeld Follies of 1919. It laments the coming of Prohibition on January 16, 1920. *"...On the day they introduced their Prohibition laws - They just went and ruin'd the greatest Shimmy dancer because - You cannot make your shimmy shake on tea - it simply can't be done, you'll find your shaking ain't taking...!"*

The first half of the twenties might be considered a "warm-up" for the "no holds barred" second half of the decade—both in lifestyles and fashion, the decade seems divided neatly in two. Both the Black Bottom and the famous (or infamous) Charleston became the rage around mid-decade, when this Party of the Century was in full swing. The Black Bottom, originally from New Orleans, was considered a scandalous dance—dancers slapped their bottoms and shook their torsos while hopping back and forth! Jelly Roll Morton's version, "The Black Bottom Stomp" (1919) created a sensation. The dance of the decade, the Charleston (named for the South Carolina city where it originated), spread like wildfire after it was featured in *Runnin Wild*, the 1923 all-black Broadway musical (see page 182).

Life had changed drastically since the beginning of the new century. America had risen to world power during World War I and the war had changed all aspects of life...the way people thought as well as the way they lived. Some two million doughboys returned from the front, many disillusioned and disheartened, prompting Gertrude Stein's remark to Ernest Hemingway, "You are all a 'Lost Generation'", a phrase that would live on in memories as the soldiers came home determined to live life to its fullest.

Zany stunts like flagpole sitting livened up life in the twenties (Alvin "Shipwreck" Kelly set a record for spending twenty-three days, seven hours perched on his pole, never sleeping for more than twenty minutes at a time). Dance marathons were all the rage; one California couple made headlines as they tangoed all the way from Santa Monica to Los Angeles! On the east coast, marathon dancers Charlestoned down Fifth Avenue. People participated in bicycle marathons and cross-country auto trips! Other crazes included miniature golf, the game of mah jongg, an import from China, and crossword puzzles (so popular stores sold crossword dresses, scarves, shoes and even stockings).

The twenties was also a decade of "youth takeover"— music, art, and fashions, as well as attitudes, were youth oriented...it was *fashionable* to be young! Both female and male physiques followed Art Deco's streamlined look as "Slim is In" and voluptuous Edwardian curves vanished. During the twenties, sports were of utmost importance; to keep their svelte figures, more people than ever before were participating in various sports, with golf, swimming, and tennis being the most popular. Spectator sports were also wildly popular, and stars like Babe Ruth were both worshiped and emulated.

"Flaming Youth" spoke a zany new language: "slang"! In 1922, *The Flapper* magazine offered these intriguing examples:

> *"Cat's meow* - great; *Cat's Pajamas, Monkey's Eyebrows, Frog's Eyebrows* - anything good. *Bee's knees* and *The Berries* - wonderful. *Ducky or Duck's Quack* - the best ever. *Hen Coop* - a beauty parlor. *Apple Sauce* - flattery. *Stilts* – legs. *Dogs* - feet. *Mug* - osculate or kiss. *Neck and Pet* - make out. *Petter* - a lovable person or one who enjoys to caress. *Petting pantry* - movie. *Goof* - sweetie. *Snugglepup* - a man fond of petting and petting parties. *Bell Polisher* - a young man addicted to lingering in the vestibule at 1 a.m. *Bank's Closed* - no petting, no kisses. *"Scram," "Go fly a kite"* and *"23 Skidoo"* all meant get lost. *Given the Air* - snubbed, stood up. *Mustard Plaster* - unwelcome guy who sticks around. *Carrying the torch* - unrequited love. *Eye-opener* - marriage. *Handcuff* - engagement ring. *Out on Parole* - Divorced. *Flat tire* - a boring person. *Hard-boiled* - mean, callous. *Heebie-jeebies* - nervous. *Billboard* - a flashy man or woman. *Whangdoodle* - Jazz band music. *Crasher* - one who goes to parties uninvited."*

Warren G. Harding was elected President in 1920; he claimed to have "no high-falutin' ideas" like "stuffed shirt" Woodrow Wilson. Harding was elected on a "Return to Normalcy" ticket. When Harding died in office in 1923 (some say due to the notorious Teapot Dome scandal), vice-president Calvin Coolidge became president, "Silent Cal's" credo being "The Business of America is Business." Coolidge remained in office until 1929, when the hapless Herbert Hoover was elected.

America was quickly becoming urbanized with just over half of its population living in towns and cities by 1920; many left their farms and moved to the cities for better incomes...and more exciting lives. Rural conservatism was bombarded with an avalanche of modern ideas— from silent films, radios, newspapers, and magazines, to "city slickers" who invaded their bucolic fields in the eight million automobiles that were on the road by 1920.

Modern Conveniences Make Housework a Breeze

In the twenties, many new modern conveniences began to make lives easier; by the end of WWI, for example, over thirty percent of homes had electricity. Even out in the country, electric lights were replacing kerosene lamps; electric refrigerators were replacing the old "ice boxes"; electric stoves were replacing wood or coal stoves; and indoor bathrooms were making the proverbial "trip to the outhouse" a memory. New electric appliances—washing machines, sewing machines, vacuum cleaners, irons, and toasters—lightened daily workloads and provided more time for leisure activities. There was better communication too, as people now chatted on "candlestick" rotary-dial telephones (telephones were half a century old; by 1920 there were approximately twelve telephones for every one hundred people). Office equipment was more efficient, with better typewriters and dictating machines. Automobiles, trains, and airplanes took people wherever they wanted to go; passenger air travel began in the mid-twenties and the grandparents of the Jet Set soon made the world a smaller place.

The price of this new all-steel refrigerator—the small-family model—is now **$215** AT THE FACTORY

New electric "refrigerators" are beginning to replace the old "ice boxes," and soon The Iceman Doesn't Cometh anymore. Just $215! (Ad, ca. 1925)

Discard your brooms, brushes and beaters—they are out-of-date. Get a Premier and

Do it with air!

"Do it with air," extols the virtues of the new electric Premier vacuum cleaner! (Ad, September 1920, *Ladies Home Journal*)

"I can run this little frock up in no time on my new electric sewing machine," this flapper beauty tells her doting husband! (Photo postcard, ca. 1922)

Presenting "The Eden" new electric copper tub washer! Though the machine washed the clothes, they had to be "wrung out" by putting them through the wringer attachment on top. (Ad, August 1920, *Ladies Home Journal*)

"Mary, I'll take these dainty things to my room and do them there with this little Hotpoint…You never have to lift this iron—simply tip it onto the attached rest…think how you are accustomed to Lift, Lift, Lift!" Note the "modern" stove with a new electric toaster on top. (Ad, August 1920, *Ladies Home Journal*)

The Fitzgeralds, A Quintessential Twenties' Couple

Legendary faces delineated the decade—musicians, authors, actors and actresses, sports heroes…and bootleggers. You'll meet many in these pages, like author F. Scott Fitzgerald who not only delineated the high life of the Jazz Age in his bittersweet novels but actually *lived it!*

Francis Scott Key Fitzgerald was named for a distant relation—the composer of our national anthem, "The Star Spangled Banner." A young man with a shining future and a lot of talent, Scott set off for Princeton in 1913, where he soon began writing for the *Princeton Tiger*. In 1918, Scott was a second lieutenant in the Army stationed near Montgomery, Alabama, where he met beautiful eighteen-year-old Zelda Sayre and fell madly in love with her. Zelda at first refused his proposals, however, feeling his prospects were dim. She relented in 1920 after Scribner's published *This Side of Paradise*, in which Fitzgerald immortalized the era's famous "flapper" as well as the "lost generation" of postwar men. The novel sold three thousand copies in three days, making him an instant celebrity.

Scott and Zelda were married on April 3, 1920 in St. Patrick's cathedral, and the young couple began to live in the decade's fastest lane. Their many zany stunts made them Jazz Age legends: Zelda often danced on tables as they caroused in trendy New York speaks; after one night of speak-hopping, Scott was spotted riding down 5th Avenue on top of a taxi. Late one evening, both he and Zelda decided to go for a dip and both jumped into the Plaza's fountain clad in full evening dress. Reflecting on these times, Scott wrote: "I began to bawl because I had everything I wanted and knew I would never be so happy again!"

In *The Beautiful and The Damned* (1922), Scott described lives of dissipation much like their own. In 1924, the Fitzgeralds moved to France to join a group of expatriates that included Hemingway and Dos Passos. While living in Europe, he wrote his most famous novel, *The Great Gatsby*, whose hero, bootlegger Jay Gatsby, found his money couldn't buy him a place in society or win him the beautiful Daisy Buchanan. In 1930, Zelda had what was then termed a nervous breakdown; she never fully recovered and spent the last fourteen years of her life in mental institutions. Zelda died in 1948. Scott tried to write between bouts of boozing; in December 1940, he died of a heart attack at age forty-four.

Prohibition

"One's host now brought out a bottle upon the slightest pretext. The tendency to display liquor was a manifestation of the same instinct that led a man to deck his wife with jewels. To have liquor was a boast, almost a badge of respectability."
—F. Scott Fitzgerald, *The Beautiful and the Damned*, 1922

Among the many factors having a major influence on life in the twenties was Prohibition. Temperance leaders and evangelists like famous preacher Billy Sunday were finally victorious as Prohibition, "The Noble Experiment," was voted into law in 1919 as the Volstead Act—the 18th Amendment to the Constitution. Prohibition went into effect at midnight, January 16, 1920, and was finally repealed in 1933.

Though Prohibition seemingly did little to stem a tidal wave of liquor, it did provide the decade with clandestine excitement and a whole lot of fun. It was parodied everywhere; cartoonists like John Held, Jr. had a field day, and corny Prohibition jokes popped up all over, like these from *The Flapper* magazine (1922):

"Did you ever see a ghost?" "No, but I've been up against some pretty bad spirits!"
"There's many a slip 'twist the cup and the lip; But a chap is more careful with a flask on his hip!"
"The trouble with some men is they have a prescription thirst with a home brew income!"
"Why do some flappers say they never drink a drop when they mean they never drop a drink?"

The Flapper also includes the following prohibition definitions:

Cellar Smeller: a young man who always turns up where liquor is to be had without cost
Embalmer: a bootlegger
Johnnie Walker: guy who never hires a cab

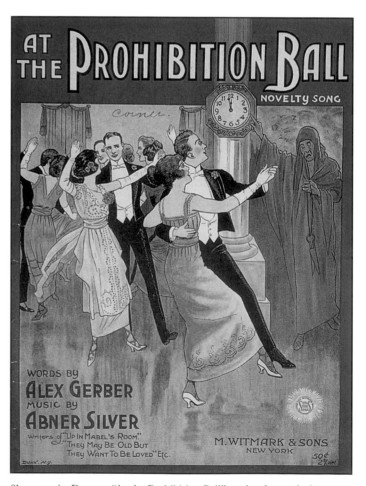

Sheet music. Dancers "At the Prohibition Ball" anxiously watch the clock—at midnight, January 16, 1920, Prohibition becomes effective. *"We'll be at the Prohibition Ball - There we'll mix with Mister Alcohol - Folks will pay their last respects to highballs and Horse's Necks - The gin we got from the Land of Cotton will be gone but not forgotten - Then we'll say farewell to old champagne - we may never taste a drop again…!"*

place to warn of raids, though the chance of being raided just added to the excitement! The speaks owned by Texas were raided many times, but when one was shut down, she simply opened another. Texas died on November 5, 1933, one month before the 21st Amendment repealed Prohibition.

Gangsters like Chicago's "Scarface" Al Capone welcomed Prohibition with open arms; by 1927 Al was realizing profits of sixty million a year! Since there was a fortune to be made supplying illegal liquor, booze was soon flowing from a vast network of "bootleggers." (The term *bootlegger* originated with the practice of tucking a flask of whiskey in a pair of boots, though there were innumerable ways to hide the hootch.) After being smuggled into the country, liquor was often watered down before bottling to increase the already enormous profits. One legendary bootlegger, Bill McCoy, was known for the unadulterated "quality" liquor he smuggled in from the Bahamas, hence the expression, "The Real McCoy."

In this photo postcard, a loving couple toasts a fond "Farewell to Old Champagne!"

"Prohibition Telephone." As the copy on the reverse of this news photo notes: *"Getting Information…Miss Julie Harrington, a New York Miss, is illustrating the use of the new style Prohibition Telephone. Getting a wrong number won't be a grievance in the future, for, inside the little box can be found a bottle of whatever you order. Your Bootlegger arrives and places it inside, taking the fee you leave there for it. Keystone View Co."*

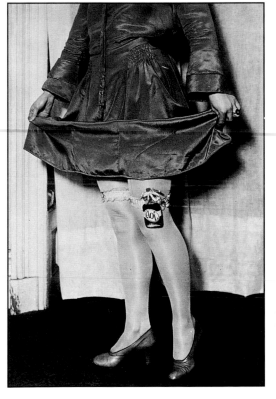

Sassy garters secure a hidden flask. "Flask – 1926 Prohibition" is noted on the back of this *International News Photo.*

Hiding the Hootch

Flagrantly flaunting Prohibition became an irresistible challenge, an exciting game of hide and seek with federal Prohibition agents. Old time saloons were quickly replaced by illegal drinking clubs called "speakeasies"…one just whispered the password ("Joe sent me") at the door and joined the party—and what a party. Hot jazz, hotter dances, and plenty of hootch! By the middle of the decade there were over one hundred thousand speakeasies in New York City alone.

Many hailed Shady Lady "Texas" Guinan as "Queen of the Speaks"—from her perch atop the piano, her raucous greeting, "Hello sucker!" pierced the air as she welcomed revelers to her rowdy New York speaks. "Texas" (formerly Mary Louise Cecilia Guinan) had left her hometown of Waco for Hollywood, where she starred in several westerns. She subsequently moved to New York to become "Queen of the Speakeasies." Her notorious "300 Club," at 157 West 54th, was patronized by the rich and famous—Rudy Valentino and Pola Negri, John Gilbert, Reggie Vanderbilt, and Walter Chrysler. George Gershwin often dropped in to play the piano, and forty fetching fan dancers entertained the patrons. Who cared if the cover charge was $25 and a pitcher of water cost $2? Speaks had alarm systems in

SSSHHHH!!! Posing as a studious student, this knicker-suited gal lets us in on her little secret—a clever book-flask! *International News Photo*, 1923.

Novelties companies came up with many clever ways to "hide the hootch." This novelty camera flask could have fooled Kodak! The top "button" is a cork stopper.

Home Brew

"Bubble, Bubble, Toil and Trouble!"
—William Shakespeare

Many concocted their own "witches' brews" with home-made stills; for under ten dollars, parts for a still could be found in any hardware store. Imaginative hootch recipes abounded; ingredients included apples, potatoes, oats, bananas, and other very strange things too terrifying to contemplate! One could also buy kits with ingredients that, when mixed together, turned to alcohol—grape juice put in the cellar to ferment for sixty days magically became wine! People often used their bathtubs to mix the ingredients, thus the notorious "bathtub gin."

As bootleg whiskey and home brews were usually too awful to drink straight, mixed drinks or "cocktails" became the decade's favorite drinks. To add to their mystique, cocktails were given naughty names. At a "cocktail party," one could choose between a "Corpse Reviver," a "Bosom Caresser," or a "Between the Sheets." Though drinking rotgut liquor was part of the "fun," many who imbibed woke up literally blind the next day due to the lethal ingredients of bad liquor.

Izzy and Moe

Federal agents tried to stem the tide, but they had their work cut out for them—there was no end to the ingenious ways of flaunting Prohibition. Izzy and Moe (Izzy Einstein and Moe Smith) were the decade's most illustrious federal agents. Izzy was a former postal clerk who spoke several languages. He soon recruited his friend Moe, a cigar store owner. On Izzy's first day on the job, he knocked on the door of a speak and said he was a new Prohibition agent. The doorman, who thought he was joking, let him in—but when he realized Izzy was telling the truth, he ran out the back door carrying the evidence! From then on, Izzy collected his evidence by pouring the hootch into a funnel in his vest pocket that led to a concealed flask.

Izzy and Moe quickly became masters of disguise. Just as imaginative as their quarry, they pulled capers that would have made a Keystone cop blush! They masqueraded as football players celebrating a win, as Cornell undergraduates to raid a speak in Ithaca, and as grave diggers to raid a speak near a cemetery. They "became" fruit vendors, ice-delivery men, farmers, and even musicians. (They often carried instruments, posing as members of a speak's band.)

Naturally, Izzy and Moe were soon making headlines, and the press kept readers amused with reports of their exploits. This press coverage eventually piqued their superior, who called the pair on the carpet, claiming all the hoopla was "not dignified" and that "you get your name in the papers all the time, while mine is hardly ever mentioned..." He cautioned them to keep in mind they were "merely subordinates, not the whole show." Though they had an impressive record (they busted over three thousand speaks and had a ninety-five percent conviction rate), Izzy and Moe were fired on November 13, 1925..."for the good of the service." When the news leaked out, one official explained that the pair really belonged in vaudeville, as they were too embarrassing to be Prohibition agents.

In his memoirs, *Prohibition Agent Number 1*, the affable Izzy apologized to the five thousand some revelers he'd arrested, saying he hoped "they bear me no grudge for having done my duty." The escapades of the duo were later made into a movie, *Izzy & Mo*, starring Jackie Gleason and Art Carney (1985).

The Silent Screen

In 1922, America had some twenty million movie theaters; by 1929, there were fifty million. During the twenties, movies were so important that theaters were "Palaces"—many survive today as opulent memorials to the Art Deco era and its unforgettable films.

Movies provided *escapism* at its most thrilling! By the teens, movies had graduated from short "flickers" to full length films that told spellbinding stories—stories whose heroes and heroines became icons then and are legends today. By the twenties, a weekly visit to the movies was a must for many families, and dreams came to life as audiences were transported to places they'd only read about. Now they could see for themselves the spellbinding lure of the orient, of ancient Egypt, and Gay Paree. They peeked into the tents of seductive desert sultans, visited the jungles of Tarzan, and fought outlaws in the wild west. Movies, silent until 1927, used printed "subtitles" with just the right music to enhance the action—thrilling, tragic, seductive—or heartrending music that brought out the hankies. Many newly arrived immigrants began to learn the language as well as the lifestyles of their new country via silent film's subtitles.

Films exerted a tremendous influence on peoples' lives, projecting more on the screen than mere entertainment. Movies served as a portal between the old world and the new, between staid Victorian lifestyles and the glorious freedoms of the unfolding new century. Movies made people laugh and made them cry, made them sing as well as dance, and gave them thrills as well as chills! Audiences could emphasize with the common man as they watched Chaplin's "Little Tramp" or they could vicariously live the lives of super heroes like Tom Mix. Films fulfilled their promise to provide "all the excitement that's lacking in your daily life"—sometimes billed as "Bold, Naked, Sensational!" and fans not only imitated their stars' fashions, they mimicked their expressions, mannerisms, and, to the best of their abilities, their very lifestyles.

Vamps and Sweethearts

Actresses were often brave but innocent "America's Sweethearts" like Mary Pickford, or teasing, tempestuous *vamps* ("vamp" being short for "vampire"!). The vamp was immortalized by F. Scott Fitzgerald in *The Beautiful and the Damned* (1922):

> "...she was in her element: her ebony hair was slicked straight back on her head; her eyes were artificially darkened, she reeked of insistent perfume. She was got up to the best of her ability as a siren, more popularly a 'vamp'—a picker up and thrower away of men, an unscrupulous and fundamentally unmoved toyer with affections."

Among the decade's favorite vamps were Gloria Swanson, Joan Crawford, Pola Negri, Mae Murray (who claimed to have copyrighted "Bee Stung Lips"), "It Girl" Clara Bow, Louise

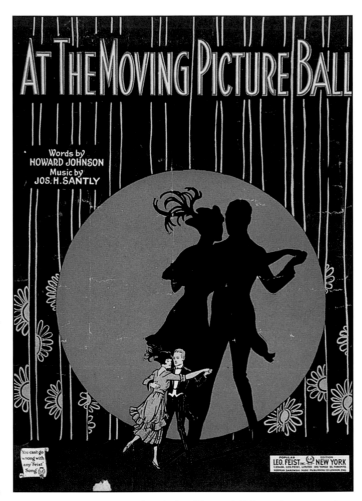

This 1920 sheet music, "At the Moving Picture Ball," pays homage to the stars of the silent screen. *"Yesterday I was invited to a swell affair - all the movie stars were there... Theda Bara was a terror, she 'vamped the little lady', so did Alice Brady; Douglas Fairbanks shimmied on one hand, like an acrobat - Mary Pickford did a toe dance grand - and Charlie Chaplin with his feet, stepped all over poor Blanche Sweet... Sennet's bathing girls were there, each one was a little 'bear'! Dancing at that Moving Picture Ball!"*

Brooks, and Norma Shearer. Vamps tried their best to vanquish any remaining shreds of Victorian prudery, often appearing nude or semi-nude like Mae Murray in *The French Doll* (1923); Gloria Swanson in *Zaza* (1923); Pauline Starke in the scandalous *Dante's Inferno* (1924); and Clara Bow in *Hula* (1927).

Movies adored "Flaming Youth," depicting a brazen, flask carrying, speed-crazy younger set. In *Our Dancing Daughters* (1928), Joan Crawford dances one of filmdom's most erotic Charlestons. In *Prodigal Daughters* (1923), vamp Gloria Swanson outlines the era's new morality as she issues "the seven deadly whims" to her startled father:

> "New lips to kiss; Freedom from conventions; A new world for women; No more chaperones; Life with a kick in it; A single moral standard; Our own latchkeys."

Naturally, men flew to vamps like moths to a flame, though they usually ended up with wholesome girls-next-door as played by Mary Pickford, Janet Gaynor, and Lillian and Dorothy Gish. Greta Garbo, the embodiment of the new, more independent woman, was introduced to American audiences in 1926; in her first American film, *The Torrent*, the Swedish Garbo played a Spanish peasant. In 1927's *Flesh and the Devil*, Garbo and John Gilbert mesmerized audiences with their sensuous love scenes. *Photoplay*, reviewing the steamy pair's next film, *Love*, reported: "It isn't Tolstoy, but it is John Gilbert and Greta Garbo, which after *Flesh and the Devil*, is what the fans are crying for…"

Actors

Actors were swashbucklers like Douglas Fairbanks, sensuous sultans like Rudolph Valentino, or rough and ready cowboys like William S. Hart and Tom Mix. Known as the "King of the Cowboys," Mix romanticized the Wild West; his flamboyant lifestyle spawned the term "Drugstore Cowboy," a prototype of Urban Cowboy. Even Tom's horse "Tony" was idolized—before his appearance at New York's Paramount Theater, Tony was photographed getting a "manicure" and a mane perm! War movies, like the 1927 classic, *Wings*, portrayed the heroic deeds of the brave men of WWI. *Wings* starred Buddy Rogers, Richard Arlen, Clara Bow, and newcomer Gary Cooper; it won an award for outstanding picture of the year.

RUDOLPH VALENTINO
in

Heart throb of the decade Rudolph Valentino in full regalia for *The Son of the Sheikh*, with Vilma Banky, 1926. Studio photo postcard.

Vamp Mae Murray posed for this studio portrait, which was used in *Photoplay* magazine's August 1920 issue. Mae was a popular vamp, starring with Rudy in 1919 in *Delicious Little Devil*; in 1920 in *Right to Love*; and in 1924, in the steamy *Circe*. In addition to her "come hither" look, Mae wears a diamante bandeau in her curly bob, long drop earrings, and a sexy slave bracelet!

Laugh and the world laughs with you...

Popular "slapstick" comedies often parodied the plight of the common man or "average Joe." Audiences laughed till they cried, as they viewed the unforgettable antics of such greats as Charlie Chaplin, the Marx Brothers, Harold Lloyd, Laurel and Hardy, Buster Keaton, and Our Gang's Little Rascals. Mack Sennett, producer of many popular comedies including the Keystone Cops, found nothing too sacred to satirize; his marvelous star, cross-eyed Ben Turpin, mercilessly parodied Valentino in 1923's "*Shriek of Araby*." And Sennett's darling but daring bathing beauties were in large part responsible for the popularity of the new figure-revealing, wool knit one-piece swimsuits.

Anyone with a claim to fame appeared in the movies—including the great Will Rogers, author, comedian, philosopher, and spokesman for the common man; "Sultan of Swat" Babe Ruth; fighter Jack Dempsey; and champion swimmer, Annette Kellerman (who starred in *Queen of the Sea* and *Neptune's Daughter*). Speakeasy Queen Texas Guinan beguiled audiences in *Little Miss Deputy*. Rin-Tin-Tin, the world's favorite German Shepherd, was a Red Cross dog in *Find Your Man*. In 1928's *Plane Crazy*, a young Walt Disney introduced his beloved, Mickey Mouse; shortly thereafter, Mickey sang, danced, and even whistled in his first talkie, *Steamboat Willie*, which debuted on November 18, 1928, at New York's Colony Theatre.

"Talkies"

On August 6, 1926, censor Will H. Hayes uttered the first words spoken on film; Hayes, introducing "Vitaphone" sound, predicted that sound would revolutionize the film industry. Bell Telephone engineers had developed Vitaphone, expanding on Edison's original experiments with sound. Warner Bros. was the first studio to realize sound's potential and begin productions using Vitaphone. In October 1927, in *The Jazz Singer*, Al Jolson spoke the proverbial line, "You ain't seen nothing yet!" to his mother, then burst into song with "Blue Skies."

The miracle of hearing their heroes and heroines actually talk on screen heralded the end of the Silent Era, and by the end of 1927, it was clear that sound was here to stay. By the spring of 1928, even bad "talkies" were outselling the best silent films. By 1929, the miracle of sound had created a mania for singing and dancing musicals like *The Hollywood Review*, which featured "Singin' in the Rain" as one of its hit tunes.

The Academy Awards were introduced in 1929; the famous gold statues were named by Margaret Herrick, an executive director of the Academy, who noted that they bore an amazing resemblance to her Uncle Oscar! The first Academy Awards were multiple; for best actress, Janet Gaynor for *Sunrise*, *Seventh Heaven* and *Street Angel*. Best actor went to Emil Jannings for *The Way of All Flesh* and *The Last Command*. Best picture or "outstanding production" awards went to *Wings* and *Sunrise*.

Film Fashion

"Film fashions of today are your fashions of tomorrow..."
—Elsa Schiaparelli

Films were a social equalizer, showing the latest fashions to millions who lived in small town and rural areas. Instead of seeing a one-dimensional picture in a magazine, fans saw many views of the latest styles worn by their favorite actresses. Increasingly, movie stars set the styles as millions of women adopted their fashions. Haute couture creations were copied or adapted by Hollywood designers, and several couturiers, including Coco Chanel, visited Hollywood. The ad world quickly cashed in on the tremendous draw of Hollywood stars and many, like Clara Bow, Joan Crawford, Louise Brooks, and Gloria Swanson, endorsed the latest fashions.

The tremendous influence of films was duly noted by *Vogue*, who warned readers to take what they saw in films with a grain of salt:

> *"Life as it is lived and life as it is screened show an amazing difference between heroines and villains in front of and upon the Screen... unfortunate authors see their stories maltreated, and the public whose opinions are so misled...raised hands against incongruities of social and fashionable life matters little...Authors' stories settings and characters are misrepresented."*

And regarding Hollywood's tendency to exaggerate or vulgarize fashion, Vogue observes:

> *The American public is learning, and they may just as well learn a fine **simplicity** as a **vulgar ostentation**."* (July 15, 1920; emphasis added)

The Automobile

> *"'Tis Summer and the urge of the wanderlust is on me...I want freedom and fresh air and the privilege to ramble wherever I please from sunset to sundown and moonrise to moonset. A twentieth century flapper and her Ford is capable of doing many things, and it is my intention to get fun, as well as education, in my little jaunt across the country!"* (Excerpt from "The Flapper Trail," a series of articles by Marie June LaVerne for *The Flapper* magazine, 1922)

In August, Miss LaVerne reports that the town of Cedar Rapids *"...looked like the Duck's Quack to me, and I decided to loaf a few days in my Flivvering trip from Chicago to the Pacific Coast..."*

Vogue observed that this new "easy mobility" was creating a new world of "Society Gypsies," as happy wanderers or "vagabonds" packed up their cares and woes and took to the roads.

The car made the world a smaller place as it brought the city to the country and vice-versa. It heralded the beginning of the "upwardly mobile" society, enabling people to move from crowded city streets to the outskirts of town—the birth of the suburbs! The "Sunday Drive" became a tradition that many still remember fondly. By 1920, there were over seven million cars on the road; by 1925, seventeen million. By the end of the decade, more than twenty-three million cars were registered in the U.S., and three of every four were bought on the installment plan. At the beginning of the decade, there were millions of miles of roads, but relatively few were paved; by end of decade, the majority had been paved. By 1920, all states had established highway departments, complete with motorcycle cops to catch speed demons—and bootleggers!

These two spunky gals change "Lizzie's" tire, "Near Charlotte, N.C., May 9, 1920" as noted on reverse. Perhaps they're heeding advice from the 1921 *Delineator* woman's motoring article, "DON'T WAIT FOR A MAN!": "She really wanted to do this work herself, for the plan of sitting by the roadside and waiting for some male motorist to arrive on the scene who was gallant enough to offer his services in her behalf was not satisfactory to her…" Instructions are included for changing tires, advising: "great care should be taken of the spare inner-tubes it is advisable to carry." After this great accomplishment, the article concludes, "Away you go, happy and independent!"

A hopeful young driver cranks up! This little guy has his work cut out for him—starting a car with a hand crank was an arduous task. Note his sturdy denim coveralls with rolled up cuffs…"he'll grow into 'em"! (Snapshot, ca. 1920)

Auto fashion, protection from the dust and dirt of the open road, was a necessity. This gallant gent adjusts his sweetie's auto goggles before she goes motoring; she's wearing a smart long duster. (Snapshot, ca. 1920-25)

14

The automobile, a source of both pleasure and pain, enjoyed a love/hate relationship with its owner—though it fulfilled one's dreams and fantasies, it was the source of endless aggravation. Motorists had to endure pitfalls aplenty, including balloon tires with inner tubes that blew out regularly and cantankerous "crank" starters. (Though Charles Kettering had perfected a self-starter in 1912 and sold it to Cadillac, many had cars that still started with hand cranks.) At the beginning of the decade, motorists had to maneuver over dirt roads with obstacle courses that included tire-eating rocks and potholes; they were often stopped dead by roadblocks of fallen trees and various farm animals. As open cars offered little protection from the grit and grime of the dirt roads, proper auto gear was necessary; this included auto dusters, caps and hats, goggles and gauntlet gloves. All the pitfalls of motoring were considered part and parcel of "The Great Adventure," and were balanced by a fabulous feeling of freedom offered by the automobile. And then, there was the RUMBLE SEAT!

Rumble Seats and Tin Lizzies

Flaming Youth saw cars as an escape from parents' watchful eyes, and the infamous back "rumble seat" became a perfect place for necking and petting!

This cute couple finds the rumble seat a cozy place to neck and pet...and the couple in the front seat isn't losing any time either! The photographer's gal poses with her hand on the fender; she's all dolled up in her chic cloche hat and fox fur neckpiece. (Snapshot, ca. 1927)

By mid-decade, one imaginative car manufacturer had taken things even further, offering a bedroom on wheels. Their promo photo of a couple necking in the back seat featured this titillating caption: "An example of back porch love in an auto—this new type offers all the comforts of your home back porch. It has reversible back seat and a curtain to draw for obvious reasons"! (See *Roaring '20s Fashions: Deco*, the companion volume to this book, for a picture of this "Petting Parlour on Wheels.") Indeed, the auto as a portable love nest contributed to the era's sexual revolution, and the birth of new "lover's lanes" resulted in the births of many babies!

By the twenties, cars came in a rainbow of colors: red, green, blue, and yellow, as well as basic black. The world watched a constant parade of runabouts, roadsters, coupes, phaetons, and broughams as Oldsmobiles, Lincolns, Pierce Arrows, Hupmobiles, Franklins, Cadillacs, and Stutz Bearcats (the supreme college car) sped by. Cars, of course, were standard shift, and Stutz advertised a "No-back" feature that prevented it from

rolling back on hills; to entice women drivers, Stutz noted: "The great army of women drivers, particularly, will welcome this innovation." Cars like the Stutz and Lincoln cost around $7,000-$9,000. The wealthiest of the wealthy favored imports like the Rolls-Royce Phantom. ("The Rolls-Royce probably costs more than any other automobile made in America. But it is worth more, too…," notes *Vogue* on April 1, 1928.) The Hispano-Suiza and Mercedes Benz started around $15,000. (Al Jolson had several—the least expensive was priced at $21,500!) Josephine Baker cruised the streets of Paris in her custom-made brown Voison, upholstered with matching brown snakeskin seats. Scott and Zelda Fitzgerald purchased a new Marmon, which Zelda promptly crashed into a fire hydrant.

Though the auto had previously been reserved for the wealthy, by the twenties Henry Ford's famous Model T, "The Car of the People," ruled the roads. The Model T, also known as the "Tin Lizzie" or "Flivver," had been introduced in 1908. Using a moving assembly line and standardized interchangeable parts, Ford made what the world had been waiting for—an affordable car that was just $290, or $5 a week on the installment plan! And Ford paid his workers very well; they were making $5 a day in 1914, while other companies paid about half that amount.

"Henry's Made a Lady Out of Lizzie," sheet music by Walter O'Keefe, 1928. "…*Everybody, Everywhere is falling for her now - I'm talking 'bout the new Ford, and boy, it's sure a WOW!... She's like all the other vamps, Pretty shape and lovely lamps - Henry's made a lady out of Lizzie!...Since he lifted up her face - she travels at an awful pace!...She once had rattles in her wheel, but now she's full of 'sex-appeal'... No more bruises, no more aches - now she's got those four wheel brakes!...No one curses, no one swears - Lizzie never needs repairs!... The horn just seems to holler out 'Toot - Toot,' they shall not pass!... She's even got a rumble seat, and lots of style and class... There's everything inside her now, except a kitchen sink - a mirror and a powder puff, a shower bath, I think!...She's not the kind who tries to get your money all at once - she only wants ten dollars down - the rest in fourteen months!"*

Votes for Women! Suffragist lectures to the crowd from an open car (1911, Syracuse, New York).

"Lizzie" could perform many duties; she was used not just for gadding about, but as a light-duty truck (bootleggers filled every speck of Lizzie's space and took to the roads with gallons of hootch) and farmers used her engine to perform many chores. Lizzie could even be transformed into a CAMPER…

On the Road…"Adventures In Autobumming"

"There is no motorist so jaded that his pulse will not quicken at the sight of the distinction of the new cars, the ingeniousness of the new luggage, and the temptation of the newly opened roads… There are seven million pleasure seeking, mile-eating motor cars in the United States, and in the summer about half of them are seized with the wanderlust or a sight-seeing fever and are off to somewhere over the best roads they can find."
—*Vogue*, July 15, 1920

To encourage these "gadabouts," Sinclair Lewis published several "Adventures in Autobumming" articles in the *Saturday Evening Post*. As millions of new car owners took to the roads, camping became a national obsession and catalogs offered tents that attached to cars for about $20. Thousands of new camp grounds sprang up, and for the not quite so adventurous, there were new hotels, motels, and "tourist homes" (early versions of the bed and breakfast).

Women at the Wheel

In a nationwide survey, one housewife declared she'd give up food rather than the car, noting: "I'd rather drive than eat!" Another woman reported she had an auto, but not an indoor bathroom; stating what she thought should have been obvious, she declared: "You can't go to town in a bathtub!" The car had a tremendous impact on women's fashions too—as women went out more, they needed fashionable clothes to wear as they motored to the movies, shops, and restaurants, or to visit friends and relatives. Now one's wardrobe had to include more than a "best" or "Sunday" dress and a few simple housedresses.

In their July 1920 issue, ever vigilant *Vogue* warns its readers that motoring can give one "a staring and strained expression"! Regarding motoring in open cars, *Vogue* lamented: "The fact that the car has made an average of 25 mph is no solace to the woman whose gown is ruined and whose hat has been assaulted by every blast of heaven." *Vogue* also complained that luggage strapped to the "outside platform" (running board) often arrives "crumpled and muddy." Their article ends with this prophetic warning: "Humans are slaves of the machine. It is not YOU who possesses the car, but the CAR which possesses you."

Women's Emancipation

On August 26, 1920, women finally won the right to vote as the 19th Amendment, or "Suffrage Amendment," was ratified after a centuries-long battle. The fight for emancipation had its birth with the country; on March 31, 1776, in Abigail Adams's famous "Remember the Ladies" letter to her husband John, she cautioned:

"…and by the way in the new Code of Laws which I suppose it will be necessary for you to make I desire you would Remember the Ladies…if perticuliar care and attention is not paid to the Laidies, we are determined to foment a Rebelion, and will not hold ourselves bound by any Laws in which we have no voice or Representation." [sic]

The fight intensified during the Victorian era; at the 1848 Women's Convention at Seneca Falls, Elizabeth Cady Stanton and Lucretia Mott shocked the nation by demanding votes for women in the "Declaration of Sentiments." Stanton and her friend, Susan B. Anthony, would devote the rest of their lives to the cause, though emancipation would not come during their lifetimes. During the teens, women became more determined than ever to win the vote, and suffragists tirelessly demonstrated…passing out handbills, marching in parades, and lecturing—even from automobiles!

VOTES FOR WOMEN

People Say:	We Say:
The majority of women don't want to vote.	The majority never wants progress.
Women will not vote when they are given the right.	Official figures show women DO vote largely wherever they have the right.
If women vote they ought to fight and do police duty.	Men who could not fight still vote; this is the age when RIGHT makes MIGHT.
If women vote they must hold office.	A woman will have to be elected to office by the men and women together. Do the men all have to hold office?
Women have enough to do without voting.	Voting takes but a few minutes and can be done on the way to market.
It would interfere with a woman's business, the care of the house.	Does it interfere with man's business in factory, store or office?
It would double the ignorant vote.	⅓ more girls than boys attend the high schools and women will soon be the more educated class.
It would double the foreign vote.	There are in the United States over 12 times as many native born women as foreign born.
It would double the criminal vote.	Only 1 in 20 of the criminals are women. It would add largely to the good vote and very slightly to the bad vote.
It would double the expense and trouble of election.	The safety of a democracy lies in giving the vote to all classes so that ALL are fairly represented, and the result will be a Fair Average opinion. Ought we to cut the present vote in half to save money?
Women can change or make laws by indirect influence.	Why be indirect when we can be direct? Why waste time and strength in beating around the bush?
A woman's place is in the home.	She leaves it to go to market and why not to vote—it takes less time.
Women are represented by men.	Would men let women represent them at the polls?
	Does a man with women to represent have more than one vote or does he cast his vote according to the majority vote of those he represents? No! Then he doesn't represent them.
	Is a man's vote given him to represent some one else's opinion or his own?

NATIONAL AMERICAN WOMAN SUFFRAGE ASSOCIATION
505 FIFTH AVENUE   Headquarters: NEW YORK CITY

This "Votes for Women" handbill was passed out to answer naysayers' concerns; it was issued by the National American Woman Suffrage Association.

"Typewriter" girl, hand colored photo postcard postmarked 1923.

New Occupations

For women, many changes came with emancipation. During WWI, many had taken on traditionally male jobs, and many were loathe to give them up when the war ended. By the early teens, *American Businesswoman* reported that there were over five million self-supporting women in the U.S. employed in around three hundred different occupations. Though most still held traditional "women's jobs" (teacher, nurse, "typewriter," shop girl, seamstress, milliner), many were now opting for careers that had previously been barred to them, becoming lawyers, doctors, dentists, engineers, clergywomen, journalists—even pilots! Women were attending college in increasing numbers to pursue their chosen occupations.

College bound: "Mildred Roberts and Hilda Floe in front of Alpha Gamma Delta House, Washington State College, 1929."

"Come hear Dr. Shaw lecture at the Long Branch casino on Thurs. Aug..." During the teens, women tacked up "Votes for Women posters"; today we tack up garage sale signs! (New Jersey, ca. 1914)

"Ready for takeoff!" Woman pilot, (?)...Stewart, employed by Essandee Air Transport. Noted on reverse: "Taken at Lincoln's Field, November 6, 1927."

"Can you ever put into words that thrilled moment when for the first time you felt no ground under your wheels..."
"As surely as the woman of yesterday was born to ride in a limousine, the woman of today was born to fly in an aeroplane."

—*Vogue*, July 1920

The intrepid Duchess of Bedford took up flying in her sixties. A Houston lady flew from Texas in less than twenty hours to shop in New York. And couturiers were so excited by flight, they created special ensembles for "aeroplaning."

With their glorious new emancipation, women yearned to be men's social equals too, to be treated as "just one of the guys." They wanted to smoke, drink, cuss...and neck and pet as well. This new woman was the legendary *FLAPPER*: "A little bit of heaven and a little bit of hell"! Born of the Jazz Age in America, she was known as a "Bright Young Thing" in England, and "La Garconne" in France.

Flapper Freedom!

Pluck your eyebrows, roll your socks
Rouge your cheeks and bob your locks
Dab your nose and dress up swell
And tell the prudes to go to...HOLLYWOOD!
　　　　　—*The Flapper* magazine, May 1922

The best description of the New Woman comes from a product of the era itself. *The Flapper* magazine, based in the Roaring Twenties' city of Chicago, came to grips with this new phenomenon, defining her independence and style.

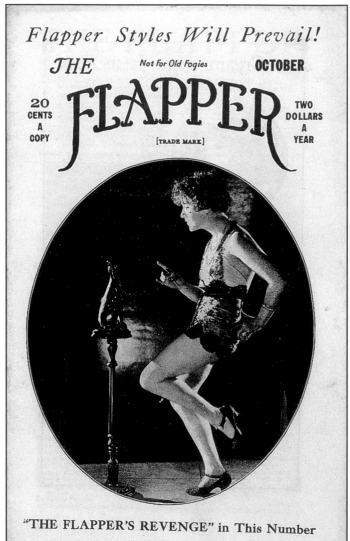

Flapper freedom...cover of *The Flapper* magazine, October 1922. Not for old fogies!

"Action!" Movie camerawoman, ca. 1927.

The Flapper, which was published from May to December of 1922, offered the following descriptions of the flapper:

> *"She's independent, full of grace, a pleasing form, a pretty face; is often saucy, also pert, and doesn't think it wrong to flirt; knows what she wants and gets it too; receives the homage that's her due; her love is warm, her hate is deep, for she can laugh and she can weep; but she is true as true can be, her will's unchained, her soul is free; she charms the young, she jars the old, within her beats a heart of gold; she furnishes the spice of life— and makes some boob a darn good wife."* (May 1922)

> *"WHAT THE FLAPPER STANDS FOR"*... *"Short Skirts. Rolled Sox. Bobbed Hair. Powder and Rouge. No Corsets. One-piece bathing suits. Deportation of Reformers. Nonenforcement of Blue Laws. No Censorship of Movies, stage or press. Vacations with Full Pay. No Chaperones. Attractive Clothes. The Inalienable Right to Make Dates. Good Times. Honor Between Both Sexes."* (August 1922)

The Flapper offered this sage advice to new flappers: "It is as natural to see powder, rouge and eyebrow pencil on girls as it is to see roses in florists' shops…" and "Never put off till tomorrow what you can take off today." Regarding controversial short skirts, *The Flapper* observed: "For the first time since civilization began the world is learning that girls, women, females, maidens and damsels have KNEES!" And concerning the controversy over rolled stockings, they took a hard line: "One season she may roll her sox, the next she may decorate them with weird designs—and the next season she may not wear any!"

Responding to cries of dismay from "old fogies," *The Flapper* issues this blistering response:

> *"Though reformers declare the flapper is 'nothing but a fad', The Flapper is here to stay! Radio is a fad, but who will be rash enough to say that it is not destined to play one of the most important parts in the future progress of mankind? As surely as horse drawn street cars, the blunderbuss and hoopskirts will never come back, so surely has the doom been sealed of the timid, trusting, retiring, servile, opinionless, unattractive, shrinking creature known as the old fashioned girl…"* (July 1922)

The term "flapper" is claimed by many. Some say the flapper was named for the bird-like flapping movements of the Charleston dance; though this is a picturesque notion, "flapper" had been in use long before the Charleston became a popular dance, ca. 1924. F. Scott Fitzgerald delineated the flapper in 1920 in *This Side of Paradise*, and the definitive *Flapper Magazine* began publication in 1922.

During 1910-1920, "flapper" was used to refer to a young teenage girl (Bonwit Teller advertises "New Flapper Modes for Spring—Girls 12-16 Years" in the April 1917 *Harper's Bazar*) and that slim, youthful, androgynous image is precisely what twenties' flappers strove to project. Perhaps the most likely origin of the twenties' "flapper" though, is that the term originated with the girls' trendy buckle galoshes— they wore them unbuckled so they "flapped" as they walked!

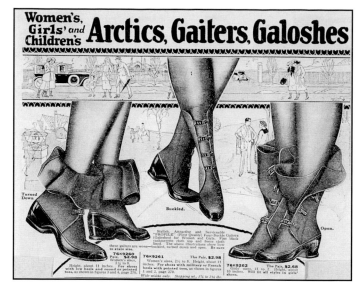

In 1922, Sears offered "Stylish, Attractive and Serviceable Four-Buckle Gaiters (Galoshes) for Women and Girls…the above illustrations show how these gaiters were worn—buckled, turned down and open"…though open and FLAPPING was the flapper's choice! As flapper readers were advised by the New York *Herald Tribune*: "We are living in a Galoshic Renaissance; the glorified galosh is one of the outstanding features of our latest civilization. The Galosh has become the pet of youthful fashion…" (January 27, 1927, reprinted in a 1927 booklet of the National Shoe Retailers Association)

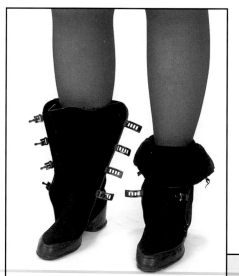

A flapper MUST— four-buckle galoshes! We've shown ours with one open and one turned down, per the Sears ad.

John Held Jr.'s famous flapper with rolled-down hose and "flapping" galoshes! Held's illustrations of the flapper and her beaux defined the decade's "Flaming Youth."

"Who is this? December 26, 1927" is noted on the reverse of this darling snapshot. This cuddled cutie demonstrates the proper way to wear galoshes!

Fashion

Our apparel oft proclaims us!
—William Shakespeare

For everyone, fashions of the twenties had to keep pace with the era's new attitude—men, women, girls, and boys demanded casual, comfortable clothes that fulfilled the mandates of *youth, simplicity* and *versatility* as they grew ever more "moderne."

In this newly casual decade, sports clothes were of utmost importance; they were the fashions that would have the greatest impact on the clothes we wear today. As women's hard won equality produced a penchant for masculine items, many twenties' women, aiming for an androgynous or "unisex" look, borrowed sportswear looks from men's fashions...as "mannish" became chic! Women often invaded men's shops, as: "These purely masculine garments are smartest when bought at a men's shop where no compromise with the feminine angle is attempted." They also raided husbands', fathers', and brothers' closets for ties, scarves, pajamas, and even robes: "For the dusty Pullman journey the serviceable lounging robe of a man is the smartest thing a women can wear..." *Harper's Bazar* advised. In many of the following fashions, vintage photos, and illustrations, the influence of men's wear on women's fashions is evident.

The influence of Art Deco on the world of fashion was extensive; its streamlined modernism was making its impact well before the famed Paris Art Deco Exposition of 1925. You'll note that during the twenties, Art Deco's geometric lines and themes pervaded every aspect of fashion, from evening gowns to the most casual sportswear!

The decade was "fashionably" split in half. For both women and men, fashions of the first half were markedly different than those of the second half. However, since women's fashions, with all their charming nuances, changed much more rapidly than men's, we've depicted them as they evolve year by year, while men's and children's fashions are shown in a separate chapter covering the entire first half of the decade. Note that since contemporary mannequins have the "wrong attitude" for twenties' fashions, dress forms have been used in this book as adult models. While imparting the shape of the human form, they don't steal attention from the garments themselves. Period mannequins have been used for hats and for boys' and girls' fashions. Also note that original twenties' expressions have been used throughout the text; for example, in the twenties dresses are "frocks"—always "chic," "modish," "fetching," "smart," "peppy," and, increasingly, "mannish"!

The twenties is a sport-loving, CASUAL decade—comfortable, practical clothes are favored by men, women and children. For girls, *National Style Book* offers this cute and casual middy blouse/knickers ensemble. (1923)

"Ready to leave for the Grand Canyon" is noted on the reverse of this darling snapshot! Demonstrating the new "Unisex" look, this loving young couple embarks on their adventure casually clad in knickers and sweaters. (ca. 1924)

The "Scooter Champions of Philadelphia" wear knickers, casual shirts, and sweaters. Note the 1st prize winner's jazzy matching sweater and socks! Noted on the reverse: "L to R: Herbert Buch and Rob Lowe, the winner and runner-up of the annual scooter race for the championship of Philadelphia held on Front Street in the 'Quaker City' recently." (News photo, ca. 1922)

Fashion and the Flapper

The twenties is considered a portal between old fashions and new, a threshold through which stepped the fashions that evolved into those of today…

An elegant Edwardian lady passes through the Portals of Fashion, shedding her tight corsets and long skirts to emerge a modern independent woman. Now her ruffles, rather than enhancing her hourglass figure, emphasize the fact that her skirts have risen to her knees! (Studio portrait, 1925)

The movement towards the flapper's famous straight silhouette began with the revolutionary designs of the "Father of Modern Fashion," Paul Poiret. In 1908, Poiret promoted his controversial new "Grecian" or "Directoire" look, featuring the "pencil slim" high-waisted gowns shown in his famous *Les Robes de Paul Poiret*, illustrated by Paul Iribe. These gowns were also known as "Empire" styles, as they were compared to the simple muslin gowns worn by the Empress Josephine at the beginning of the nineteenth century. At first controversial, by 1911 they'd banished the fussy froufrou and wasp waists of the Edwardian "hourglass" era and paved the way for the all-important *SIMPLICITY* to follow.

Vintage fashion fanciers have often noted the marked size difference between the tiny Edwardian gowns of the turn of the century and the tubular chemise frocks of the twenties—in just one generation, women seemed to have acquired a totally different shape. As the wasp waist disappeared and the new straight, slender line evolved, one commentator observed: "…our bodies actually seem to change in response to the times and new designs and fashions that are created…"

As fashions steadily simplified to become multi-purpose, fewer changes per day were needed. Before World War I, a lady of fashion changed several times a day, requiring correct clothing for each occasion: boudoir gowns or peignoirs for breakfast; informal "morning" dresses; tailored suits for shopping; dressy gowns for luncheon; and afternoon "calling" dresses, or, if receiving callers at home, perhaps a luxurious tea gown. After tea, of course, she changed yet again into a formal reception or dinner gown. For special evening events like balls and operas, the most formal (and decollete) gowns were required.

The Great War changed everything. As noted in *Harper's Bazar*:

> "The war seems to have cleared away so many unnecessary things; it has swept away all the efforts to be recherché, it has killed the blasé, the supercivilized so to speak, and has brought back the simple and natural. The perfect dress of today is the dress that appears to have been created with the least effort. The lines must be simple, unaffected…women today are coping with the realities of life; the Artificial is out of date." (May 1915)

The Chemise Dress

The war necessitated styles with *FREEDOM* that women of the twenties were loathe to give up. The chemise, an ancient tubular style revived around 1908 by Paul Poiret and other couturiers, is the look most associated with the fashions of the twenties. It's important to note, however, that fashion is not static, rather it is constantly evolving. As Elsa Schiaparelli once noted, "As soon as a dress is born, it has already become a thing of the past"! Thus, during the first half of the decade (depicted in this book) you'll see the chemise evolve to its "arrow straight" apex by 1924, while in the second half of the decade (depicted in the companion volume, *Roaring '20s Fashions: Deco*), the chemise segues into a more feminine look, with new emphasis on the bust, waist, and hips. The bias cut pioneered by Madeleine Vionnet was one of the most important methods used. As Vionnet proclaimed: "The dress must not hang on the body but follow its lines…and when a woman smiles, the dress must smile with her!" While observing the evolution of the twenties' fashions as shown in both books, you'll note that

this fascinating decade goes full circle…beginning with natural waistlines and trailing "tails," and ending with them too, but with a much different look. *Vive la difference!*

Art Deco's tremendous influence on fashion is evident not only in the angular, geometric cuts of the clothing, but also in the era's "moderne" Deco prints, the best designed by well-known artists who also created designs for fabrics. Artists like Sonia Delauney and Raoul Dufy created prints for such prestigious French manufacturers as Rodier, Bianchini-Ferier, Ducharne, and the Successors of Albert Godde et Baude (which published the fabulous pochoir fashion magazine *Art Gout Beaute*).

By the twenties, fashion was no longer reserved for the rich. Several factors played a role in its "equalization"—including movies, fashion magazines, better transportation, more active lifestyles, the growing number of working women, the tremendous growth of ready to wear…and the simple style of the chemise dress!

The Twenties' Chemise

> "I make clothes women can live in, breathe in, feel comfortable in and look young in."
>
> —Coco Chanel

*Simple, youthful, versatile, comfortable…*the tubular chemise was perfectly suited to twenties women's active lifestyles! In the past, the word "chemise" had referred to an undergarment worn next to the body, under a corset—a plain, straight, knee length slip-like garment that sometimes doubled as a nightgown. The twenties' chemise frock was as straight and "simple" as the age old garment it was named for.

The chemise dress is perfect for active sports—like golf! This marvelous Art Deco pochoir embodies the spirit of the twenties…free and easy and streamlined for action. By Bonfils, from *Modes et Manieres*, 1920.

By the beginning of WWI in 1914, several couturiers had begun to simplify Poiret's tubular Grecian dresses even further, creating fashions with ever simpler lines. As early as 1916, *Vogue* was heralding the chemise as "The Modern Dress!" Though Lanvin, Vionnet, and Chanel all experimented with this new look during the teens, the chemise would come to be most associated with Chanel. *Harper's Bazar* took note of Chanel's "simple" creations as early as 1915 (though they misspelled her name), advising readers that "the woman who has not at least one costume by Chenel (sic) is hopelessly out of the running in fashion." In the fall of 1916, Chanel presented her first complete collection: svelte black jersey chemises, loosely girdled and richly embroidered. In April 1917, *Harper's* rhapsodized: "This season the name of Gabrielle Chanel is on the lips of every buyer…!" In 1919, prophetic *Vogue* observed that Chanel's chemise gown "…is imbued with the sort of simplicity that always has been and always will be expensive."

This grandmother of modern aerobics ad appeared in the May 1921 *Delineator*. It exhorts women to: "Get Thin to Music! At Home! With your own phonograph!"

By the beginning of the twenties, the chemise's straight silhouette was well established. Though the early chemises were often *loosely* belted or "girdled" at either the natural waist, slightly above, or slightly below, they exhibited a much straighter line than was previously fashionable. The chemise's main competition was the decade's alternative silhouette, the full-skirted "robe de style" or "picture frock," introduced by Lanvin ca. 1914. The robe de style was a "romantic" youthful fashion, very popular for evening and afternoon events such as dances, teas, garden parties, and weddings; it remained popular throughout the twenties. You'll note that even these full robe de style gowns have the twenties' famous dropped waistline.

To carry off the tubular chemise dress, a slender figure was a must, and women of the twenties are often described as being "ethereally slender," their streamlined bodies corresponding with the streamlined images of Art Deco. In *Antic Hay* (1923), Aldous Huxley's ideal woman is: "…fairly tall but seemed taller than she was by reason of her remarkable slenderness…a founded slenderness…flexible and tubular like a boa constrictor…dressed in clothes which emphasized her serpentine slimness…"

Sportswear for Women

The straight, uncluttered lines of the chemise made it a practical sports frock. At the turn of century, most Edwardian women had simply dabbled in sports; vigorous activity was not considered "ladylike." By the twenties though, women had become active *participants* rather than spectators. They enjoyed tennis, golf, swimming (as opposed to bathing), hiking, and even such traditional men's sports as basketball, baseball, lacrosse, hockey, racing, and crew! Naturally, their sportswear had to be chic as well as comfortable.

By the twenties, sportswear had become such an important part of a woman's wardrobe that couturiers devoted large segments of their showings to it. Many featured special "Sports Departments," and opened boutiques featuring sports clothes in exclusive resorts like Deauville and Biarritz. Among the couturiers most noted for sportswear are Patou, Chanel, Vionnet, Jane Regny, Jenny (founded by Jenny Sacerdote), Mary Nowitsky, and, by the late twenties, Schiaparelli.

For the average women, both department stores and mail order catalogs offered a wide variety of sportswear. Some stores were devoted exclusively to sports: Abercrombie & Fitch, "The Greatest Sporting Goods Store in the World" as their logo declared (in New York at Madison Ave & 45th) sold sportswear for both men and women; Amelia Earhart, Ernest Hemingway, and the Prince of Wales were among their illustrious customers.

Women of the twenties were justly proud of their sports heroines, including American Gertrude Ederle, who swam the English Channel in 1926, knocking two hours of the world record. Famous Australian Annette Kellerman overcame childhood polio to become a champion swimmer and movie star. French tennis star Suzanne Lenglen won the singles championship six times from 1919 to 1925; sassy Suzanne was known to sip brandy between matches. Dressed by Jean Patou, Lenglen revolutionized tennis dress when she marched onto the courts in a short-sleeved, short-skirted frock with a bright orange bandeau, rolled stockings—and NO GIRDLE! Beautiful American tennis champ Helen Wills was also dressed by Patou; she's often pictured in her trademark eyeshade.

Due to the flappers' love of active sports, more of the body began to be bared as clothing became less restrictive, and it didn't take long for sports clothes' scanty features to creep into day wear: sleeveless day dresses, shorter skirts, and lower necklines all began with sportswear. And you'll note that though chemise dresses are pictured for sports like golf and tennis, women were increasingly donning *pants* for sports!

Pants for Women

Pants for women had been promoted as a "reform fashion" in the mid-nineteenth century, when Amelia Bloomer attempted to replace the era's restrictive dress with more practical clothing. In her publication, *The Lily*, she pictured an outfit with wide, full-length pants worn under a full, knee length dress. The famous "Bloomer" pantsdress was worn by only a handful of brave women, as it was greeted with outraged scorn by the majority of men—and women!

In the early teens, the innovative Paul Poiret made a valiant attempt to popularize pants for women. He introduced the famous "lampshade" tunic ensemble with baggy Persian pantaloons at his "1002 Night Fete" in July 1911, and followed that with his "jupe culotte" pantdresses for day wear. These early teens pants were quite controversial, and were worn only by the avant garde. During the second half of the teens, however, many couturiers were beginning to show luxurious at home "lounging pajamas," which the bravest women even wore to parties. By the late teens and early twenties, women's penchant for pants had spread to sportswear, as women began to adopt men's knee-length knicker pants for sports like golf, hiking, skiing, and skating. As early as 1920, *Vogue* pictured a smart knicker ensemble for gardening, noting: "Tragedies and romances have begun with dress, and since the garden is the setting par excellence of romance, at all times it behooves every fair gardener to look well to her modes."

Also as early as 1920, forward-thinking couturiers were showing wide leg pants outfits such as Chanel's "Yachting Costume." And by mid-decade, Paul Poiret would see his dream of LONG PANTS for women become a reality, as lounging pajamas left home to go to the beach as "beach pajamas," the first *fashionable* long pants to go out in public!

"Jupes Pantalons" a la Paul Poiret. These modest pantdresses were considered scandalous! On May 1, 1911, "Charlotte" sent this fashion postcard to Mr. Christian Christoffersen, 1628 N. Rockwell St., Chicago; it's postmarked Paris. She noted "Newest fashion" on the front.

Beauty and Bobbed Hair!

"'I want to be a society vampire you see,' she announced coolly, and went on to inform him that bobbed hair was the necessary prelude."
—F. Scott Fitzgerald, *Bernice Bobs Her Hair*, 1920

One of the most prominent symbols of women's "Declaration of Independence" was their newly bobbed hair. In the early twenties, millions of women celebrated their intoxicating new freedoms by succumbing to the scissors and shearing their long locks for the "boyish" new bob. Though this famous hairstyle had been introduced in the teens, it wasn't until the twenties that it became the rage.

Soon to be sheared long locks are shown in this ad for Fashionette Invisible Hair Nets. (*Ladies Home Journal*, August 1920)

Gros Temps! (Stormy weather). An avant garde pants ensemble *pour le yachting*, by Zinoview for *Gazette du Bon Ton*, 1920. Though not noted on the plate, it was perhaps a Chanel design; in 1920, she was designing avant garde "yachting costumes."

"The Boyish Bob," as featured in the August 1924 issue of *Harper's Bazar*.

To bob or not to bob? Short vs. long! (Snapshot, ca. 1925)

25

Both dancer Irene Castle and couturier Coco Chanel claim to have "invented" the famous bob, ca. 1914. Castle, the epitome of youth and beauty, was a fashion icon in the teens and early twenties; she graced the pages of countless fashion magazines. In her autobiography, Mrs. Castle states she was the first to "bob" when she cut her hair short in 1914 prior to an appendix operation. To look glamorous for news photos during her recovery, she placed a seed-pearl necklace around her forehead—thus "inventing" both bobbed hair and the famous flapper "headache band" or bandeau. She claimed that by the next week, 250 women had copied her bob and by the week after, 2,600 women had followed suit.

Coco Chanel claimed that as she was dressing for an opera during the teens, a heater exploded and her hair was singed. Undaunted, Chanel proceeded to cut the damage off with her nail scissors, and since everything she did was fashionable, her new "bob" caught on immediately!

Through the teens, however, the bob remained very avant garde; it wasn't until 1918 that *Vogue* pictured their first "bob" in the magazine.

Prospective "bobbees" often invaded that male bastion, the barber shop, for the proper "mannish" look. The bob was followed by the "shingle" (invented by Antoine, a French hairdresser Saks coaxed to New York in 1927); then by the middle of the decade, the ultra short and brilliantined Eton crop. The almost mandatory cloche hat was a factor in the decision "to bob or not to bob"—cloches fit so snugly that long hair was impossible.

Men's barber shop, ca. 1925. This young "Bernice" has invaded a men's barber shop for a proper "boyish bob." Note her chic cutout Mary Jane pumps!

Beauty Shops and Cosmetics

Beauty shops were as popular as speakeasies in the twenties. They offered not only haircuts and permanent waves, but also facials, massages, manicures, and pedicures. Women also flocked to beauty shops to have their hair colored; inspired by the gorgeous red locks of Clara Bow's famous curly bob, many had their hair "hennaed" RED, one of the decade's most popular shades!

"Red Hair," sheet music dedicated to Clara Bow by Elinor Glyn. Partial lyrics:

"Red hair, they tell me spells 'danger'
Because it's the color of fire…
Red hair, red hair, there's none with you can compare
Lock my heart in with a lock of your hair
I'll never care if your love is there…

Makeup was of utmost importance during the decade, as lipstick, rouge, eye makeup, and nail polish had all become de rigueur. By 1927, there were over eighteen thousand makeup firms, including Elizabeth Arden, Helena Rubinstein, Revlon, Ponds, Tangee, and Delica Laboratories; by the end of the decade, women were spending around $750,000 annually on makeup.

Advertising was imaginative and enticing: "Liquid Lushlux means luxuriant lashes that last whether you go swimming or weep at the theatre!" Woodbury promised "You, too, can have 'A Skin You Love to Touch'" while Delica Laboratories offered a "Kissproof" lipstick designed to last through a lengthy session of necking and petting! Vivaudou's "Ego Creme Wrinkle Remover" ("not only removes wrinkles but molds the skin into a firm, smooth surface!") sold for $5, "because of its costly ingredients."

"Gloria Swanson's BEAUTIFUL EYES are framed in long, silky, luxuriant EYELASHES and well-formed EYEBROWS, and these are largely responsible for the deep, soulful, wistful expression..." declares this ad for Lash-Brow-Ine. (*Pictorial Review*, 1921)

Nail polish became very popular after a long-lasting version was developed (earlier nail polishes often ran when hands were wet); devastating colors included pink, red, blue, green, and even purple. Suntans become the rage as soon as Coco Chanel stepped off the Duke of Westminster's yacht sporting a glowing tan.

As checking one's makeup—even in public—was an absolute necessity, a wide variety of compacts, vanities, and makeup cases also became available.

In this hand colored photo postcard, a flirty bobbed beauty applies ruby red lipstick with the help of her hand mirror. Note her smart "headache band"... and that Chinchilla coat!

Drian, one of the era's most illustrious artists, captures the excitement of a haute couture opening in his sketch of Chez Worth for *Vogue's* April 15, 1923 issue; note the "...important representatives of American houses, sketching and deliberating."

Clothing Manufacture

Clothing is made in two ways: "Bespoke" or custom made to a specific individual's order; and mass produced for non-specific customers, that is, "ready to wear" (also "ready made," "off the rack" or "prêt-à-porter"). Custom made clothing includes the exclusive custom designs created for individual haute couture clients; in-house store designs and professional dressmakers' creations made for specific clients; catalog clothing that's made up to a specific customer's measurements; and dresses sewn at home to fit an individual's measurements. The vast majority of the clothing we wear today is mass-produced ready to wear—and by the twenties, American ready to wear couldn't be beat!

Ready to Wear

Ready to wear has a long history. As early as the Renaissance, haberdashers and milliners sold trimmings and accessories like hats, gloves, stockings, garters, and even petticoats ready made; in the 1660s, Samuel Pepys writes that he visited

Paternoster Row to buy his wife a ready made striped silk petticoat! By the eighteenth century, hooped petticoats, quilted petticoats, cloaks, and shawls were available ready made in shops (though still, of course, fashioned by hand). Dresses, however, were still custom made. In December 1798, Jane Austen agonized over the construction of a new frock, writing to a friend: "I wish such things were to be bought ready-made!" Dresses wouldn't be mass produced until around the beginning of the twentieth century.

In America, as early as 1830, Brooks Brothers store sold ready made clothes for working men who didn't have the time (or money) for tailor made. In the 1850s, Levi Strauss made ready made pants for gold miners—sturdy pants of serge de Nimes or "denim," double top-stitched and riveted for strength.

By the mid-nineteenth century, the combination of practical sewing machines and paper patterns facilitated the phenomenal growth of the ready to wear industry. Thimonnier, Elias Howe, and Isaac Singer all contributed to the development of the sewing machine, and by the end of the Civil War there were over one hundred thousand in use. Sized paper patterns, invented in the 1850s by Mme. Demorest and followed in 1863 with Ebenezer Butterick's version, were a huge success—by the 1870s some ten million paper patterns were being sold annually. At the end of the Civil War, quite a wide variety of ready made clothing was available.

At the turn of the twentieth century, the famous American Gibson Girl was making her contribution to ready to wear! In her favorite ready made shirtwaists, skirts, and tailored suits, this elegant beauty created a craze for the first *American* fashions; in 1907, the *New York Times* observed that her fashions were even being copied abroad! As more women entered the workforce, they found it practical to dress in her comfortable, ready made fashions; suffragists also found her styles fit their needs...and soon department stores, shops, and mail order catalogs were selling millions of ready made shirtwaists, skirts, and suits called "tailor-mades."

During the teens, ready to wear advanced via new mass production techniques and new electric machinery...and the simpler tubular cut of the decade's new fashions. By WWI, many women were purchasing ready made clothes for day and sportswear, and selecting custom made gowns for fancier afternoon or evening events. And some women who formerly bought only custom made clothing were reportedly removing those telltale labels from their new ready to wear purchases!

By the twenties, ready to wear had become the rule rather than the exception...the average woman was most often clad in stylish, ready made fashions!

Fashion's "Pyramid of Style"—From Haute Couture to Home Made

> *"...There is not a woman who does not dream of being dressed in Paris..."*
>
> —*Art Deco Exposition Catalogue*, 1925

Parisian haute couture has been considered the pinnacle of fashion's pyramid since the mid-nineteenth century, when the "Father of Haute Couture," Englishman Charles Frederick

Worth, began designing for the French Empress Eugenie and her court. Worth also treasured his American clients; he once remarked that they had the "three 'Fs': Faith, Figures, and Francs!" Haute couture was, of course, exclusively custom made up until ca. 1920, when couturiers began to offer some ready made or "instant couture."

Traditionally, couturiers exhibited new creations at two main shows a year: in February for the following Fall/Winter season, and in September for the following Spring/Summer. Fashions were modeled on live "mannequins" (who, though they wore the world's most glamorous clothes, were often paid less than maids!). By the twenties, there were also mid-season showings.

The top ten couturiers of the twenties (in arguable order) are: Chanel, Patou, Vionnet, Lanvin, Molyneux, Lelong, Poiret, Worth, Jenny, and, by the late twenties, Elsa Schiaparelli. Other prominent couturiers of the decade include: Anna, Agnes, Augustabernard, Alice Bernard, Bechoff, Beer, Bernard et Cie, Berthe, Boue Soeurs, Callot, Chantal, Paul Caret, Cheruit, Yvonne Davison, Doeuillet, Doucet Drecoll, Goupy, Nicole Grault, Jeanne Hallee, IRTE (Russian Prince and Princess Youssoupoff), Lenief, Louiseboulanger, Lucile (Lady Duff-Gordon), Jean Magnin, Madeleine et Madeleine, Martial et Armand, Mary Nowitsky, Miler Soeurs, Joseph Paquin, Phillipe et Gaston, Premet, Redfern, Jane Regny, Renee, Suzanne Talbot, YTEB. Artists who also designed include Erte and Sonia Delauney.

At a French couture house or "maison," each client was assigned a "vendeuse" or special saleswoman, to help with her order from the moment she arrived until her items were ready for delivery—her vendeuse arranged for her to see the collection, suggested the most flattering styles, fabrics and colors, and oversaw the necessary fittings. The vendeuse also coordinated accessories to ensure that every detail of her client's total ensemble was perfect. She often became her client's confidant, entrusted with as many of her secrets as her hairdresser.

By the twenties, haute couture not only catered to individual clients seeking custom made creations, but increasingly relied on "The Trade"; that is, buyers from clothing manufacturers that came to Paris to purchase styles to copy ("reproductions") or adapt ("adaptations"). As these commercial buyers paid well and required less attention than individual clients, they became the "bread and butter" of haute couture, and were greeted appropriately. "A Seat at the Paris Openings," from *Vogue*, offers a glimpse of the excitement:

> *"...As the month of January drags to an end...window displays on the rue de la Paix and on the grands boulevards show tickets worded in both French and English...American banks put up prominent placards giving the exchange for the day in dollars... HARK, HARK, the Dogs do Bark - the Buyers have come to town! They have come exclusively and uniquely to buy models, and from the first to the 15th of February they are occupied in a perfect orgy of inspection and purchase. At the popular houses the crowd is suffocating and every place is taken long before the first mannequin comes writhing her way between the serried ranks of chairs."* (January 1923)

Now—when the shops are smart with all that is newest and most fashionable—now is the time to purchase one's complete hosiery wardrobe for the autumn and winter season.

McCallum

Y O U   J U S T   K N O W   S H E   W E A R S   T H E M

"Now—when the shops are smart with all that is newest and most fashionable..." With supreme self-confidence, ladies clad in the latest styles stroll through the aisles of one of New York's fine department stores. The thrill of shopping in the twenties is captured in this McCallum Hosiery ad by M'alaga Grenet (*Ladies Home Journal*, October 1925)

Couture Pirates

Haute couture fashions have long been imitated. So powerful was haute couture's influence that by the turn of the century, it was common practice for many exclusive shops to sew faux French couture labels into their gowns; one of New York's most prestigious shops excused this practice, remarking that the French labels were necessary as the French had brainwashed American women into thinking that only French fashions could be "chic."

The simpler styles of the twenties made it easy for fashion pirates to copy a couture design *without paying for it*...an enormous problem for haute couture. If a trade buyer wanted to copy a design for reproduction *legally*, he had to pay by buying (or in some instances "renting") the desired design. Pirates could quickly sketch a couture piece at a show or simply copy a couture design from a fashion magazine to make their own reproductions or adaptations. Shops and catalogs also vastly increased their sales with ad copy like "Inspired by...," "Influenced by...," or "After a...,"—couture names popped up everywhere!

Though the *Chambre Syndicale de la Couture* was formed to keep piracy at bay, their efforts were not too effective. Vionnet's magnificent creations were often too complicated to copy, but she had her thumb print put on her couture labels. Chanel, to make copying more difficult, sent her models through her showings at a fast clip. Patou, in one of his 1927 programs, issued a warning to pirates on a page headed "*Tres Important*":

> "The sale of our models to the Commercial Firms includes only the licence (sic) of reproduction and sale outside Paris. Our buyers are kindly asked to inform their customers of the limitation. All tailored suits, coats and wraps; all the gowns, all my fur models are made in my workrooms and are copyright subject to the law of 1909. I intent by all means in my power to sue any copyists and their accomplices that I may discover..."

Though pirated copies could mock couture, the meticulous, impeccable work of a maison couture was not easily duplicated, and, as haute couture declared in *Harper's Bazar*: "Fashion interpreted by copyists is no longer art but confection." (August 1924)

American Couture

Of course, only the wealthiest women could afford to visit Paris twice a year for haute couture fashions, but with modern transportation—trolleys, trains, cars, and buses—American women visited fashion meccas like New York and Chicago for the latest fashions.

New York was the undisputed capitol of American style. A true shopper's paradise, it had everything: gigantic department stores, exclusive custom/import shops, and some fine American designers. During WWI, when French couture became more difficult to obtain, these American designers began to make their own fashion statements.

Though American women had long *followed* Parisian fashions, they often *adapted* them to suit American lifestyles. As early as the Victorian era, *Godey's Lady's* magazine was promoting adapted or "Americanized" fashions. By the early twenties, *Vogue* was proclaiming:

> *"GONE ARE THE DAYS WHEN ONE OR TWO GREAT FRENCH DRESSMAKERS DICTATED A FASHION...It is the fashionable—no matter how snobbish one feels in saying it—who set the fashion. The would-be fashion maker, particularly in America where we are now aspiring to create models of our own, should remember this; that no novelty is worth creating simply because a novelty... The desire for originality must be backed by a feeling for beauty."* (February 1922)

Vogue and *Harper's Bazar* were the acknowledged arbiters of American fashion, and *Vogue* described "fashion" as:

> *"What persons of taste wear with taste at appropriate times...a beautiful gown becomes ridiculous if worn on an inappropriate occasion...all fashions do not agree with all people, and only as much of them as will fit one's particular* individuality *ought to be taken...The happy medium, the adaptation of costume to character and condition always with an eye to the prevailing trend of the times, is safe, smart..."* (February 1922)

Though both magazines featured French haute couture, they increasingly paid homage to American designers and shops. In their May 1923 issue, *Harper's* extolled the benefits of shopping at New York's exclusive specialty shops:

> *"New York Houses Show the Cream of the Paris Collections...There is a certain advantage in viewing the New York showings of the Paris collections rather than seeing the openings in Paris. At a single establishment here one may review the most important models of a score of French designers instead of going about to each individual French Maison, and here one sees only the choicest costumes selected with infinite care from the complete French collections by connoisseurs—the Creme de la Creme!"*

A few years later, *Vogue* lauded New York shops that offered their own Paris replicas as well as couture originals, featuring in their "Shops" section: "...fashions chosen by *Vogue* in Paris and imported and copied in this country by the shop mentioned in each instance." (1926)

Both magazines pictured socialites, debutantes, and actresses as well as models in the latest styles. Both also offered "Shopping Services": "Each month *Harper's Bazar* shopping service selects merchandise that is smart and typical of the mode: send check or money order with size, description and issue to Harper's Bazar Shopping Service". (October 1926).

In addition to featuring exclusive, expensive fashions, *Vogue* appealed to women of more modest means with "Dressing on a Limited Income" articles, noting: "*Vogue* conducts this department to meet the needs of the woman with a limited income; if any special problem confronts you write to *Vogue* and it will answer individual questions on dress and suggest ways of altering frocks." (Though *Vogue's* idea of a limited income might not have seemed very "limited" to some, as it notes "a dress of this kind might be made for $100"!) *Vogue* also offered patterns in "Designs for Practical Dressmaking...Patterns may be obtained from any shop selling Vogue-Royal patterns or by mail from Vogue Pattern Service." (February 15, 1925). By 1927, these pattern designs were featured in colored fashion plates on heavy matte paper.

American Designers

Jessie Franklin Turner, one New York's most revered designers, first opened in Greenwich Village, moving to 280 Park Avenue in the early twenties. In addition to being a talented designer, Turner created her own fabrics. Valentina (Russian-born Valentina Sanina) opened her first couture house in 1925; her exquisite designs made her an instant success. In 1928, the legendary Charles James opened a shop in New York, selling hats and dresses. (In the early twenties, he'd had a millinery shop in Chicago, featuring hats under the "Charles Boucheron" label). Nettie Rosenstein, Elizabeth Hawes, and Jo Copeland (of Pattullo) are also well known American designers.

Many of New York's exclusive import/design shops offered creations by their own "in-house" designers as well as importing Paris originals and selling their own copies and adaptations of Paris originals. Irene Castle endorsed the creations of Evelyn McHorter, J.M. Gidding's talented house designer. Stein & Blaine's famous designer, Miss E.M.A. Steinmetz, created fashions that were thought more American in design than Parisian. Miss Steinmetz was also a noted fashion illustrator and, in addition to designing, she also illustrated her fashions in Stein & Blaine's ads. Hattie Carnegie, Lily Dache, and Peggy Hoyt all designed as well as imported, as did the flamboyant Herman Patrick Tappe, who also wrote for *Harper's Bazar*. Joseph (an exclusive import shop at 2 West 57ᵗʰ) was another, "who, unlike the majority of New York houses, subordinates importation to the creation of original models…" (*Vogue*, November 1917). Actress Marion Davies frequented Kurzman's exclusive shop; Kurzman sold their own designs as well as Paris imports. (Kurzman's Parisian reproductions were priced around $100-$500.) Gervais, another high end shop, was noted for chic, custom made versions of such luminaries as Vionnet, Chanel, and Patou; and Thurn's prestigious establishment was often mentioned in *Vogue* and *Harper's Bazar*.

Harper's lauded the services of these chic "little shops of New York" thusly:

> *"What is the chief charm of the Paris frock? There are many models produced each season in the Rue de la Paix. Are they all perfect? Perfect perhaps, but not just in themselves. They are designed for individuals and sold only to women to whose type and temperament they are suited. That is what the little shop in New York can do so well for its customers. There you will find leisure and consideration for the needs of your own personality…Between your trips to Paris, find out for yourself how near to the rue de la Paix and Place Vendome Harper's Bazar's list of shops can bring you…"* (October 1926)

Department Stores

The department store is "a store of individual shops," providing the ultimate in shopping convenience. In an issue of *Vogue*, Bergdorf Goodman offered this marvelous description of a twenties' department store:

> *"Here, under one roof, women of delicate perception in fashions may arrange their complete ensembles in the height of the autumn mode…frock, wrap, hat, fur, scarf, stockings, bag, flower, handkerchief, even cigarette case and perfume…a blessing in this season when perfect chic means perfect harmony of detail in every point"!* (October 1928)

New York's glittering department stores offered a wide variety of fashion choices and prices—imported Paris originals, store copies and adaptations of Paris designs, and the store's own in-house designs. Most also had dressmaking departments where a customer could select a pattern and fabric for the store to make up (or baste, to be finished by the purchaser). Most stores offered mail order shopping services and "charge accounts are solicited"! Many top stores also featured fashions shows on a regular basis.

During the twenties, Fifth Avenue was Fashion Avenue! Many fine department stores and exclusive specialty shops lined Fifth Avenue in New York. A 1922 building announcement from J.M. Gidding noted that:

> *"…it is fitting this part of Fifth Avenue, so recently the home of women around whom centered the fashionable life of the whole country, should…be given over mainly to houses full of beautiful things, for the service of those women and their daughters."*

And, as if all this wasn't enough, New York even had "Style Consultants": "Katherine Kaelred will select for your individual requirements the most advanced creations of leading couturiers… [she] brings Paris to you" (30 W. 51ˢᵗ Street). Elizabeth Osborne (41 Fifth Ave) also advertised as a "Consultant in Dress."

Dress manufacturers also advertised regularly in magazines like *Vogue* and *Harper's Bazar*; they included Barbara Lee ("Costumes for women and misses shown exclusively at shops listed here for $39.50!"); Bedell ("sold exclusively in 19 Bedell shops coast to coast"); Rosemary Dressmakers ("sold at but one store in each city," in New York at Franklin Simon); Davidow (exquisite ready made clothes available "at your favorite shop"); Golflex (by Witkin & Adler, "a great many of the best stores throughout the country feature Golflex styles!"); Betty Wales ("at good stores everywhere, smartness without extravagance!"); Princess Pat ("Now on sale in one carefully selected store in each town, $39.75"), Mangone ("individualized versions of the mode, procurable at better shops in over 200 cities"); Printzess (styles that "embody the newest mode approved by Paris"); Madelon ("clothes merit the unanimous endorsement of 50 fashion experts," priced around $40); Max Schwarz ("at better stores everywhere, write for style book"). Hart Schaffner & Marx, the famous men's clothing manufacturer, also made fine outerwear for women.

The Appendix to this book (see page 234) contains a list describing many of the fine New York stores, along with some of their original ad copy from *Vogue* and *Harper's Bazar*.

Window Shopping—Dreams on Display

"Fifth Avenue and Forty-fourth Street swarmed with the noon crowd. The wealthy, happy sun glittered in transient gold through thick windows of the smart shops, lighting upon mesh bags and purses and strings of pearls in gray velvet cases; upon gaudy feather fans of many colors, upon the laces and silks of expensive dresses…

Working girls, in pairs and groups and swarms, loitered by these windows, choosing their future boudoirs from some resplendent display which included even a man's silk pajamas laid domestically across the bed. They stood in front of the jewelry stores and picked out their engagement rings, and the wedding rings and their platinum wrist watches, and then drifted on to inspect the feather fans and opera cloaks; meanwhile digesting the sandwiches and sundaes they had eaten for lunch."

—F. Scott Fitzgerald, *Tales of the Jazz Age* (1922)

Window shopping was a favorite pastime in the twenties, as crowds admired the latest fashions displayed in stores' huge new plate glass windows. Life-size wax mannequins often modeled "The Fashions Dreams are Made Of!"

"Working girls, in pairs and groups and swarms, loitered by these windows…" longing for "Fashions Dreams are Made Of!" This photo by Gainsborough of an unidentified store window is ca. 1920-22. Note the feathered "Restaurant Hat" on the standing mannequin, and her fashionable mesh bag. While both mannequins wear chic Louis-heel pumps, pictured beneath the bench are a pair of smart high-top dress boots.

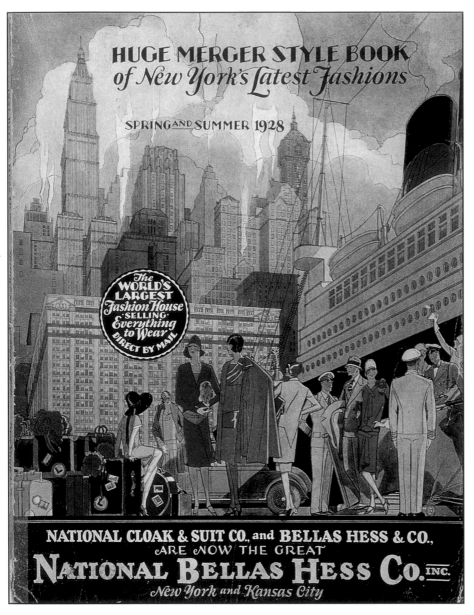

Huge Merger Style Book of New York's Latest Fashions! This exciting cover announced the 1928 merger of two mail order giants, National Clock & Suit Co. and Bellas Hess & Co., to form National Bellas Hess. Inside is an invitation from the President, H. Bellas Hess:

"From our windows we can see the gigantic transatlantic liners docking. The French Line bringing the new styles from Paris, the Cunard and White Star Lines from England… The sight of the world's largest ocean liners lying at the wharves beneath the world's tallest buildings is a sight that once seen will never be forgotten. When you come to New York be sure to visit us and from our sixteenth floor look out upon this wonderful panorama of mighty ships and towering skyscrapers."

Catalog Shopping…"Wish Books"

Mail order catalogs like Sears' famous *Wish Book* were great fashion equalizers, making it possible for women who lived far from cities to dress in nearly the same styles they'd seen in the movies. Sears (1896) and Montgomery Ward (1872) were two mail order giants that sold just about everything and featured practical, utilitarian, ready made clothing. Unbeatable advertising, catch phrases, standout illustrations, and even fashion photos made readers yearn for their wares—and prices were *reasonable!* By the mid-twenties, Sears claimed to be the "World's Largest Store," with some nine million customers buying "New Styles, Correctly Priced; Styles of Rare Beauty, Chosen for YOU!"

Since the 1870s, catalogs had offered ready to wear as well as custom "made to measure" (buyers sent in measurements for bust, waist, and skirt length). By the twenties, catalog clothing had become quite stylish. As clothing historian Stella Blum observed in her introduction to *Everyday Fashions of the Twenties*:

> *"When one compares the fashions shown by Sears during this time with* Vogue *or* Harper's Bazaar, *it's interesting to note there is only about a year's lag in the mail order fashions, which have a surprising amount of Chic!"*

Bellas Hess, National Style Book, and Chicago Mail Order catalogs were a bit more "modish" than Sears and Montgomery Wards. They focused mainly on clothing, with outstanding illustrations and fashion photos accompanied by clever, enticing ad copy. They featured clothes for men, women (even maternity fashions), children, and teens—fashions for "Sunday Best," work, going out and staying home, including sportswear, coats, "intimate apparel," and house or "porch" dresses. Many offered free shipping, vowing "Merchandise mailed within 24 hours or less!" Today, period catalogs are one of the best ways to find what the average woman wore…and how much she paid.

Custom Made Clothes

Professional Dressmakers' Creations

In small towns as well as large cities, many women of the twenties continued to patronize professional dressmakers; they were still in demand despite advanced mass production techniques and the growing number of home sewers that the decade's simpler styles and electric sewing machines had produced. Professional dressmakers designed their own creations or copied/adapted couture designs, as well as making up designs brought in by their customers.

Home Sewers

Many cost-conscious and/or creative women of the twenties preferred to make their own clothing. Home sewers could buy fashionable tissue patterns with deltors (instructions) and quickly run up stylish versions of the latest fashions on their new electric sewing machines. Popular pattern magazines like the *Vogue Pattern Book, Butterick Quarterly, McCalls, Delineator,* and *Pictorial Review* offered not only patterns, but also savvy advice on the latest fashion features...as well as where (and how) they should be worn, and with what accessories. There were patterns for almost every type of clothing: dresses, coats, lingerie, "Fashions for the Future Mother...and layette for Future Child"! There were patterns for the man of the family too: suits, knickers, robes, and even underwear.

Convenient dress kits were also available, which included pattern and fabric, thread, etc. Some kits even had pre-cut fabric: "simply stitch it up on your sewing machine and add embroidery or other finishing touches." Pre-beaded and/or embroidered dress fabrics were available in lengths so that one could make up a stunning gown for afternoon or evening in a jiffy!

This Book is Illustrated by Three Methods

This charming trio will guide us on our odyssey through the Jazz Age of the early 1920s:

Vintage Photos

Snapshots, studio portraits, and photo postcards charmingly depict the lifestyles as well as the fashions of the decade with unerring accuracy.

Professional Photos of Existing Garments

John Dowling's combination of artistic talent and technical skill are evident in his photos of these existing twenties' garments. John was a photographer for the Syracuse newspapers for many years before opening his own studio; he has a Master's Degree in photojournalism from Syracuse University.

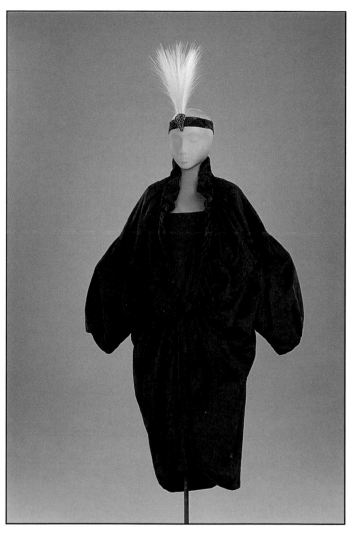

Professional photos. In John Dowling's marvelous photo of an early twenties' theater coat, you can almost feel the sumptuous red panne velvet!

Vintage photos. Louis Daguerre's miraculous daguerreotype photograph debuted in 1839, but photography was such a painstaking a process that it was largely reserved for professionals until the late Victorian era. It wasn't until the turn of the century that advancements made photography a practical hobby for amateurs...and moments that would have been impossible to record previously could now be captured in "snapshots." In 1900, Kodak introduced the Brownie camera, so simple to use that Kodak advertised even children could take great pictures. It used roll film, and at the end of the roll, the whole camera was sent to Kodak for processing and reloading. The price was right too, just one dollar! In this marvelous snapshot, the photographer has captured a great "Kodak Moment"—a young photographer taking a picture of his brother and sister. (ca. 1922)

LE CINE

Artists' illustrations. Off to *Le Cine* to see a silent film staring Charlie Chaplin! This fabulous pochoir fashion plate by A.E. Marty appeared in the French publication *Modes et Manieres* in 1919; the lady at left is wearing a "cocoon" theater coat similar to ours. These exquisite French pochoirs were often very witty, and in addition to showing the latest haute couture fashions, they offered a fascinating peek at the lifestyles of the era.

Artists' Illustrations

These have been culled from many period magazines, including exclusive French pochoir publications, American fashion magazines, and pattern magazines. (It's interesting to note that in the twenties, the fashions shown in fashion magazines were quite similar to the fashions worn by women in vintage photographs.)

Pochoir magazines depict the finest haute couture creations; the most famous are *La Gazette du Bon Ton*, published from 1912 through 1925, and *Art Gout Beaute*, published monthly by the French textile firm of the Successors of Albert Godde et Baude from 1920-1933. Pochoir plates resemble exquisite water colors; they're made from a series of finely cut stencils, hand colored to reproduce the exact colors and textures of the artist's original painting. Each color had a separate stencil cut from very fine zinc or copper or thin oiled card. Colors were applied with a brush or textured sponge, and each print involved up to thirty-two stencils.

Fashion magazines like *Vogue* and *Harper's Bazar* kept American women abreast of the latest fashions, with articles on the latest in French couture and the news from exclusive New York shops. In 1909, Conde Nast took over a small American magazine called *Vogue*, and it quickly became one of the leading arbiters of fashion. Published bi-monthly, it cost $6 a year for twenty-four "Numbers" in 1920. *Vogue* appealed to everyone, offering articles on dressmaking and "Dressing on a Limited Income," as well as haute couture. *Harper's Bazar*, first published in 1867, was a popular monthly. In the late 1890s, its readership declined, however it was rejuvenated in 1913 by William Randolph Hurst and during the teens and twenties it was in the forefront of fashion. During the twen-

ties, *Harper's* featured Erte covers and illustrated articles; its cost was $.50 a copy or $4 for a yearly subscription. Pattern magazines, very helpful as they describe the cut of the clothing and the terms used, include *Butterick Quarterly*, *Ladies Home Journal Fashion Quarterly*, *Delineator*, *McCalls*, *Pictorial Review Fashion Book*, and *Vogue Pattern Book*.

Values

Values in this book are based on consultations with dealers (including websites), auctioneers, and appraisers from around the country. Also taken into consideration are such factors as:

Location – where the item was purchased. Prices vary not only in different parts of the country, but also among antique shows, auctions (including Internet auctions), small shops, large antique malls, flea markets, and local tag sales.

Condition – If an item is torn, soiled, untrimmed or trimmed recently with inappropriate material, its price would be accordingly less.

Rarity – Of course, the harder an item is to find, the higher the price.

Trends – In the field of antique clothing, items that are currently "trendy" bring higher prices. For example, "car wash" beaded flapper dresses and lavish twenties' lingerie are currently hot items.

Labels – Labeled items are most desirable, with haute couture of course, being the ultimate goal of discriminating collectors.

Chapter One

1920 Women's Fashions

Timeline

In 1920, the American Civil Liberties Union is formed by such luminaries as Helen Keller and Clarence Darrow. Baseball's Shoeless Joe Jackson and Eddie Cicotto confess to fixing the 1919 World Series; the "White Sox" become the "Black Sox," banned from baseball forever.

January 10: First meeting of the League of Nations is held to ratify WWI's Treaty of Versailles.

January 16: The 18th Amendment, Prohibition (also known as the Volstead Act after its author), becomes effective at the stroke of midnight.

January 20: The Red Sox sell the great Babe Ruth to the Yankees for $125,000, beginning "The Curse of the Bambino," which the Red Sox endured for eighty-six years (until the 2004 World Series, when the Sox finally beat the Yankees). Yankee Stadium becomes "The House That Ruth Built." Babe, also known as "The Sultan of Swat," also stars in silent films and cheerfully endorses a multitude of products.

February 13: Negro National Baseball League is formed.

February 17: A woman called Anna Anderson is taken to a Berlin hospital after a suicide attempt; she claims she's Russia's Grand Duchess Anastasia.

May 5: In Massachusetts, Sacco and Vanzetti, two Italian immigrants, are arrested for the April 15 payroll robbery of a shoe factory where two guards were shot and killed, even though evidence was by no means conclusive and both had alibis. Their trial, which would become one of the most controversial in history, began May 31, 1921, before Judge Thayer.

May 13: Women's Suffrage leader Carrie Chapman Catt founds The League of Women Voters to keep newly enfranchised women voters abreast of the issues.

August 26: The 19th Amendment to the Constitution, the Suffrage Amendment (passed June 4, 1919) is ratified by Congress.

November 2: For the first time, women go to the polls to vote in a Presidential election. Warren G. Harding defeats James M. Cox (Governor of Ohio).

November 2: Radio has arrived! The first presidential results are broadcast by Station KDKA in Pittsburgh; new radio stations soon spring up all over and sales of radios skyrocket.

On the Silent Screen

Charlie Chaplin and little Jackie Coogan beguile audiences in *The Kid*. (Jackie reportedly saw his chance when he spotted Chaplin at a Los Angeles railroad station—he winked at Chaplin and was promptly awarded the starring role.) Douglas Fairbanks thrills in *The Mask of Zorro*; John Barrymore terrorizes in *Dr. Jekyll & Mr. Hyde*; and famous magician Harry Houdini astounds in *Terror Island*. Edgar Rice Burroughs's beloved *Tarzan of the Apes* is made into a movie starring Gene Pollar, and "The Babe" (Ruth) stars in *Headin' Home*. Vamp Pola Negri plays a steamy seductress in Ernst Lubitsch's *Passion*, and sexy Olive Thomas teases in Selznick's racy *The Flapper*. Comedian Fatty Arbuckle stars in Paramount's comedy *The Round Up* and a relative newcomer, Rudolph Valentino, stars in *Four Horseman of the Apocalypse*. In an early scene, Valentino dances a torrid tango; he's soon to become the most seductive man of the decade!

Favorite New Recordings

Music hits include "Crazy Blues," (the first gigantic blues hit), by black singer Mamie Smith; "Love Nest" by John Steel; and "Whispering," by the Paul Whiteman orchestra.

In Literature

Several novels that are classics today are released this year, including F. Scott Fitzgerald's *This Side of Paradise* (which defined the Jazz Age "flapper" as well as modern mores), and Edith Wharton's epic *The Age of Innocence* (which wins a Pulitzer Price in 1921). Wharton's hero, Newland Archer, notes the profound changes that occur after WWI: "The new generation has swept away all the old landmarks and with them the signposts and the danger signal." Sinclair Lewis's controversial *Main Street*, a biting commentary of small town life, is published to great acclaim. British author Agatha Christie introduces Hercule Poirot in her first novel, *The Mysterious Affair at Styles*, written while she was nursing during WWI. A Pulitzer Prize is awarded to Eugene O'Neill for his play, "Beyond the Horizon."

In Fashion 1920—Couture Confusion!

As the decade opened, fashion was still in transition as it continued to evolve from styles introduced during WWI; among couturiers, there was much speculation as to what would become *The Look* of the twenties. Two alternative silhouettes coexisted—the emerging tubular chemise and the romantic bouffant "robe de style" or picture frock, introduced by Lanvin ca. 1914.

Many couturiers looked to history for inspiration, and their creations showed influences of past eras: medieval, eighteenth century, Directoire, and Victorian touches were all evident. Of fashion's penchant for the past, Chanel once remarked, "Only those with no memory insist on their originality," though she gained fame looking forward instead, creating elegantly simple, easy to wear "modern" clothing. The flamboyant Chanel was always in the news—readers were fascinated not just by her fashions, but by her exciting lifestyle!

Couture Trends

Vionnet offered a fascinating tubular chemise with a provocative handkerchief hem. Chanel cleverly combined fashion's two silhouettes with a chemise tube under a full, sheer hooped cage. Bustle effects abounded, but as *Vogue* advised, "...the hint of bustle might be, oh, so subtle." (They noted that Parisians call their bustle frocks "robes a' pouf"!) Long wide ribbon sashes adorned many frocks, "because, you know, they make such lovely trains!" And, as *Vogue* noted in their July 1920 issue, "The art of the couturier is now often devoted to the back of the costume, and the charm of a woman, like the might of the Parthians, is most apparent as she departs!" Backs were often bared ...Molyneux, who opened in 1919, stunned with his glamorous evening gowns, the daringly bared backs held up with narrow beaded straps.

For day, sportswear was becoming increasingly important, and haute couture was beginning to devote more of their showings to sports fashions. The comfortable, clingy jersey knits popularized by Chanel in the teens were now extremely chic. Jersey, an "elastic" fabric knitted in tricot or "stockinette stitch" had had a long history—it was worn by fishermen from the Isle of Jersey as early as the fifteenth century. By around 1880, jersey had become a fashionable fabric for women, often used for the tight basque bodices (blouses) then worn.

Smart Shops and Catalogs Interpret the Mode for the "Average Woman"

While couturiers experimented, the average fashionable woman increasingly favored simpler, more comfortable clothing. *Butterick Spring Quarterly* extolled the "Simplicity that Brings Distinction," with "interesting silhouettes...straight lines relieved by side 'frills,' cascade ruffles, tiers and bolero effects"...frocks with pleats, vestee inserts, fluttering draped panels ("pouf-pannier draperies"), apron panels, scallops, fringes, and so on! The waistline wandered; waists were natural, slightly above (Empire), or slightly below.

With "simplicity" a mandate, fashions were increasingly designed with enough versatility to take one from morning into afternoon...and afternoon styles went through the dinner hour. To facilitate this concept, frocks, tailored suits, and

The 1920 *Butterick Quarterly* welcomed Spring with this marvelous cover by Maud H. Bogart (mother of Humphrey Bogart), which depicts the latest Spring fashions. Note the chic tiered skirt and surplice wrap bodice of the blue dress; the woman wearing the dress carries the almost mandatory fox "scarf." The frock is described as "a draped surplice waist with sash ends, body in one with sleeve; gathered straight skirt with three gathered ruffles." At right, the young lady's pink frock features a vestee style bodice, flowing sleeves, and "cascade drapery" skirt; she carries a sprig of pussy willows, a symbol of spring. *Butterick's* notes this frock is "for misses or small women, consisting of a waist (bodice) with vestee and two-piece straight skirt with draped frill inserted in each seam, attached at 'empire waistline.'" (The waistline is slightly above normal). The little boy's sailor suit "...consists of blouse to be slipped over the head, with or without shield; straight trousers attached to an underbody." The girl at extreme left wears "a junior's dress in empire style, draped jumper with sash ends; attached gathered straight skirt."

interchangeable separates were paired with accessories that could quickly change the look of an ensemble.

Ladies' magazines enticed movie stars to model their gowns. The *Ladies Home Journal*, for example, featured Lillian Gish in "a lovely, transparent robe de style which incorporates many important fashion features: a satin vestee and four-flounced skirt...with narrow squirrel bands edging the surplice and sleeves and top every flounce...a cut-to-measure pattern can be supplied."

The *Journal* offered comments on haute couture, stating that Chanel's frocks "have undoubtedly delighted in their simplicity and charm...she has demonstrated the beauty and adaptability of fine, colorful embroideries by the yard this season, using them for panels and aprons, even for entire overslips." They also offered patterns for "The Ensemble," described as "a one-piece frock with matching coat"; this is one of most important concepts of the entire decade. Included as well was an article on how to "Make Our Old Clothes New, commenting that alterations are easy "…as long, supple straight lines prevail at all the leading houses." Fashions for the new working woman were also pictured, along with the following advice on "correct" clothing for the "Business Woman":

"No Tea Gowns for the office!" Frivolous frills and furbelows should be eschewed, as should extremely **mannish** *clothing. The earnest business woman of today would never make good through sex appeal. She insists on meeting men competitors on an equal footing, asking no favors because she is a woman."* As the *Journal* further notes: *"the average business woman pins her faith to the Tailored Suit…"* (Carolyn Trowbridge Radnor-Lewis, *Ladies Home Journal*, October 1920)

1920 Fashions

"Simplicity Brings Distinction!" proclaimed *Butterick's* of the mode in Spring 1920, though as *Butterick's* advised, the simple, straight lines of their new "interesting silhouettes…are softened by a variety of frills, tiers, cascade ruffles, 'pouf pannier draperies,' tunic effects and boleros!"

Close-up of the exquisite roses on the lilac organdy dress. Various catalogs and brochures gave complete instructions for making these lovely trims.

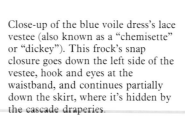

Close-up of the blue voile dress's lace vestee (also known as a "chemisette" or "dickey"). This frock's snap closure goes down the left side of the vestee, hook and eyes at the waistband, and continues partially down the skirt, where it's hidden by the cascade draperies.

"Never have fluffy frocks been more alluring with their dainty ruffles and crisp shirrings!" (*Butterick Quarterly*, Spring 1920)

The charming transitional summer dress at left is blue voile, printed with white carnations with pink-tinged edges. Nineteen rows of gathered tulle ruffles, edged in blue picot, form the vestee bodice and the sailor collar; a concealed snap closure is at left. The natural waistline is outlined in pink satin piping, and a double row of pink satin covered buttons adorns the center front; they're repeated on the sleeves' bell cuffs, which are reminiscent of eighteenth century styles. The "short" mid-calf skirt features the popular side cascade draperies, which are edged in pink picot. Ca. 1919-22. Though this frock is custom made, B. Altman's 1921 catalog pictures a similar style for $48! Now, $300-$400.

At right, for a young miss, is a charming two-piece afternoon dress in lilac organdy. It features a separate back-buttoned bodice over a "frock skirt" (combination slip and skirt). Rows of self ruffles adorn the top's neckline and cuffs. The skirt portion features an overskirt that alternates exquisite self-fabric roses with rows of ruffles; the frock skirt's hem beneath is bordered with rows of ruffles. Ca. 1920-22. In 1921, B. Altman's offers a similar frock, "a girlish mode of great charm," for $9.75. Today, $300-$400.

The endearing child's sailor suit has spanned many decades—it's been a favorite since a Bond Street tailor designed one in the 1850s for Queen Victoria's sons. This fine two-piece example is sturdy white cotton duck. The sailor top fastens to knee pants with decorative navy buttons; it features navy cord side laces, a navy cord tie, and welt pocket. Small navy buttons trim the knee pants, which close with two hidden buttons at each side. The pants have two pockets and a small fly opening (no buttons or zipper). Label: *Manhattan, Standard of Merit, Fast Color.* Worn with a jaunty striped wool tam. Ca. 1915-25. In 1920, Macy's advertises a similar "English Middy Suit" priced at $6.49. $75-$150.

"A wide hat of horsehair completes this charming summer toilette!" This magnificent capeline of transparent lilac horsehair is embellished with a spectacular garden of original silk flowers. Ca. 1920-25. $500-$800.

Silent film star Jean Paige poses in a delightful organdy frock. Jean's about to choose between the two wide brim hats on the couch beside her. In 1920, she appeared in Vitagraph's *The Fortune Hunter*.

Close-up of the "flower garden," modeled by "Caroline," a wax milliner's mannequin named for Caroline Reboux—one of the most famous milliners of all time. These wax mannequins are very hard to find today; prices for one in very good to excellent condition may range between $2,500-$5,000.

As "dinner dancing" and "tea dancing" are all the rage, the latest fashions often debut at restaurants, so Caroline Reboux created a "Restaurant Hat" trimmed with feathers that's very similar to this dramatic black velvet; it features a wide brim trimmed with ostrich feathers in a circular design, with a sky blue velvet underbrim. Ca. 1918-1924. Label: *Mme. LaVine, Millinery Imports, Madison & Orange Sts., Syracuse, N.Y.* $350-$500.

Casual Day Wear

As women of the twenties began to embrace more active lifestyles, practical, comfortable clothing became a necessity. Haute couture, realizing the tremendous impact women's new lifestyles will have on fashion, began to devote more time to casual day and sportswear.

As their knicker-clad caddies stand by, two lovely ladies are poised to putt! Beautiful dresses, and very typical of the late teens to early twenties…but too restrictive for golf. No wonder women would soon be wearing more practical ensembles such as the one featured next. (Snapshot, ca. 1920)

RENTRONS

Robe de plage, de Beer

Gazette du Bon Ton — N° 4   Mai 1920. — Pl. 28

Tailored Suits

The "mannish" tailor-made suit or *tailleur* had been introduced by Doucet in the 1880s. Noting women's growing interest in sports like yachting, bicycling, and tennis, Doucet had realized the need for a more practical ensemble and created a smart combination of bodice, skirt, and jacket. This versatile ensemble also met the needs of the growing number of working women. By the twenties, the tailored suit was a mainstay of every fashionable wardrobe.

The 1920 *Butterick Spring Quarterly* depicts several smart tailored suits, advising that "suit coats vary in length." Suits are pictured with blouses, separate vestees, or jabots (see page 48). You'll note that skirts of the twenties are slimmer and straighter, not quite as full as they were in the late teens. Waistlines are generally at natural level, and loosely belted, while skirts hover just below midcalf. Note the smart hats, bags, "high" dress boots, and "low" shoes. At B. Altman's exclusive New York store, similar ready made *tailleurs* are priced between $42-$89. (1921)

Rentrons! (Let's go back inside…). This beautiful pochoir from *Gazette du Bon Ton* depicts a stylish suit from de Beer—casual enough for a variety of activities, including a walk on the beach! (May 1920)

This smart summer *tailleur* is "…simple enough for country wear and quite smart enough for a town luncheon…" It's fashioned of silk satin fabric that's as soft and supple as jersey. Typical of the early twenties, this suit features a black hip-length jacket with a notched collar and cuffs that match its bold plaid skirt; the style is similar to the one Butterick pictures at lower left (on the previous page). The jacket and belt are fastened with large faceted black glass buttons, which also trim the big patch pockets; a lace-trimmed separate collar jabot is worn beneath. The diagonal plaid skirt, worn at mid-calf, is slightly gathered to a wide grosgrain inner waistband; it's fastened with both hook and eyes and snaps. This smart ready made tailleur is labeled: *O'Malley's, Paris, Syracuse* (NY). $500-$600. It's shown with a chic black straw tricorne hat with wispy feather aigrette, $150-$250.

Close-up of the skirt's bold plaid fabric and wide separate belt with carved mother-of-pearl buttons hand-painted with polka dots.

Below:
A black and white "tapestry" or "carpetbag" purse with art deco "Aztec" motifs complements our smart suit. Its silver-plated gate top frame features scenes of Holland, with Dutch boys and girls and windmills. It measures approximately 9"x 9". $50-$75.

These three gals pose in stylish suits, ca. 1920-22. Note their chic hats and high-lace boots, also the tasseled reticule bag carried by the gal on the left.

Anita Loos, popular author, socialite, and avant garde trend setter, has selected a smart tailored suit that covers all the bases—the jacket has a short bolero front graduating to a dramatically lower back. Anita is the author of the 1925 classic, *Gentlemen Prefer Blondes*. *Women's Home Companion*, October 1920.

Right:

This impeccable navy wool gabardine suit is quite similar to Anita's. Its jazzy jacket has a short bolero front that graduates to long in back, with deep rounded tabs. Exquisite Art Deco embroidery in red and navy silk floss trims the tabs, collar, and edges all around. Beneath the Peter Pan collar are narrow self ties that end in small ball tassels, a detail that's very popular from the late teens to early twenties! Side darts gently shape the bust, and two welt pockets adorn each side. The sleeves are long and narrow with one button at the wrist. The bold satin lining has a wavy windowpane check pattern. The mid-calf skirt is softly gathered to an inner grosgrain waistband, fastening with both hook and eyes and snaps. The skirt also has small front welt pockets, and a narrow attached belt fastens with a single covered button at center front. This splendid suit, in excellent condition, is old store stock; its original tag reads: *Navy blue & red, #277, WALLER Cloak and Suit Mfg. Co., Style 1036, Size 36, Cost $79.75* (the equivalent of around $800 today). $600-$800.

Close-up of the front of the embroidered bolero jacket.

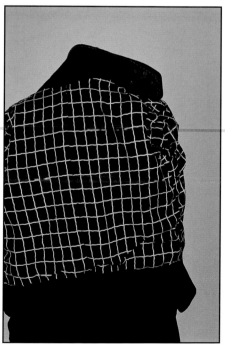

The windowpane checked lining.

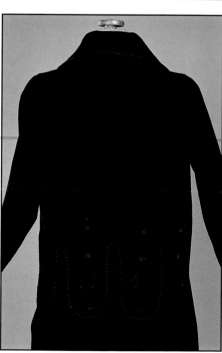

Back view of the jacket, showing the embroidered tabs.

43

Accessories

Shoes and Hosiery

Fashionable shoes to complement 1920s suits and dresses were "HIGH or LOW—Take Your Choice! Both are stylish, becoming and attractive!" (*Bellas Hess*, 1920)

Dress hosiery of the early twenties was offered in rather sedate colors, while sport hose was positively riotous! (See page 102)

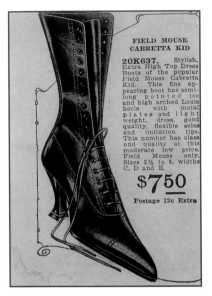

High-laced "dress boots" are very chic from the mid-teens to the mid-twenties. The 1920 *Bellas Hess* catalog offers these stylish high tops in "Field Mouse" brown kid leather for just $7.50. Note the "semi-long" pointed toes, and graceful Louis heels (named for the seventeenth century's resplendent Sun King, Louis XIV). Dress boots for women had been popular in the early nineteenth century; in the 1830s, two-tone side lacing boots called "gaiters" or "Adelaides" (named after William IV's Queen, who reigned 1830-37) were all the rage. By mid-century, high-button styles were favored. By WWI, the high-button styles with their rounded toes had been replaced by high *laced* styles with svelte pointed toes; they remained popular throughout the first half of the twenties.

Depicted here is a nice selection of "low" shoes in "the very styles Fifth Avenue's most exclusive shops are now showing," including T-straps, oxfords, and Mary Janes in a choice of one, two, or three straps. *National Style Book*, 1922.

As *National's* notes: "Satin pumps are always popular," and this lovely pair of satin T-straps is ever so chic! Outlined in silver kid, with graceful "Baby Louis" heels, they close with small embossed brass shoe buttons on each side. $75-$150.

To complement a modish *tailleur*, a lady might select these elegant white kid dress boots, with chic pointed toes and black Louis heels (also "French" or "Spool" heels). Black leather straps extend from the instep to crisscross over the vamp. They lace with seventeen rows of eyelets. These boots are old store stock, never worn. Manufactured by the Rall Shoe Co. of Cedar Rapids, Iowa, they were offered for sale by Harry H. Gray Shoe Store, Syracuse, New York. $300-$500. (Plainer and/or previously worn versions from $75)

The 1920 *Bellas Hess* selection of the "Finest Silk Hosiery" is shown here. Stockings were available in pure silk, "thread silk," "artificial silk" ("rayon" after 1924), cotton lisle, and "combed cotton." Though nude or flesh colored hose was still considered somewhat racy, by 1921 *Bellas Hess* was promoting a nude/tan shade called "Russian Calf."

Two pairs of early twenties' stockings in white silk and black lisle. Both have back seams. (Seamed hose had replaced unseamed hose; it was more expensive, but fit the leg more closely.) Artificial silk hose was priced about $1.00; mercerized lisle, $.75; and combed cotton, $.30. Today, early twenties' stockings range between $20-$40. Stocking boxes often had delightful graphics; they're popular with today's collectors. This hosiery box depicts a pert flapper lass, her shapely legs clad in sheer "Finery Hosiery"! Note her stylish bob and smart Mary Jane pumps. $40-$55.

Handbags and Vanity Boxes

The right bag for one's ensemble was a must, of course, and with makeup becoming a ritual rather than a rarity, vanity bags, boxes, and cases were also essential for quick touch-ups.

Lovely leather Arts & Crafts bags and cases remain as popular in the twenties as they'd been in the teens! This rare leather vanity case features a marvelous Art Nouveau motif of giant Philodendron leaves and berries. It's a roomy 7" x 7-1/2".

The vanity's interior is lined in mauve moire. It has a large makeup mirror in the lid, and handy elasticized side compartments. $200-$300.

With vanity cases in hand, these two flappers gals unabashedly apply makeup—in public and outdoors! (Snapshot, ca. 1920)

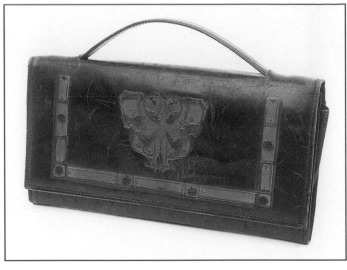

A delightful blend of Art Nouveau and Art Deco, this envelope bag is both hand-painted and embossed with a "butterfly" of twining Nouveau oak leaves and acorns, surrounded by an Art Deco border. In faint script on the kid lining, its original owner has written: "Mrs. Peter White, Monroe Co., R.F.D. #1, Pa." There are three inner compartments, the center compartment snaps open, and the top carrying strap slides flat when not in use. $100-$150.

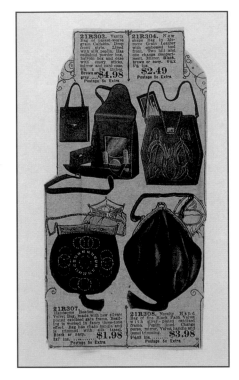

Top row: *Bellas Hess* offers a vanity box similar to the one on the preceding page: "Moroccan-grain leather with embossed tooled front; two bill and one change compartments." According to catalog descriptions, these cases typically contained: "mirror, rouge or powder box, comb and brush, inside money compartment and memo book and pencil!" Bottom row: Pictured are two popular pouch or reticule-style handbags with jaunty tassels: the bag on the left with a "gate frame"; the bag on the right with an arched "cathedral" frame. (*Bellas Hess* 1921)

This flat purse, often called an "envelope" or "clutch" bag, was to become *the* purse of the decade! It was either carried in the hand "clutch" style, or by a strap attached to either the top or back. *National Style Book*, 1920.

From the turn of the century through the 1930s, tooled or embossed leather Arts and Crafts handbags were favorites! These lovely bags featured graceful Nouveau motifs on steerhide or "Morocco" leather, goatskin-laced edges, green suede linings, and gunmetal frames. Jemco and Meeker were two of the finest manufacturers. Our bag is by Jemco; it features columns of vines and flowers tooled in leather on both sides. It closes with Jemco's patented "turnloc" mechanism (turning the tab releases the snap opening). Large button-top openings that lifted to open were also used, especially on Meeker bags. $150-$250.

46

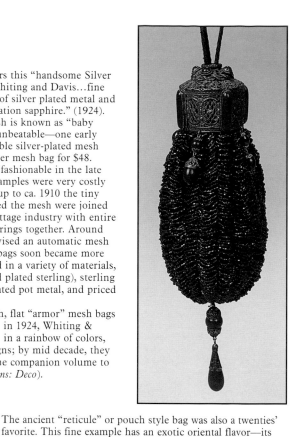

National Style Book offers this "handsome Silver plated Mesh Bag made by Whiting and Davis...fine handsomely engraved frame of silver plated metal and clasp furnished with an imitation sapphire." (1924). This extremely fine ring mesh is known as "baby mesh." *National's* price was unbeatable—one early purse catalog lists a comparable silver-plated mesh bag for $8, and a sterling silver mesh bag for $48.

Mesh bags had become fashionable in the late nineteenth century. Early examples were very costly and completely hand made; up to ca. 1910 the tiny interlocking rings that formed the mesh were joined by hand. This was often a cottage industry with entire families working to link the rings together. Around 1910, inventor A.C. Pratt devised an automatic mesh making machine, and mesh bags soon became more affordable. They were offered in a variety of materials, including gold, vermeil (gold plated sterling), sterling silver, German silver, and plated pot metal, and priced accordingly.

In addition to ring mesh, flat "armor" mesh bags were also popular. Beginning in 1924, Whiting & Davis began advertising bags in a rainbow of colors, with fantastic Art Deco designs; by mid decade, they were the "cat's meow" (see the companion volume to this book, *Roaring '20s Fashions: Deco*).

The ancient "reticule" or pouch style bag was also a twenties' favorite. This fine example has an exotic oriental flavor—its filigreed brass "Persian" top is adorned with red and green glass cabochon beads; the sassy, swinging tassel features a round red glass bead followed by a large red teardrop. The body is comprised of horizontal swags of amethyst-colored glass beads. It's lined in purple silk. $400-$500.

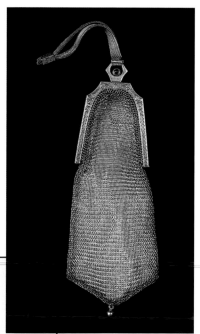

A fine Sterling baby mesh bag with an embossed cathedral frame, sapphire clasp, and bracelet style slide handle. The frame is stamped: *Sterling, AM CO, Made in U.S.A.* $150-$250.

Beaded bags, beloved for centuries, were updated in the twenties with "moderne" Art Deco designs, and this beautiful example proclaims its era with a spectacular Deco motif! Its faux tortoise celluloid frame has a lift-button closure. Note that many of these bags originally had bottom fringe...sometimes snipped off when damaged by a careless flapper! $300-$400.

Lifting the reticule's jeweled top provides access to the drawstring opening.

Vestees

"So interesting are the new French vestees that one could hardly be censored for planning a costume around them…" exclaimed the 1921 *Delineator*. The popular vestee was available separately as well as being an integral part of a dress. Detachable vestees, "collar jabots," and collar and cuff sets provided that all-important *versatility*, while adding a soft, feminine touch to a variety of frocks.

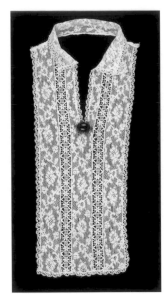

This lovely lace "vestee-and-collar" (similar to that second from bottom right in the ad), has a V-neck that could be worn open or closed. Snaps along the sides fastened it to one's frock. $25-$50.

Close-up of the vestee's lace, and the cabochon "ruby" turtle brooch.

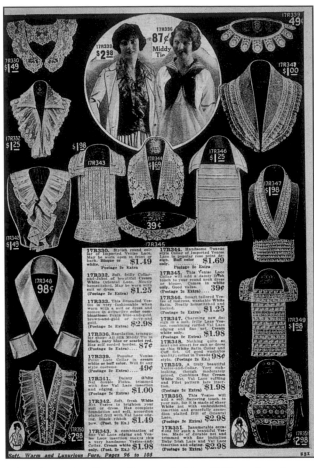

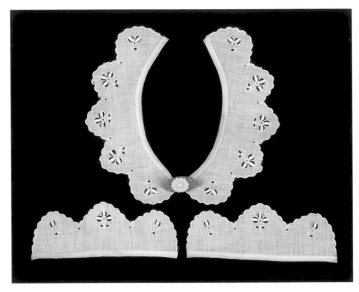

"Many Interesting Vestees Come to the Front"! These charming separate vestees, jabots, "collar jabots," and collar and cuff sets were pictured in the 1921 Bellas Hess catalog. They were often worn with the exceedingly popular tailleurs, as they changed the *"mannish"* look to a bit more feminine one. Note the "Regulation" tie for the sporty Middy blouse pictured—just $0.87!

A chic linen collar and cuffs set with eyelet embroidery—the perfect tailored, yet feminine touch! $20-40. It's worn with a celluloid floral brooch.

Detachable net and lace jabot, trimmed with Val lace, and with a center of Irish Crochet. $20-$40. A carved "simulated ivory" celluloid Art Deco brooch provides a nice accent.

White net and lace vestee, similar to that at center left in the ad above; *Bellas Hess* describes as: "a soft, fresh white net vestee to brighten your suit or dress…has complete foundation and soft, accordion plaited frill with Val [Valenciennes] lace edging." A period cameo brooch accents the v-neck. Vestee, $25-$50.

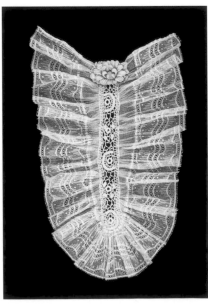

Gloves

For both day and evening, gloves like these added an elegant finishing touch to one's ensemble. For day...

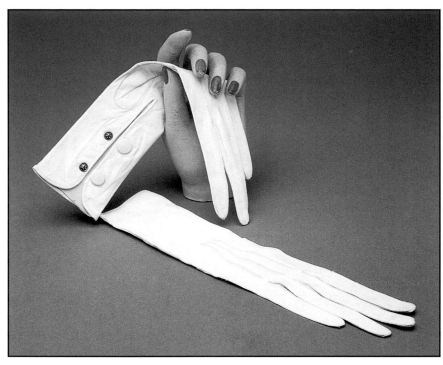

These fine kid leather day gloves are old store stock; the left still has the original cardboard insert inside. They have three rows of "fancy stitching" on the backs, and fasten with two celluloid buttons. $25-$45.

"Perfect-fitting" and available in a variety of fashionable colors, *National's* "very desirable" day gloves boast three rows of neat stitching on the backs; they close with two snap clasps, and have "double finger tips" for extra wear. For day, gloves of leather, silk tricot, or "washable chamoisuede" are very popular. Some styles have one snap closure, others two. Adjacent is information on how to order the proper size, plus instructions for washing.

For evening...

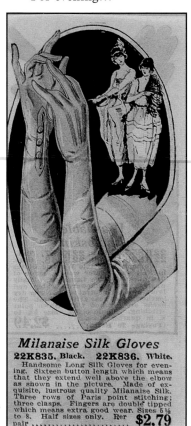

Milanaise Silk Gloves
22K835. Black. 22K836. White.
Handsome Long Silk Gloves for evening. Sixteen button length which means that they extend well above the elbow as shown in the picture. Made of exquisite, lustrous quality Milanaise Silk. Three rows of Paris point stitching; three clasps. Fingers are double tipped which means extra good wear. Sizes 6½ to 8. Half sizes only. Her $2.79 pair ....

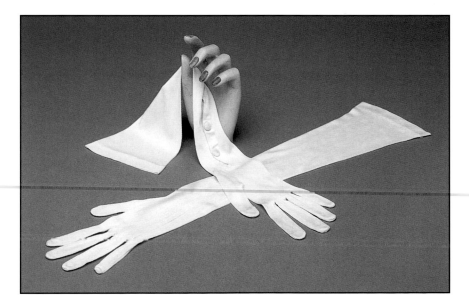

A pair of fine silk evening gloves in 19" length (or "twelve button length," as noted in the catalog). Fingers are double tipped; closure is with two self fabric covered snaps. $35-$50.

For dressy events, the 1920 *Bellas Hess* features "Handsome Long Silk Gloves...of exquisite, lustrous quality Milanaise Silk...Three rows of Paris point stitching; three clasps..." They're "sixteen button length which means that they extend well above the elbow..." Period catalogs also refer to these long gloves as *Mousquetaires*, a "Frenchy" word for Musketeer! While these Milanaise Silk Gloves are $2.79, a similar pair in kid leather, "Made in France," is priced at $4.98.

The Undercover Story—"Intimate Apparel" or LINGERIE

"Lingerie," a French word referring to ladies' underwear, was first mentioned in *Godey's Lady's Book* in the mid-nineteenth century, according to historian Ruth Turner Wilcox. It was a time when undergarments were more discreetly referred to as "unmentionables" or even "indescribables"! Victorian ladies wore a variety of cumbersome unmentionables, including chemises (slip-like garments), corsets, corset covers (camisoles), full knee-length "convenience" drawers (underpants), and petticoats, with, as fashion decreed, a variety of supporting wire hoopskirts, bustle forms, or crinolettes. Early attempts at dress reform met with little success. By the turn of the century, though the wire hoopskirts and bustles had gone out of style, the early Edwardian lady's hourglass figure still demanded a very tight corset. Her undergarments also included a variety of frilly petticoats, slips, camisoles, and drawers ("knickers"), plus camisole/knickers combination known as "camiknickers."

During the teens, this curvaceous Edwardian beauty would become an impractical creature. Ridiculed rather than emulated, the Gibson Girl with her "wasp waist" would soon be swept away by the advent of the new "Grecian" or Empire gowns. Popular teens' lingerie included the straight, slip-like "envelope chemise" (which replaced the camiknicker); knee-length "bloomers" (which replaced knickers or underdrawers); and the "brassiere," which would eventually replace the camisole. Though brassiere-like garments were as old as time, the "modern" teens' version was claimed by Paul Poiret, created for his mannequins to wear beneath his Empire dresses. Teens' brassieres were more fitted than a camisole; waist length, they were usually boned at the front and sides. Though both Poiret and Vionnet claim to have "banished" the corset in the teens, most women then still considered it a necessary "foundation"—it wouldn't be until next decade that many women would cease to wear one.

By the early twenties, lingerie was needed that didn't interfere with the era's ever straighter silhouette. Teens' favorites like the envelope chemise, brassiere, and bloomers were streamlined as lingerie grew ever more sensuous—briefer, and sheerer! Favorite fabrics included silks like "glove silk," crepe de chine, satin, silk tricot, and pongee, and lightweight cottons such as batiste, nainsook, sateen, dimity, lisle, and ribbed cotton knits. The new "artificial silk" (dubbed "rayon" by 1924) was increasingly used for lingerie.

"Foundation Garments"—The Controversial Corset

During the teens, the movement to abolish the corset had steadily been gaining ground. Daring dancer Isadora Duncan did much to promote a corsetless body beautiful, performing not only sans corset, but almost *au naturale*! Several prominent couturiers, including Paul Poiret and Madeleine Vionnet, continued to advocate for the abolishment of the corset. Vionnet, criticized because her designs "revealed too much of the body," responded: "I have never been able to tolerate corsets myself, so why should I inflict them on other women?"

At the beginning of the twenties, however, even after enduring centuries of torturous corsets, many women still continued to think them necessary. As a result, the corset's demise was gradual, with publications like *Fashionable Dress* advocating a "modified" corset:

"There was a time when corsets were looked upon as necessary evils, a time when each woman endeavored to rival her sister in the matter of waistlines and an eighteen inch circumference was aimed at by one and all. That was in the days when the hourglass figure was the reigning mode...women suffered in silence and heaved a sigh of relief when night time came and the straight jacket could be removed...

"It is a well known fact that the continual absence of a corset does cause the figure to spread and in time become sloppy and shapeless... *In this day of enlightenment, with corset designers and manufacturers working hand in hand with doctors, there is no legitimate reason for the uncomfortable and trying corset...for the slender, there are any number of corsets light in weight and boned just enough to provide proper support, yet the wearer is scarcely conscious of the garment. For the stout woman, there are models so cleverly combined that they are really works of art; they cover up and smooth out ugly lines of flesh, they appear to lengthen the waistline and flatten the hips and abdomen, and at the same time care for the bust...yet there is no sensation of being bound in whalebone."* (1922; emphasis added)

For "full-figured" women, a corset was essential to provide the proper foundation for the decade's slender, tubular silhouette—a corset that didn't curve in at the waistline, but rather emphasized the mode's straight lines. And throughout the entire decade, slender yet conservative women continued to cling to the corset. My grandmother, who was a lithe young mother at the beginning of the twenties, used to say she "needed the support of her corset"; she didn't feel "properly dressed" without it.

Though briefer corsets or "girdles" were advertised early in the decade, the avant garde was already beginning to go sans corset or girdle; they simply rolled their hose over elastic garters! *The Flapper* magazine, of course, railed against corsets, advising:

"Flappers don't wear corsets. Why should they? Name one reason why a girl should wear a corset and I'll name fifty why they shouldn't. Do you remember way back when women strapped themselves in corsets, using fifty pounds of tension? That was to give them a figure. ***The flapper says the human figure is quite all right.*** *She does not believe in artificiality, excess baggage or a coat of armor. She gets along without them. She is returning to nature. She is civilizing herself by ridding her body of junk."* ("The Flapper From the Physician's Viewpoint," by Julius I. Mandel, M.D., article published in *The Flapper*, July 1922)

Throughout the decade however, catalogs and magazines continued to advertise a wide variety of corset styles: "guaranteed hip and thigh reducing corsets" that "bring out in full the charm of your dress or suit"! Corsets came in sizes "slender to medium," "medium to full," and "stout"! (*National Style Book*, 1920). Most corsets shown in the first half of the decade begin just above the waist, though a "bust forming" longline corset-brassiere combination (the "corset/bandeau") was also offered. The most popular fabrics for corsets were sturdy cotton coutil or brocaded broche; both were reinforced with elastic. Corsets featured front-hooking "spring metal" busk fasteners, a method used since the mid-Victorian era; many had additional lacing at front, back, or sides.

As fashion's silhouette grows ever straighter and slimmer, *National Style Book* offers "New York's Latest Style Note," the "Corset Bandeau," a practical combination of brassiere and corset in one, designed for "slender and medium figures…excellent for outdoor sports, housewear, dancing and general wear." *National's* notes that it could also be worn by those with "heavy figures" over the ordinary corset to provide a smooth fit. (1922)

Pink Brocade and Elastic
2 V 756—Splendid value. New style Brassiere or Corset Bandeau of fancy Pink Cotton Brocade and pink elastic. Takes the place of a corset for slender figures. Makes an excellent Brassiere for larger women. Four elastic hose supporters (two front and two back). Elastic sections at sides of front insure trim fit. Hooks in back. PINK. 32 to 48 bust.
Postage 3¢ extra. **$1.29**

$1.29

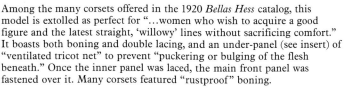

Among the many corsets offered in the 1920 *Bellas Hess* catalog, this model is extolled as perfect for "…women who wish to acquire a good figure and the latest straight, 'willowy' lines without sacrificing comfort." It boasts both boning and double lacing, and an under-panel (see insert) of "ventilated tricot net" to prevent "puckering or bulging of the flesh beneath." Once the inner panel was laced, the main front panel was fastened over it. Many corsets featured "rustproof" boning.

A most formidable "reducing corset" in sturdy pink coutil, featuring a strong, elasticized inner panel, with a front hooking spring metal busk closure, and long outer panel which laces over it. Both inner and outer panels have "extra strong front steels" to "prevent breaking over the abdomen." The corset is constructed in eleven sections; double boning separates each section. Stockings are held up with four attached "hose supporters" (garters). Label: *Welfit, Proper Posture*. $75-$150.

Girdles Are All the Rage!

Sports-loving, active women often opted to wear the new, much briefer, foundation garment—the "GIRDLE"! Made for slender to medium figures, it was touted as the "Newest Tendency in Corsetry" and was advertised using a variety of names: "corset-girdle," "girdle-corset," "semi-corset," "comfort corset," "girdle belt," "hip confiner," and even "college corset"!

Many flappers claimed they considered even these brief girdles a hindrance when dancing a wild dance like the shimmy; thus they "parked" their girdles in ladies' rooms and rolled down their hose before hitting the dance floor. When the evening was over, the girdles were reclaimed and put back on in case mom or dad decided to wait up…!

A brief new Girdle in flesh pink coutil, with elasticized panels over each hip and short, flexible boning and four attached garters. Label: *Hickory, A. Stein & Co., Chicago, New York, 26 (waist).* $35-$50.

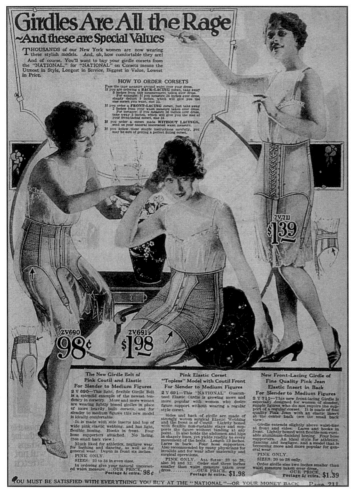

As *National's* proudly points out, "Girdles Are All the Rage"! They offer three new girdles that "thousands of New York women are now wearing…" (*National Style Book*, 1922)

The Envelope Chemise

The teens' practical "envelope chemise"—a combination of chemise and drawers—was still a favorite during the first half of the twenties. It was not only comfortable, but brief enough not to interfere with fashion's straight silhouette. By mid-decade, the envelope chemise would grow briefer still, and adopt a new name: "The Teddy"!

Center right:
A fine envelope chemise in sheerest cotton batiste, trimmed with delicate floral embroidery. The hem is finished in scalloped, embroidered "handkerchief" points—similar to the figure at right in the adjacent ad. A pink flowered ribbon drawstring adjusts the top, and the filet lace straps were based to size. Called a "step-in" style (see small insert illustration in ad on page 53), it simply slipped over the head and buttoned with a flap closure. $75-$125. It's shown with a pink silk boudoir cap with pleated cockade trim, $35-$50.

Right:
Close-up photo of the delicate embroidery and pink satin drawstring.

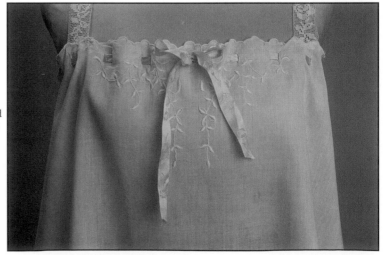

The 1920 *Bellas Hess* catalog offers two delightful envelope chemises at just $2.98. They are "lavishly trimmed in Val lace…with buttoned flap closures."

These young gals just have to be flappers—daring enough to be photographed in their scanty camisoles! (Snapshot, ca. 1920-24)

Camisoles

The waist-length camisole (formerly "corset cover") was another favorite undergarment option. This delightful Edwardian holdover was worn with a petticoat, bloomer panties, or step-in drawers that were almost knee length. By the mid-twenties, the camisole had been largely replaced by the briefer bandeau or "brassiere." Note that although the *Bellas Hess* camisoles are reasonably priced, women with more expensive tastes could spend up to $59.50 for a "Paris Handmade Vest Chemise" in Franklin Simon's "New Trousseau Room"; matching "Step-in Drawers" were priced the same! (*Harper's Bazar*, May 1923)

Bellas Hess offers lovely "Camisoles and Caps"—the embroidered satin camisoles are "slip-over" styles with "satin shoulder straps" and "elastic at waist." The sweet boudoir caps are: (left) "Satin with Venise and Shadow lace, $.59"; and (right) "satin and net, $.69." In pink, rose, blue, and lavender. (1920)

A lovely trousseau camisole with a bust of sheerest lace; the lace medallions are hand-appliquéd to extend onto the silk below. Adjustable with satin ribbon drawstrings. The embossed floral ribbon straps are basted to the desired length, and the waistband is elasticized. $75-$100. It's worn with a charming lavender satin and lace boudoir cap with tiny rosettes. $35-50.

Boudoir Caps

Boudoir caps, another teens' favorite, were the rage throughout the twenties. They came in both an enveloping "cap" style (a direct descendant of the eighteenth century "mobcap") and a flat "bandeau" style, which encircled the head and tied in back.

This beautiful sheer silk lavender cap with silver lamé stripes echoes its eighteenth century ancestor! It's trimmed with a wide band of pleated lilac satin bordered with Val lace. $75-$100. *Courtesy of Margaret Brzostek.*

A flat bandeau style cap in peach silk, lavishly trimmed with pale blue satin ribbon and tiny pink rosettes. This charming cap was part of a trousseau ensemble worn by Connie Lathey (see page 60). $50-75.

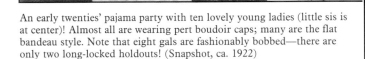

An early twenties' pajama party with ten lovely young ladies (little sis is at center)! Almost all are wearing pert boudoir caps; many are the flat bandeau style. Note that eight gals are fashionably bobbed—there are only two long-locked holdouts! (Snapshot, ca. 1922)

A turquoise satin boudoir cap with hand-crocheted brim and top, adorned with long, trailing ribbons. Adjusted to size with a satin drawstring. $35-50.

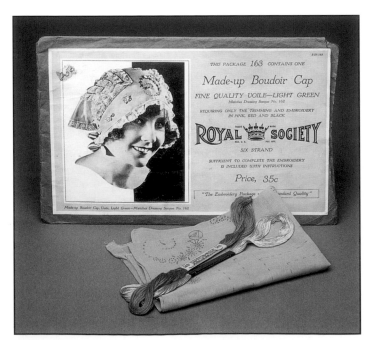

In addition to purchasing these charmers, ready-made boudoir cap "kits" were also available. For just $.35, *Royal Society* offered this "Made-up Boudoir Cap" kit, which included pre-stamped fabric ("fine quality voile—light green"), six strand floss "sufficient to complete the embroidery," and instructions. $35-$50.

Brassieres & Bloomers—The Twenties' Dynamic Duo!

Brassieres paired with bloomers were one of the most popular twenties' lingerie combinations. Often worn in place of a slip or petticoat and camisole, the brassiere/bloomer set offered comfort as well as brevity, and was perfect for sporting activities.

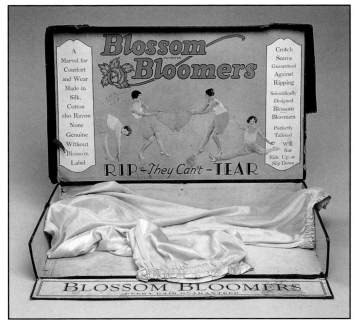

This display box for Blossom Bloomers once graced the counter of the "Intimate Apparel" department of a twenties' store. $150-$200.

Although both the camisole and the brassiere were worn during the first half of the decade, the svelter brassiere was beginning to replace the camisole—the camisole was fuller, loose-fitting, unboned, and elasticized at the waist, while the brassiere was more fitted. It was often boned at the sides, and hook and eyed up the back or side, presenting a smoother line under the straight new fashions. As *Vogue* noted: "Brassieres have come into greater prominence than ever, by reason of the flat bodices indicated by fashion." (June 1, 1922) Early brassieres were also known as "bandeau brassieres." A rather suggestive "flesh pink" was the color of choice. As most were discarded when they showed signs of wear, they're hard to find today.

Bloomers had a long and fascinating history! During the mid-teens through the twenties, the term "bloomers" generally refers to a knee-length *undergarment*, though bloomers were originally *outer wear*. In the mid nineteenth century, they were the trousers portion of the famous "Bloomer" ensemble, named for Amelia Jenks Bloomer, editor of *The Lily*, a suffrage magazine. In the February 1851 edition, Mrs. Bloomer describes this reform ensemble:

> *"We would have the skirt reaching down to nearly half-way between the knee and ankle, and not made quite so full as is the present fashion. Underneath this skirt, trousers made moderately full...coming down to the ankle (not instep) and there gathered in with an elastic band."*

This revolutionary woman's trouser ensemble had been introduced to Mrs. Bloomer by her friend, Elizabeth Smith Miller, daughter of famous abolitionist Garret Smith, who'd seen a similar ensemble while visiting a Swiss health spa. Though these early bloomers blazed the way to acceptance of pants for women, they initially met with hilarity...or outrage! With the growing popularity of sports like cycling in the 1890s, they gained some grudging acceptance, however, and women brave enough to wear them were known as "Bloomer Girls."

By the twenties, bloomers as undergarments had replaced the frilly "drawers" of the Victorian and Edwardian eras. It should be noted that, confusing though it may seem, the favorite twenties' *outer wear* knee-pants are referred to as "knickers," not "bloomers"; bloomers as outer wear referred to gym suits or bathing suit bottoms.

Bellas Hess offers "Brassieres, Bloomers" in this ad. The "Neat, serviceable, practical brassiere" in "strong, flesh pink rep" is lightly boned and fastens in front. The "Women's Knee Length Bloomers of good quality, soft Batiste in Flesh Pink" have an elastic waistline and elastic knees, finished with scalloped ruffles. They are "closed" style as opposed to the old-fashioned open-crotch "convenience drawers." (1920)

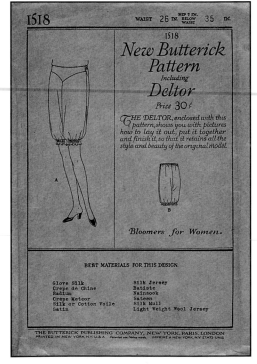

With your trusty sewing machine, some fabric, and "a new Butterick Pattern including Deltor" (layout and instructions), you could run up a pair of sassy bloomers in no time! Note the yoke waistline. Pattern, $15-$25.

"No matter how slim you are these days, you probably wear a bandeau brassiere," exclaims Miss Gould, *Woman's Home Companion's* fashion consultant, in the February 1920 issue. This fine example is never-worn old store stock, a Bien Jolie brassiere in cotton mesh, with a four hook and eye fastening in back. The sides are lightly boned and slightly gathered; the top width adjusts with a cord drawstring. At bottom center is a labeled "corset tab" with metal hook (which seems, according to former flappers, to have been as vestigial as an appendix). $50-$75. The silk crepe de chine bloomers, lined in sheer cotton, were home sewn, perhaps using a Butterick pattern! They feature a narrow yoke waist in front and back, and cased elastic at the waistband and knees. The knees are edged in Val lace. $50-$75.

Five frolicking flappers hike up their skirts to expose their bodacious *bloomers*! (Snapshot, ca. 1925)

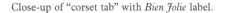

Close-up of "corset tab" with *Bien Jolie* label.

Period catalogs also offered "bust-reducing" elastic brassieres, for the unfortunate busty woman. Ads claimed that these bust reducing elastic brassieres would "reduce the bust without injury." As *National's* advises, this bust-reducer can be worn with or without a corset. (1923) Note: These "reducing" brassieres are sometimes referred to as "breast binders."

A form-fitting knit "vest" or undershirt was a popular alternative to a brassiere or camisole.

Bellas Hess offers this "bodice style Vest for Winter wear, especially during the vogue of sheer waists." Knit undershirts were also worn by men and children. (1921-22)

A fine ribbed cotton vest or undershirt with a crocheted lace neckline. $30-$50.

During the coldest months, the age-old favorite "Long Johns" kept out winter's chill...

Bellas Hess offers women's cotton Union Suits or "Long Johns." (During the twenties, "union suit" referred to both long and short combination undergarments for winter and summer, though today many think of union suits as these warm, full-length, body-hugging undergarments...with the convenient "extension flap seat" in back. (1921-22)

Petticoats & Pantalettes

Petticoats and "Pantalettes" (a longer versions of the bloomer) were also options, and you'll note that the old Edwardian lacy white petticoats have been replaced by narrower but more colorful styles.

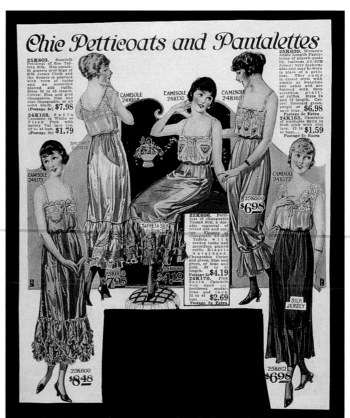

Bellas Hess pictured this lovely color ad for "Chic Petticoats and Pantalettes" in their 1921-22 catalog. Petticoats in glowing, iridescent colors like "blue and gold changeable" feature flounces with "accordion plaited ruffles." At top left, note the "Smuth-fit" gussets over the hips! At top right, the silk jersey Ankle Length Pantalettes are longer versions of bloomers; they're "...very fashionable and may be worn in place of a petticoat..."

Robes

A cozy woman's Beacon robe in an Art Deco pattern of stylized daisies and ivy leaves climbing a brick wall. In white on "Copenhagen blue," with two-tone cord outlining the long roll collar, cuffs, and patch pockets; wide blue satin ribbon trims the lapels. It's missing its original "fancy rope girdle cord"; we've used a contemporary replacement cord. Older looped Beacon label: *Made of Beacon Blanket*. $100-$200.

"For Boudoir or Lounging"… a nice selection of robes from the *1921-22 Bellas Hess* catalog, including two blanket robes, so warm and cuddly their descendants are worn today! Beacon brand robes were most desirable; note that the genuine Beacon (top row, second from right) is $8.98, while the "blanket robe" at lower left is only $4.98. Beacon's description boasts:

"'*Beacon' is all you need know about a blanket robe to know that it is the very best. It is the highest standard make of blanket cloth, is warm, comfortable and washable and particularly attractive in the model pictured. Designed with comfortable width, finished with heavy silk robe girdle and richly trimmed with matching wide satin ribbon on collar, bell shaped sleeves and large patch pockets…*"

Of course, warm blanket robes were worn by men and children too. (See men's robes, pages 164-165)

This style felt slipper was a favorite that spanned many decades, from the turn of the century on. These sweet slippers are old store stock in blue wool felt with pompom toes, and corduroy hounds-tooth check trim. $25-$45. The slipper box has charming graphics, depicting an early twenties beauty admiring her new pompomed felt slipper! The edges of the box have scenic illustrations of the four seasons. $40-$50.

For Descriptions, See Opposite Page

159

Nightgowns & Boudoir Jackets

The "dainty" Edwardian nightie had grown a bit more sensuous by the twenties, and was now offered in colors like "flesh pink," blue, and orchid.

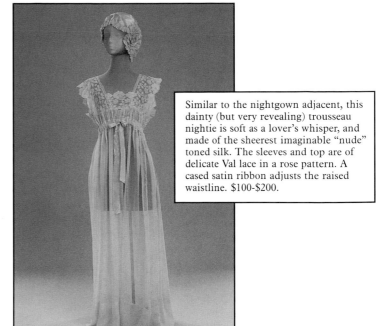

Similar to the nightgown adjacent, this dainty (but very revealing) trousseau nightie is soft as a lover's whisper, and made of the sheerest imaginable "nude" toned silk. The sleeves and top are of delicate Val lace in a rose pattern. A cased satin ribbon adjusts the raised waistline. $100-$200.

Two exquisite "Dainty Night Gowns" offered by *Bellas Hess* in 1920. At left is "a hand embroidered nightgown of fine, soft batiste," and at right, "an exquisite nightgown made of silk crepe de Chine…daintily trimmed at top with fine Val lace…" Both are ankle length. Ladies with more expensive tastes could find "Paris Handmade Lingerie with Real Laces" in Franklin Simon's "New Trousseau Room," featuring "Paris Nightrobes…$9.75 to $175.00." (*Harper's Bazar*, May 1923)

Look what's happened to the ancient "combing jacket" of Marie Antoinette's day. While it's kept its eighteenth century charm, it's been updated to the twenties and given a new name, the "dressing sacque." *Sooo Frenchy!* Perfect to slip on while combing your bobbed tresses and applying your make-up. These charmers were also known as boudoir or bed jackets.

Close-up of the exquisite ribbon rose.

A marvelous dressing sacque in crepe de chine, trimmed with lavish ecru Val lace and a tiny ribbon rose bouquet. Note the graceful, flowing dolman sleeves. The satin ribbon tie is rose pink on one side and flesh pink on the other—a favorite ribbon treatment. Label: *B. Altman & Co., Paris, New York*. (B. Altman originally opened in 1864 on Third Avenue in New York; by the twenties they were located on Fifth Avenue at Thirty-fourth Street). $150-$200.

This marvelous illustration from an eighteenth century *Galerie de Mode* pictures a beautiful lady at her toilette wearing a lavish combing jacket. Eighteenth century themes were flapper favorites!

Pajamas

"Pajamas" (also "pyjamas") derived from the Hindu "paejama," meaning a leg covering. Originating in India and Persia, they were brought to the west by the British, who adopted them for men's sleep and lounge wear in the late nineteenth century. By the twenties, the "new woman" considered pajamas a symbol of freedom...they had just the right touch of the avant-garde and were definitely not for "old fogies"!

Pajamas were worn for "lounging" as well as sleeping; by mid-decade they'd become the rage. By 1927, lounging pajamas would become the first long trousers popularly worn in public, stepping from the boudoir to the beach as "beach pajamas" (see companion volume, *Roaring '20s Fashions: Deco*).

Haute couture even took pajamas to glamorous *evening* parties, and though Poiret, Callot, and Patou were among the couturiers known for spectacular evening pajamas, Baron de Meyer, in one of his *Harper's* "chats," notes: "It was Molyneux who started the modern craze for this attractive and exotic looking garment called 'pajama'...Molyneux, who made a special feature of his famous English tea gown and its modern development, the trousered lounge gown, seems to be the authority on the subject." In a subsequent interview with de Meyer, Molyneux observed: "Pajamas are nowadays quite the thing for private dinner parties...they suit the modern women with bobbed hair, are boyish and young, and fit into the picture. There will be several in my next collection." (*Harper's Bazar*, 1924).

24K134. Women's Two-Piece Pajama Suit made of fine Flesh Pink Batiste. Exquisitely hand embroidered on front and on the two pockets. The slip-over jacket is shirred on front, and the neck and short sleeves are finished with blue stitching. The pajama pants have hemstitched ruffle at ankles and elastic at waist and ankles. Flesh pink only. Sizes 14 to 17 neck. Sale price. (Postage 5c Extra) $3.79

Bellas Hess offers this darling two-piece "pajama suit" with hand embroidered "slip-over" jacket and pajama pants with "hemstitched ruffle at ankles." Cased elastic waistband and ankles. Note her adorable mule slippers! (1920)

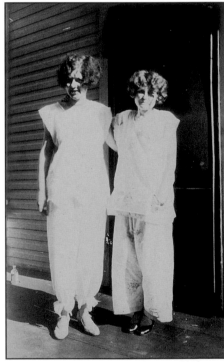

Two jazz babies show off their "pajama suits" in this darling snapshot taken ca. 1922-25. Note that the pajamas at left boast "ankle ruffles," while the pair at right have straight legs.

This fine peach silk crepe de chine pajama suit and cap set was part of Connie Lathey's wedding trousseau. Ecru Val lace edges the neckline, wide sleeves, pockets, and handkerchief hem of the top, as well as the bottom ankle ruffles. Ribbon rose bouquets adorn both patch pockets, and the sides of the ankles. The matching bandeau cap is also shown on page 54. $200-$300.

Tea Gowns

The comfortable yet flattering tea gown was a holdover from the Victorian era, originally designed to give ladies a little relief from their tight corsets during afternoon tea, before they dressed formally for dinner. With their long medieval sleeves floating like specters, these enchanting tea gowns lingered into the first half of the twenties before being ousted by the daring "lounging pajamas." To give readers an idea of tea gowns' original prices, Bonwit Teller pictures Tea or Hostess Gowns "For the Leisure Hours" priced from $17.50 to $44. (*Harper's Bazar*, May 1923).

FOR TEA OR THE REST HOUR

Butterick Quarterly offers home sewers this beautiful array of tea gowns "For Tea or the Rest Hour."
(1920 Spring/Summer issue)

A rare early twenties' photo of a lovely black woman in her boudoir. She's a vision in a tea gown that's lavishly trimmed with lace, satin ribbons, and ribbon bouquets. She lifts her skirt to show off satin slippers with rhinestone buckles. Her little toy poodle rests on the satin comforter, behind the novel she's been reading.

An aqua silk satin tea gown with medieval (or gothic) sleeves of translucent georgette, tipped with chic silver tassels. Two lovely ribbon rosettes adorn the band above the gathered bust, and a pink satin ribbon belt is threaded from behind through slots to tie in front. $300-$400.

Close-up of the sleeve tips, showing the metallic silver tassels.

Close-up of the ribbon rose bouquet on the gown at right.

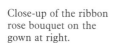

Lady Duff's couture label.

The famous couturiere Lucile was an English Lady—Lady Duff Gordon; this lovely pink tea gown bears her "Lady Duff" label. Her couture house had branches in London, New York, Chicago, and Paris. This tea gown is a sheer delight in pink silk georgette; it's trimmed at its wide flowing sleeves and tunic hem with a band of magnificent Val lace that's 11" wide. It features a picot-edged tunic front over an attached slip of pink silk pongee; it has a bloused back and sides of sheer georgette. An exquisite ribbon bouquet adorns the loose waistline, with three satin ribbon streamers falling to the hem. $500-$700.

Evening Gowns

Evening wear of the early twenties includes both the full-skirted eighteenth century-inspired robe de style gowns and gowns with the still evolving tubular silhouette. The tubular gowns often incorporated eighteenth century features as well, such as panniers, bustles, and trains to add panache to their simple silhouette. Tantalizing trains—trailing "tails"—could be placed at back or side. These long tails dwindled by 1923, only to reappear at the end of the decade as the popular "peacock tail" gowns.

In July 1920, *Vogue* rhapsodizes over the new evening gowns:

> *"It is clear that the mode has been hinting things behind woman's back… for six whole months at least, it has been whispering hints, beguiling, intriguing hints of the eighteen century mode of bustles…As for sashes, there is no end to the puffs and bustles and trains which are accomplished by ribbons that start out…with a pretense of being mere sashes."*

As this exquisite studio portrait illustrates: "The art of the couturier is now often devoted to the back of the costume, and the charm of a woman, like the might of the Parthians, is most apparent as she departs"! The model pauses before she steps into the spotlight, wearing a breathtaking gown of shimmering lace, its tubular lines softened by a low, bloused back with a long trailing train. (Photo by Charlotte Fairchild, of 5 East 47th St, New York, ca. 1920 22)

Back view of a frock to rival a moonbeam in shimmery, silvery, luminescent lamé—a twenties' favorite! It's a fine example of the new tubular silhouette, with a huge pouf pannier bow or choux at left that loops under and extends to an extravagant trailing "tail." Metallic silver and sequined lace forms the straps and adorns the neckline, the top of the pouf pannier bow, and the tail's border. This gown would definitely make a dramatic departure! This back view shows the train and pannier pouf on the left, as well as the gentle draping employed to accentuate the hips. The silver lace and sequin straps extend into the lamé to end in a deep "V", accenting the natural waistline at back. Concealed hook and eye closure is on the left.

Front view of the lamé gown below, showing its exquisitely simple tubular lines. It's shown with a long rope of faceted crystal beads, and an evening turban-headdress composed of period materials: green gauze ribbon, an ostrich aigrette, and fringed silver medallion. $400-$500 (reflecting light tarnish and a few reinforced splits to the lamé). Note that although lamé is lovely, it has a tendency to tarnish in places as it ages; it may also separate in places of stress. It should be stored separately in buffered acid free paper (see appendix).

Actress Nella Regini wears a similar gown with a huge bejeweled pouf pannier bow and rhinestone straps. She carries a favorite twenties' evening accessory (see next section) —a marvelous ostrich fan!

Note that headdresses, NOT hats, were often worn with formal evening wear. Fashioned of matching or contrasting fabric, they wound around the head turban-style, and were embellished with a variety of jewels, aigrettes, and medallions. A fashionable woman might also elect to wind jewels through her hair, or add a dramatic Art Deco hair comb.

A marvelous example of a twenties' turban headdress, complete with aigrette, medallion, and dangling bangles! This lovely flapper graces the cover of a French perfume box, *Parfum Exquis Qualie' Royale*.

Evening Accessories

Flirtatious feather fans were an important evening accessory and pearls of every size and length were so popular in the twenties they were just about mandatory! You'll note a plethora of pearls in both vintage photos and magazine illustrations. The new cultured pearls were relatively inexpensive, and "very lustrous"!

These fans are all the rage! The 1920 *Bellas Hess* catalog depicts a lovely lady about to depart for a night on the town. She's carrying her favorite accessory—a flirtatious ostrich feather fan! From left are: a "Four-Plume Opera Fan (length including sticks, 20"); a "Six Plume Evening Fan…each plume has turned over curled Amazon tips" (22"); and the most expensive, an "aristocratic and elegant fan for evening wear, made of fourteen superb flat curled ostrich feathers…Has very wide spread when opened." All are mounted on "Peruvian Tortine" (faux tortoise) sticks. These fans are offered in "Chinese Jade Green, Orange, Cerise, Black…," though fans of red, pink, purple, and lavender were also very popular. Fans had to coordinate with many different colored evening gowns. Note this gal's chic rhinestone hair comb!

This magnificent magenta ostrich feather fan was found in its original art deco box from *Galeries Lafayette*, the famous Paris emporium. A full 22" tall, it boasts nine superb ostrich plumes with "turned over curled Amazon tips"; sticks and guards are faux tortoise. New York's Best & Co. advertised a similar fan for $25 in *Harper's Bazar*. Fan and box, $300-$400. Note that feather fans range from wide fourteen stick examples to one simple but elegant plume. In addition to ostrich fans, Art Deco coq feather fans and paper advertising fans are very collectible; many of these are shown throughout the text, placed with appropriate gowns.

Lovely "F. Bertini"* poses with her "aristocratic and elegant" ostrich fan, ca. 1920. She's accessorized with a plumed evening turban and she's draped ropes of precious PEARLS around her. (Studio photo postcard).
*Francesca Bertini was a popular Italian silent film star; in 1921, she married a Swiss count and gave up her film career.

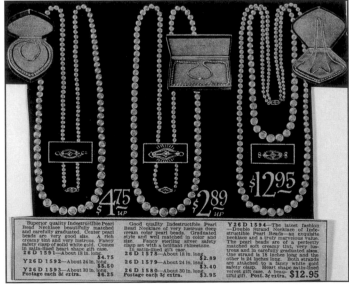

National Style Book offers a nice variety of "superior quality indestructible Pearl Bead Necklaces beautifully matched and carefully graduated." They're offered in a choice of 18" to 30", and pictured at right is "The latest fashion—Double Strand Necklace" (one strand is 18" long and the other is 24"). (1924)

64

Hair Combs and Switches

"Pretty Novelty Combs"! Flappers used these wonderful celluloid art deco hair combs to "...Enhance the Latest Fashionable Coiffure." They were available in all shapes and sizes, in both hand-carved and rhinestone studded versions. Since these lovely combs added a Spanish flavor, they're named appropriately. Today, they may range from $50-$200, depending on design and condition. Though most have lost a few rhinestones over the decades, their beauty is still compelling. They're also known as "back combs."

National Style Book offers this nice selection of "Pretty Novelty Combs" in "shell or amber finish," picturing both "hand-carved" and "sparkling Parisian rhinestones" examples. The Spanish "Espanita" and the "Carmencita" are pictured at right. (1921)

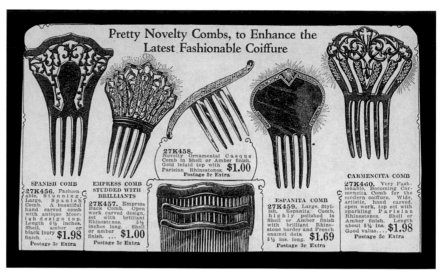

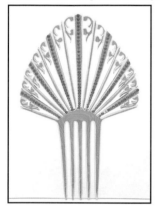

A lovely triangular Deco comb in pale and dark green, studded with green rhinestones. $50-100.

A chic amber celluloid comb studded with red rhinestones. $50-$75.

A circle within a circle! This beautiful shell finish comb is studded with blue rhinestones. $50-75.

Similar to the "Carmencita," this fan-shaped, shell finish comb is studded with blue rhinestones. $50-75.

Many "bobbed" flappers resorted to a hair piece or "switch" to secure their beautiful hair combs. During the first half of the decade, switches were often used, especially for evening coiffures. The 1920 *National Style Book* offers this luxurious "Three-Strand Switch with Guaranteed Permanent Wave."

This wonderful vintage news photo pictures "Mildred O'Connell displaying the familiar bobbed tresses." Mildred peers in her hand mirror as her hairdresser adjusts her magnificent Spanish comb to just the right angle. This photo was taken at the "Hairdressers Convention at Hotel Pennsylvania," by Pacific & Atlantic Photos, Inc., 25 Park Place, New York City, 9-10-23.

Sequin Evening Gown

Perhaps we have accumulated a hunger for lovely colors, gossamer tulles and the glow and sparkle of crystal and jet...
— *Butterick Quarterly*, 1920

Love 'em and leave 'em! Washing beaded and/or sequin dresses is NOT recommended; early gelatin sequins can melt or "wave" when washed or stored in too warm a place. If washed, the material inside glass bugle beads may wash away, leaving just clear glass, and sometimes staining the fabric. Dry cleaning, no matter how careful, involves chemicals that may weaken and damage fabric often weakened by the weight of the beads.

In magazines like *Vogue* and *Harper's Bazar*, prices for exclusive evening gowns were not often given; offered in catalogs by upscale shops like B. Altman's, couture *inspired* ready made evening gowns were generally priced from $75 up (about $750 today).

This lovely starlet wears a large Spanish hair comb on top of her bobbed locks. She's posed for her studio portrait in a beautiful (and quite revealing) tubular sequin gown; note her tight satin vestee bodice with its draped tulle and sequin trim. On the sequin skirt portion, tulle ruffles accent the train, which trails to the floor on her left. On her pretty feet, she wears pointed silver opera pumps. This interior shot is also an excellent example of early twenties' art deco décor...note the Harlequin portrait and the feisty rooster figurines!

A marvelous tulle and satin tubular gown that's entirely encrusted with jet, sequins, and bugle beads! It incorporates many popular features of the early twenties, including a deep vestee bodice with tulle sleeves that float from shoulders to waist. The tunic overskirt is worked in a spectacular art deco pattern, a combination of black/purple/blue iridescent bugle beads, black jet beads, and cobalt blue iridescent sequins, with a hem ending in handkerchief points that are bordered with dangling jet bead fringe. The iridescent sequins are sewn in two different directions to enhance their shimmer and emphasize the deep "v" of the skirt's design. Focusing attention on the fashionably "straight" waist is an exotic Deco flower in cobalt sequins, outlined in jet bugle beads, with a faceted jet bead center. All tulle is picot-edged. Its black satin underdress snaps at left. It's shown with a tasseled jet necklace and plumed aigrette bandeau of period materials. Dress, $600-$700.

Close-up of tunic overskirt and Art Deco flower, showing the gown's exquisite workmanship. Beading was often applied to dresses using a tambouring technique; the beadworker applied a pre-strung string of beads one by one to the fabric. On the reverse, this work resembles a chain stitch, which can easily unravel when threads are pulled.

An intriguing couture touch—ball-tipped jet fringe, to swing, sway, and "shimmy"!

Presenting the Alternative Silhouette—The Robe de Style

Inspired by the wide "Robe a la Francaise" of the eighteenth century, Jeanne Lanvin first showed her full-skirted "robe de style" ca. 1914. Providing a romantic alternative to the straight tubular silhouette, it was a youthful fashion, immensely popular for afternoon and evening events throughout the twenties. Though Lanvin is most associated with the robe de style, most twenties' couturiers had their own versions, alternatively known as "picture frocks," "1840s frocks." "second empire gowns," and even "infanta gowns."

This charming paper souvenir fan, ca. 1920, depicts a masquerade, with an Art Deco illustration of an eighteenth century courting couple. The reverse reads "With Compliments of Hotel St. Regis, New York." $150-$200.

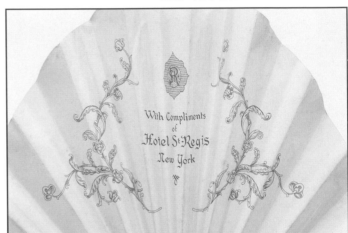

Eighteenth century fashion illustrations, like this 1778 plate from *Galerie de Mode*, "Marie Antoinette in a grand habit de cour" (court robe), provided the inspiration for the twenties' robe de style.

Eighteenth century deja vu! This witty and wonderful pochoir fashion plate by Pierre Brissard, "They Didn't Recognize Me," depicts a Jeanne Lanvin robe de style. Note this gown's resemblance to the eighteenth century plate from *Galerie de Mode*. (*Gazette du bon ton*, 1921)

ILS NE M'ONT PAS RECONNUE

TRAVESTI. DE JEANNE LANVIN

Fox Studios' starlet Elinor Fair wears a gauze turban headdress similar to that shown with the gown. On the back of this publicity photo, Elinor notes: "Having photos taken in costume of my next picture, The Yankee Clipper, and will be glad to send one to you and any of your friends who might write for one."

Below:
The full skirt's incredible silver lace border is a marvelous example of the fine handwork that echoed that of the eighteenth century. Seventeen inches wide, it's a masterpiece of exquisite, hand-applied, variegated pink ribbon rosettes that alternate with trailing vines and flowers—all adorned with mercury glass beads, crystal bugle beads, tiny silver sequins, and silver soutache. This silver lace border is hand appliquéd to the skirt, with winding crystal beadwork extending another 2" onto the pink taffeta. (This gown is shown with a pink silk gauze ribbon, bugle bead and rhinestone headdress fashioned of period materials.)

One of the finest existing examples of an early twenties' robe de style! This gown, though lacking its label, exhibits the hallmarks of haute couture it may have come from the house of Lanvin. It was owned by Helen Louise Edwards Smith, the wife of Smith-Corona typewriter magnate Elwyn Lawrence Smith. They were married on April 23, 1919, and spent much time abroad, where Mrs. Smith selected her wardrobes from the most prominent French couturiers.

This marvelous gown is a lavish rose pink silk taffeta, with a slightly lowered, piped waistline that has two rows of fine shirring beneath. The elongated, rather fitted bodice is slightly shirred along the side seams, and three darts at the piped armscyes provide a bit of bust emphasis. The silver lamé turnover bateau neck continues to a surplice V-back, ending in trailing ties that are silver lamé on one side and pink taffeta on the reverse. The bodice has an attached white silk inner camisole with a grosgrain waistband. $8,000-$10,000.

Men's Formal Wear

"In the foyer of the theatre they waited a few moments to see the first-night crowd come in. There were opera cloaks stitched of myriad, many-colored silks and furs; there were jewels dripping from arms and throats and ear-tips of white and rose; there were innumerable broad shimmers down the middles of innumerable silk hats; there were shoes of gold and bronze and red and shining black; there were the high-piled, tight-packed coiffures of many women and the slick, watered hair of well-kept men—most of all there was the ebbing, flowing, chattering, chuckling, foaming, slow-rolling wave effect of this cheerful sea of people as tonight it poured its glittering torrent into the artificial lake of laughter."

—F. Scott Fitzgerald, *The Beautiful and the Damned*, 1922

Impeccably tailored men's fashions originated from London's famous Savile Row, not Paris, as women's fashions did. During the twenties, two styles were worn by men to formal evening events, and invitations specified whether the occasion would be "white tie" or "black tie."

The most formal evening events required the sartorial splendor of "white tie and tails." This consisted of a tail coat and matching trousers worn with a white shirt with a wing-tip collar, white bow tie, and vest (waistcoat). The trousers, with braided side seams, were uncuffed. The shirt fastened with pearl studs; the vest was most often single-breasted with mother-of-pearl buttons. Patent leather oxfords or pumps were worn with black silk hose. Outerwear consisted of an elegant silk top hat or "topper," a velvet-collared Chesterfield coat, or an evening cape. A white silk scarf, white gloves, and elegant cane completed the ensemble. Popular since the 1850s, this splendid attire saw only minor changes through the decades.

Georges Lepape's stunning cover for *Vogue's* July 15, 1920 issue depicts a stunning robe de style with daring back décolletage. The lady's headdress is a bejeweled evening turban. Her escort is splendidly attired in formal "white tie and tails."

This evocative portrait captures the elegance of formal evening attire for the twenties' man. Here, George Mereditte out-Gatsby's Gatsby in his elegant "black tie" attire. He wears his tuxedo with just the right air of *savoir faire*...slicked hair, wing-tip collar, breast pocket handkerchief, cigarette, and, of course, cuffs with cufflinks! In the early twenties, he was a hopeful young actor and had this portrait taken for his portfolio; noted in script on the reverse is: "George Mereditte, 6 ft 2", 180# - light brown - brown eyes." Photo by *Empire*, L.A.

Less formal or "black tie" evening events required the tail-less "dinner jacket" or "tuxedo" (later shortened to "tux"). This style originated in the 1880s when the Prince of Wales (later Edward VII), wore a short, tail-less dinner jacket when dining on his yacht at Cowes. He subsequently introduced this style to James Brown Potter, a guest from Tuxedo Park, New York, who in turn introduced it to the members of the exclusive Tuxedo Club. This dinner jacket created a sensation when it debuted October 28, 1886 at the Club's Autumn Ball, worn by young Griswold Lorillard and several of his friends. Horrified, a reporter from *Town Topics* exclaimed that Lorillard "looked exactly like a royal lackey," and that he and his friends "should have been wearing straight jackets"! By the turn of the century, however, the dinner jacket, then known as the tuxedo, was commonly worn by men desiring more comfortable dress for such semi-formal events as "small dinners." John Chapman Hilder, author of a *Ladies' Home Journal* article on "The Man and His Clothes," favored the tuxedo, commenting: "The dinner jacket, or tuxedo, which to my mind is far more becoming to men in general than the tailcoat, and which will, I hope some day supplant that fantastic garment, should be neither too snug nor too loose…Men should avoid the appearance of being corseted." (One can only imagine what the proper Mr. Hilder might have said if his crystal ball had told him that the tuxedo style would be usurped by avant garde twenties' women in the second half of the decade—a design by the French couturiere, Anna!)

The tuxedo suit was of either black or midnight blue worsted wool, and consisted of a matching jacket and trousers with braided seams, worn with a white shirt and *black* bow tie. As Mr. Hilder advises: "With a tuxedo, a turnover collar may be worn, though the wing is preferable…The tie should always be black." Regarding hats, he notes that with the tuxedo, "the silk hat should never be worn; the derby or soft felt (a homburg or fedora) may be chosen." The single-breasted tuxedo jacket was worn with a vest, but by the mid-twenties a double-breasted style, worn with a cummerbund belt instead of a vest, had become very popular.

Formal Day Wear

Formal day wear included a cutaway coat, vest, black and grey striped trousers (uncuffed), worn with white shirt with wing-tip collar, striped four-in-hand tie with a pearl stickpin, or an ascot. Accessories were gloves in white or gray, black or gun-metal oxford shoes and a cane or walking stick. For outerwear, a Chesterfield overcoat and silk top hat was worn. Of the cutaway, Mr. Hilder remarks: "The stately frock coat, attributed to Prince Albert, has fallen from grace…supplanted by the cutaway. Black, or dark oxford gray jackets are favored, and there should be a marked difference between the gray of the coat—if it happens to be gray—and that of the trousers. These ought to be lighter and of a very fine stripe…Fancy waistcoats are permissible with the cutaway. The collar should be a wing; the tie a four-in-hand, ascot or bow. Light pearl gray, fawn or white spats, chamois gloves and a silk hat, always a silk hat, complete the picture." Formal day wear was worn at weddings, to the racetrack, political events, and other special daytime occasions. Four decades later, President John F. Kennedy wore a cutaway and top hat to his 1961 inauguration.

THE MAN AND HIS CLOTHES

By John Chapman Hilder

A Dinner Jacket Should Fit Like a Well-Cut Sack Coat

Evening Dress Should be Devoid of

The Cutaway Has Supplanted the Stately Frock Coat

Formal men's attire as illustrated for John Chapman Hilder's article, "The Man and His Clothes," appearing in the October 1920 issue of *Ladies' Home Journal*. Left to right: the tuxedo or dinner jacket (black tie); full evening dress (white tie and tails); and for formal day wear, "the cutaway." In his article, Hilder offers men the following advice: "In choosing evening clothes, it is wise for a man to take the plainest he can possibly get, sedulously avoiding all fancy touches…good materials and workmanship, good fitting—given these three essentials a man is assured of a suit that will remain in style for years." He also comments that the "aversion of the male toward formal dress springs partly from laziness and partly from hypocrisy…deep down, Henry rather fancies himself in full dress," despite his protestations.

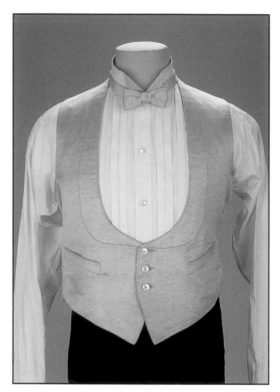

A splendid formal "white tie and tails" suit, superbly tailored in black worsted; a label on the inside pocket notes that it was made for a Mr. "C.A. Knippenberg." The black trousers, of course, have braided side seams and are not cuffed; like all trousers of the twenties, they have a button fly, not a zipper. It's worn with a single-breasted silk brocade vest, pleated shirt with detachable wing-tip collar, and white silk faille bow tie. $300-$500.

Close-up view of the pleated shirt, silk vest with three mother-of-pearl buttons, and white silk bow tie. As Mr. Hilder advises: "...for full dress, the tie should **always** be white..." He goes on to note: "a white tie is **never** worn by a well-dressed man with any except evening clothes..." This pre-tied bow tie is stamped: "Spur Tie, Pat. June 13, 1922." The shirt is labeled: "Arrow - Cluett Peabody & Co.,", and the collar, "Tuxara," 16 ½.

Back view of the tailcoat, showing the tails that come to approximately the back of the knees. Mr. Knippenberg was a man of large stature, standing about 6' 2"!

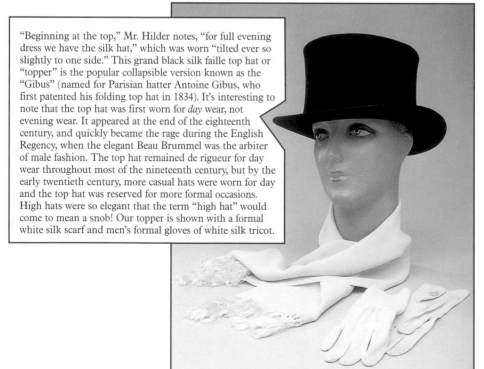

"Beginning at the top," Mr. Hilder notes, "for full evening dress we have the silk hat," which was worn "tilted ever so slightly to one side." This grand black silk faille top hat or "topper" is the popular collapsible version known as the "Gibus" (named for Parisian hatter Antoine Gibus, who first patented his folding top hat in 1834). It's interesting to note that the top hat was first worn for *day* wear, not evening wear. It appeared at the end of the eighteenth century, and quickly became the rage during the English Regency, when the elegant Beau Brummel was the arbiter of male fashion. The top hat remained de rigueur for day wear throughout most of the nineteenth century, but by the early twentieth century, more casual hats were worn for day and the top hat was reserved for more formal occasions. High hats were so elegant that the term "high hat" would come to mean a snob! Our topper is shown with a formal white silk scarf and men's formal gloves of white silk tricot.

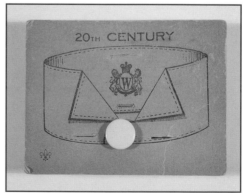

A flat collar button, like this store stock example on its original card, fastened the wing tip collar in front as shown; another button secured it in back. $20-$25.

The coat's label: *C.H. Ziehlsdorff, Duluth, Minn.*

In November 1920, an epic event takes place—for the first time in history, women go to the polls to vote in a presidential election! In Haskell Collins's poignant illustration, "The Mystery of 1920," a confident young woman enters Voting Booth No. 1 to exercise her newly-won right to vote. It's cold in November, so she wears a warm coat with a large fur cape collar and her flame-red feathered hat reflects her indomitable spirit. (*Leslie's Magazine* cover, September 11, 1920)

September 11, 1920

Price—15 Cents
Subscription Price $7.00 a year

Leslie's
Illustrate   paper

VOTING BOOTH NO 1

The Mystery of 1920

Caroline models a similar early twenties' red straw toque, trimmed with an assertive band of flame-red ostrich feathers. It's lined in black silk, with a tiny bow to mark the back, and labeled: *The Edwards Store, Syracuse and Rochester*. This was an extremely popular style ca. 1918-1922, before the clamor for the cloche crescendo! $250-$350.

Women's Outer Wear, Coats, "Jacquettes," Capes, And Neckpieces

Coat styles, like dress styles, were transitional in the early twenties, and fashions that had put in an appearance in the late teens lingered into the early twenties. Coats are either full or three-quarter length, and both belted and unbelted styles are shown. Belted styles feature natural waistlines or even slightly raised; some belts button cross-over style, while others tie, often ending in decorative tassels. A very popular late teens style, the unbelted "cocoon" coat (wide through the body, narrowing at the hem) remains a favorite. Many coats feature "convertible" collars, which can be worn high, "muffled up" Directoire style, or open. Winter fabrics include a long-napped velvety "Plush," a softly-napped wool with a diagonal-weave known as "Bolivia," and a heavy gabardine in "Poiret Twill." Fabric coats are trimmed with lavish embroidery and/or a wide variety of decorative buttons, tabs and oriental tassels—and, of course, FUR!

Fur had been popular since cave people first slung pelts around their shoulders for warmth. During the nineteenth century, however, fur was used as a luxurious *lining* for coats; it wasn't until around 1880 that the famous couturier Doucet created quite a stir with coats featuring fur worn on the *outside*. During the twenties, the fur coat was considered the ultimate in warmth…and luxury! Mink, sable, and ermine were the most desirable, but mink, sable, and ermine were, of course, reserved for the wealthy.

73

Five smart gals, perhaps also on their way to the polls, in a delightful variety of fur and fur-trimmed coats and "jacquettes." Penned at the bottom: "Part of 'The Family,' Mary, Eve, Mabe, A.B. and Dot." (Snapshot, ca. 1920-22)

This "coat of many colors" is perfect for a chilly November day—it's a magnificent silk velvet dress coat with vertical stripes in luminous shades of green, navy, red, and gold. The convertible fur collar of Russian bear—or perhaps "Black Manchurian Wolf"—an be worn three ways: Directoire, muffled high; medium, Peter Pan (shown); or open. The fur trim is repeated on cuffs and hem. Front closure with two sections of large, round covered buttons, which also fasten the wide attached belt. Self-piping outlines the belt, and also emphasizes the shoulder seams. Lined in black satin with a couture label: *Francois, Inc., 589 Fifth Ave, New York*. $450-$600. (In 1922, B. Altman offers a similar fur-trimmed coat for $58!)

For the average woman, twenties' catalogs like *Bellas Hess* advertised a variety of less expensive furs, with such compelling ad copy such as:

> *"Why Furs are Like Diamonds…I once heard a man advise another to go to Tiffany—the high class Fifth Avenue jeweler—if he wanted to be sure that the diamond he bought was just as represented. Furs are like diamonds in that it is hard for the average woman to know the real quality of the fur she buys and the value it represents. Here at* Bellas Hess *only perfect furs are chosen—furs that our experts have carefully examined and that we guarantee to give full satisfaction in every respect."* (1921)

"Genuine" furs were advertised—muskrat, seal, fox, bear, raccoon, skunk, squirrel, stone martin, opossum, and fitch (similar to mink)—as well as inexpensive furs that masqueraded as expensive, with clever, catchy names (and often startling origins): "Japanese Mink" ("a short-haired, rich, sturdy brown fur with darker brown markings, resembling the high priced genuine Mink"); "Manchurian Wolf" ("a durable, long-haired, silky fur"); "Manchurian Lynx" ("Manchurian Wolf-Dog"); and "Chinese Raccoon" ("one of the most dependable of the inexpensive furs"). "Chinese Goat" imitated "Russian Bearskin," and Nutria "resembles the expensive South American Beaver Fur." "Hudson" Seal was sheared, dyed muskrat. The ubiquitous Coney (rabbit) imitated just about anything and everything, including "Muskrat-coney," while Seal, "Near seal" or "Sealine fur" is described as "a sheared coney, rich fine glossy fur closely resembling genuine Alaska Seal at a fraction of the price.". "Leopard-coney" is "Coney dyed in fashionable leopard skin effect."

The favorite collegiate fur was, of course, the famous Genuine Raccoon Fur Coat! *National's* offers a full-length version for $56.95: "A handsome big coat of sturdy natural raccoon fur is just what you want to defy the winter's cold. It is an ideal garment for driving" (especially in an open car!).

Furs came in styles to fit all shapes and pocketbooks—coats in full length or three-quarter length, capes, hip-length "jacquettes," fur neckpieces, and the smallest fur "chokers." Those with modest incomes could also splurge on fabric coats with lavish fur trim! Prices for both genuine and faux furs include a "natural leopard three-quarter coat," $169.50; a three-quarter length "Russian Marmot," $159.00; and a full-length "Genuine Muskrat," $99.75, while a full-length "Sealine Coney" is similarly priced at $98.75.

Bellas Hess offers three modish belted coats on the back cover of their Fall/Winter 1920/21 issue. The center coat, a style similar to ours, is described as a "dress coat of lustrous Egyptian Plush" with collar, cuffs, and hem of "black Manchurian Wolf fur"…it's just $29.95! Note that waistlines are about natural level; hems are around mid-calf on the two full-length coats, while the coat at right is three-quarter length.

Erte's stunning Art Deco painting, "Love's Captive," graces the cover of *Harper's Bazar's* Christmas issue for 1921. His lady wears a voluminous, unbelted coat with a high, muffled "Directoire" fur collar. One of the most famous Art Deco artists, Erte (Russian-born Romain de Tirtoff) produced many stunning covers for *Harper's Bazar* during the twenties. Multi-talented, he designed both sets and costumes for opera, theater, and ballet, including the Ballet Russes. He also created extravagant fantasy costumes for the Ziegfeld Follies and the French Folies-Bergere. Josephine Baker, the beautiful black American entertainer who took Paris by storm in the twenties, wore some of Erte's most erotic creations.

"It's beginning to look a lot like Christmas…"! A marvelous photo of a flapper gal in a luxurious, high-collared fur coat of mink, sable, or muskrat. It's an unbelted style with horizontal bands of fur providing a wide border. She carries the requisite "brown paper packages tied up with string" and there's a little trimmed Christmas tree to her right. Note her chic (but not too practical) T-strap shoes—she'd be better off with a pair of stylish gaiter-topped boots! By professional photographer William Kollecker, Saranac Lake, New York, ca. 1920-24.

Right:
Close-up of the early twenties' toque of batik-printed silk faille trimmed with seal, and the plush coat's Directoire collar "muffled up." The collar has four self fabric loops, and two smaller matching Bakelite buttons in addition to snaps placed under the collar to secure it when worn muffled up. Toque hat, $150-$200.

A smashing unbelted winter coat in a toasty silk/wool plush that imitates seal. *Bellas Hess* describes a similar coat as: "Fit for a princess is this wonderfully becoming Directoire wrap coat of 'Peco Seal Plush,' which has a beautiful glow and lustre that so closely resembles the genuine seal fur that it is almost impossible to distinguish the difference…its graceful lines and handsome appearance proclaim it a masterpiece of designing and tailoring." The very large convertible collar is quilted in wavy Deco lines, as are the wide cuffs. This style narrows at the hem in the "cocoon" silhouette so popular in the teens and early twenties. Dramatic dolman sleeves enhance its lines. Closure is left of center with two large carved Bakelite buttons. Lined in purple satin, it has inner ties and a *Worthwhile* label (*Worthwhile* coats were advertised in *Vogue*); *Vogue's* "Shopping Service" features a similar style at $79.50. (July 15, 1920) $300-$400.

Spats, Gaiters, and Boot Tops—A "Necessary" Accessory!

"Fashionable gaiters represent one of Broadway's latest fads!" trumpets *Bellas Hess* in 1920, "For fall and winter wear, it is almost necessary that your wardrobe contain at least one pair of gaiter boot tops!" Variously known as "spats," "gaiters," or "boot tops," these items were supremely chic during the teens through the first half of the twenties. They were usually worn over dress boots, but were also seen over oxfords and even pumps. While they came in various heights from just above the ankle to over the knees, the most common hovered below mid-calf in ten button to fifteen button ("extra high to carry out fashion-favored short skirts") styles. Most were wool felt, "kersey" (a coarse, ribbed wool first manufactured in Kersey, England), canvas, or linen, though *Bellas Hess* even offered gaiters of black satin, "which New York's smart set endorses as the very latest style." "Very pretty" colors include: "beaver brown," "field mouse brown," dark gray, and black, with prices ranging from $.48- $3.49.

Gaiters had enjoyed a long life. As *guetres*, they had been worn in eighteenth century France; in England they'd been called *spatter-dashes*, later shortened to "spats."

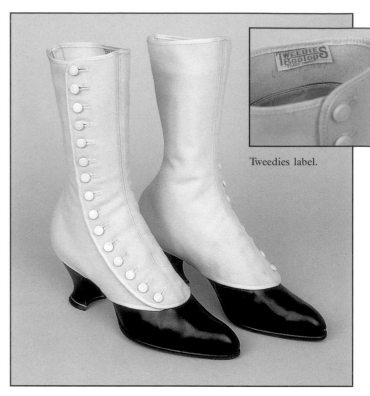

Tweedies label.

A dashing pair of white felt "Tweedies Boot-Tops" that fasten with fifteen white textured buttons. Can you imagine lacing nineteen rows of eyelets on the dress boots beneath, then buttoning thirty spat buttons before venturing out?! $50-$75.

Depicting a gigantic pair of spats sauntering by New York's Public Library at Fifth Avenue at 42nd Street, this witty Art Deco ad for "Tweedie Boot-Tops, More Than a Spat" appeared in the November 1920 issue of *Ladies' Home Journal*. The ad copy proclaims: "Stylish – Comfortable – Practical, and all at the same time. There's a wonderfully satisfying delight in feeling properly dressed for the occasion and the weather that goes with Tweedies—none of the careless-fitting faults of just spats, for Tweedies are super-spats!"

This pert young miss models Tweedie's "latest invention"—new 12" spats named "The Tweedie Putter." (Department store display photo, ca. 1922-24)

Capes

The cape remained popular throughout the decade; as *Delineator* notes: "Why is it that the cape, after years in the dust-bin of social oblivion, is having such a tremendous success this Spring? Is it because all good styles are slated to return once within a certain cycle of years? The cape is charming and women wear it morning, noon and night..." (March 1922)

LE RETOUR DES AUTANS
Tailleur et Robe d'après-midi, de Doeuillet

Gazelle du Bon Genre. Nº 7. — Planche 35

Le Retour des Autans (The Southerlies Return)! Simeon's charming pochoir depicts two smart Doeuillet creations for fall: at left a *tailleur* with a three-quarter length jacket with "muffled" fur vestee and cuffs. At right is an early example of the famous ensemble concept: a Directoire collar coat and dress ensemble, the chic plaid coat trim of the same fabric as the dress beneath. (Chanel was one of the most prominent promoters of the ensemble concept). *Gazette due Bon Ton*, ca. 1920.

A waist-length mink cape or "scarf" is so luxurious, and so warm when cold winter winds begin to blow! In this example, the pelts are vertically placed to end in a border of tails and paws; two mink pompom buttons adorn the front. It can be worn fastened via the pompom buttons, closed higher with hook and eye closures, or off the shoulders and secured by an inner chain. The silk brocade lining is trimmed with embroidered featherstitching; no label is present. It's 20" long and measures 60" around the hem. Cape, $200-$350. The cape is worn over Wanamaker's caramel-checked tailored suit, and topped by a transparent lace brimmed hat, trimmed with fall bittersweet berries and orange glass balls, labeled: *The Jardine Hat Company, 42 West 38th St., NY*. Hat, $250-$350.

The 1920 *Bellas Hess* catalog offers a similar "scarf" cape and muff, "trimmed with tails all around." Their scarf is "genuine dyed black skunk...one of the season's most fashionable furs...," offered at $46.75. The muff is described as "a large Canteen shape muff of high grade dyed black skunk to match cape-scarf described above...," $26.95. They offer a similar cape-scarf in fox for $79.95, and matching muff, $52.95.

This huge "Canteen" muff measures 15" wide by 21" long. A full pelt "critter," complete with head, paws and tail encircles each end; at left, a tasseled rope of braided silk is attached for carrying over the arm. Silk satin lining. $100-$150.

The ultimate! Store stock dress boots in caramel kid and black patent leather lace with seventeen rows of eyelets. Note the graceful, curving design on the heels. Manufactured by "Duttenhofer" with a trade-mark griffin stamped on the soles; sold by "C. Sautter's Sons, Utica, N.Y." as stamped inside top edge. $400-$700.

A sporty tailored "walking" suit for fall in caramel-checked wool from the prestigious John Wanamaker's. The hip-length jacket is double belted in a smart Norfolk variation; the front is accented with vertical plackets topped with mother-of-pearl buttons, which is repeated on back and cuffs. The skirt, slightly full, has a back snap closure with inner grosgrain waistband, labeled: *John Wanamaker, No. 25164, size 38*, [original] *price $48.50*. Ca. 1919-1922. $600-$800.

Back view of suit, showing the intricate detailing of the Norfolk belts and vertical plackets with pearl buttoned tabs.

Two chic gals in luxurious fur "jacquettes" and smart early twenties hats! While the gal on the right wears trendy galoshes, her companion has opted for dress boots and spats (also note her coat's chic cross-buttoned belt). (Snapshot, ca. 1919-23)

National's advertises a similar fur jacket: "Fashionable Fur Jacquette, New York's Favorite," claiming, "there is no style that enjoys quite so long a season as the fur jacquette. With the very first autumn winds right up to the last breath of spring, Fifth Avenue is just flooded with fur jacquettes!" *National's* prices are: "genuine muskrat," $57.95; "muskrat coney," $22.50; "sealine coney," $44.75. (1924)

Fur Neckpieces or "Scarves"

The fox neckpiece or "scarf" was one of the flapper's most beloved accessories—an absolute *must*, it remained popular through the entire decade. During the twenties, one-pelt "single animal effect" pieces with "...animal head and paws at one end and tabs and bushy tail at the other" were most fashionable. They're pictured in zillions of period fashion plates, and countless vintage photographs show them worn both winter and summer—even at the beach! Since genuine fox scarves were quite expensive, catalogs offered a range of faux favorites as well.

Note that though these "critter" neckpieces may seem bizarre today, they'd been worn for a long time prior to the twenties; they were favorites during the Victorian era, and many Victorian photographs picture ladies wearing similar fur pieces, complete with heads and tails. Though single pelts were favored in the twenties, by the thirties and forties four to six pelt scarves were all the rage, and the craving for these critters continued into the 1950s!

National's offers this "Fine Russian Fox" neckpiece: "...a very high grade fur neckpiece for year-round wear...rich lustrous appearance of the fur will delight you no less than its good wearing quality...with fur on both sides...trimmed with four paws and a tail, with animal head snap and ball snap chain fasteners." (1924)

A flapper's delight! This luxurious silver fox scarf measures a full 50". Naturally, it has the requisite "animal head and paws at one end and tabs and bushy tail at the other"; the head has glass eyes. It fastens with crocheted ball snaps on the left front and back paws; under the head is a crocheted spring or "animal head snap." $150-$250.

This smartly dressed flapper looks bemused as her beau completes his puzzled perusal of her fox's anatomy. You can almost see her thinking, "*Men!!!*" (Snapshot, ca. 1927)

The smallest version of the neckpiece-scarf was the chic "choker scarf."

Caroline's modeling a magnificent mink "choker-scarf." Small but sensational, it's complete with a tiny glass-eyed head at one end and tail at the other; it's bordered with black and white ostrich feathers. Choker, $100-$150. Her dashing black satin hat is trimmed with iridescent coq feathers and simulated sequin birds. Hat, $300-$400.

Close-up photo of Caroline's hat with the sequin birds!

Bellas Hess offers a similar "Smart Choker Scarf of high grade American Marten fur...in single animal effect with head at one end and tail and paws at the other," $10.75. Note her smart tricorne hat, and modish tasseled belt. (1920)

The lovely gal in this early twenties' hand-colored photo postcard is wearing a smart choker scarf—no wonder she's receiving so much attention from her beau!

Feather Boas

Chic feather boas, at just $2.98, are much more modestly priced than fur pieces. Versions of these flattering feather neck pieces had been favorites for centuries.

Bellas Hess offers: "A charming, becoming, up-to-date neck piece or boa...finished with long silk cord tassels..." As *Bellas Hess* advises, it "gives good wear and is just as effective as an expensive fur piece." (1920)

Sooo flirtatious! This becoming royal blue ostrich boa is also "...finished with long silk cord tassels." Boa, $75-$100. (Her cloche is also pictured on page 203).

Chapter Two

1921 Women's Fashions

Timeline

In 1921, famous black scientist George Washington Carver addresses the House of Representatives on methods he developed to benefit agriculture in the South; Albert Einstein wins the Nobel Prize for Physics; and Coco Chanel introduces her famous Chanel No. 5 perfume—named for her birthdate (and lucky number).

April 2: Albert Einstein lectures on his revolutionary new "Theory of Relativity" at Columbia University.

May 19: Congress passes the Emergency Quota Act, restricting immigration.

May 23: *Shuffle Along*, an all-black musical, opens on Broadway—it's a smash hit. In 1922, young Josephine Baker joins the road show, and she's on the road to stardom!

June 20: Alice Robertson of Oklahoma becomes the first women to preside over the House of Representatives, filling in after the death of her husband.

July 14: A jury finds anarchists Nicola Sacco and Bartolomeo Vanzetti guilty of murdering two guards in a shoe factory robbery in South Braintree, Massachusetts; the verdict prompts mass protests as many believe the two did not receive a fair trial due to inadequate evidence and that the conviction was because of their anarchist leanings.

September 7-8: The first Miss America beauty pageant is held in Atlantic City; lovely Margaret Gorman, just sixteen years old, is the happy winner!

On the Silent Screen

Rudolph Valentino steams in *The Sheik*; women swoon in vicarious ecstasy when he carries Agnes Ayres off to his tent. *The Sheik* is so popular that soon guys are known as "Sheiks" and gals "Shebas"! Douglas Fairbanks swashbuckles in *The Three Musketeers* and Little Jackie Coogan charms in *Peck's Bad Boy*.

Popular comedian Roscoe "Fatty" Arbuckle is arrested September 5, 1921 for the rape and manslaughter of twenty-five-year old starlet Virginia Rappe at a Labor Day weekend party at the St. Francis Hotel in San Francisco. During the party, Virginia passed out, and though the hotel doctor concluded she was simply drunk on bootleg liquor, she died of peritonitis three days later. Arbuckle was charged, though the autopsy results showed no evidence he had assaulted her or played any role in her death. Arbuckle claimed that when she passed out, he'd simply tried to revive her. The scandal was

"I am afraid I am going to wake up and find this has all been a dream," declared Miss Margaret Gorman as the judges presented her with the chief prize for the first Miss America pageant—the $1,500 trophy, a golden mermaid! An all-American beauty, Miss Gorman is shown here wrapped in the flag and wearing a beautiful beaded gown with a Statue of Liberty crown. The back of this 1921 news photo notes that Miss Gorman and her parents lived in Washington, D.C.; her father was executive clerk to the Secretary of Agriculture, and she'd starred in several government films.

front page news; William Randolph Hurst said the Arbuckle story sold more papers that the *Luisitania* disaster. Today, many historians believe Arbuckle was unjustly accused. There were three trials; the first in November 1921 ended in a hung jury, with a vote of 10 to 2 to acquit. At the second trial, Arbuckle did not testify, and the jury deadlocked, 10 to 2 for conviction. At the third trial, in March 1922, Arbuckle took the stand and the jury not only came back with a verdict of not guilty, but also issued a statement declaring: "…We feel that a great injustice has been done him…" In April 1922, Will Hayes banned Arbuckle from films, and though the ban was subsequently lifted, his career was in ruins.

Favorite New Recordings

Popular tunes include "All By Myself," by Ted Lewis and his Jazz Band; the "Wang Wang Blues," by the Paul Whiteman orchestra; and "Margie," by Eddie Cantor.

In Literature

Published this year are John Dos Passos's *Three Soldiers*, Rafael Sabatini's *Scaramouche*, and *Alice Adams* by Booth Tarkington. James Joyce's controversial *Ulysses* is published in Paris, though it's promptly banned in America and Great Britain. Edith Wharton wins the Pulitzer Prize for *The Age of Innocence*. Elinor Glyn, avant guard author (and sister of famous couturiere Lucile, Lady Duff-Gordon) laments in the November 21 *Cosmopolitan* that there seems to be:

> "...a great spirit of dissatisfaction and unrest which appears to be abroad among the young women of all classes...There is a feverish chase after some unknown desired thing which eludes them...do they ever think, these beautiful young girls? Do they ever ask whence they have come, whither they are going? It would seem not. Their aim appears to be to allure men, and to secure money...Has the American girl no innate modesty—no subconscious self respect, no reserve, no dignity?"

No shrinking violet herself, Glyn's racy novel, *It*, is adapted for a silent movie starring Clara Bow.

In Fashion 1921—The Tube Predominates, The Waist Creeps Lower!

Though the tubular silhouette was predominant, fashion was still in transition with several styles prominent. *Delineator's* Anne Harrison Black advised in 1921: "No one style is strong enough to be called the dominant fashion of the season. Frocks emphasize the youthfully straight and slender outline, as well as the quaint bouffant line of the full wide skirt [of the robe de style]." She also observed that although "Normal is the high-water mark for the fashionable waistline, many of them [are] lower than that." In August, *Art Gout Beaute* succinctly sums up: "...Diverse, unstable, wide, narrow, long, short, who knows?"

Couture Trends

Couture continued to vary the tube in several ways. Skirt portions with fluttering "cascade" draperies that trail below the hemline continued to add excitement; tiers and apron panels were also chic. Smart surplice fronts often gathered on the hip to drape in folds to the hem. Pointed "handkerchief" hems and scalloped hems were in vogue. *Vogue* lauded Vionnet's exquisite new Restaurant Frock "with a skirt of an infinity of double PETALS..."; versions of this flattering Petal Skirt endured through the second half of the decade. Trailing trains remained favorites for evening. The beloved vestee was a prevalent feature, and high "Vionnet" Directoire collars were also seen. Of course, the penchant for pleats continued in the mode.

Many couturiers showed "arrow straight" tubes, even unwaisted styles—as "long, straight lines help to give the impression of slenderness"! To this end, *Pictorial Review* bannered: "Fashion Favors Princess Lines!" as couturiers revived that supremely slender classic, the unwaisted "Princess" dress (a style originally named for a gown created by Charles Frederick Worth for the Princess Alexandra in 1875).

Lanvin's full skirted robe de style remained a youthful favorite for afternoon and evening. In 1921, Lanvin's "Rivera Collection" featured marvelous Aztec embroideries. Embroidery was everywhere, shown for both day and evening. "Palm Beach is sanctioning embroidery on frocks of every type," the Spring 1921 *Pictorial Review* advised; they also observed that "beguiling lingerie dresses of voile and organdy are prevalent at Palm Beach." Soutache braid applied in vermicular designs was ultra chic, and fringe trims were yet another smart touch. Black and white was a favorite color combination this year.

Regarding that all-important hemline, the May 1921 *Delineator* advised:

> *"In a season of conflicting silhouettes, Paris has at least agreed on certain important details of the mode...skirts are of a moderate shortness that shows malice toward none, since they do not insist on a juvenile brevity that is unkind to many women, nor a length which is maturing to all. They vary above and below the ten-inch-from-the-floor length **to suit the individual**."* [emphasis added]

Though most skirts were shown about mid-calf, they were shorter, of course, at Chanel.

Smart Shops and Catalogs Interpret the Mode for the "Average Woman"

"Every *Bellas Hess* dress is designed and made in New York, the style center of America," this smart fashion catalog advised in its Fall/Winter 1921/22 issue! Catalogs like *Bellas Hess* showed frocks with both the natural and the new, slightly lowered waistlines. Tubular dresses from *Bellas Hess* were shown either loosely belted with a narrow belt or ribbon just below the normal waistline, or alternatively, with wide sashes that tied at the left hip. Narrow cross-over buttoned belts were also chic, especially on tailor-made suits. Beading and embroidery were not just for evening and afternoon—many day dresses were so ornate they'd be considered evening wear today.

Sportswear Trends

> *"While we are playing tennis, golfing and motoring, dressed in our smartest sports frocks and top coats, Mistress Fashion is pointing the way toward a season of extreme **Simplicity** and offering us a choice of many modes to reach this end."*
> —Anne Harrison Black, *Delineator*, June 1921

For sports like golf, the new knicker suit was quickly becoming the rage, and middy blouse knicker combos were even more casual. For tennis, *Delineator* advised: "we must be sure to combine comfort with looks, neither need suffer. All white from head to foot always looks best (please don't wear dark stockings with a light skirt). Simple turnback collar high at neck to avoid sunburn, no tie as it flaps when I run which is most annoying...Our national shoe, the sneaker, is by far the best. It is light, you can run faster and turn more quickly." For swimming, the "dress-style" bathing suits and the clingy "California-style" knit suits vied for favor. The dress style was more suited to sunbathing, while the athletic knits were for actual "Swimming, Not Bathing"!

1921 Fashions

Day Frocks

Exquisite Frocks of Simple Design

Dress 3238   Dress 3227 Embroidery 10557   Dress 3229   Dress 3251 Embroidery 10558

As you can see in this lovely illustration from *The Designer's* June 1921 issue, frocks continue to grow straighter and "simpler," though the waistline still wanders. Many frocks simply "slip-on" over the head, and most are worn a little below mid-calf. Sleeveless frocks for day wear, previously too risqué, are beginning to appear (second from left).

Left to right: #3238: "Paris wears frocks whose chief charm frequently lies in trimming with self fabric, an effective and thrifty way to turn out a smart costume. This model combines that feature with the new tendency for the slightly raised blouse line of the Directoire Mode." #3227: "A welcome change is offered by Paris dressmakers for the slender figure in this semi-princess frock which slips over the head and is shirred at the waistline. It is delightfully simple, being sleeveless, with shoulder line emphasis suggested with contrasting color binding." #3229: "The accommodating slip-on basque (blouse) and straight two-piece skirt is given an air of fashion importance when made of two fabrics. Lace and taffeta are used together in this instance..." #3234: "This simple style slip-on frock with long blouse and tucked skirt depends much for its charm on the fabric selected. Edging the tucks with ruffling in contrasting fabric emphasizes its summery daintiness. The flat collar and cuffs are embroidered in eyelet edging..."

Note also the charming toques and bicornes, so popular before a cloche takeover, and the graceful parasols, an accessory fashionable for eons that's soon to fade from fashion's scene.

A delightful pink velvet toque in a style popular from the late teens through the early twenties. It's shaped like a tiara, with a shallow, fitted crown; the veined velvet leaves are quite detailed. Similar to the hat second from left in the previous illustration. $175-$250.

Front view of the velvet toque, showing the detailed leaves.

Another favorite early twenties' style—a magnificent, curvy bicorne hat in shiny black straw! $150-$250.

A sweet Spring accessory! This blue gingham parasol is bordered in solid blue; the "streamlined" handle is maple wood as is its long finial tip. $100-$150.

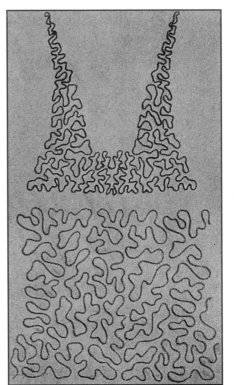

"Embroidery and Braiding Trim Exclusive Models for Spring!" trumpets *Pictorial Review* in Spring 1921, noting: "Embroidery expresses itself in many forms and mediums this season, the variety of choice allowed being little short of bewildering." Their "Newest and Smartest Trimmings" include this transfer pattern, "...worked out attractively in silk soutache."

Perfect to go from afternoon to early evening! This stunning frock has chic couture touches; it was made by an accomplished dressmaker after a haute couture design. Note the evolving silhouette with its lowering waistline, quite similar to the blue frock in *The Designer's* illustration. Ours is black silk taffeta, covered with white soutache braid applied in the fashionable vermicular "scrolly" design. The waist is encircled with a black ribbon band adorned with small red ribbon rosebuds that meet at center in a large bouquet of roses in the center; the bouquet's red and black ribbon streamers descend to the hem. The bell sleeves feature soutache on transparent tulle to the elbow, then alternating bands of sheer georgette and black velvet. Beginning at hip level, the slightly gathered skirt alternates horizontal bands of black taffeta and velvet to the mid-calf hem. A black silk inner bodice fastens with hook and eyes. While Bonwit Teller's "blouse coat" with similar "all-over appliqué of scroll braid" is priced at $94 in 1923, today's collectors may pay $600-$800.

Close-up of the scrolly soutache braid work and exquisite ribbon rose bouquet. These scrolly designs had a long fashion history; they were very popular during the Civil War era too. It's yet another example of "what was old is new again!"

Wedding Attire

A simple circlet of flowers, popular in medieval times, was a favorite headpiece.

This lovely silk pongee frock, ca. 1921-24, was worn to an informal afternoon wedding. Its slightly lowered waistline is accented by a wide "girdle" adorned with silk rosettes. Sheer knife-pleated panels float from the sides; the knife pleating is repeated around the wide bateau neckline. The short sleeves are slit at the sides and trimmed with small bows. This lovely frock is a "slip-on" style, and an inner camisole lining is attached at the waist. $300-$400. R.H. Macy offers a similar afternoon frock with "effective knife pleated side panels which fall below the skirt" for $29.75 (about $300 then!). (*Harper's Bazar*, May 1923)

PSYCHÉ

ROBE DU SOIR, DE WORTH

N° 9 de la Gazette du Bon Ton.   Année 1921. — Planche 68

Psyche! Gazette du Bon Ton's marvelous pochoir is from Greek mythology, depicting Psyche searching for Cupid, her lost love! This "robe de soir" (silk gown) is from the venerable House of Worth—a tunic style worthy of any Grecian goddess. Its graceful, flowing lines are accented by the lowered waistline's silk rosette girdle and the beautiful metallic silver lace of the tunic's underdress. Psyche has adorned her stylish bob with a circlet of matching rosettes. (1921) This Worth gown would make a lovely wedding dress!

Her first Kiss as a *Mrs.*! The bride wears a simple silk tulle veil with a floral circlet.

Caroline models a similar circlet of orange blossom buds, with side "wings" of Alençon lace. $125-$200.

"The Great Adventure"! This illustration by Walter Beach Humphrey graces the cover of *The Designer's* June 1921 issue. His pretty, pensive bride ponders her future. For her headpiece, she's selected a circlet of wax buds and orange blossoms.

For a more formal wedding, a gown with a long train was selected.

L'Epousee aux Dentelles (Bride with Lace). Alexandre Rzewuski's Art Deco pochoir depicts a magnificent formal wedding gown from Maison Worth. It's a very new and daring style—note the surplice front, erotically draped to the huge brooch at her waist. It's described as: "Bridal gown of silver tissue over white lace, caught at the waist with a pearl brooch; white lace veil decorated with sprays of orange blossoms." (*Gazette du Bon Ton's* 1921 Marriage issue) Note the comparison between this haute couture creation and the gowns offered for the average fashionable woman, as pictured next. These gowns, designed for the home sewer or professional dress-maker, are not as startling as the haute couture example but still exhibit chic couture touches.

L'ÉPOUSÉE AUX DENTELLES
ROBE DE MARIÉE, DE WORTH

Nº 2 de la Gazette du Bon Ton..   Année 1921. — Planche 14

Blouse 2992
Skirt 2808   Dress 3100   Dress 2896
Embroidery 10553   Dress 3084
Embroidery 10543

New Ways To Dress The Bride

The Designer offers four lovely wedding gowns: "New Ways to Dress the Bride!" Original descriptions, left to right: 1) #2992,2808: "The summer bride chooses lace and gracefully drapes it (tunic-style) over a satin overslip. The very simple line of the surplice blouse is girdled with white satin and satin peeps beneath the caught-up lace skirt in back." Note the cascade-drape "barrel" skirt so popular in the teens and early twenties, and her high laced pumps. 2) #3100 "The short skirt and long basque (top) characterize this wedding dress as the newest mode for the summer bride. The scalloped outline of the skirt and the (bateau) neckline are daintily trimmed with self-fabric ruffling and a floral wreath joins the skirt and basque." She wears smart t-strap shoes. 3) #2996: "Alluringly lovely is the bridal gown of satin and chiffon. The chiffon tunic in pointed outline is cleverly arranged at the top to form drapery. The square cut neckline is filled in (vestee) with bead-trimmed chiffon and diamond-shaped bead motifs weight the tunic. Embroidery is worked in seed pearls, iridescent or crystal beads." It's shown with "Colonial tongue" pumps. 4) #3084: "Simple in design, this satin bridal frock is lavishly embellished with beadwork. French knots may be used instead of beading; also outlining or couching embroidery. The one piece skirt and sleeveless blouse mark it as a particu-larly easy dress to make." She wears marvelous high strap "Roman Sandals." Note the variety of stylish headpieces and, of course, the pearl necklaces.

This beautiful bride posed for her formal wedding portrait ca. 1920-24. Note her formal gown's extremely long train, with floral trim and a square cut hem, covered by the voluminous illusion veil. She wears a modish bonnet-style headpiece, trimmed no doubt with wax orange blossoms…and note her beautiful satin slippers! Her very large bridal bouquet is typical of twenties' wedding bouquets. Photo by Bernard Studio, Syracuse, N.Y.

Close-up of the opalescent crystal beadwork of the exquisite satin wedding slippers worn by Mrs. Hulbert W. Smith. The kid lining is stamped: *Flint & Kent, Buffalo* (NY). $200-$300.

Full view of the wedding slippers. Note the narrow, rather pointed toes and the graceful curved "Baby Louis" heels. This was a style popular ca. 1918-24.

Fashionable attire for the smallest attendants is shown here.

The *Ladies Home Journal Fashion Quarterly* pictures a darling rosette and lace-trimmed frock for a young flower girl. For the ring-bearer, they suggest an elegant velveteen "Eton suit," with knee pants and pleat-trimmed shirt. It's the twenties' version of the famous "Little Lord Fauntleroy" suit that was named for the hero of Frances Hodgson Burnett's popular 1886 children's book. (1922)

Harriet, our flower girl, is wearing the sweetest dress—sheer handkerchief linen, with hand-appliquéd blue trim adorned with embroidered pink French knot roses. Every tiny stitch in this little dress and matching slip was done by hand…probably by a loving mom! $75-$125. Jimmy, our ring bearer, looks splendid in a black velveteen suit consisting of a short, collarless Eton jacket, knee pants, and silk pleated shirt. Small gray mother-of-pearl buttons trim the cuffs and sides of his knee pants; the pants button to the shirt with pearl buttons. Pants for very young boys typically had a small placket fly opening, with no buttons (and of course, no zipper). $75-$125.

Close-up of the skirt appliqué, pink silk floss French knot roses on blue linen. Note the hemstitching that connects the yoke to the skirt and adorns the hem.

Presenting the new "Mr. and Mrs. Kewpie!" These twenties' bisque Kewpie cake toppers are dressed in crepe paper—the bride's radiant in a tunic gown, bonnet headpiece, and veil; her groom's resplendent in white tie and tails…and top hat! Chubby-cheeked and cherubic, the irresistible Kewpies were so popular they became a symbol of their time. Conceived by Rose O'Neill, famous artist, author, and leader of Greenwich Village avant garde society, Kewpies debuted in *Ladies Home Journal's* December 1909 issue. In 1913, Rose obtained a patent for Kewpie dolls, and her Kewpie earnings soon made her a millionaire. By the twenties, Kewpies and their look-a-like kin were everywhere—even on wedding cakes!

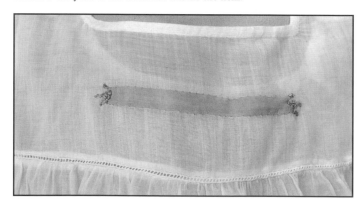

Close-up if the appliqués and embroidery on the front yoke.

Garden Party Dresses

This cream-colored silk slip was worn beneath the dress at lower left. Very typical of the slips of the early twenties, it features a square neckline, adjustable drawstrings, and very deep "shadow-panel" hem. The gathered sides provide ease of motion. Straps were basted to size. (Adjustable strap devices did not appear until the next decade.) Decorative hemstitching or fagoting work is placed under the casing. The attached original tag reads: *E.W. Edwards & Son, Syracuse, NY* and in script: *9/10/22, 8.98.* $50-$75.

Artist Marcelle Pinchon's fabulous Art Deco pochoir depicts two full-skirted *Robes de Garden Party*—they're perfect for a garden wedding! (*Gazette du Bon Ton*, July 1921)

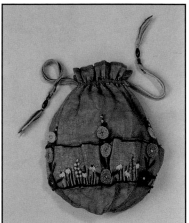

A lovely flower garden in multi-colored wool yarns is embroidered in the Arts & Crafts style on this hand-made reticule of pink gauze over lilac sateen. $100-$150.

Close-up of the skirt's embroidery, ecru on rose pink organdy, embroidered vertical center bands, and narrow self ruffles.

An incomparably lovely robe de style "Garden Dress" of rose pink organdy, trimmed with narrow self ruffles and embroidered in Aztec or perhaps Egyptian motifs. The neckline, shoulder seams, and center panels are embroidered bands outlined in white piping; the lowered waist is emphasized with a self belt also outlined in white piping. The skirt features alternating rows of extraordinary embroidery, separated by tiers of narrow ruffles that also comprise the short "cap" sleeves.

In 1921, robe de style Queen Jeanne Lanvin presented her famous "Rivera Collection"... magnificent gowns embroidered in Aztec motifs; there is no label present in this exceptional robe de style however. A prestigious store like B. Altman's may have offered their "replica" of a similar haute couture original for around $80 (comparable to $800 today). $800-$1,000.

Petal Skirt Frocks

The flattering, fluttering petal skirt was a popular new look this year—its many versions would reappear throughout the decade! This trio gives you an idea of how quickly haute couture fashions were copied or "adapted." These frocks were worn for both afternoon and evening occasions.

It was inevitable that a look as irresistible as the petal skirt would be quickly copied. Here, the Spring 1922 *Butterick Quarterly* presents their version of the petal skirt in yellow with beaded, teardrop petals and openwork sleeves. It's a pattern with deltor (instructions) for a: "Ladies' slip-over dress having a waist, Petal Skirt and two-piece slip," requiring "3/1/8 yards of material." Today, a similar dress would be $400-600.

Dress **3353**

For evening...embrace on the balcony! Pochoir artist George Barbier illustrated a bouffant version of the petal skirt for the exclusive French publication, *La Guirlande* (1921). Note her large, bustle-like trailing bow, high heeled evening slippers, and evening bandeau, plus his elegant white tie and tails, gloves, and evening pumps.

For afternoon to early evening, Madeleine Vionnet presents a tubular version of the petal skirt—a "Restaurant Frock" with "an infinity of double petals." It's worn with a Reboux "restaurant" hat. (Sketched for *Vogue*, July 1921)

(Left) A restaurant frock created by Vionnet for Mme. de Mier's trousseau is of mauve silk crêpe with a skirt of an infinity of double petals and a bodice shading from light to dark. Black crin and fine lace make the wide Reboux hat

A Beaded Evening Gown

FAITES-MOI CELLE-CI
ROBE DU SOIR, DE DŒUILLET

N° 7 de la Gazette du Bon Ton.   Année 1921. — Planche 56

Faites-Moi Celle-Ci (Make me this one!) Every bride dreamed of selecting her trousseau in Paris, and no trousseau was complete without a magnificent evening gown! Pierre Brissand illustrated this stunning beaded gown for *Gazette du Bon Ton* in 1921. At left, an elegant lady makes her selection at Maison Doeuillet. The mannequin models a fabulous evening gown with a chic uneven hemline, its vertical beading emphasizing fashion's slim tubular lines. The lowered waistline is accented with a smartly draped satin sash, which matches the bodice's small vestee insert. Note the client at center background—for her visit to Doeuillet, she's selected a smart *tailleur* accessorized with a fox scarf, matching muff, and ever-so-elegant small toque. (1921)

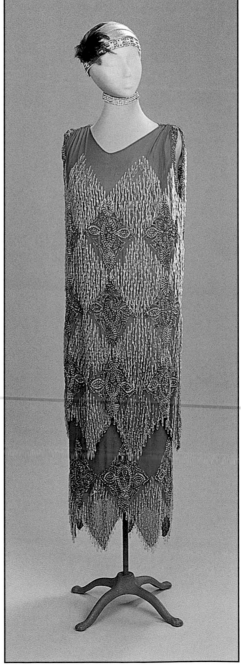

Left:
This magnificent beaded evening gown exhibits the evolving tubular silhouette at its most dramatic, and it's perfect for dancing the shimmy! Literally thousands of beads— mercury glass and rhinestone medallions and crystal teardrop loops— almost completely cover this gown's vibrant silk georgette. It's designed tunic-style; the bottom's pointed border is affixed to the long tunic top. The gown is shown with a turban headdress of period materials: a silver lamé turban bordered with rhinestones and a sassy green father aigrette. Though no sash was included, it perhaps was originally worn with one. (ca. 1921-24) $1,000-$1,500.

Far left:
Close-up of the mercury glass and rhinestone medallions, and crystal loop teardrops. Note that in the early twenties, the Cornaly needle (like a tiny crochet hook) was adapted for use in beading gowns; the fabric was stretched over a type of tambour frame and beads were applied by hand with the adapted needle, using a type of chainstitch.

91

Separates

"Every day one notices the influence of sport upon clothes…," observed couturier Jean Patou…and sporty separates are of utmost importance! "Separate Blouses and Skirts are sanctioned by Dame Fashion…" trumpeted the 1921 *Pictorial Review*. Fashion commentator Anne Harrison Black noted:

"Summer is the outdoor playtime of the year for all of us but Mistress Fashion, who never rests. While we are playing tennis, golfing and motoring, dressed in our smartest sports frocks, Mistress Fashion is engaged in pointing the way toward a season of extreme simplicity, and offering us a choice of many modes to reach this end…" (*Delineator*, June 1921)

Blouse (also called "waists" or "shirtwaists") and skirt combinations had come into their own during the 1890s as a favorite of the Gibson Girl. With their smart versatility, simplicity, and comfort, they'd become a staple of every woman's wardrobe by the twenties, worn for both work and *play*!

Skirts

"You will see a great many separate skirts worn this fall, because they are very fashionable and the styles are prettier than in previous seasons," the 1921 *Bellas Hess* catalog advised. Skirts had narrowed since the teens, and two styles were most worn: pleated skirts, and skirts softly gathered to a wide waistband, dirndl style. Pleated skirts had either wide or narrow pleats, or combinations of both. One of the smartest pleated skirts was the new "Prunella," described as "an exceptionally dressy and smart skirt, box-pleated all around, disclosing between the box pleats a checked pattern that contrasts very effectively with the solid." Skirt prices in catalogs ranged from about $2.98 to $9.98, while similar styles advertised in *Vogue* were often $16.50 to $19.75.

Presenting the popular new "Prunella" skirt…this version of the sassy Prunella is black silk crepe with ecru and black checked inner pleats, side snap, and hook and eye closure. The self-belt is fastened with a smoky gray mother-of-pearl button. It's worn with a sheer, crisp handkerchief linen blouse that's pintucked and embroidered (note the wide Peter Pan collar). A medium-brimmed velvet cloche with metallic floral appliqués completes the ensemble. Prunella skirt, $75-$150; linen blouse, $45-$75; cloche, $250-$350.

Though many skirts and frocks have self belts, separate belts or "girdles" were also smart.

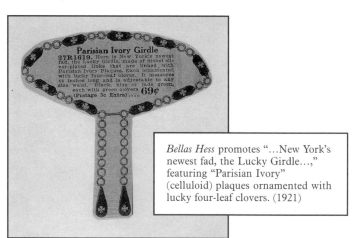

Bellas Hess promotes "…New York's newest fad, the Lucky Girdle…," featuring "Parisian Ivory" (celluloid) plaques ornamented with lucky four-leaf clovers. (1921)

Brise Du Large (Sea breeze). This romantic pochoir depicts Doeuillet's casual yet elegant skirt, blouse, and jacket ensemble "For the Honeymoon Voyage," as pictured. (*Gazette du Bon Genre*, 1921)

This exotic looking Parisian Ivory girdle belt would grace any skirt—or frock! Black and ivory celluloid plaques with brass links; the ivory is studded with faceted "rubies." A long mesh tassel trims the center plaque. $100-$200.

Bellas Hess's all-wool Prunella with "striped fancy checked effect…, one of the Fall's latest models, is very dressy and at the same time very serviceable, $9.98"! (*Bellas Hess* 1921-22)

Very typical of the early twenties, this delightful yellow woven plaid skirt keeps to the tubular silhouette in a softly gathered, dirndl style. Fashioned of the era's favorite soft, supple jersey, it features front pockets trimmed with rows of mother-of-pearl buttons. Note the hemline, just below mid-calf. Inner grosgrain waistband with left side snap closure; striped ribbon sash belt. It's worn with a sheer white batiste blouse with lace trimmed and embroidered collar and front closure, and a yellow straw medium-brimmed cloche, trimmed with original yellow chenille "puffballs" and edged in brown velvet. Skirt, $75-$150; Blouse, $45-$75; Cloche, $300-$400.

"This skirt and blouse are Paris suggestions which you can develop at home…" the June 1921 *Designer* advises, noting that the skirt is slightly gathered beneath the wide, sashed waistband.

This lovely gal, in her smart Prunella skirt and crisp "Armistice" vestee blouse, is keeping a close eye on her two cute kittens! (Snapshot, ca. 1919-22)

"Kollecker's Kareless Kodak Krew" reads the sign held by one of the employees from William Kollecker's photography shop in Saranac Lake, New York! The two women employees are dressed for work in practical but stylish skirts and blouses; the gal on the right wears a belted cardigan sweater with a sailor collar. (Professional photo, ca. 1920-24)

Blouses

"Dainty New Blouses – In Appropriate New Styles for Every Occasion"

"Real New York Blouse Styles – Worthy Complements to Your Skirt or Suit"

"Fashions from Fashion's Blouseland at Amazingly Low Prices"

"When You See These Beautiful Blouses You Will Appreciate What Marvels of Value They Are!"

These are just a few of the enticing headlines that extol the latest blouses. Favorites included beaded georgettes in every color of the rainbow; embroidered "Russian" peasant blouses; and vestee-effect "tuxedo" or "Armistice" blouses (named in honor of the Armistice ending WWI, signed Nov. 11, 1919). Favorite necklines included the "becoming bateau" (a wide, rounded neckline) and the modish V-neck. Collars included simple turnovers, sailors, Peter Pans, "tuxedo" shawl collars, and floppy, ruffled jabot collars. Embroidery, beading, lace, and ruffles were the smartest trims.

Blouses were either tucked in or worn over the skirt, overblouse or tunic style. "The overblouse is one of the latest New York styles," notes *National's*; they were shown either waist length or long like the modish "hip blouse" (often belted). Many overblouses tied at the back or sides; some featured cummerbund-type waistbands. The nautical middy blouse (see pages 104-105) remained a "MUST" for many sporting activities.

"Hootch earrings!" is noted on the reverse of this *International News Photo*. Though this flapper may look demure in her crisp gingham blouse with a Peter Pan collar, she's pouring a shot of hootch from her ingenious flask earrings! Her blouse is quite similar to *National's* illustration at top left. (ca. 1920-24)

6V63 Pongee $1.98

6V62 Embroidered Tricolette $2.98

6V60 Voile $1.98

6V64 Embroidered Crepe de Chine Overblouse $3.98

6V66 $4.98

6V61 Crepe de Chine and Lace $3.98

6V65 Hand-Embroidered All-Silk Georgette $2.98

New York's Latest Style Peasant Sleeves Paisley Trimming With Hand-Embroidery

See Opposite Page for Descriptions and Other Colors of These Charming Blouses
YOU MUST BE SATISFIED WITH EVERYTHING YOU BUY AT THE "NATIONAL"—OR YOUR MONEY BACK   Page 61

"In the well-planned wardrobe, smart blouses and new collars appear in profusion…" *National Style Book's* dazzling array of the newest blouses includes: a smart silk pongee blouse with Peter Pan collar and pintucked front, upper left; an embroidered "Hip Blouse," lower left; and the latest hand-embroidered "Peasant Blouse," lower right. At upper right is an exquisite voile Armistice blouse. (1922)

Note that though the catalogs' blouses are reasonably priced, haute couture blouses are much costlier; at Franklin Simon's exclusive "French Blouse Salon," an "Indo-Chinese Tapestry Blouse" is priced at $55! (*Harper's Bazar*, April 1923)

A very smart beaded overblouse in navy silk pongee with a collar insert of burnt orange crepe; it features sassy side ties and elbow length sleeves. The style is quite similar to *National's* "new and very becoming Basque Blouse" at top center. The beadwork is applied in a geometric Deco motif, with iridescent navy and orange glass beads. It's worn with a medium brimmed horsehair cloche, trimmed with original silk and velvet tulips. Blouse, $75-$125; cloche, $400-$600.

Two flapper gals enjoy ice cream cones on a fine summer's day, ca. 1920-24; they wear blouses and skirts similar to those pictured.

A lovely Armistice blouse of sheer handkerchief linen; the vestee insert, long "tuxedo" collar, and cuffs are lavishly trimmed with Irish crochet and filet laces. The shoulders have inverted pintucks to provide fullness. *National's* describes theirs as "having a dressy air…a rich and dressy trimming is provided by the Tuxedo collar of beautiful embroidered voile trimmed with Irish crochet pattern lace. Pin-tucked vestee is finished at top to match the collar; lace trims the turned back cuffs." $125-$200.

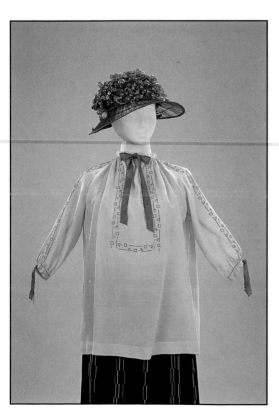

Left:
A nice example of the chic "Russian Peasant" look. This blouse is peach silk pongee, with cross-stitch embroidery on the front and along the sides of its ballooning sleeves, which are "gathered into narrow band cuffs." The narrow collar is tied with picot-edged brown faille ribbon, which also trims the cuffs. This blouse can be worn as an overblouse with a narrow tie belt or tucked inside the skirt. $50-$75. Note that colorfully embroidered white gauze peasant blouses were also popular, as were peasant frocks.

Right:
A sheer delight in silk georgette that's woven with a subtle plaid stripe. Self ruffles hide the snap closure, which is topped with a "mannish" bow tie. Note the full sleeves and waistband. $55-75.

Sweaters

"There was a time when a sweater was—well just a sweater; a worsted garment with no particular style, intended merely as a protection against the cold. But nowadays a smart, becoming sweater is an indispensable adjunct to every well-dressed woman's wardrobe!"

—*Bellas Hess*, 1920

Toasty sweaters came in both pullover (slip-on) styles, and cardigans. (The versatile cardigan, originally a knit worsted wool jacket worn by British officers during the Crimean War, 1854-56, was named for the 7th Earl of Cardigan, who led the disastrous Charge of the Light Brigade.) During the twenties, Coco Chanel and Jean Patou were among the couturiers famous for their striking Art Deco sport sweaters.

Bellas Hess, with tempting ad copy, extols: "Smart Sweaters—Just Like Home-Knitted and MUCH Less Expensive!…New Sweater Styles are Practical and Charming—It's more satisfactory to buy a sweater than to knit one!" And note those chic matching knit tams! Pictured left to right are: #32K105: "Slip-on sweater of warm worsted with tuxedo collar and turned back cuffs; trimmed with contrasting stripes"; #32K111: "Fashionable Tuxedo coat model sweater of soft, pure wool. Front lapels and bottom in fancy rack stitch; turned back cuffs, pockets" (note the chic slip-through button belt); #32K119: "Warm, pure knitted worsted sweater, medium heavy weight without bulkiness. Has smart belt, two pockets and square (sailor) collar trimmed as pictured"; #32K125: "Sweater of warm wool, deep collar in contrasting color…turned back cuffs, ribbed at waist; ripple effect at bottom."

Syracuse University coeds pause on the steps of the Student Store in 1921. The gal on the left wears a smart jersey pullover, and the gal at right, a warm, pocketed cardigan. The poster in the window advises there's a "Regatta Ball, Saturday, May 8th"! Syracuse had progressive leadership; the following appeared in the November 1922 *Flapper* magazine: "'Marry a modern girl!' is the advice to young men of Mrs. Charles Wesley Flint, wife of the new chancellor of Syracuse University, and Mrs. Florence E.S. Knapp, dean of the College of Home Economics."

These cute roller skaters wear warm cardigans, middy blouses, and short skirts! (Snapshot, ca. 1920-24)

Pullover sweaters paired with mid-calf white skirts look chic yet comfortable on "Gussie" and "H.W.B.," while "Evelyn" (center), has opted for a chic print frock. Note the blouses' large collars pulled over the sweaters, and their early cloches. (Snapshot, ca. 1920-22)

Ready for takeoff! It's bound to be cold up there, so for her flight this gal has selected a warm cardigan sweater. Neither person is named, but this marvelous photo is date-stamped: *5/31/22.*

MOTOR

50 Cents

Ruth Eastman

A fashionable sweater in the twenties' favorite jersey, with a ribbed shawl or "tuxedo" collar ending in knotted, fringed trim. It has two roomy front pockets, long cuffed sleeves, and a self-belt trimmed with two large tassels. *National's* describes a similar sweater as a "light weight knitted 'Coat Blouse'... one of the most popular spring and summer styles. It is a fashionable Tuxedo model of light weight Fiber Silk (later "rayon"), the Tuxedo collar and revers [lapels] give becoming long lines!" Shown with a large, floppy-brimmed straw cloche with a striped silk band. Sweater, $75-$150; straw cloche, $125-150.

With her racket and warm sweater tucked under her arm, this dashing young woman motors off to the courts. Note her mannish tie and floppy-brimmed straw cloche. Artist Ruth Eastman illustrated this marvelous cover for *Motor* magazine's July 1921 issue.

Sweaters for hiking! "What was left when we got home from the hike. Esther, Dorothie, Todd and me 1/21" is noted on the back.

Sweater vests are also chic…

Two charming young gals; the one at
left wears a plaid vest with a chic beret!
(Snapshot, ca. 1920-24)

This marvelous beret is a licensed replica of an Agnes design. (Agnes is
one of the decade's top French milliners.) Glowing rust velvet is overlaid
with black silk soutache in a triangular pattern; soutache daisies and buds
are appliquéd to the center of each pie-shaped section. The finishing
touch is a wispy curled feather aigrette! Label: *Agnes, 6 Rue St. Florentin,
Paris, Reproduction*. $250-$350.

Sporty canvas shoes com-
plete our ensemble. They were
the forerunners of today's most
popular footwear: "sneakers"!
Throughout the twenties,
white canvas shoes are extremely popular for sportswear.
National Style Book refers to
them as "Outing Shoes" and
offer a wide variety of both
high-laced and low-laced versions for the whole family. For
women, canvas shoes were offered in sporty oxfords, T-
straps, cross-straps, Mary
Janes and even pumps. Both
flat and military heels are
shown.

National's "Serviceable White
Canvas Lace Oxford, very attractive
for summer wear," and just $2.75!
With "leather military heels." (1920)

A silk jersey vest in an earth-tone plaid of rust, gold, blue, and black. Front
closure with five smoky gray mother-of-pearl buttons. It's bordered in tan,
which also trims the buttoned patch pockets. The back of the vest is solid color
tan. It's worn with the skirt and blouse pictured on the next page. $75-$100.

A pair of sporty canvas oxfords with military heels, three-eyelet ties, and
leather soles. They were worn by a lady named "Hubert" as noted in script
inside, and judging from the rather worn soles, they were well-loved! $50-$75.

Casually clad in a summer skirt and blouse with a "mannish" tie, this cute flapper holds her sexy, "saxy" jazz man's arm with one hand and her smart cloche with the other! The saxophone player is "Lawrence Harris," as noted on the reverse. (Snapshot, ca. 1920-24)

A very similar skirt and blouse! The casual summer skirt is cotton gabardine, modishly trimmed with soutache braid patch pockets. It's fashionably slim, slightly gathered at the waist, and has a self belt which closes with a large mother-of-pearl button. Left snap closure with inner grosgrain waistband. Label: *Korrect, Trade Mark*. The blouse is crisp white pique embossed with small Art Deco triangles; it has a Peter Pan collar and long sleeves. A wide finished waistband enables it to be worn either tucked in or as an overblouse. Worn with a coral rayon knit tie. Skirt, $75-$125, Blouse, $45-$75; Tie, $20-$45.

Close-up of soutache braid pocket.

"The New Knickers for Ladies…!"

During the early twenties, knickers (short for "Knickerbockers") became the first pants to be *commonly* worn in public by women. These knee-length baggy pants got their name from the character "Dietrich Knickerbocker," the "narrator" of Washington Irving's *History of New York* (1809). During the nineteenth century, they were extremely popular sportswear for men and boys. In the 1890s, the most avant garde women had worn them teamed with Norfolk jackets for bicycling. By the twenties, they'd become a symbol of women's new freedom, and were worn by women whose mothers and grandmothers would never have dreamed of wearing pants in public. Pattern magazines offered them as "The New Knickers for Ladies"; of course, they could also be purchased ready made from stores and catalogs.

As many "old fogies" continued to think women's knickers indecent, *The Flapper* magazine printed many letters to the editor in their favor. A Mrs. A.R.M. of Richmond, Ont., Canada wrote:

"I look forward to the day when every female, fat or lean, will walk the highways in her knickerbockers and be proud of it. Continue your good fight and we may yet see the day."
—*The Flapper*, November, 1922.

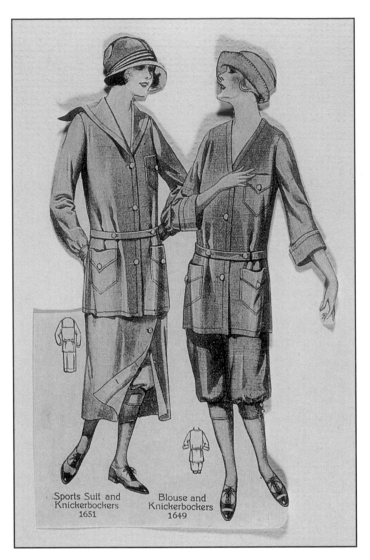

A versatile "Sports Suit and Knickerbockers" and "Blouse and Knickerbockers" offered by the 1922 *Pictorial Review* pattern magazine. This charming skirt/knickers ensemble permitted more conservative ladies to hide their new knickers under their skirts!

A priceless snapshot of three gals at a wienie roast; the granite wear coffee pot's already on the fire. The gal at left, casually clad in a skirt and blouse, holds up a string of wienies; her friend at right, wearing a bold new knicker suit, has found a stick for roasting. The gal in the center, in a skirt and belted cardigan, stirs the embers. (ca. 1920-24)

A window display for Schmelzer's Sporting Goods features an attractive knicker suit for golf, ca. 1920-24. Note the mannish shirt and tie, also the cloche hat at right.

Bold and beautiful—a smart striped tweed knicker suit, complete with button-cuff knickers and belted Norfolk jacket with roomy flap pockets! Buttons are faux camel hard plastic. This suit is old store stock, never worn; paper labels in both jacket and pants are printed: *Lot*, *Age*, *Price*, but no manufacturer's label is present. It's worn with a striped rayon knit tie, and velvet embroidered "crusher" hat, page 190. Suit, $400-$600.

Close-up of back, showing the vertical pleats at the shoulders, center placket, belt, and center belt loop.

Knickers are also purchased separately, and paired with blouses and sweaters. They're worn with sporty oxfords and snazzy hose!

Women's linen knickers in a smart cream and brown windowpane check, perfect for all types of sporting activities—golf, tennis, motoring, hiking and camping! Typical of women's knickers, they have a button closure down each side of the waist, welt pockets, and buttoned knee bands. They're worn with a heather green wool cardigan woven in a windowpane check; its collar and hem are trimmed with caramel stripes and there are two front pockets. Label: *Princeton, Mills Richmond, Calif.* Knickers, $75-$125; Cardigan $75-$100.

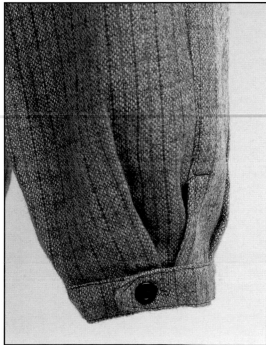

Close-up of the pleated buttoned knee band and striped tweed fabric.

In 1921, this shy young miss posed in a similar knicker/cardigan ensemble.

Sport Shoes and Hose

A wonderful pair of perforated spectator "wing-tip" oxfords in white suede and brown leather, with original brown and white checked laces. They're stamped "Collegebred—Your Footprint in Leather." $100-$200.

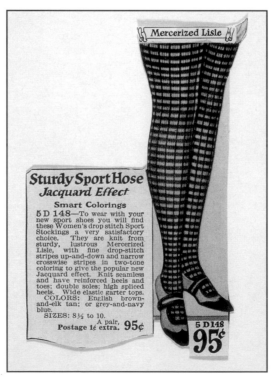

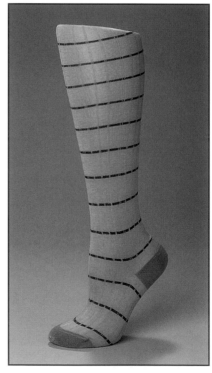

Three flirty flappers show off their knickers and flamboyant "sport hose," though their shoes seem a bit too dressy! Note those "mannish" ties too. (Snapshot, ca. 1920-24)

A great pair of "jacquard effect" sport hose in yellow cotton lisle, with contrasting black horizontal stripes. $50-$75.

Knickers on the go, summer and winter!

"Ready to leave for Grand Canyon" is noted on the reverse of this great snapshot—this amorous young couple is off on their honeymoon! Both wear knickers. Note her striped sport hose and cloche, and his smart argyle sweater and cap. (1920-30)

Skating at "Humboldt Park, February 18, 1923" shows two gals in warm woolen knickers and two in plaid skirts. Younger brother, in the center, wears long pants. All wear thick woolen sweaters.

At the Adirondack's posh Lake Placid Club, Amanda Siegel and her two friends are ready to hit the slopes. On the reverse, Amanda has written: "Here we are—just look how nice we look in our ski costumes…we are three experts now. February 20, 1923." (Note that the gal at left wears riding breeches while her friends have opted for knickers.)

The Twenties' Favorite "Dynamic Duo"—Middy Blouses and Knickers!

For vigorous outdoor sports, a pair of knickers and a middy blouse could not be beat! The athletic yet appealing sailor or middy blouse had been an item since the turn of the century, and by the sports-crazed twenties, it was all the rage! It was advertised as "a regulation middy blouse—a copy of those worn originally by U.S. Navy Midshipmen, complete with 'official' insignia." Summer fabrics included sturdy cotton duck, jean and "linene" ("a serviceable cotton material resembling linen in weave and finish.") For fall and winter, warm wool flannel or wool serge middies were favored. As advertised, "Middies will tub splendidly!"

The middy was generally worn outside the pants or skirt, at about hip length; though most had a plain hem, some had a wide waist band. Appealing to the throngs of new college girls, *Bellas Hess* offers "The New Co-ed Middy, presenting a neat, smart appearance" with "buttons placed effectively on the Co-ed lower band." (1921) Middies are shown both with and without "smart sailor bow ties"; some featured lace-up ties and some had detachable ties. The beloved middy was also paired with a skirt, and middy dresses were also worn.

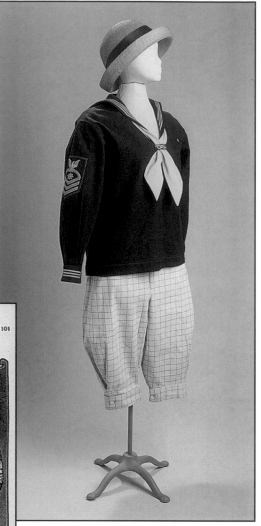

A magnificent regulation middy in brown wool flannel, with gold "service stripes on sleeves." There's an insert (welt) breast pocket, the cuffs and collar are trimmed with stripes of gold soutache braid, and there are gold star appliqués on the collar's back corners. An "apprentice knot" at v-neck held the sailor tie in place (the gold poplin tie is a replacement). $75-$150.

"At Last—A Dependable Flannel Middy...who doesn't want one?...for sportswear or college campus, outdoors or gym..." These resplendent middies in red, green, and navy are "fashioned in true regulation style—complete with chief rating badge, service stripe and apprentice bow knot." This "Goody Middies" advertisement exhorted readers of *Ladies' Home Journal* to buy these Kantikoy Flannel Middies, manufactured by "Samuel Goodman, Paca and Lombard Sts. Baltimore Md.; 1182 Broadway, New York." (August, 1920)

As these vintage photos prove, middies and knickers go *everywhere*!

Rowing! (and sneaking a smoke) "June 17, 1923—Thousand Islands."

Tennis!

Necking!

Motoring! "End of trip to Montreal."

At the beach, complete with bamboo parasol!

Camping! "Washing Breakfast Dishes."

Mountain climbing! "On Carpenter Mountain."

The Equestrienne

Almost as long as horses have been around, there have been "equestriennes"—free spirited, athletic women who ride like the wind! For centuries, artists have depicted women on horseback riding three different ways: sidesaddle, pillion (behind a man), or astride (cross-saddle). Since "Days of Old, When Knights Were Bold," sidesaddle was thought the proper way for ladies to ride. Since they were considered too delicate to ride astride, they perched somewhat precariously on the saddle with both "limbs" down the same side of the saddle…"sidesaddle." It was long considered not only scandalous, but even "damaging" for a woman to ride astride, or "cross saddle."

During the Renaissance, Queen Elizabeth I was an avid, accomplished horsewoman. In private, "Good Queen Bess" reportedly rode astride, though in public she rode sidesaddle. By this Elizabethan era (the second half of the sixteenth century), ladies had begun to wear ensembles designed exclusively for riding, which would become known as "riding habits." Riding habits generally followed the lines of the fashions of the times, often with "military" features. The redingote, French for "riding coat," originated in the eighteenth century; it was adopted by the daring horsewomen of Marie Antoinette's day, known as "Amazons"!

Throughout the staid Victorian era, though riding was one of the few sports women participated in, any position other than sidesaddle was unthinkable. Victorian riding habits were quite somber, though very form-fitting; Elizabeth, the beautiful Empress of Austria, was actually sewn into her habit's jacket! *Godey's Lady's Book* of August 1849 describes a proper habit: "A closely fitting waist (jacket) of dark merino or cloth, closed to the throat with the darkest mother of pearl buttons; linen collar fastened by a knot of plain ribbon. Small-brimmed riding hat and plume. Skirt of any light and suitable material, very full and long." A revolutionary new habit appeared in the early 1880s; the popular *Peterson's Magazine* included a fashion plate complete with a pair of *trousers* under the habit's skirt! (June 1882)

As late as the 1920s, for more formal events like the hunt, sidesaddle was still the proper way to mount; the huntswoman traditionally wore a three quarter length coat over a narrow divided "apron skirt," which draped to the knee. For more casual occasions though, by the late teens riding astride had become very popular, and the habit's traditional skirt was replaced by mannish pants, known as "breeches" or "jodhpurs." Naturally, many viewed those who rode astride with distaste—some thought it "unladylike" even into the thirties! In their February 1922 issue, *Vogue* featured an article by Belle Beach entitled "Good Form on Horseback." She first issues age-old warnings:

"It comes to this: women cannot ride astride because most of them are not built that way…their knees are not made for breeches, they are usually too round and too large!"

She then goes on to advise:

"If a woman insists on riding astride, she should first consult a doctor."

Recognizing, however, that bucking the tide to ride astride may well be futile, she continues:

"I do not say all women cannot ride astride, for there are many who do and know how to dress and how to ride just as well as their brothers, husbands and fathers, but I say comparatively few look well doing so…"

She also offers advice on "looking well" when riding astride:

"When I see a decent horse, I feel like riding up to him and saying, 'don't be downhearted. I'll tell your rider how to be worthy of you by looking smart and chic'!…A horsewoman should dress like a gentleman, not like a chorus girl all ready to go on to the pony-ballet."

To ensure a proper fit, Ms. Beach advises:

"Coats should not be too short, nor breeches too baggy in the thighs or loose in the knees; breeches should fit the knee and the leg absolutely, there must be no wrinkles or bagginess. The flare should start three inches above the knee; they must fit perfectly in the crotch. The coat may have two or three buttons and must come to the point of the knee when the rider is in the saddle; being neither too tight nor too loose, and should follow the lines of a well-made man's riding coat."

Boots with Cuban heels should not be used, but they are; and, regarding the newly fashionable sleeveless riding vests, she notes:

"Sleeveless coats are as bad as bad can be for ordinary riding…but I have actually seen girls in the park, poor dears, wearing such coats while riding in the bridle-paths, and they looked at the well-habited woman as if they thought she was a bit old-fashioned!"

And, of course,

"Jewelry is out of place in the saddle, and earrings entirely wrong!"

It should be noted that riding breeches, or "jodhpurs," were also worn for other sports, including "aeroplaning," golf, skiing and hiking. (The name "jodhpurs" came from the area in northwest India where they originated; worn for riding, they were quickly adopted by the British.) Riding breeches are reinforced with patches at the crotch and inside the knees.

Schmelzer's Sporting Goods store featured this smart riding habit in their window ca. 1920-24. Note the smart top riding hat at left, and knockabout cloche at right. Derbies and knockabouts were popular for informal riding events.

Butterick Quarterly offers this pattern for a smart "Cross-Saddle Riding Coat and Breeches for Ladies." As noted, it can be made up in many different fabrics, including "heavy linen." (1922)

2255—Cross-Saddle Riding Coat and Breeches for Ladies, Misses and Girls. 8 to 18 Years and 34 to 44 inches Bust—12 Sizes. For 36 inches bust, 3½ yards of material 54 inches wide. Use tweeds, heather mixtures, homespun, heavy wool jersey, men's-wear serge, cheviot, velours, checks, wool khaki, heavy linen, crash, etc.

A custom tailored "cross-saddle" or astride linen riding habit, consisting of a thigh-length jacket and breeches or jodhpurs. The jacket, which fashionably flares from the waist, has a two-button front closure and two welt pockets; three buttons trim each sleeve. Outer seams are top-stitched; inner seams bound. A back vent extends from waist to hem to provide ease of motion; it fastens at inside center with one button.

The breeches close at either side of the waist with four hard plastic buttons; more buttons in the traditional "step" pattern fasten to the knees. Two side slash pockets. Reinforcement patches are placed at the crotch and inside the knees. A script notation inside the waistband notes the number and owner's name: *S1046, C.G. Buffin.*

Habits were also available ready made; the Spring/Summer B. Altman catalog offers a similar habit: "coat and breeches of tan linen…the unlined coat has two pockets and the breeches are reinforced with self material, $21.00." Today, $350-$500.

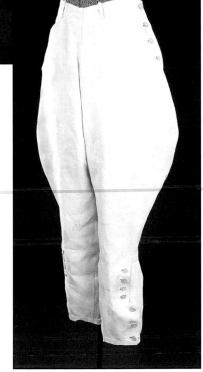

Close-up of the habit's riding breeches, showing the extremely baggy thighs that narrow to stepped buttons at the knees. Note the side-buttoned waist closure typical of women's pants at this time.

Riding astride! In this marvelous photo, Ringling circus star Minnie Taylor rides astride in a chic cross-saddle habit. It's autographed on the reverse: "Love from Minnie Taylor, Ringling Bros." Note that Minnie's chic riding hat is very similar to the one in Schmeltzer's window! By Wichita Studio, Wichita Falls, Texas, ca. 1920-25

Bathing Suits and *Swim* Suits—A "Brief" History

The bathing suit has always been a fashion trendsetter. Swimwear, more than any other type of clothing, has blazed the trail for freer, briefer fashions—inhibitions were shed with cumbersome clothing as bathing "melted reserves" and offered escape from rigid rules that "old fogies" fought to preserve.

The earliest recorded bathing suits, ca. 300 B.C., are depicted in ancient Grecian artwork—brief versions of the famous Greek chiton, though it was common for ancient Greeks to swim and exercise nude. The ancient Romans wore toga-like garments for bathing, garments that were adapted for swimming for centuries afterwards. A stunning mosaic from the Piazza Armernia in Sicily, ca. 400 A.D., depicts a pert young girl in a *two-piece bikini-like suit*, and it's interesting to note that it took civilization way over a thousand years to return to this style!

In the long interim, since many thought swimming synonymous with Sodom, various methods were employed to properly preserve modesty. Men and women often used separate areas to bathe (men often bathed naked; women wore toga-like tunics). In the late 1600s, voluminous swimsuits of "fine yellow canvas with great sleeves like a parson's gown" preserved a lady's modesty. "The water fills it up so that its borne off that your shape is not seen..." Men wore "drawers and wastcoates *[sic]* of the same sort of canvas." (*Traveler* 1687)

The ultimate in bathing modesty was achieved with the amazing eighteenth century English "Bathing Machine," a portable dressing room on wheels that was taken to the water's edge; a "modesty tunnel" opening permitted its occupant to enter the water unseen! Considering the extreme décolletage of the eighteenth century dresses, this might seem somewhat incongruous...

By the Victorian era, "bathing" had become a popular sport. Men and women bathed together, dressed in modest swim wear. In their August 1849 issue, *Godey's Lady's Book* features a rather licentious print by a Mr. Croome entitled, "Scene at Cape May." It depicts men and women frolicking in the waves together—some even embracing—though all are clad in cumbersome clothing. Beneath was noted this irresistible advice:

> *"It cools and refreshes to look at a scene like this, and to feel, in imagination, the shock of the inpressing surf, so often felt in reality. Have you been to Cape May this season, pent-up denizen of the hot city? No? Then shut up your ledger, close your office, cork up your inkstand, and, carpet-bag in hand, step on board a swift-gliding steamer, and hasten away to snuff the ocean breezes, and take a plunge in the invigorating waters!"*

The "bathing dresses" in this scene resemble the famous bloomer reform outfit, with knee-length dresses worn over ankle-length pants (pants being either "Turkish" bloomers, gathered at the ankles, or wide, straight-leg "trowsers" *[sic]*). By the 1870s, pants pictured in *Harper's Bazaar* had shrunk to knee length. Victorian bathing dresses were most often flannel; favorite colors included scarlet, navy, and "pearl." Accessories included capes (called "mantles" or "bathing cloaks"), bathing hats or caps, and plain or laced slippers. Men's suits were considerably more practical, with short-sleeved tunic tops that extended over knee-length pants. During the Gay Nineties, wasp-waisted bathing beauties were photographed wearing merciless corsets under their bathing dresses, which had large leg-of-mutton sleeves and full, knee-length skirts and were accessorized with capes, ruffled mobcaps, slippers, and the mandatory stockings.

By the turn of the century, athletic women like Australian "Diving Venus" Annette Kellerman had begun to rebel against constricting, impossible-to-swim-in suits. Annette had started swimming as a child to strengthen legs weakened by polio; she was soon winning competitions against Australia's best male swimmers. When she was fourteen, her family moved to England and, to promote her career, her father announced to the press that Annette would swim from Putney to Blackwell—twenty-six miles! She competed against men in events held in the English Channel, the River Thames, and, in Paris, the Seine. Annette performed at London's Hippodrome, thrilling audiences with daring diving feats and exhibitions of synchronized swimming. And, declaring "I want to SWIM!", she adopted a brief racing suit that left her legs, arms, and neck bare! In 1907, Annette toured America; among other stops, she performed at an amusement park in Boston's Revere Beach. After her performance, she strolled out on the public beach in her brief black swim suit (it was without sleeves or the mandatory skirt, though it had bloomers or pantalettes that ended just above the knee). A proper Bostonian matron, outraged on spotting Annette, immediately notified the police and Annette was arrested for "indecent exposure." On being advised by the court that she'd exposed too much skin, she promptly attached black stockings, sleeves and a tucker to her suit... and created a *one-piece bathing suit!*

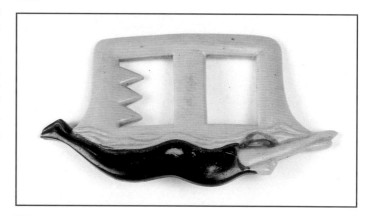

This clever celluloid belt buckle pictures Annette Kellerman slipping through the surf in her famous one piece knit suit and red bathing cap.

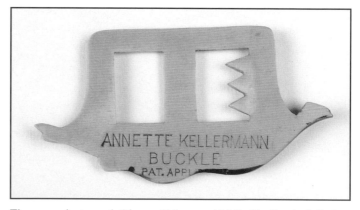

The reverse is stamped: *"Annette Kellermann* (sic) *Buckle, Pat. Appl. For."* $75-$150.

"Hollywood's Latest Thrill—The Bain de Champagne—Perfumed with the Rarest French Fragrance...A Bevy of Noted Film Stars Enjoying a Luxury Which Even Cleopatra Could Not Afford," reads the caption for this delightful publicity photo, taken in the early twenties. This beautiful bevy of starlets posed in a array of the very latest swim wear, including both "dress" styles and one-piece knits. The charming photo is from "Ames & Norr, Film Star Publicity Service, 1133 Broadway, N.Y." The copy notes:

"Ruth Clifford's new swimming pool in Hollywood was the scene recently of a 'Bain de Champagne Party', in which many leading movie stars participated. A new French perfume, put up in champagne bottles and champagne in everything but taste and fizz, was used to perfume the entire pool. The group (from left to right) upper row: Helen Ferguson, Mary Philbin and Laura LaPlante; lower row, Gertrude Olmstead, Ruth Clifford and Patsy Ruth Miller..."

Note that though most mail order catalogs didn't offer swim suits until the second half of the decade, they're often advertised in *Vogue* and *Harper's Bazar*. Franklin Simon offers "California wool swimming suits," as well as dress style bathing suits: "Salt Water Bathing Apparel that goes both to Sea and to be Seen!" for $10-$20. (*Vogue*, June 1, 1922). Since salt water suits had to be more durable, manufacturers attempted to design fabrics that would withstand exposure to ocean water. Couturier Jean Patou was noted for his efforts to create swim suits of materials that would stand up to the sea.

During the teens, Hollywood discovered the bathing beauty, and Mack Sennett's gorgeous girls became the darlings of the silent screen. They appeared in the revealing new one-piece "California-style" knits, and, by the end of the teens, millions of movie fans had "followed suit." Since their suits exposed the *entire arm*, sleeveless suits soon caught on. In homage to the "bathing beauty," Madison Square Garden declared May 26, 1916 "Bathing Suit Day," with a parade of the latest fashions for the beach—it was a tremendous success! Throughout the teens, though the move to briefer suits seemed as inexorable as the tide, many cities enacted "modesty laws" and hired beach censors to keep a watchful eye on bathing beauties who crossed the line. For example, Atlantic City's beach law mandated the wearing of stockings, and on many beaches one could be arrested for wearing a one piece knit suit that was too revealing or lacked the concealing "modesty skirt."

By the beginning of the nineteen twenties, active *swimming* rather than *bathing* had become a new health craze. To fit into fashion's mandatory "slim silhouette," women needed to be fit and trim…and swimming was a perfect way to get in shape. With the growing number of fashion-conscious active swimmers, suits needed to be attractive as well as practical; as *Vogue* noted: "Gone are the days when a bathing suit was simply a covering that would wring out well. Today, one's individuality must be considered."

During the first half of the twenties, there were two popular styles of swim wear. Haute couture favored fabric "dress style" bathing suits, perhaps a bit more suitable for lolling on the beach and sunning in the sands, while athletes preferred a suit similar to the one Annette Kellerman had worn—the streamlined one-piece "California style" knit suit that Jantzen was promoting "for *swimming*, not bathing!" However, even though most one-piece knits featured a short modesty skirt or tunic to cover the groin, "old fogies" continued to think them "immoral." Until around mid-decade, many areas continued to restrict one-piece knit suits, and beach censors continued to remove the most daring deviators.

These restrictions outraged *The Flapper* magazine, which had of course come out in favor of the figure-hugging "California Style" knits. As this poem relates:

A Beach Romance

Two flappers at Jersey went out for a flop,
But met the beach censor, who told them to stop;
'Your costumes are shocking to decent folks here;
Go back to your rooms, keep away from the pier'.
They went to a dance in their costumes so shocking,
With never a petticoat, never a stocking;
And nobody cared, not the tiniest bit
They won the first favor by making a hit
(By "A.W.A.," *The Flapper*, November 1922).

To combat the "indecent" image of the one-piece knits, the Jantzen Company designed ads promoting an all-American, wholesome, healthy look. In 1921, artist Cole Phillips created Jantzen's famous diving girl symbol—an athletic young miss, she was soon appearing everywhere in her smart red suit and pompom cap. Their ad copy was outstanding: "THE SUIT THAT CHANGED BATHING TO SWIMMING"; "guaranteed perfect fit regardless of body type"; "you can slip through the waves in a Jantzen as in your own skin!"

Jantzen had developed their knit suit in the early teens, when rowers approached Carl Jantzen and his partner John Zehntbauer, for a practical, comfortable suit, "ribbed like a sweater." They came up with their "elastic rib stitch" that provided twice the elasticity of jersey. Jantzen (until the early twenties, the "Portland Knitting Co.") sold 4,100 suits in 1919;

by 1930, they were the world's largest manufacturer, producing over a million and a half suits. In 1921, their booklet *Jantzen Yarns* promoted "Learn to Swim Week," and swimming clubs popped up all over. By 1926, the Jantzen Swimming Assn. was offering color charts with accessories, belts, caps, and shoes all coordinated to match the swimmer's hair color and complexion.

Other popular swimsuit manufacturers of the era include:

Catalina: formerly Bentz Knitting Mills, in 1912 they added knit swimwear and changed their name again, first to Pacific Knitting Mills and then in 1928, to Catalina. In 1920, they introduced a shockingly brief, bold striped "Chicken Suit" and also a "Speed Suit" for men, a sexy one-piece with deep armholes and angled trunks. Catalina suits were designated as the Miss America Pageant's official suit.

Cole: Cole was formerly West Coast Knitting Mills. Fred Cole designed a sensational suit called "The Prohibition Suit," with a low U-neck, deep armholes and a very short modesty skirt. Cole became famous designing suits for screen sirens.

Bradley: "Slip into a *Bradley* - and Out-of-Doors!" The Bradley Knitting Company of Delavan, Wisconsin, claimed: "Half your joy in swimming depends on the beauty of your suit—all your comfort rests on its correct proportions…". Bradley made very stylish knit suits, dashingly illustrated by artist Coles Phillips. They also published the "Famous Swim Book, written by Mr. Harry Hazelhurst, Swimming Coach of Chicago Athletic Assn." Bradley's promoted suits for the swimming pool: "You'll be delighted with the novelty and smartness of the new summer styles…Even if they have to build pools to wear them, people want Bradley Bathing Suits! Ask us how to go about having a pool built-if yours is an inland locality. We'll gladly send literature, without obligation."

Le Lecon de Natation ("The Swimming Lesson"). A marvelous Art Deco pochoir from the 1921 *Gazette due Bon Genre*. Depicting a "Costume and Cape for Bathing," it's a charming example of the voluminous capes and dress-style bathing suits favored by haute couture. The bathing cape had been a popular accessory for ages; twenties' versions were often made of rubberized silk, satin, corduroy, terry, and chenille plush. As *Vogue* notes: "For those women who may like to swim long distances and who may prefer the more abbreviated suit, but desire protection when they emerge on the beach, the makers of bathing costumes have devised the yoked and high neck bathing capes…" (June 1, 1922)

LA LEÇON DE NATATION
COSTUME ET CHALE, POUR LE BAIN

N° 6 de la Gazette du Bon Genre.   *Année 1921. — Planche 41*

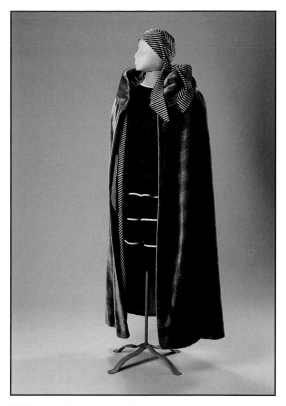

"This wrap is the sort of thing that Diana, or any of those athletic Olympian girls would have just loved to toss on after a strenuous dash around Parnassus!" *Vogue* exclaims of a cape similar to that in the pochoir print on page 110. This warm cape is a velvety, long napped plush, a blend of silk and wool, with horizontal stripes of dark gray and mushroom brown. Mushroom silk lining (fraying) with arm loops. $200-$300.

Back view of cape. The large convertible is gathered from a yoke under the collar.

A flapper *MUST*! "On the beach, the promenade at smart resorts, or even for walks in country lanes, the Parasol, entering a season of renewed favor, flourishes in particular abundance....At the beach they reach proportions never seen before, stoutly handled to resist rough winds and waves." (*Vogue*, July 1, 1922). These parasols are as intriguing on the inside as they are on the outside; this photo shows the parasol's intricate construction as well as its Art Deco design. Such parasols were outrageously popular during the teens and twenties, but note that repros abound today. $100-$200.

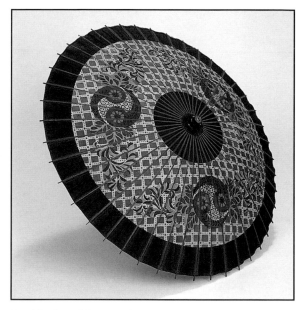

Outside view of the parasol.

Beach capes and "Persian" parasol! H. Messerole's charming illustration pictures three elegantly clad bathing beauties, noting: "When the bather leaves the water, further protection is afforded by the capes, of lavender rubberized moiré satin and a rubberized Roman striped silk and flannel cape." (available for $29.50). (*Vogue*, June 1, 1922)

Dress Style "Bathing" Suits!

Bloomers bared! This daring young athlete offers an excellent view of the bloomer pants worn under the dress style bathing suits. Note the turban cape and those rolled stockings, mandatory on many beaches in the early twenties.

All decked out for a day at the beach in a dress style suit with a vestee tucker, huge piped pockets, and tie belt. Note her rolled stockings, high laced bathing slippers, and bathing cap. (Snapshot, ca. 1918-22)

A wonderful dress style bathing suit in black satin, with a three-tiered scalloped skirt edged with white piping; the bateau neck and armholes are also piped. Pearl buttons fasten the left shoulder, and also decorate the sides of the skirt's tiers. It's worn with a self-belt. This suit is constructed with an inner camisole with hook and eye closure; it's attached at the waistband (see next photo). $200-$300. The suit is worn with a striped turban constructed of period taffeta. Note that these dress style suits are harder to find than the more popular one-piece knits.

View of the suit's inner camisole.

In addition to being purchased ready made, bathing suits were often made up by home sewers...they could also be RENTED!

On the boardwalk in Atlantic City, professional photographer William Kollecker points out that rental bathing suits are just $.25!

Patterns for smart dress style bathing suits from *The Designer's* June 1921 issue. Note that the two suits on the left feature straight-leg pants, while those on the right are gathered bloomer-style. Left to right: 1) "The slip-on upper part is easily made, and girdled with a wide sash at the normal or low waistline, it is extremely effective"; 2) "...a smart suit of gingham, bind the scallops with pique..."; 3) "The possibilities of being well dressed on the beach are shown in this bathing suit with matching cap. The length of the skirt is chic"; 4) "This suit is designed on girlish lines...the straight, gathered skirt and blouse are joined to a deep belt, through which is run the sash." The *Designer* notes that "Surf satin, sateen, taffeta, jersey and gingham are desirable fabrics."

California Knit "Swimming" Suits

The popular "California Style" knit one-piece suits, for women and men! Left: A woman's ultra chic purple wool knit one-piece suit, featuring smart chartreuse and purple stripes at the neck, sleeves, skirt hem, side godets, and modish cross-over button belt. (These belts, very popular in the early twenties, were also worn with jackets and suits.) It's a slip-on style, with a pearl button closure on the left shoulder. Just visible under the skirt is the pants portion, which is attached at the waist. Ca. 1918-22. $200-$400 (plain color knit suits range around $50-$100). Few of these wool knit suits have survived without moth damage, which of course affects the price. Right: A man's one-piece knit suit, bordered with tan stripes. You'll note that men's and women's knit suits are similar, almost unisex; men's suits also feature the brief modesty tunic! Button closure, left shoulder. Though pure wool is most common, this suit is a more comfortable cotton jersey knit. $75-$100.

"Evelyn and Fredrica with Chippie" at Long Beach, Long Island, ca. 1918-22. Fredrica's suit is quite similar to the purple striped knit above!

113

Annette Kellerman label.

This form-fitting black knit Annette Kellerman suit is almost as brief as those worn at Deauville, shown below! It's very eye catching, with contrasting turquoise knit drawers that are attached at the waist beneath. Worn with a bright orange rubber bathing cap. Kellerman suit, $200-$300; cap, $25-$50.

"Frolickers in the Surf" photographed at Deauville. In France, of course, the Briefest of the Brief is worn! This photo appeared in the June 1921 *Designer*, along with this vivid imagery of golden days in the sun:

"The hour of the bath at Deauville is an hour of sunshine, of sport and laughter... thousands of pleasure seekers, from all classes of society come to this popular watering-place to disport themselves, and on a bright day the beach presents a kaleidoscopic panorama of color, fashion and verve...

"Here beautiful women and debonair men, chic mademoiselles, and comely matrons may be seen daily promenading the sunny terrasse which skirts the immaculate beach, frolicking in the laughing surf, or lying in the white sand, shaded from the sun by huge, colorful parasols... And, as night falls they begin to drift leisurely in the direction of the brilliantly lit casino or to the Grand Hotel..."

Beach Shoes

Beach shoes were necessary accessories, and both high and low styles were worn.

This wonderful Art Deco ad for "Beach Kicks, The Really Satisfactory Bathing Shoes" vows that "their soles never come off." They offer "low shoes—oxford and strap pump styles—or the trim snugness of laced high shoes…" (*Vogue*, June 1, 1922)

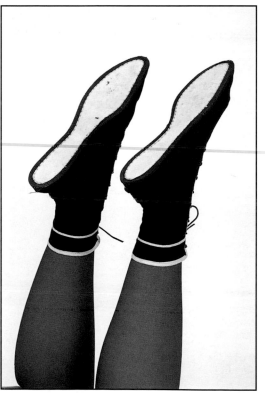

High lace beach shoes in cotton sateen, trimmed with white piping. Nine eyelet laces, flexible rubber soles. $75-$150.

These four flappers have selected a variety of smart "laced high shoes." They're worn with stockings rolled to just below the knees. Three of the girls wear clingy one-piece knit suits, while the gal at left wears a chic dress style suit that laces up the front. All wear stylish caps! (Snapshot, ca. 1920-24)

Hand loomed purple cotton purple bathing slippers trimmed in yellow, the soles made from Goodyear tires. $75-$125.

Low beach slippers in ankle tie and Mary Jane strap styles, from "Beach Kicks" ad. (*Vogue*, June 1, 1922)

"Isn't She a Darling?…Introducing Miss Antoinette Folta of Michigan City Ind. who copped the beauty prize in the state of Indiana which is noted for its beautiful women. She was awarded the prize at the recent tri-state aquatic convention held in Michigan City, and fifteen thousand people seconded the selection of the judge by vociferous applause. (Photo and original text from Keystone View Co.). Note Antoinette's chic Mary Jane strap low beach slippers!

Chapter Three
1922 Women's Fashions

Timeline

Former film star Texas Guinan opens this year at New York's famous Cafe des Beaux Arts...though she's hired as singer, she quickly becomes the decade's favorite "Speakeasy Queen," greeting guests from atop her piano with a raucous "Hello sucker!" Louis Armstrong leaves New Orleans for Chicago to join King Oliver's Creole Jazz Band. *Physical Culture* magazine awards twenty-eight-year-old Charles Atlas, a former "97 lb. weakling," the title of "The World's Most Perfectly Developed Man." Atlas develops a popular isometric physical fitness program; one of his most famous ads advises a skinny "weakling" that after an Atlas course, a bully will never kick sand in his face again!

February 8: President Warren G. Harding becomes the first president to do a radio broadcast from the White House.
April 7: Harding's Secretary of the Interior, Albert G. Fall, grants Mammoth Oil Company exclusive rights to the Teapot Dome government reserves in Wyoming. On April 16, the Senate begins an investigation of what's become "The Teapot Dome" scandal.
August 28: Radio "sponsors" initiate radio COMMERCIALS!
October 3: The first woman to become a U.S. senator, Rebecca Felton, is appointed by the Governor of Georgia to fill the vacancy left by her husband's death—*for only one day!*
October 31: Benito Mussolini, "Il Duce," comes to power as his "Black Shirts" march on Rome.
November 7: British archaeologist Howard Carter and his financial backer, Lord Carnarvon, prepare to enter King Tutankhamen's tomb, untouched since his burial. When news of this astounding discovery reaches the public, "*TUTMANIA*" ensues!

On The Silent Screen

Ex-postmaster Will Hayes is appointed a censor in an attempt to clean up the film industry, which is largely ineffective until the stricter "Hayes Code" of 1934. Jackie Coogan is beguiling in Dickens's *Oliver Twist*, Gloria Swanson vamps in *Her Gilded Cage*, and Ramon Novarro thrills in *The Prisoner of Zenda*. In *The Young Rajah*, Valentino appears in a titillating knit brief that leaves little to the imagination; he also stars in another desert thriller, *Blood and Sand*. Warner Bros. makes a movie version of Fitzgerald's *The Beautiful and the Damned*. Philosopher, comedian, columnist, and folk hero Will Rogers stars in a screen version of Washington Irving's *The Headless Horseman*. America's sweetheart Mary Pickford struggles valiantly as *Tess of Storm Country*, while husband Doug Fairbanks swashbuckles in *Robin Hood*. Sisters Lillian and Dorothy Gish emote in D.W. Griffith's *Orphans of the Storm* and the first of Hal Roach's very popular *Our Gang—Little Rascals* kid comedies is released. Technicolor is introduced in *Toll of the Sea*, a film version of Puccini's *Madame Butterfly*—glorious, but proves too costly for widespread use.

Favorite New Recordings

Hit tunes include "April Showers" and "Toot Toot Tootsie Goodbye," by Al Jolson; "Hot Lips" and "It's Three O'Clock in the Morning," by the Paul Whiteman Orchestra; and "Way Down Yonder in New Orleans," by Margaret Young.

In Literature

F. Scott Fitzgerald's second novel, *The Beautiful and the Damned*, is published; also a second collection of his short stories, *Tales of the Jazz Age*. T.S. Eliot's epic poem, "The Waste Land," describing the after effects of World War I, is published to great acclaim. The Pulitzer prize is awarded to Booth Tarkington for *Alice Adams*. Sinclair Lewis's *Babbit*, a biting commentary on life in the twenties, is overwhelmingly successful. James Joyce's controversial *Ulysses* is published in Paris in February; several hundred copies are burned by the New York Post Office as obscene and it's banned in Britain and America. Emily Post's *Etiquette in Society, in Business, in Politics and at Home* is published.

In Fashion 1922—Hemline/Waistline Wars!

Hemlines as well as waistlines were vacillating this year, so there was much conflicting advice. Sage *Vogue* advised the decision should be personal:

> "*The question of the waistline, like that of the length of skirts, is to a great extent an INDIVIDUAL matter, which should be decided first by the proportions of the individual figure, then by the type of gown...The secret is knowing one's self. It is not to be denied that skirts have lengthened, though in general, this lengthening has not been in the least exaggerated. Women are coming to recognize that there is no 'fashionable' length, that one cannot give a definite measure of so many inches from the ground which will be invariable for all figures... All*

women seem to agree that the revival of the really long skirt for street wear would be a great mistake." [emphasis added]

Vogue also noted that "...it was, of course, the war...which led to the introduction of the very short skirt for street wear." Of the eagerly awaited new Spring styles, *Vogue* rhapsodized:

"In the spring, just as a young man's fancy is apt to turn to thought of love, a young woman's, in fact, turns automatically to the spring wardrobe. No matter how many mistakes she has made about clothes during the long hard winter, she feels sartorial hope surge within her at the return of the robin." (February 1922)

Couture Trends

Though many couturiers were showing longer, straighter fashions this year, women were clearly reluctant to give up the freedom (and sexiness) of the short "simple" skirts that brought Chanel fame. Regarding the waistline, *Vogue* noted that frocks "may have slim, draped lines or be bouffant and circular, but all favor low waistlines." *Vogue* advised women to take full advantage of the great variety of several new fashions: "One can be draped medievally or classically toga'd; or rustling in 1840 [robe de style] flounces at night; one can go marketing in the morning in a tightish short skirt and wide paneled jacket or short, loose jacket with the ever-comfortable chemise frock under it, and any and all of these will be equally smart." (February 1922)

Couture highlighted *fantastic* sleeves this year with flowing, swooping, even slashed versions that gave dresses a romantic, medieval flavor. As *Fashionable Dress* observed: "The heart of the Parisian designer is still very much on her sleeve...they can not very well go further in the matter of width of length or shortness, for the very short sleeve just covering the top of the arm is used a great deal." (October 1922)

Vogue also praised "Fashions of the English Middle Ages": "The mode adapts from masculine costume, the Crusaders' surcoat and cote-hardie [fourteenth century] and the houppelande [a fifteenth century garment with long, wide flowing sleeves, belted in folds at the waist by a jeweled girdle]." *Vogue* also mentioned that "...the princess frock came to England with the Normans." (February 1922) The Crusaders' open-sided "Tabard" styles, so popular in the late teens, were also seen, lending their distinctive medieval touch.

"Evening gowns...have suddenly become almost invariably long, except for the very young women who adore dancing...with youthful insistence, the debutante demands the bouffant dancing frock." Lanvin, Patou, and Poiret were among those showing extremely wide robe de style frocks. Of note this year was Callot's straight, tubular evening frock with an overskirt of detached "gladiator-like" tabs hanging from its lowered waist, a feature that was much imitated during the second half of the decade (sometimes called "Car Wash" dresses today). Molyneux's new models were "simplified to meet the needs of the smartest women who absolutely refuse to countenance any eccentricity at present";

many were designed to be worn "for afternoon—or continue into evening as informal dinner gowns." Poiret's bold evening pajamas, black satin pants with a yellow and green printed satin blouse, created a sensation. "Frocks that are draped at one side lead the fashions of spring,"... and frocks with either pleated or fluttering drapery panels were very much in vogue. Sashes and bows continued to accent backs and/or sides. First seen in the teens, frocks with flattering "petal" skirts, formed of many overlapping "handkerchief" points, retained their popularity.

For day wear, the "peasant look" with its magnificent embroidery made headlines. "From the devastated frontiers, a soldier brings back a piece of Balkan embroidery...before one know it, gowns are being made and embroidered like Balkan chemises." Chanel's latest creations were dripping with colorful "Balkan" embroidery. *Vogue* showed Lebreton models: "Silk tricot covers itself with the glory of vivid embroidery as a background for the Arts and Graces of strange lands and far-away peoples." Regarding couture's "inevitable" monkey fur fringe, *Vogue* observed: "Monkey, which is considered by the Parisienne more as a trimming than a fur, is certain to keep its place in the mode...it is used by every creator in Paris." (February 1922) Rows of decorative buttons also trimmed stylish frocks. *Vogue* noted that "Especially smart are Redfern's frocks of hemstitched geometric squares..."; this treatment was another example of the influence of Art Deco on fashion.

Coat dresses were both smart and practical. *Vogue* advised: "The coat-dress of simple line is certain of an honored place in the coming mode." And the new "Suits for spring are simple enough for country wear and quite smart enough for a town luncheon." Short suit coats were shown at Jenny's, "a house which frequently gives a lead to the mode of the hour," while Patou preferred hip length flared jackets over tubular skirts, and Lanvin's "newest southern models keep the straight, short coat belted low with a belt often made of braided strands."

"Frocks with matching capes make fashion news," as *Fashionable Dress* noted. "...it is small wonder women wear them morning, noon and night!" *Vogue* also went cape crazy: "The new frocks of spring arrive with matching capes of coats in delightful variations of wool jersey or tweed and in soft, becoming colours that blend with vernal scenes." Capes were shown in various lengths: full, three-quarters, or just below the waist.

As to fabrics, "Prominent in the Rodier collection are Kasha, and woolen and cotton crepes; all-over hemstitching plays an important part on all these materials..." Rodier's "Kasha" was a soft, silky blend of wool and goat's hair. Tweeds, of course, retained their chic, and Chanel's favorite jersey, "the hardy perennial, returns every season with renewed vigor." It's a material that would "withstand any amount of wear." Crepe is "too becoming, too practical and too appropriate to the demands of modern life to be abandoned." Vibrant new printed fabrics were also praised: "Spring silks are Gay as Swaying Lanterns...bright in New Persian and printed designs..."; Lanvin showed Persian designs printed on crepe de Chine. *Vogue* noted an "almost CUBIST design of cream-white splotches dotted with fuchsia red" [emphasis added]; and "Batik combinations of vermilion and magenta, poison green and orange dazzle the eyes." Bold plaids and checks were also smart, on coats, day dresses and suits. For evening: "...there is nothing more exquisite then brocaded georgette crepe with the brocaded pattern carried out in a darker shade than the crepe itself." (February 1922) By summer, *Vogue* advised: "Typical of the Paris mode for summer is the combination of two fabrics and colours." Premet combined "almond green" crepe de Chine with white chiffon, while Cheruit offered painted frocks in foulard, crepe de Chine and chiffon, "brilliantly colored as tropical birds"! (June 1922)

Fashionable Dress also offered advice on "What to Wear" and how to wear it:

> "There is a proper dress for afternoon wear, another for evening functions. There are certain costumes for wedding, and others for the garden fete. It makes receiving an invitation as fascinating as playing a game...And one whispers in true Shakespearean manner, 'What to Wear and What Not to Wear—That is the Question!'
>
> "An invitation to tea requires one's prettiest afternoon frock—except for the hostess, who will need to choose something inconspicuous as it would hardly be hospitable to outshine one's guests! For the theatre, one selects a becoming street frock or smartly tailored suit, because it looks so chic with the new draped turban. An afternoon dance invitation requires careful planning for the correct frock; the very young might select a gown of bouffant youthfulness, while the older woman a gown more suited to her years in taffeta or crepe de chine; though colors may be subdued, trimming should have a note of gayety. Long gloves of silk or kid and a light afternoon wrap complete the ensemble. At informal dinners, a semi-evening dress is suggested, under no circumstances should it be decollete; if one does not have a semi-evening dress, an attractive afternoon frock is appropriate.
>
> "Formal invitations include a formal dinner, the theatre, and opera, the musicale or formal, ceremonious tea...to a formal dance where 'all's a giddy whirl of colors and costumes' one wears one's most elaborate styles. Lustrous satins and taffetas for youth; handsome brocades and velvets for the more mature. When attired in conventional evening dress, one wears one's hair arranged somewhat more elaborately than usual. Accessories are important; an ostrich fan to match the gown, pumps of satin or lame; long gloves of white silk or kid. When selecting jewelry, remember that a gaudy display is in bad taste. HATS ARE NEVER WORN to a formal occasion. For the evening wrap, velvet with a collar of white fox is charming; for more economically minded, a dark, loose coat of satin.
>
> "For the business woman, in a good tailor-made [suit], with several blouses one can always look neat and well dressed. For the office, high necked satin blouses are excellent. A soft fluffy georgette transforms the suit into an appropriate costume for visiting or entertaining...
>
> "You can always recognize a well dressed woman because of her poise, self-confidence and dignity. She is never self-conscious, never uncomfortable, never conspicuous; she is always well dressed... One should always remember that 'there's a time for every dress and every dress in its time.'" (October 1922; emphasis added)

Smart Shops and Catalogs Interpret the Mode for the "Average Woman"

Modish catalogs quickly picked up on the latest couture trends. Trendy *Chicago Mail Order*, "Parting the Curtain of the Stage of Fashion, Presents the Smartest PARIS DRESS STYLES OF 1922, at America's Lowest Prices," offering a modified medieval sleeve frock "...of Paris inspiration that shows in every line and fold the handiwork of a master designer...great cuffs hand beaded and hand embroidered, drape themselves over the forearm and flutter, like great butterfly wings, at every movement of the body...A splendid dress for semi-formal occasions that can later be transformed into a simple day-time frock by simply removing the cuffs—$19.97."

The 1922 Spring/Summer *National Style Book* presented a wide array of the latest fashions, including: "All the Rage in New York...The Cape is Fashion's Favorite"! A green and white ribbed knit cape with a large turnover collar was "only $5.75—what a bargain," and a smart cape and dress ensemble with a full, hip-length cape and matching tasseled scarf was just $6.98! Waistlines were low, and many tied loosely with narrow self belts. The usual panels, tiers, and tunics were well-represented; embroidery, lace and buttons were favorite trims. Though couturiers were stressing longer styles, most dresses in *National's* were shown around mid-calf. Prices ranged between $3.98 for a gingham housedress to $21.50 for an "elaborately beaded silk crepe de Meteor" afternoon dress. Jumper styles were popular, as "New York's most smartly dressed girls and young women are all wearing the jaunty, becoming jumper dress, so smart with a semi-tailored blouse."

Ladies Home Journal's "Fashion Quarterly of the Home Pattern Company" adapted couture features for the home sewer:

> "The silhouette for winter is long, slender and graceful. With the dignity of the lengthened skirt has come a craving for flowing sleeves and straight draperies. Skirts are often made of two straight pieces, the front extending and forming a cascade on one side, while an extension of the back performs the same office on the other side. Clever placing of panels accomplishes many delightful effects, giving the costume individuality and character as well as softness of line. Circular side sections and circular panels are also features of some of the new frocks... and in time will probably succeed the draped effects so prevalent now." (Fall/Winter 1922)

The Great Hemline War!

By 1922, "The War of the Fever-chart Hemline" began in earnest as couturiers longed for long dresses to fulfill their newest aesthetic visions, and *re*fill their purses! However, many women, accustomed to the freedom of the shorter skirts, were loathe to give them up. Generally, casual day and sports clothes were rather short (a bit above mid calf), while more formal afternoon and evening dresses hovered just above the ankles. As *Vogue* advised: "Fashions, like food, must be properly assimilated, and only such of them as agree with one's individuality should be assimilated!"

Long vs. Short—Long Skirts

In one corner, representing haute couture...the great Paul Poiret! During a 1922 visit to America, Poiret had sparked a huge controversy; in a *New York Times* interview, he'd remarked that American designers didn't have "the spark of genius necessary" and that American women appeared to be three years behind the times. Nathaniel Giddings of the *Times* defended American style ("Fifth Avenue shops are superior to the rue de la Paix ten to one.") and subsequent letters to the editor praised American women as not being slaves to Paris fashion!

This chic young miss models couture's controversial favorite—a long, ankle-length pleated frock.

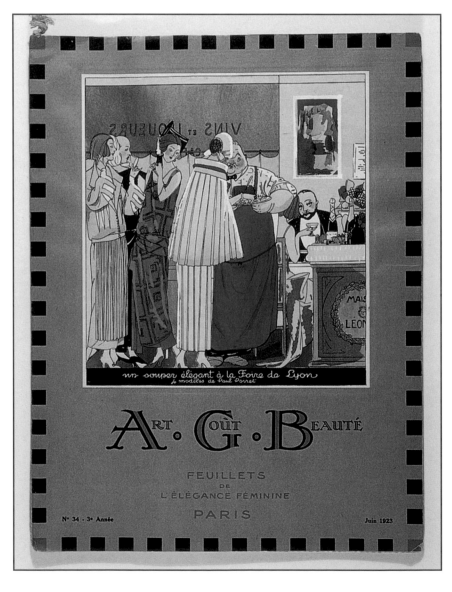

This wonderful pochoir fashion plate graced the cover of *Art Gout Beaute*. It depicts long dresses designed by Paul Poiret; Poiret himself is pictured at right, sipping champagne with a lovely companion.

Short Skirts—The Flapper's Choice!

And, in the opposite corner...*the flapper!*

An avid advocate for the short skirt, *The Flapper* magazine, which debuted in May 1922, relentlessly expressed outrage at the longer styles from Paris. Comparing The War of the Hemline to the American Revolution, *The Flapper* quoted *The Toledo Blade* under a banner of "Our Sentiments Too":

> *"Paris seems determined that our girls shall wear long skirts, but the Declaration of Independence was not written in vain...everyone to his or he own taste is our motto, and if some of our fair ladies have limbs that do not show to advantage in short skirts, they are at perfect liberty to cover them up. But legs are made to walk with, and therefore **we are heart and soul behind the sensible American girls who insist on freedom in movement before anything else.**"* (June 1922)

In October 1922, *The Flapper* proclaimed: "The flappers have rebelled...they have hurled the gauntlet in the face of the Parisian dictators of style and declared that from now on they are going to use their own minds in the matters of dress..."; and, "as one flapper puts it: 'Why in the name of common sense do the manufacturers of ladies' clothing insist upon girls wearing long skirts when we simply don't want them?'"

The Flapper's ire was directed at Paul Poiret, who "...has seen fit to take up the cudgels on behalf of the long skirt." Poiret was quoted as stating: "When fashion has outlived its purpose it should be related to the scrap heap and something new tried." *The Flapper* scathingly retorted: "Not fashion, Monsieur Poiret, but the designers of senseless modes are the ones who will ultimately be relegated to the scrap heap!" *The Flapper's* statement was prophetic; as the decade progressed, Poiret, unable to keep pace with the spirit of the twenties, saw his fortunes dwindle and was eventually forced to declare bankruptcy. It's interesting to note that *The Flapper* also stated that "as a sop" Poiret predicted "that in 1927, or perhaps 1925, short skirts will come back, shorter than ever"...and, of course, history proved him right.

By November 1922, *The Flapper* had declared victory, headlining:

> *"Short Skirts Win...Of hundreds of votes on modern styles all but one was recorded in favor of short skirts, so we guess that makes it pretty nearly unanimous. The great majority of the votes were also cast in favor of rolled sox, bobbed hair, knickers, low-heeled shoes, and against corsets, with a few declaring that the latter is merely a matter of taste...!*

Definitely in favor of short skirts, these two leggy flappers are vaudeville actresses, posing beside Kearney Theater's "WORLD'S BEST VAUDEVILLE" poster. (The Kearney theater was located on Fulton Street in Brooklyn; the photo was taken by the stage door, in back of the theater on Livingston Street.) Dated on reverse: October 20, 1921.

Five flamboyant flappers demonstrate their love for short skirts and rolled "butterfly" stockings as they hold their *Flapper* magazines aloft! Cover, *The Flapper*, June 1922.

FLAPPERS' DICTIONARY in This Issue

THE Not For Old Fogies JULY

FLAPPER

[TRADE MARK]

20 CENTS A COPY
25c in Can.

TWO DOLLARS A YEAR
$2.50 in Can.

Photo by Phil F. Stahl

What is Home Without THE FLAPPER? Impossible!

The Flapper also helped guide potential flappers; as Dorothy Garner of Chicago writes in her letter to the editor:

I am just a new reader of The Flapper, *but I am a flapper and I think it is the berries. I was almost tempted to let my hair grow and wear my skirts longer with high heels, but I won't now; I am going to stay a flapper!"* (November 1922)

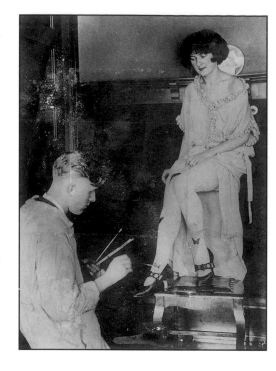

It's a tough job…! Noted on the back of this Keystone View Co. photo is: "A Prize Winner… when Marie Galewski, of Milwaukee was adjudged the winner of a recent 'Beautiful Leg' contest, she gave a little dance, and exposed the fact that part of her costume was paint. Here we have a young artist painting butterflies on her limbs…" (ca. 1922-25)

"AU REVOIR, MON AMOUR…"
ROBE D'APRÈS-MIDI, DE PAUL POIRET

1922 Fashions

By 1922, the tubular look is well established. Many couturiers show frocks at ankle length—some with very low waistlines and some with no waistline, "princess" style.

Benito's pochoir plate "Goodbye, My Love.." for a 1922 *Gazette du Bon Ton* illustrates the new long, tubular look from Paris with its ankle-length skirt and markedly lower waistline, exemplified in this day dress by none other than Paul Poiret! Note the extravagant wide sleeves that complemented the tubular look. American publications took a more middle of the road approach, showing dresses that hovered between ankle and mid-calf.

The March 1922 *Delineator* describes the Worth dress at left as: "A coat dress from Worth ignores the waistline altogether and goes straight to conclusion of its monkey-skin fringe. The material is black craquelinette trimmed with monkey fur and worn over a waistcoat of white satin." The jacket and skirt outfit at right is a bit shorter: "Again, the jacket apparently at odds with the skirt, for the black satin tunic almost hides the skirt of red duvetyn which matches the short scarlet jacket banded with satin and embroidered with jet. From Worth."(Note the high Directoire collar.) At Franklin Simon, a similar ready made "replica" is priced at $85 (*Vogue* 1922). Both models wear strappy "high heel" pumps and chic wide hats.

Wide "airplane" hats looking like they're ready for takeoff pay homage to the miracle of flight. Note that creations of Parisian milliners, like Maria Guy's hat "of airplane inspiration" are quickly copied and offered by catalogs like *Bellas Hess*.

In their October 1920 issue, *Ladies' Home Journal* depicts Maria Guy's extravagant "all day hat…of airplane inspiration."

Back view of a smashing draped black velvet "airplane hat," a chic variation of Maria Guy's creation. It's distinctive even from behind; the back boasts vermicular scrolls of black silk chenille over gold lamé. Label: *Style Square Distinctive Hats, New York-Paris-Chicago*. $200-$300.

Front view of the airplane hat!

Very similar to the Worth creation shown in the *Delineator*, this custom made coat dress trimmed in monkey fur exudes STYLE! As *Vogue* advises: "Monkey, which is considered by the Parisienne more as a trimming than a fur, is certain to keep its place in the mode…it is used by every creator in Paris." (February 1922) Fashionably long, this unwaisted princess style silk crepe dress is fully lined; it closes surplice style, just below the natural waistline with a single covered button. Two tiers of monkey fur fringe adorn the wide, open sleeves; monkey fur "fringe" is repeated around the hemline. The collar can be worn open or closed. $300-$500. It's worn with a V-necked tulle "vestee," and a black satin bicorne cloche. $250-$350.

Bellas Hess offers their version of the "New Aeroplane Turban— one of the smartest of New York's Fall styles… gracefully draped in jaunty wing points at either side; a very becoming model at an exceedingly moderate price…$2.87." (Fall/ Winter 1921-22)

Casual "Country Club" Frocks

"With the Advent of Spring Comes New Gingham Frocks," announces Butterick Quarterly in 1922. "Gingham might be a fabric woven by Dame Nature herself, with the wide world for her loom...greens of the hills, brown of the road and all the colors of wayside posies are used...gingham is the wash material which never loses sway over feminine hearts and fashions!" (Parkhill Ginghams ad, *Ladies Home Journal* 1920)

Right:
Worn to a casual luncheon at the country club are three of the newest tubular frocks; their lowered waists marked by narrow belts. Descriptions, including original prices: (Left): "a frock of French voile in many lovely colours is decorated by drawn-work and a jabot descending to the hem, $39.50...worn with a pink and white French crepe hat with picot edge and pink satin ribbon, $30. (Center): "Green and cream carabola homespun dress, fringed at the hem, $45; the sailor hat is of natural, rough, pressed straw, $10. (Right): A dull blue, red and green printed cotton frock copies old printed linen and is finished in white linen, $39.50; the mushroom hat is of moiré ribbon, $22.50." (*Vogue* June 1922)

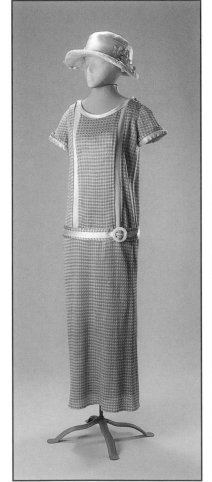

So long, lean...and *tubular!* This pink gingham-checked confection in outrageously popular silk jersey* epitomizes the long, low-waisted silhouette so fashionable by 1922. White satin trim emphasizes its vertical lines and trims the bateau neck, cuffs, and self belt. It's a slip-on style, but with two snaps at the left shoulder. Shown with a white satin cloche with a medium brim of nubby boucle; satin orange blossoms spill over the edge on each side. Dress, $300-$400; cloche, $300-$400
*Note that Chanel had made jersey a favorite during the teens, and by the twenties it had become a classic: "...jersey, that hardy perennial, returns every season with renewed vigor and is a material that will withstand any amount of wear." (*Vogue* 1922)

"All Decked Out," three flapper gals enjoy sunning in their deck chairs, 1922. Note their cloche hats, which have now become the rage!

Ready to go motoring, this pert young miss wears a checked gingham frock in a style quite similar to those above. Note her stylish bob and low oxford shoes! (Snapshot, ca. 1922)

Maternity Clothing

Clothing designed especially for maternity wear became popular during the teens. During the Victorian era, it would have been considered unseemly to be seen in public while pregnant, so regular clothing was often altered to accommodate an expectant woman. By the teens, it had become common for pregnant women to venture out and the "maternity dress" was born! By the twenties, catalogs and pattern magazines pictured stylish maternity frocks that followed the lines of fashionable day dresses.

National Style Book offers four "Stylish Maternity Dresses," in batiste, gingham and "linene." As noted: "All 'National' maternity dresses are made so that they can be worn **after the maternity period** without any alteration." To accommodate pregnancy's increasing girth, *National's* notes: "The fullness is adjusted by a self-material sash belt long enough for any adjustment," or "a loose front panel held at the waistline by a detachable sash belt." (Spring/Summer 1922)

Unbelievable as it may seem today, maternity corsets were thought to be *beneficial* as late as the 1920s! *National's* offers three versions with "scientifically designed" features. "The corset is the most important article of maternity apparel...the support of a corset is necessary, but an ordinary corset will not do after the third month. Its abdominal compression is dangerous!" *National's* claims their "scientifically designed maternity corset supports without binding...is easily adjustable to the changing figure, gives freedom from pressure and protects both mother and child..." Their maternity corsets provide for expansion with "elastic webbing inserts" and/or by "side lacings and abdominal lacings."

House Dresses

Dainty house or "porch" dresses are advertised as "Fashions for the Land of Pots and Pans." These delightful frocks, crisp as a spring breeze, are "tubbable," and they're perfect for almost any informal morning activity. Note that they're shown quite a bit shorter than dresses worn for more formal occasions.

These lovely gals posed beside their Model T, ca. 1922. Both wear crisp gingham frocks, perhaps ordered from *National Style Book!*

National's offers "New York Dresses... Just as Sweet and Dainty as They Can Be." The blue voile dress (second from right) is similar to ours; it boasts a "crisp white organdie used for the novel vestee." Note the green frock at center, advertised as the "stylish new Jumper Dress." The ribbon bow ties are a very popular twenties accent. (Spring/Summer 1922)

Above left:
An adorable house or morning dress in blue plaid cotton batiste, with an embroidered, pleated organdy vestee; rows of pearl buttons trim each side of the vestee. The organdy sailor collar, cuffs and patch pocket flaps are also embroidered with dainty spring flowers. The side snap closure is at left of vestee. The (replacement) grosgrain belt may tie at back or side. These popular frocks were also called "porch dresses" and you can almost taste the fresh-squeezed lemonade! $125-$175.

Above right:
Back view, showing the sailor collar.

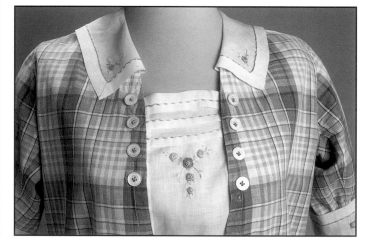

Close-up photo of the embroidery and button trim.

126

Afternoon Dresses

Parisian afternoon dresses exhibit longer skirts and fantastic "medieval" sleeves. As *Delineator* exclaims, "The heart of the Parisian designer is still very much on her SLEEVE...!" (March 1922) And *Vogue* observes the influence of "Fashions of the English Middle Ages," noting "...the mode adapts from masculine costume the Crusaders' surcoat and cote-hardie..."

In a fetching plaid morning dress, Carol Spoor Broom enjoys a summer sunny morning with her little daughter. Carol's dress has a crisp white collar and cuffs, and a row of pearl buttons down the front. Note her chic wide brim cloche and pointed pumps. Her daughter wears a practical romper (playsuit), and white canvas (?) Mary Janes. (Studio portrait, ca. 1920-24)

«COMBIEN DE MORCEAUX DE SUCRE?»

ROBE D'APRÈS-MIDI GARNIE DE DENTELLE "A LA MARÉCHALE"

N° 1 de la Gazette du Bon Ton.   Année 1922. — Planche 2

Combien de Morceaux de Sucre? ("How many sugar cubes?") Illustrating couture's enchantment with all things medieval, this charming pochoir by Carl Erickson (who later sketched for *Vogue* as "Eric") appeared in *Gazette du Bon Ton* in 1922. Note the gown's long skirt, low waistline, and enormous "Guinevere" sleeves. Fashionable women dressed for tea; as the October 1922 *Fashionable Dress* advises: "An invitation to tea requires one's prettiest afternoon frock—except for the hostess, who will need to choose something inconspicuous as it would hardly be hospitable to outshine one's guests"!

This enormous black ostrich feather fan is a full 27" long from handle to tip; it's mounted on a single faux tortoise (celluloid) handle. $200-$300.

Full length back view of the gown.

"In Days of Old, When Knights Were Bold…" fair maidens wore medieval gowns that were still being revived hundreds of years later! Here, a twenty-first century "Guinevere" models a magnificent 1920s "medieval" afternoon or tea gown; the fabric is exquisite, with an ancient pattern of twining flowers, leaves, and buds. Though *Vogue* describes these fabrics as "Cut out velvets on transparent grounds," today they're often called "burnout" or "cut velvets." The incredible Dolman sleeves are cut in one with the bodice portion, which is open at the sides in the twenties' version of the medieval tabard that had been so popular in the teens. Ornate silk chenille braid extends from the bateau neckline to and around the wide sleeves; it's also placed under the bustline, and emphasizes the low waistline. Adorning the waist just left of center is a rose formed of layers of silver lamé and self fabric, from which a medieval "chatelaine" of chenille ribbon streamers tipped with burnout buds extends to the hem. The long skirt is draped gracefully across the front to the flower. This dress is just as fascinating from the back, where two smaller chenille-edged flowers also trail chenille streamers and buds to the hem. The black silk underdress is typically cut straight across; it has a left snap closure. Her period accessories include a long jet necklace, satin cross-strap shoes, and a black ostrich plume fan; her contemporary sequin headache band has a wispy feather aigrette! Dress, $500-$800.

Close-up of the silver lamé rose, chenille leaves, and "chatelaine" streamers.

The sleeves extended. It's obvious "…the heart of the Parisian designer is still very much on her sleeve!"

Robe de Style

Delineator tempted shoppers with this lyrical advice as Spring approached:

> *"Days are dipped in yellow sunshine, the cold sweet scent of the street corner violets falls on the air, motors drone like hives of lazy bees, and in the shop windows of Fifth Avenue and the Fifties dresses of rose and silver gauze and primrose yellow spread their skirts and await the invitation to the Easter dances at Sherry's and the gay little suppers at the so-called clubs where New York gathers after the theater..."*
> (March 1922)

The bouffant robe de style remained a favorite for spring and summer. It was a youthful fashion, as *Fashionable Dress* advised: "An afternoon dance invitation requires careful planning for the correct frock; the very young might select a gown of bouffant youthfulness..." (Spring 1922). And *Vogue* declared, "...with youthful insistence, the debutante demands the bouffant dancing frock"!

Against an appropriate background of an old-fashioned garden, these two bouffant silhouettes are very beguiling. Rose organdie trimmed with white net has broken tucks defined by a contrasting line of navy blue faille. A knot of flowers at the waist is repeated on the immense organdie hat shading, momentarily, two lovely heads

Cockades of navy blue ribbon are picturesque touches on a gown of lavender organdie, trimmed with bands of navy blue organdie. Handkerchief linen makes a tucker and tiny frills at the sleeves. Like all Lanvin's full-skirted frocks, these models all but touch the ground and have a natural or slightly lowered waist-line

LANVIN

PARIS FROCKS GIVE SUMMER A VIVID RAISON D'ÊTRE

"Paris Frocks Give Summer A Vivid Raison D'etre"! This Art Deco fashion plate by A.E. Marty is a marvelous illustration of the bouffant robe de style made famous by Jeanne Lanvin. Here, *Vogue* notes: "Like all Lanvin's full-skirted frocks, these models all but touch the ground and have a natural or slightly lowered waist-line." Referring to the dress on the right, *Vogue* advises that the round "cockade" trims "add picturesque touches..." (June 1922)

Harper's Bazar also sings Lanvin's praises as Baron de Meyer declares: "The periods between 1830 and 1880 have given her renewed inspiration for pictorial robes de style... decorated by the marvelous embroideries and ornamentations for which this house is justly famed...embroidered wheels of cut-out work, extraordinary cockades...are seen on many of the models." (April 1923)

Close-up of one of the gown's Art Deco cockades.

"The bouffant silhouette is beguiling—and perfect for a summer afternoon…" This pale pastel robe de style might have stepped from the pages of *Vogue*. Perfect for an afternoon dance, it's fashioned of silk "paper" taffeta with an iridescent sheen. Embroidered cockades of silk tulle ruffles in shades of light pink and rose, with Art Deco centers of gold soutache, form the skirt's scalloped hem and climb the left side to above the low gathered waistline. Backed with heavy gold lamé, they're hand appliquéd to the frock. Sheer silk tulle forms the rounded neckline and slightly capped sleeves. The second neckline, where the tulle and taffeta meet, is delicately embroidered; first with a row of metallic silver beads, then with a row of delicate fleur de lis— this embroidered double row also extends around the armscyes. Self piping emphasizes the low waistline, and the tulle neckline. As its label attests, it's from one of New York's most prestigious shops: *Jay Thorpe Inc., 57th Street West, Paris, New York.* $800-$1,000. Shown with a matching wide brim horsehair cloche, $300-$400.

"Mabel," a sweet young lady from Cedar Rapids, Iowa, models a charming robe de style with full gathered skirt and piped low waist (though she's evidently not wearing panniers or a supporting petticoat beneath). The gown's lace "Bertha" bodice has slightly capped sleeves; the skirt's lace border ends in handkerchief points. Note her long beaded necklace and t-strap shoes. (Photo postcard, ca. 1920-24)

Popular throughout the twenties, wide brim cloches or "capelines" made a flattering frame for the face—as this pretty French lady demonstrates! (Photo postcard, Leo, *Made in France*, ca. 1920-24)

Evening Wear: Lavish Dresses and Lush Capes!

A dramatic jet beaded "girdle" belt with a floral hook and eye closing and medieval-ish strands of jet that trail to the hem. $100-$200.

"A giddy whirl of colors and costumes…" is pictured in this selection of evening wear offered by the 1922 *Ladies' Home Journal Fashion Quarterly*. Note the smashing red robe de style at upper right and the increasingly more tubular gowns with their "Soft Draperies…" The pale green tubular gown at lower right is a very popular style. Draped at the waistline with a fancy "hip brooch," it cascades beyond the hem; she carries a pink ostrich fan mounted on a single tortoise stick. To her left is a sheer gold medieval gown ending in modish "handkerchief points," a floral girdle accents the waist. Several other gowns emphasize low waists with decorative "girdle" belts: the silver lace tunic gown at lower left has a girdle of roses with hem to match, and a lovely lace tunic overskirt that ends in softly draped points. (She's draped in a voluminous red evening coat, trimmed with fur, and note her chic carved Spanish comb.) Just above, the yellow gown at top left features a girdle of modish monkey fur for a bold, dramatic touch; she's also wearing a sensuous "slave bracelet."

The belted tubular brocade coat adjacent has a lavish fur collar and cuffs, while the elegant velvet cape to its right is more bouffant—and quite a bit shorter than the dress beneath. You'll note that the cape has no front closure other than a collar fastening, a style that prompts the *Ladies Home Journal* to observe:

"Paris insists that you hold your coat in place. You grasp the left edge high in front with the left hand. With the right hand low on the right edge you fold it over the left, or huddle into your wrappings. Of course you cannot do a thing in the world except wear your coat…but if you could look as (Miss Stevens) looks, you wouldn't ask anything more, would you?" (November 1920).

Note that for ladies who prefer to purchase evening capes ready made, Franklin Simon's prestigious New York store has similar styles for $124.50. Most skirts are pictured either ankle length or just above for evening, and note the charming array of "…headdresses rather than hats worn to a formal occasion."

An exciting "diamante" tiara in an Art Deco
design with prong-set rhinestones on brass
mesh; back hook fastening. $150-$250.

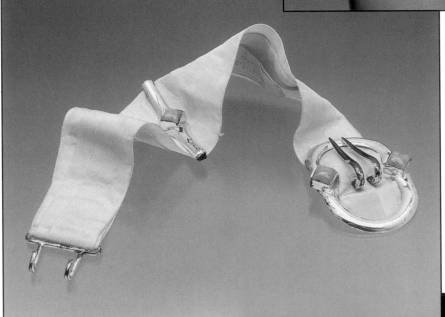

A marvelous Art Deco pleated ivory faille
slave bracelet, with jade and "quadruple
plate" silver buckle and center support.
Label: *Trade Mark, F/A Co. (emblem),
Assurance of Correct Style and Excellence of
Quality.* $150-$200.

Just the thing to emphasize a draped
cascade—a prong set rhinestone "hip
brooch" in a Deco design of
intertwining circles. $75-$125.

Back view, showing the gathered shoulder yoke.

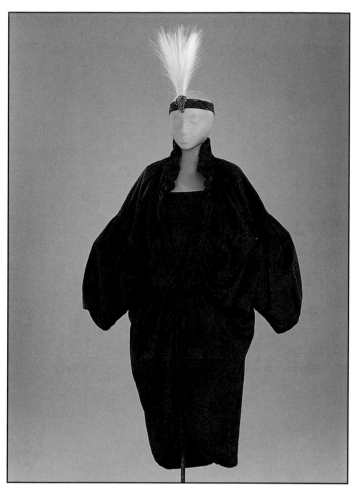

A glowing ruby red panne velvet evening coat in the popular cocoon style so chic in the late teens through the early twenties! It features a wide, gathered yoke that also forms the upper part of the huge sleeves. Self ruffled trim around the front opening dips to the enormous oriental frog at the waist. From the waist, the front curves gracefully to the hem. Shown with a bandeau headpiece with period aigrette and brooch. Ca. 1918-24. $700-$900.

Close-up of the oriental frog closure.

A bit late for the cinema…and it's a Charlie Chaplin film! An usherette lights the way as she leads this stylish trio to their seats. The lady at left wears a coat very similar to ours. *Le Cine* was illustrated by Andre Marty for *Modes et Manieres*, 1919. Pochoir plate, $300-$500. This plate was accompanied by an ode to the cinema (translated):

I would like, as I take up my lyre, o Muse,
In honor of Cinematography, to pluck her golden strings…
The film is good, What fun it is! It is bad—what a bore!

The Art Deco Influence

As the decade progresses, Art Deco becomes a more integral part of fashion via magnificent printed fabrics as well as applied designs.

I. Miller's window display at their Brooklyn store, 498 Fulton St., features these stunning "Avedon Gowns." As the sign in the window notes, they were "worn by Miss Brooklyn, Ethelda Kenvin, judged 'second most beautiful girl in America at Atlantic City Beauty Contest,' and Miss Peggy Sheldon, 'voted by *Evening World* the most beautiful girl in New York.'" Note the incredible Art Deco prints used for these gowns, the graceful draping of their tubular skirts, and their low waistlines emphasized by cleverly draped "girdles."

Beadwork, sequins, and even celluloid bangles or "bubbles" also give frocks a look that screams ART DECO!

Close-up of a magnificent piece of Art Deco artwork: geometric celluloid "bubbles"!

This intriguing silk georgette evening frock features hundreds of green and black celluloid "bubbles," hand-applied in geometric patterns. "Draperies Characterize the Evening Gown," as *Ladies' Home Journal Fashion Quarterly* declares, and this gown's tubular lines are complemented by floating draperies that extend from shoulders to waist, and from the waist to points that fall well below the hem. These draperies are formed by two overlapping rectangular panels of georgette (picot edged). The left shoulder snap opening continues to the low waistline (which has old cased elastic basted beneath). Original black satin underdress. $800-$1,200. (Shown with a draped evening turban headdress with wispy aigrette formed from period materials.)

This exciting Art Deco fan must have caused quite a sensation! It's a full 23" tall, with green and black coq feathers mounted on eighteen amber celluloid sticks. $300-$500.

Chapter Four

Men's Day & Sportswear Fashions
Children's Fashions, 1920-1924

" J'AI FAILLI ATTENDRE "

COSTUME VESTON, DE LUS ET BEFVE

Nº 4 de la Gazette du Bon Ton.　　　　　　Année 1922. — Planche 26

J'ai Failli Attendre ("I almost waited"). Impeccably attired in the newest powder blue double breasted suit, this elegant gent checks his watch as he impatiently awaits his lady—he's the epitome of *savoir faire*! Note the stylish silhouette of the early twenties: trim waist, naturally contoured shoulders, and slim, cuffed pants. His light fedora matches the spats he wears over his narrow-toed shoes, and he carries a walking stick. Powder blue, a "soft greyish blue," is one of the smartest colors of the early twenties, as *National Style Book* exclaims: "London applauds, Paris Approves and New York adopts Powder Blue!"

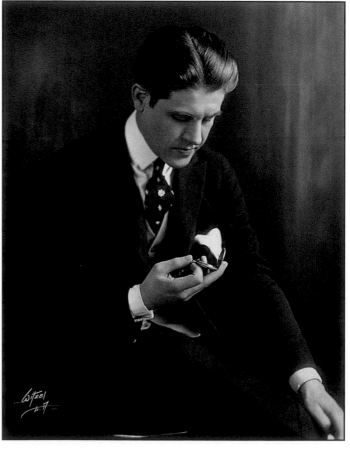

Sartorial splendor! Hugh D. Elder also appears concerned about time slipping away as he checks his pocket watch. He's a living fashion plate in a smart suit with contrasting vest and bold polka dotted tie. Note the trim, natural lines of his jacket, his sharply creased pants, and shirt with detachable "turnover" collar. Hugh's hair is immaculately "slicked," as was de rigueur for a fashionable young man of the day. F. Scott Fitzgerald defines the "Slicker" in *This Side of Paradise* (1920); his Princeton-bound hero, Amory Blaine, notes:

"The Slicker was good-looking or clean-looking; he had brains, social brains, that is, and he used all means on the broad path of honesty to get ahead, be popular, admired, and never in trouble. He dressed well, was particularly neat in appearance and derived his name from the fact that his hair was inevitably worn short, soaked in water or tonic, parted in the middle and slicked back as the current of fashion dictated..."

This marvelous portrait is by Witzel of N.Y.; Hugh's telephone number, "Brdwy 3321," is noted on the reverse. It's interesting to note that country folks often referred to a flashy urban fellow as a "city slicker"!

Men's fashions from most of the first half of the decade emphasized a slim and *youthful* look, a look that went hand in hand with the slender silhouette of women's styles. Though men's fashions changed far less often than women's, they too were evolving into simpler, more casual clothing. Doughboys who'd just returned from WWI simply weren't willing to endure the stuffy, uncomfortable styles of the Edwardian era; they refused to wear something just because it was "proper"…comfort triumphed over tradition, slowly but surely. London, rather than Paris, was the capitol of men's fashion; as the prestigious *Men's Wear* exclaimed in their February 7, 1923 issue: "London is more famous in the sartorial world than it has ever been since pre-war days."

"Beau" Brummell and Modern Male Dress

The most elegant men's styles, custom-made or "bespoke," originated from London's Savile Row, as they had since the days of the dashing Regency dandy, George "Beau" Brummell, who banished the ornate rococo fashions of the eighteenth century and established the modern male attitude towards dress. The Beau began his reign as indisputable King of Fashion at the beginning of the nineteenth century, his credo being the "elegant simplicity" created by immaculate, impeccable tailoring. The Beau, feeling that "the severest mortification a gentleman could incur was to attract observation in the street by his outward appearance," insisted that clothing be stripped of "any adornment that in his opinion might ruin the appearance of the cut." On being complimented at Ascot, the Beau haughtily replied: "I cannot be elegant since you have noticed me." Author Virginia Woolfe would later write of the Beau: "His clothes seemed to melt into each other with the perfection of their cut and the quiet harmony of their colour…everybody looked overdressed or badly dressed beside him…"

The Beau was not royalty, but from the middle class. His father was secretary to the Prime Minister, Lord North; his grandfather, William Brummell, ran a lodging house on Bury Street. The Beau's reputation as the ultimate "Dandy" was established at Eton and Oxford. He soon began to move in circles that brought him to the attention of the libertine Prince Regent, "Prinny" (George IV from 1820-30). The fashion-conscious Prince was awed by the elegant Beau, and invited him to join the royal regiment. He completely understood when the Beau soon resigned his commission; after all, the regiment had been ordered to leave London and the Beau's social life would have been severely curtailed. With Prinny's patronage, the Beau's success was assured, and his fame as supreme arbiter of fashion grew with his arrogance.

With a single-minded fervor that was almost a religion, the Beau and his Dandy Disciples began to demolish the age-old belief that extravagant ostentation was the epitome of splendor, and soon the embroidered and bejeweled satin suits of previous centuries were replaced by clothes that merely whispered wealth and power.

The Beau's patronage of Savile Row tailors established the reputation Savile Row has enjoyed to this day. Though he terrorized his tailors by critiquing the cutting of his clothes, they ultimately agreed he'd improved on their cut. Although long pants for men had been worn by the *sans culottes* of the French Revolution, they weren't considered fashionable un-

George Bryan "Beau" Brummell 1778-1840, from the original 1805 watercolor portrait by Richard Dighton.

til the early nineteenth century—due in large part to the Beau, who cut such an elegant figure in his skintight long "trowsers," he's credited with abolishing knee breeches. His jackets were so well cut that Lord Byron was heard to remark: "You might almost say the body thought."

Innumerable Beau legends have drifted down through the centuries, some plausible and some to be taken with a grain of salt. Beau is said to have spent upwards of six hours on his toilette before venturing out! Beau advocated daily bathing (including a milk rinse) and clean linen underwear, unheard of at the time. He popularized clean-shaven chins and short, neoclassical "Brutus" haircuts. (One legend claims Beau employed three separate hairdressers: one for the front curls, one for the side curls, and yet another for the back.) The Beau asserted that for a matchless patina, his tasseled Hessian boots were polished with the "froth of the finest champagne." He advocated changing gloves at least six times a day. Fanatically fastidious about his gloves, Beau considered that three glove makers were necessary; one for the fingers, one for the palm, and yet another for the thumb. Beau was fond of snuff, and deemed it necessary to have a different snuffbox for every day of the year.

The Beau's skill in tying a cravat was unparalleled; it would have been unthinkable for him to appear in public if his cravat was not perfectly knotted under a collar so high it partially obscured his cheeks. He developed his own formula for lightly starching his cravats to achieve the desired degree of perfection. Tying the cravat was perhaps the most painstaking operation of the day; Beau legend claims his valet once explained, "Those are our failures" to a visitor who'd noted a pile of wrinkled rejects. When Beau's cravat was tied to his satisfaction, he then thoroughly examined the effect in his mirror, gyrating his jaw to further adjust the cravat to more natural contours. Since the Beau felt a cravat should be changed three times daily, one might wonder if there were enough hours in his day for cravats alone.

On completion of his dressing ritual, the Beau often sauntered to White's Gentlemen's Club. Operating since 1763 as a private club, White's was dedicated to wagering, whist, dining, *and* establishing male fashions—though not necessarily in that order. In 1811, White's installed a large bow window, which would come to be known as the "Beau Window." White's is located at 37-38 St. James Street, London; their facade remains unchanged and one can still look out on the world from the Beau Window.

As the Beau's fame grew, so did his audacity. From the Beau Window he preached sartorial sermons, spiced with scathing sarcasm directed at anyone less elegantly attired (everyone). No one, not even the Prince, was spared. Eventually the Beau made one comment too many, rashly remarking to one of the Prince's entourage, "Who's your fat friend?" Beau was immediately ostracized, and creditors began clamoring for long-overdue payments. In 1816, at age thirty-eight, the Beau, elegant even in exile, hired his own boat for a flight to France. Unable to reconcile himself to his ignominious plight, he began to suffer delusions of his former grandeur, and, possessed by phantoms of his prominent past, he carried on imaginary conversations with these sartorial specters until, in 1840, he died a pauper in a French insane asylum.

"Prince of Wales leaving Chateau Frontenac for his ranch, September 13, 1923… Della in the corner" is noted on the reverse of this photo postcard. The prince is casually but immaculately attired in a vested suit and homburg hat; every detail is perfect. Note the snappy fedora on the man to his right and Della's chic cloche! (The famous Hotel Frontenac is located in Quebec, Canada.)

Though Beau's legends have undoubtedly been embellished over the last two hundred years, his impact was so great that his name became synonymous with elegant men's attire. Beau's credo of "Elegant Simplicity" has left a legacy to men's fashions that has endured for the past two hundred years, expressed one hundred years later by actor Adolph Menjou: "When people overdo things, the smartly dressed shy to the other extreme." Over the decades, many men's wear manufacturers, shops, and articles of clothing (particularly ties) have been named for him. So enduring was his fame that some two hundred years later, pop singer/philosopher Billy Joel would long to be "…a real Beau Brummell"!

By the twenties, another English trendsetter was the arbiter of men's fashions…

The Prince of Panache!

In the twenties, casual clothes for men were of utmost importance. They were given a certain *cashet* by the Prince of Wales, heir to Beau Brummell's sartorial crown as well as Britain's. (This Prince of Wales would become "abdicating" Edward VIII; he renounced the throne in 1936 to marry American divorcee Wallis Warfield Simpson.) Edward followed in the fashionable footsteps of his grandfather, "Bertie," who'd been *the* style setter of the Edwardian era. (Bertie, Queen Victoria's eldest son, was a bon vivant whose paramours included Lily Langtry and Sarah Bernhardt; he became King Edward VII after Victoria's death in 1901, and reigned until 1910.)

The fashionable young Prince favored elegant but casual fashions, styles with considerably more panache than was formerly thought "proper." His visits to America fomented a fervor of excitement; his wardrobe made fashion headlines wherever he went. The famous *Men's Wear Magazine* noted: "The average young man in America is more interested in the clothes of the Prince of Wales than the clothes of any other individual on earth."(September 1924) Style-setting favorites of H.R.H. included: patterned Fair Isle sweaters, baggy "plus-four" golf knickers and floppy golf caps, elegant Panama hats and large "snap-brim" fedoras, sporty oxford brogues and cocoa brown bucks. He popularized four-in-hand ties with large double "Windsor" knots, and created a sensation when he wore a flamboyant *red* tie, previously thought too effete. He favored suits of Glen Urquhart check (also known as the "Prince of Wales check"), and also popularized the double-breasted dinner jacket (tux).

By 1924, the Prince was sporting roomier suits with broader shoulders and wider trousers, a style that would replace the slender, fitted suits of the early twenties during the second half of the decade. Canny advertisers used the Prince of Wales's name to market anything and everything—even suspenders!

No sporty gent could resist these natty blue Prince of Wales suspenders with their Art Deco arrow design! Store stock, $25-$50.

Twenties' men obtained their clothing in several ways; the pinnacle of men's fine garments, of course, being custom-made or "bespoke" clothing purchased from one's favorite tailor. The Prince of Wales patronized Frederick Scholte of Savile Row, who dressed such other luminaries as the Duke of Kent and Rudolph Valentino. Scholte was responsible for the broad shouldered "drape" suit which became the rage during the second half of the decade, a style that evolved into the business suit of today.

Most men during the twenties, however, wore ready-made or "off the rack" clothing, manufactured by such fine firms as Hart Schaffner & Marx, Kuppenheimer, and Hickey-Freeman, and available at local department stores, specialty shops, and haberdasheries. Ready made clothing had had a long history; some items like capes, hats, and accessories had been available during the Renaissance. In the War of 1812, soldiers wore ready made uniforms manufactured by the US Army plant in Philadelphia. The famous Brooks Brothers men's store opened in 1818, and they soon advertised ready-made fashions for civilians, "having on hand a very large stock of ready-made clothing, just manufactured with a due regard to fashion, and embracing all of the various styles of the day." (In the twenties, Brooks Brothers was located the corner of Madison Avenue and 44th Street in New York City with branches in Boston and Palm Beach.) The invention of the sewing machine in the 1840s helped bridge the fashion gap between rich and poor, and stylish, affordable ready-made clothing was soon available to all. By the second half of the nineteenth century, ready made clothing could be purchased from mail order catalogs; Montgomery Wards' first catalog was issued in 1872, Sears Roebuck followed in 1896. In the twenties, catalogs like *Bellas Hess, National Style Book,* and *Chicago Mail Order* offered stylish clothing for men as well as for women.

Twenties' men also wore clothing that their wives, mothers, and sweethearts made from patterns. Magazines like *Butterick's Quarterly* and *Pictorial Review* offer patterns for men under such headlines as: "Clothes that Make the Mere Man Comfortable." (1922 *Pictorial Review*) They include suit coats ("sack coats"), pants and shirts, smoking jackets, lounging robes, pajamas, nightshirts, even underwear (delicately described as being for "The More Intimate, Practical Needs of the Man of the Family").

Favorite male ad words included "snappy," "jazz," "smart," and of course, "handsome." As *Vogue* advised, women wanted their escorts to be "correctly attired on every occasion and at all times," adding, "…So get pretty or beat it if you want to be loved by one of today's fair maidens."

During most of the decade's first half, men's fashions followed the trim, natural contours set during the teens: suits exhibited "Snappy Formfitting Lines!" Interestingly, the beginning of this "Slim and Youthful" look in men's styles coincided with the slim silhouette of women's fashions. Men's suits with "tailored shapeliness" had jackets with "military high waists" and natural, unpadded shoulders. Though single-breasted styles were prevalent, double-breasted suits were also worn by dashing young men. *National Style Book* advocated their "snappy double-breasted model with an air of real New York Style." (1922) Double-breasted suits were also quite fitted, and noticeably contoured at the waist; they were advertised as "Chesty Models with Plenty of Snap"! Suit jackets were either "sack coats" or sportier Norfolk jackets ("belters"). A "sack coat" was like today's suit coat, a coat without a waist seam; it evolved from the Victorian lounging or smoking jacket. The sporty Norfolk jacket was either belted all around, or belted only in back. Both style jackets had been popular since the mid-nineteenth century, and in the twenties, both were popular in single and double breasted styles. Vests remain favorites, and came with many suits.

Early twenties' suit jackets paired with slender "daddy long-leg" trousers that were rather short, ending just below the ankles. Trousers had a pressed center crease, a custom that's believed to date to the Victorian era, originating with Queen Victoria's son, Bertie, who appeared in ready made trousers (which were stacked creased) after a hunting mishap. During the early twenties, trousers were most often cuffed, though uncuffed styles were also available. Some historians attribute cuffed trousers to Bertie too; he reportedly set this trend by turning his cuffs up during a rainstorm and forgetting to turn them back down.

For increasingly important sporting events, the Knicker Suit was a favorite with participants and spectators alike. Baggy knee pants or "knickers" were paired with matching Norfolk jackets. Practical and versatile, they were often purchased in three and four piece sets (jacket, knickers, trousers, and vest). Sporty gents could go to the office in trousers, jacket, and vest, then head for the links by simply changing to knickers and adding golf hose. Tweed knickers were favored for cooler weather, and white linen or Palm Beach cloth for hot summer days. On the course, golfers often substituted sweaters for Norfolk jackets for more freedom of movement; since the Prince of Wales favored Argyle plaids and jacquard Fair Isles, naturally they became the rage.

Goodall's famous "Palm Beach" suits, made from Goodall's patented blend of cotton and mohair or worsted, were an essential part of every stylish man's summer wardrobe. The *1920 National Style Book* offered a variety of "Genuine Palm Beach Suits, Guaranteed to be made of the Genuine Palm Beach Cloth—The Ideal Suit for Hot Weather Wear." *National's* described the Palm Beach fabric as: "a light weight fabric, woven of a mixture of hard-twisted worsted and cotton in equal proportions. It is porous in texture, and permits free circulations of air." *National's* also noted that "These suits will launder splendidly and retain the original handsome appearance." *National's* offered: "the newest models, ranging from the snappy belter to the dignified business suit." In addition to traditional white, colors included: "dark grey with lighter grey making a pin-check pattern; dark green blended with dark maroon, giving a stylish two tone effect; and dark green striped." Catalog suit prices ranged from $14.98-$16.98.

"Mix and match" was also a popular men's concept in the twenties: for instance, a favorite suit jacket may have been worn with contrasting trousers, or a Norfolk jacket paired with non matching pants or knickers. White flannel trousers paired with dark suit jackets were such a popular combination that *Men's Wear* noted it was "almost a uniform." In 1924, *Men's Wear,* reporting from the Henly Regatta, one of England's most fashionable events, observed snappy dressers wearing light trousers with nautical, double-breasted sports "Blazers"—inspired by the jackets originally worn by seamen on the H.M.S. Blazer in the 1860s.

Today's favorite blue jeans or denims were worn as work clothes for farmers, factory workers, mechanics, and railroad men. They were not a fashion statement, but were "Hard Working Pants," as they had been since Levi Strauss first produced his sturdy riveted jeans for the "49ers"—men who flocked to California's gold fields during the gold rush of 1849. The 1920 *National Style Book* advertised "National Work Clothes of white-backed Indigo Blue Denim"; the forward-thinking *National's* declared they're "The Most Practical Garments of All"! "Wear proof" features included: "triple-stitched seams, riveted non-rust buttons, and rip-proof button-

Hard working man in hard working denim pants! (Snapshot, ca. 1920-30)

holes" and, of course, large, practical pockets and button flies. *National's* also advised that their roomy denim pants "can be worn over your suit pants, making a very convenient and comfortable type of garment to work in." Styles included classic jeans (referred to as "waistband overalls"), bib overalls, coveralls ("overall suits"), and work jackets. Denim was also favored for boys' rugged playwear.

With the decade's emphasis on "Flaming Youth," college students' favorite fads made a significant impact on fashion. To predict what would become the styles of tomorrow, *Men's Wear* regularly sent scouts to Princeton and Yale, considered the decade's most fashion-conscious universities. In the first half of the decade, yellow rain slickers, sometimes decorated with John Held Jr. type drawings, were all the rage with both young men and women. Slickers were often paired with the era's ubiquitous unbuckled galoshes or "Artics," and for football games and motoring, both Sheiks and Shebas bundled into raccoon coats.

In England, undergraduates at Oxford University—to circumvent a "no-knickers-in-class" edict—adopted wide, baggy trousers that could easily be worn over their favorite forbidden knickers. By 1924, these wide trousers had been spotted by the ever-vigilant *Men's Wear*, who reported seeing "very loose flannel trousers" at England's Henly regatta. The following spring, Wanamaker's New York store began advertising: "OXFORD BAGS...The trousers that have created such a furore in England." John Held, Jr. immortalized these Oxford bags in his cartoons of "Flaming Youth" and they remain a symbol of the Roaring Twenties to this day.

Catalogs also took note of the trend for wider pants; by the fall of 1924, *National Style Book* was offering: "All wool flannel Bell Bottoms...Young men's wide bell bottom dress trousers of fine all-wool flannel with new slanting side pockets and plain bottoms, suitable with any dark coat, $5.69!" By

1924, young college men, following the lead of the Prince of Wales, were wearing suits with both wider pants and roomier jackets. *National's* trumpeted: "Young Fellows—Here's the suit you want made in the Correct English Style; the two-button sack coat with full loose lines...the trousers are cut full, wide and roomy...in the new Powder Blue or Brown."

Three smart suits offered by *National Style Book*'s 1922 Spring/Summer issue, illustrating the early twenties' slim, fitted lines with rather short jackets and pants. *National's* ad copy is enticing. Left to right: 1) "a favorite three-button Sack Suit with good lines—a suit you can wear for almost every occasion and can count on for good hard service...all wool worsted in the popular herringbone stripe weave. The single-breasted coat is well tailored in every detail. Correct lapels; flap pockets and welt breast pocket...regulation five-button vest; correctly cut trousers with cuff or straight bottoms." 2) "You fellows who want a summer suit that means comfort on the hottest days, combined with real style—here's a new two-piece suit designed just for you. The big patch pockets, the notched lapels, and splendid tailoring make this an unusually smart style, and think what a bargain it is at only $9.98! In corded mohair, a cool, crisp finished fabric well known for its serviceability and one of the most comfortable of summer materials. Two button coat, cuffed bottoms." 3) "The old reliable, and a big honest value at $15.95! You can always depend on an all-wool worsted navy blue serge suit...it is the well dressed man's choice for all around wear...The style of this suit too will appeal to men who want a quiet, conservative suit of good quality." The three-button sack coat features "the correct narrow peaked lapels"; it comes with a five button vest of "correct height"; trousers are offered in your choice of straight or cuffed. Note their striped shirts with detachable collars, striped Rep ties, and sporty hats—a trim fedora, a Panama straw in Optima style, and a snappy straw boater or "skimmer!"

140

It's "August 26, 1922" and this smart couple's enjoying a beautiful summer day at Atlantic City! Note his slim, trim "sack suit," striped four-in-hand tie, and snappy straw boater. His lady wears a chic capeline cloche and a fox neckpiece, and carries an envelope bag.

Norfolk jackets or "belters" were named for a hunting jacket worn in the early eighteenth century by the Duke of Norfolk; their distinguishing features are still evident two hundred years later, including box pleats down each side in front and back and handy flapped patch pockets. By the mid-nineteenth century, the Norfolk had become a favorite of the English country squire and was worn for golf, hunting, bicycling, and croquet. By the turn of the century, the Norfolk jacket and knicker pants combination was tremendously popular, often advertised as a "golf suit."

Knickers, originally "knickerbockers," were descendants of the ancient knee breeches that disappeared during the French Revolution—when revolutionaries or *sans culottes* adopted full-length trousers. They were the most popular sports pants of the twenties, and were still worn in the thirties.

Breeches or jodhpurs, another popular type of pants for sport, were the pants of choice for both horsemen and aviators!

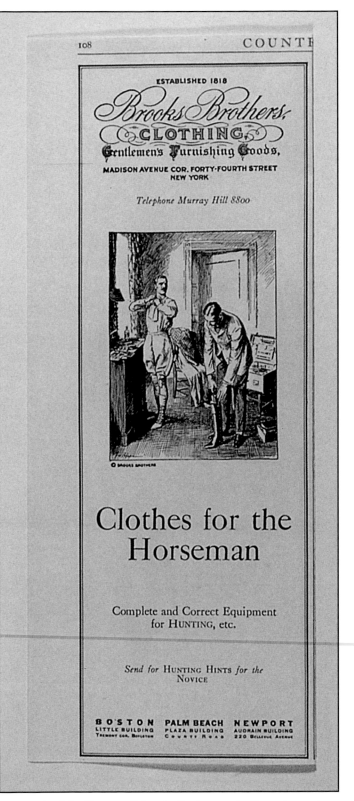

Breeches for "The Horseman"! Brooks Brothers carries "Complete and Correct Equipment for Hunting, etc." The uninitiated may send for their helpful pamphlet, *Hunting Hints for the Novice*. (Ad, *Country Life*, October 1927)

For casual wear, a snappy gent may have selected a versatile wool tweed suit like the one shown here with two pairs of pants: long cuffed pants for the office, and "Tee Top Knickers" for golf. The baggy knickers fasten with chrome buckles at the knee bands. Of course, both the long pants and knickers have a button fly. (Zippers in men's pants were not in general use until the late thirties.) The suit jacket has a three button front, notched lapels, and flapped patch pockets; its belted Norfolk back has deep side pleats for ease of motion. Jacket label: *Rothschild-Greenfield Co., Locust at Sixth, Saint Louis*. In 1922, B. Altman's offers a "men's 4-piece golf and sports knicker suit," knickers, long trousers, coat, and waistcoat, for $55 (comparable to about $550 today); its current value would be between $600-$800. *Courtesy of Janet Schwarz and Ken Weber.*

Close-up of the trousers' button fly.

Tweed suit, long pants: "A chesty model with plenty of Snap"! The three-button Norfolk jacket is belted in back only; note the notched or "peaked" lapels and large flapped pockets. The slim trousers, not pleated at the waistband, end in narrow cuffs; they have belt loops as well as inside buttons for suspenders.

Three smartly suited "slickers" shooting craps in front of a men's sporting goods/smoke shop in Saranac Lake (the Adirondacks), New York. Taken by professional photographer William Kollecker, ca. 1920-24.

The knicker's label: *Tee Top Knicker—Golfers Delight!*

Far left:
The tweed suit worn with its "Tee Top Knickers." Knickers are so important one shop advises: "Every golfer should have at least three pairs—one in the locker, one at home, and one in the laundry"!

Left:
Back view of the knicker suit, showing the jacket's belted Norfolk back, with wide pleats at the side seams to ensure ease of motion. Note the buckle fastenings on the knicker's cuffs.

Below:
Brown wool ribbed stitch knicker socks with snappy Argyle tops. $50-75.

Knee length golf hose or "knicker socks" were mandatory with knickers and sweaters that often coordinated or matched. In February 1924, *Men's Wear* reported from St. Moritz: "80% of the men are wearing Fair Isle jersey pullovers, many with matching or coordinating socks…Americans are calmly wearing patterns and colors unthinkable previously…no doubt this arises from the Fair Isle vogue…" They're imported from England, Norway, and Spain, in checks, stripes, and zigzags, in addition to the "Fair Isle jacquards."

National's 24/5 catalog offers fine English all-wool "Imported Golf Hose" with Fair Isle style turnover tops, proclaiming: "Men everywhere wear these handsome golf socks with knickers for golf, hiking and all outing wear."

Far left:
Hand-knit heather green ribbed knicker socks with the Fair Isle tops. $75-100.

Left:
Close-up of the Fair Isle knit.

As noted earlier, another favorite casual ensemble—light trousers with a contrasting dark jacket—was so popular it was "almost a uniform." Teaming light trousers with dark jackets had been fashionable since men adopted long pants; this classic duo often appears in men's nineteenth century fashion plates and is a timeless ensemble, still worn today.

Jazz King Louis "Satchmo" Armstrong models the casual classic "uniform" of white flannels with contrasting dark jacket. His wife Lil is decked out in a smart plaid frock with the requisite fox scarf. (Snapshot, ca. 1924-25)

"A Phone Booth in July" illustrates why Goodall's patented Palm Beach suit was a necessity for the smart twenties' man. As the guy in the booth swelters, "well, the man to your left is clad in a suit of GENUINE PALM BEACH!" Goodall's description is persuasive: "Its open porous weave, its clean, fresh appearance, its airy lightness make living a joy, even when the old thermometer is dizzily climbing around the hundred mark!" (*The Literary Digest*, July 17, 1920) Palm Beach clothing was available in shops and catalogs; as Goodall notes: "Every conscientious clothier can, and will, show you the Genuine in a full variety of colors and with the Trade-Marked Label inside the coat." While Goodall first manufactured just the fabric, they were shortly offering suits "Tailored by Goodall" as well. Palm Beach suits often had labels in the trousers advising that they "readily wash or dry-clean."

Palm Beach Suits

By the early twenties, the Goodall Worsted Company had developed a "washable" lightweight blend of cotton and mohair for summer wear—their patented "Palm Beach" fabric. They began an extensive ad campaign, and soon every well-dressed man's wardrobe boasted at least one Palm Beach suit. Classic white was favored, but Palm Beach fabric came in a wide range of colors and patterns, and was made into a variety of clothing.

The Literary Digest for July 17, 1920 83

A 'Phone Booth in July
will quickly wilt the freshest smile and darken the brightest disposition — Unless —
Well—the man to your left is clad in a Suit of
Genuine Palm Beach

Palm Beach
THE GENUINE CLOTH
MFD. ONLY BY GOODALL WORSTED CO.
Genuine Palm Beach Suits are shown in many patterns—in dark colors as well as light.

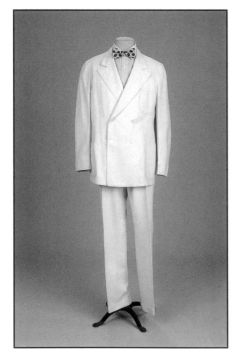

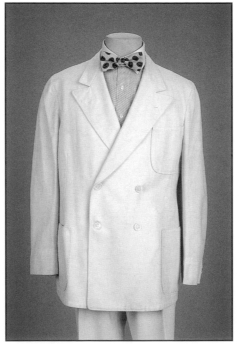

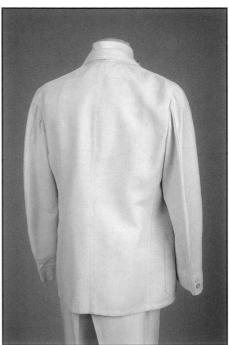

This impeccable Palm Beach suit is a nice example of the snappy double-breasted styles favored by the Prince of Wales. These roomy, masculine styles were becoming quite popular by 1924, and they remained so for decades. The trousers have wide, 20" cuffs, a watch pocket, belt loops, and a five button fly. We've paired our suit with a twenties blue pin-striped shirt with detachable collar. (The snappy pre-tied yellow and blue paisley tie is contemporary). Suit, $500-$800.

Close-up of the double breasted suit jacket, roomy but with subtle shaping via long front darts. Note the wider, notched lapels, four original pearl buttons, and three large pockets (not flapped); sleeves have two smaller pearl cuff buttons. Seams are top-stitched.

Back view of suit jacket, which has a topstitched center seam, and no center vent.

The suit's famous Goodall label.

144

Men's Shirts

In the twenties, shops that sold men's clothing and accessories were known as haberdasheries!

Awaiting the first customers of the day! Pictured left to right in this splendid early twenties photo: on top of the display case, long four-in-hand ties and "Grayco" bow ties ($.50); inside the display case, the top two shelves contain collarless shirts; on the bottom shelf, caps are stacked. On the shelves behind the male clerk, boxes of BVD underwear are piled high. The display case below the clerks contains both low and high-top shoes, socks, and gloves. To the right of the woman clerk is an ornate brass cash register; on top is a poster for "Mule Gloves" and to the right, a Shinola (shoe polish) sign. Over the woman's head, on top of the shelves, is a poster for "Miller Work Shirts." A large ledger book sits on the counter at the extreme right; and on top of the shelves is a sign for "Hood Athletic Indoor Footwear." The table in the foreground is piled high with slacks. Note the male clerk's trim jacket, smallish bow tie, slicked back hair, and the lady's chic cloche hat and blouse with Peter Pan collar.

The formerly mundane male shirt had become something of a sex symbol by the early twenties, due in large part to Cluett Peabody's famous "Arrow Shirt Man." Their ad copy was nothing short of erotic; he was described as "a hunk of male magnificence"…with "languorous lid, the eyes piercing. The chin noble, the mouth innocent. Overall, an air of imponderable calm. Ah, but what power beat at that gate of purity?" This hunk of male magnificence had been introduced in 1905 by illustrator J.C. Leyendecker; he made such an impact that he soon received more fan mail than a movie star—some letters included marriage proposals!

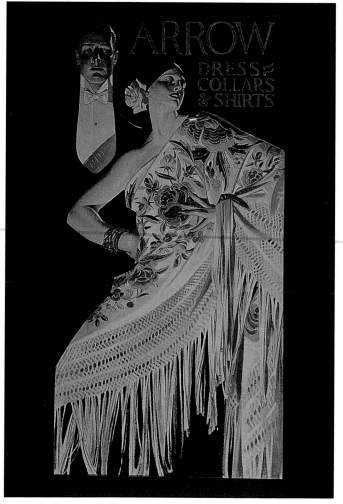

Proving that his Arrow Shirt man can emote as erotically as Rudy Valentino, artist Leyendecker portrays him admiring his lady's seductive Spanish shawl…with a look of barely controlled passion! Note her Spanish mantilla haircomb and bangle bracelets. (1922).

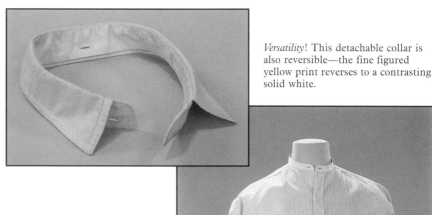

These two detachable-collar shirts are "Extra Big Values for You Men Who Appreciate Quality": a woven-stripe madras with "fast color stripes woven through," and a small check with "separate collar to match" in a choice of blue, lavender, or green check. (1923 *National Style Book*)

Two handsome gents show off their snappy detachable-collar striped shirts, worn with short striped knit ties (see page 149). Note they're wearing belts rather than suspenders, and white canvas outing shoes or "sneakers." (U.S. Rubber developed "Keds," an early sneaker, in 1917.)

During the first half of the decade, the majority of men's shirts had detachable collars, though shirts with attached collars—in both "button down" and turnover styles—were gaining ground, as were casual shawl-collared "sports shirts" (also known as "outing shirts"). "Soft shirts" had largely replaced the previous stiffly-starched shirts, which were now worn by old fogies or "stuffed shirts"! These new softer shirts were often called "negligee shirts" in period catalogs.

The detachable collar proved difficult to oust...it had been around a long time! Esquire's fascinating *Encyclopedia of Men's Fashions* notes that the detachable collar was "invented" by a Mrs. Hannah Montague of Troy, New York, when one day in 1820, thoroughly sick of scrubbing, she snipped the collar off her blacksmith husband's shirt and washed it alone. By the first half of the twenties, period catalogs often pictured shirts that included matching detachable collars; some reversed to a contrasting solid white. Detachable collars were also purchased separately and were available in a wide range of styles. Removable "collar buttons" attached collars to shirts at the center back and front openings (see page 72).

Versatility! This detachable collar is also reversible—the fine figured yellow print reverses to a contrasting solid white.

A splendid butterscotch yellow shirt in a very fine figured gold and white print; the fabric is woven in vertical stripes. Note the white collar band with collar buttonholes, the front closure with the button facings only part way down, and the button cuffs. Label: *E&W Trade Mark*. $75-$125.

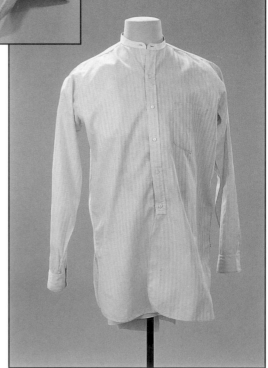

Neat as a pin and cool as a cucumber! A snappy blue pinstriped shirt with a detachable white turnover collar, button cuffs, and front chest pocket. Label: *E & W, Trade Mark*. $50-$100.

Of the increasingly popular shirts with attached collars, the button-down was a twenties' favorite. Destined to become one of the most popular shirts of all time, the button-down shirt has a fascinating history. This classic shirt originated in England, where it was originally worn by polo players. To keep collar points from flapping in players' faces during the game, they were fastened with small buttons. In the mid-1890s, John Brooks of Brooks Brothers men's store noted these distinctive shirts while attending a polo match in England; he bought several and sent them to Brooks Brothers for their sports line. By the early twenties, the button-down shirt had become so popular many manufacturers had come out with their own versions. Brooks Brothers claims their original has never been successfully duplicated, however; their classic is oxford cloth, with collar points measuring exactly 3-3/8 inches.

Twenties' shirts came in a variety of fabrics and a rainbow of colors! There were "smart" solids, snappy "novelty" checks, small prints, and outrageously popular stripes—wide stripes, narrow stripes, and every combination thereof…stripes were also woven into fabrics. Favorite fabrics included washable "tub" silk, the new "artificial" or "fiber silk" (rayon), and of course, mercerized (shrink-resistant) cotton. Cotton/artificial silk blends were common. Cotton fabrics included madras, oxford cloth, broadcloth, percale, and poplin. Pongee was also desirable, finished in both silk and cotton, and shantung. In period catalog layouts, shirts were often pictured with appropriate contrasting ties (priced separately). To keep out winter's chill, there were flannel, wool, and corduroy shirts "for sport or outdoor wear."

Period catalog shirt prices ranged from about $1.00 (cotton) to $10.45 (silk broadcloth), though buyers were advised to keep in mind "THE BEST IS ALWAYS CHEAPEST IN THE END"! (1922 *National Style Book*)

"Buddy's Best"! A chocolate brown button-down shirt in fast color broadcloth. This is a never opened store stock shirt with its original tag, picturing a young man wearing a button down shirt, red tie, and knickers! Since button-downs have been popular for many decades, it's hard to find an old example that's labeled. $75-$125.

Close-up of *Buddys Best* original tag.

A true sports shirt, this early twenties "outing shirt" was meant to be worn *without a tie*! It's "lustrous white pongee" with a washable silk striped collar, buttoned pocket, and short sleeves. "A popular shirt for summer wear," this casual style was a favorite throughout the decade, worn by both men and boys. (*National Style Book*, 1920)

"Here You Are Men!" The 1923 *National Style Book* offers "The Most Popular Shirt of the Season," featuring the "Attached Buttoned-point Collar." *National's* offers this "coat style shirt of our best quality Mercerized Cotton Pongee" in white, tan, or light blue. It has a "convenient patch pocket with buttoned flap" and the soft cuffs are buttoned also; there's "no need to bother with cuff links."

Men's Ties

The *piece de resistance*...the TIE!

Since the days the fastidious Beau Brummell spent hours tying his cravat, the tie has literally been close to a man's heart, adding a touch of individuality to clothing otherwise mandated to uniformity. The tie undoubtedly had practical origins; perhaps cave men flung sinew ropes around their necks to leave their hands free to hold their weapons. Some historians believe that Roman legionnaires wrapped a type of tie or neck scarf around their necks to prevent sunburn and chafing caused by their armor (which also came in handy to wipe off bloody swords). After the Renaissance, with the disappearance of the era's huge lace ruffs, men seemed to feel a need to adorn the shirt's opening with something, and a neck scarf or "cravat" fit the bill. Famous historian Ruth Turner Wilcox notes in her classic *The Mode in Costume* that the earliest recorded mention of the cravat was in 1660, when it was worn by Croatians visiting Paris to celebrate their victory over the Turks, wearing "colorful linen neckerchiefs called 'royal cravattes.'"

During the twenties, ties were mandatory. They were worn with almost everything except utilitarian work clothes...an "AN UNTIED MAN IS EVER AN UNTIDY MAN!", as Sears proclaimed in the early 1900s. (Sears offered over three hundred different patterns of neckties or "scarves," including "handsome brocades in Persian effects, oriental designs, scotch and highland checks...")

Twenties' men wore both long four-in-hand ties and "snappy" bow ties. Of the four-in-hands, the successful businessman preferred rather conservative ties, including regimental diagonal stripes, "reps" and small-figured foulards. Collegiate trend setters often selected one of the sportier boucle knit four-in-hands—and the brighter the better! Four-in-hand ties were available with bias wool interlinings, rather than flannel, which kept the shape better. In addition to the popular silk foulards, other fabrics included silk blends ("silk-mixed") and the new "artificial silks" (rayon). Conservative four-in-hands generally end in a point, while the sporty knits are cut straight across.

Bow ties, a very popular alternative to the long four-in-hands, were available in both "ready-made" and tie-your-own styles. Bow ties had also been worn throughout the nineteenth century. The ingenious pre-tied bow tie dates to the 1850s, when the bow was pre-formed and sewn on to the front; it was fastened in the back with a strap and buckle, a method that continued into the twentieth century. Of course, bow ties were also required for formal wear; solid white worn with the tailcoat, and black with the tuxedo or dinner jacket.

Rather conservative "office" four-in-hand ties, typical of the early twenties, as offered by the 1922 *National Style Book*.

Four fine four-in-hand ties of the early twenties. Left to right: 1) a luxurious brocade with an Art Deco pattern of orange and blue stylized flowers on a cinnamon brown ground; 2) a diagonally striped "rep" in shades of forest to light green accented with white; 3) a snappy red silk with slate blue Deco geometrics; 4) a conservative navy silk foulard, with a fine-figured print of white and lighter blue squares. The rather flashy red tie would have been considered "foppish" before the Prince of Wales had the audacity to wear one...then they soon became the rage! None of these ties have labels; all are unlined. Their colors are so lustrous as to be almost iridescent. $35-$75 each.

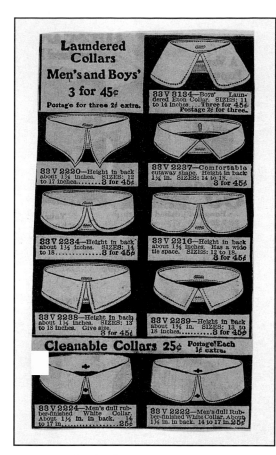

The 1922 *National's* offers a variety of detachable "Laundered Collars, Men's and Boys'." Note the two "cleanable...dull rubber-finished white collars" at bottom, and the popular boy's "Eton" collar, top right.

Bouclé knit ties are a smart alternative to the smooth fabric ties. 1922 *National's* offers three popular striped knits in both all-silk and the new synthetic artificial silk ("rayon" after 1924); note the price difference, just $.44 for the artificial silk. Knit ties were sportier, and more colorful; they're offered in vibrant blues, purples, and greens as well as more sedate colors. Flappers favor knit ties too, and often buy them at men's haberdasheries!

An original box of colorful knit ties from an old store! $25-$45 each.

Bow ties are the Cat's Meow in the twenties; 1922 *National's* offers both pre-tied "Ready-Made Band Bows," with adjustable elastic banded buckle back fastener, and—for traditionalists—tie-yourself bow ties...the one pictured is "fancy figured artificial silk." During the first half of the decade, bow ties are rather small and neat, to complement the trim suits of the day.

Below left:
Pictured are: 1) A detachable "Hallmark" soft collar stamped *Hall, Hart, Well & Co. Of Troy, N.Y.,* size 15. $10-$20. 2) a pre-tied "fancy figured" bow tie with adjustable back elastic, buckle and hook closure, metal clips secured the tie in front. $25-$45. 3) a gold silk tie-your-own bow tie with diagonal black and white stripes, the back marked "Adjustable" in increments from 13 to 16 inches, facilitated by a sliding buckle. $25-$45. Many men opted for pre-tied styles, as tie-your-owns caused as much angst as they did in the Beau's day, described in the following "Sonnet to an Obstinate Bow Tie":

Oh, that there were such vivid words to say
that I could scare this tie into a bow!
Here I've been wrangling with it half a day,
And all I have is a wrinkled silk to show!
I've no technique, and, too well-bred to swear,
I vent my rage in molten beads of sweat,
Restrain the inside urge to take and tear
This puny thing that's caused so much regret.
Were I not going to a dance tonight,
I'd wear my usual modest four-in-hand,
But that, worn with a Tux, would be a sight,-
And so, defying more the mode's command,
I'll buy, if still I cannot tie this tings,
One on the end of an elastic string.
—Robert R. Wallstein, *Life Magazine,* June 2, 1927

Hats for Informal and Sports Wear

During the twenties, hats remained the mark of a civilized man—they were so necessary an accessory one might think they were all that separated twenties' men from Dark Ages barbarians! The most popular hats of the first half of the decade included the homburg, derby, fedora, cowboy or "Carlsbad," and foldable felt "pocket hats" or "crushers." During the hot summer months from May to September, snappy straw boaters and prestigious Panamas were worn; another summer alternative was the straw fedora. Caps were worn to all types of sporting and informal events.

Most of these styles had been established in the nineteenth century; many had even earlier origins. The homburg, derby, and fedora were very popular from the mid-nineteenth century on. The fedora, perhaps the most beloved of all hats, took its name from *Fedora!*, an 1880s play by Emile Sardou, which starred Sarah Bernhardt. The soft peaked cap had been the mark of the Renaissance era's working man. In the late eighteenth century, Admiral Horatio Nelson made a round straw sailor hat regulation for summer; the English called it the "boater" and by the 1890s it had become a sporty summer hat for civilians. The elegant (and expensive) Panama was woven by hand; the finest were made in Ecuador. The western "cowboy" hat was a descendent of the Mexican "sombrero" (Spanish for shade), dating to as early as the fifteenth century. Variations of the cowboy hat had been worn during the Civil War, and by Teddy Roosevelt's Rough Riders during the Spanish-American War in 1898. During the twenties, stars like Tom Mix and William S. Hart made the cowboy hat a rough, tough favorite.

To determine the size of a hat that's unmarked, measure the inside circumference to the nearest 1/8", then divide by 3.15; e.g., a 22" circumference would equal a size 7 hat. The center indentation in the homburg and fedora is usually referred to as the central "crease." The smaller indentations on either side of the hat's central crease are called the "pinch." Cowboy hats were often creased or pinched at the top too; a large horseshoe shaped pinch was called a "mule kick."

There were many well-known hat manufacturers during the twenties, including: Adam, Borsalino, Cavanaugh, Churchill, Disney, Dobbs, Knapp, Knox, Lion, Mallory, Milbrae, Rogers Peet, Resistol, Sarnoff-Irving, Stetson, and Wormser. Brooks Brothers was the New York agent for the illustrious British hatters Messrs. Herbert Johnson & Co., and also for J. & G. Locke (or Lock) of St. James St., London. Locke's was founded in 1676; they moved in 1764 to #6 St. James Street, where they were still located in the twenties. The largest English firm was the prestigious T.W. Christy & Co., Ltd., founded 1773.

The homburg and the derby (English "bowler") are dignified, dressy hats. For day wear, they're the choice of "successful businessmen"; for evening, they're worn with a tuxedo to semi-formal events.

The *handsome homburg!* With its central crease and curved brim, the homburg became popular in the mid-nineteenth century after Queen Victoria's son, "Bertie," then Prince of Wales, wore it while vacationing at his favorite spa in Homburg, Germany. The homburg was manufactured there, thus its name. To salute the hat's Tyrolean origins, Bertie stuck a bright feather in its band, and this colorful custom was soon passed to the fedora as well.

Close-up of the Borsalino label.

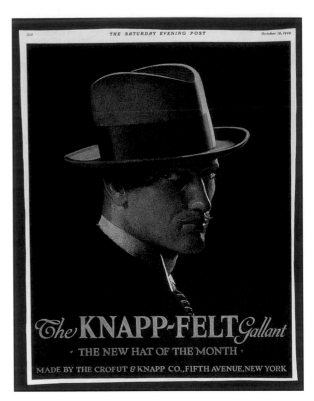

This elegant homburg, "The Knapp-Felt Gallant / The New Hat of the Month," was advertised in *The Saturday Evening Post*. Note the wide grosgrain crown band, slightly rolled brim, and central crease (without a "pinch" on each side). In this illustration, it's shown with the semi-formal "wing-tip" collar and conservative striped tie. (October 19, 1929)

From the "World Famous" Borsalino hatters, a magnificent grey homburg with central crease, rolled brim, and slightly tapering crown. The grosgrain crown band is 1-3/4" wide; grosgrain also edges the brim. Stamped in gold around the leather sweatband inside: *Borsalino, Grand Prix Paris 1900; Antica Casa 1857; Savioli Celso, Via Ugo Bassi No. 4/1, Angolo Via Della Zecca, Bologna. Tab (size) 4 1/2.* Note the Tyrolean feather accent! $150-$200. (Borsalino hats command higher prices than other manufacturer's hats; prices may be doubled.)

The *dignified derby*! The derby or bowler is a dignified but dashing, hard-crowned felt, with a narrow, slightly curved brim and rounded crown. It debuted in 1850, designed by Locke's of St. James St. at the request of feltmakers Thomas & William Bowler, as there was a need for an "in-between" hat—a hat less formal than the top hat, but not as sporty as the soft felts. During an 1888 visit to the United States, the 12th Earl of Derby appeared at Epsom Downs race course in an elegant gray bowler with a black band, thus giving his name to the American version of this stately hat.

The derby remained very popular throughout the twenties and thirties. A snappy brown derby was the trademark of New York's Governor Al Smith, "The Happy Warrior," who ran against Herbert Hoover for President in 1928 to the tune of "On the Sidewalks of New York." The world's largest "derby" is also one of the most famous restaurants—Hollywood's Brown Derby! Silent movie comedians mercilessly poked fun at conservative businessmen; their favorite derbies were parodied by the likes of Charlie Chaplin and Laurel and Hardy.

This classic Derby bears the emblem of Sarnoff-Irving Hat Stores, "est. 1893." Note its slightly rolled and bound brim, and the grosgrain crown ribbon with classic bow on the left. As the inside of the crown attests, it's "Nutriafelt Quality." (Many fine hats were made from nutria fur; Sears offered nutria hats of "hare and rabbit.") Inside the leather sweatband, stamped in gold, is: *The United Hatters of North America—Union Made, Registered.* $50-$100.

Perhaps the most famous derby-donner of all time! Charlie Chaplin as the "Little Tramp" spoofed the successful businessman by wearing his derby two sizes too small!

The Sarnoff-Irving label.

More casual, sporty hats include fedoras, straw boaters or sailors; Panamas, foldable felt crushers or "pocket hats," and western cowboys or "Carlsbads."

"Follow the Crowd to Hat Headquarters"! *National Style Book* offers a variety of casual favorites, including a "Real Fifth Avenue Style" fedora (top right); a "Correct Sailor of Sennet Straw" (bottom left); a high-crowned Western Carlsbad just like Tom Mix wears (center row, second from right); and a felt "crusher" that "can be rolled without injury" (bottom right). At center left, a "Genuine South American Panama" in Optimo shape is $4.95, while the Japanese-made "Toyo Panama" at center right is just $2.29. (1923 Spring/Summer issue)

The *fedora*, a sportier cousin of the homburg, is arguably the most popular men's hat of all time! The fedora features a "pinch" or dent on each side of its central crease; homburgs generally do not. Soft felt hats had become very popular after the invention of a felt making machine in the 1840s. Fedora-styles were also known as Alpines, Tyroleans, and Trilbys.

Though the fedora came in several variations by the first half of the twenties, the most popular was a neat, small-brimmed style with a slightly turned up brim that complemented the close-fitting suits. By 1924, the Prince of Wales was seen in a wider "snap-brim" fedora that would become the classic worn till this day. In 1924, *Men's Wear Magazine* advised that both newsreels and newspapers showed the snap brim to be a favorite in both town and country; they noted that the brim was considerably wider, and the higher crown tapered more to a point. Paying homage to the Prince of Wales, *Men's Wear* observed: "This is still another minor but new and correct change in the detail of men's wear sponsored and introduced by the Prince of Wales." (October 1924). Summer straws and Panamas were also often shaped fedora style.

The *cowboy* or "ten gallon" hat was designed to provide protection from the blazing southern sun. As noted earlier, this practical hat was a descendant of the Mexican "sombrero" and was later adopted by cowboys of the American west—they waved these large hats to help turn their cattle. According to western legend, the cowboy hat also substituted as a drinking gourd for both man and mount...thus the "ten gallon" name. Stetson is famed for their version of the cowboy hat, which dates to the 1870s. Cowboy hats often have a central crease and/or a variety of "pinches"; a large horseshoe shaped pinch was affectionately known as a "mule kick"!

Western hero Tom Mix with his six shooter, bandana, studded chaps, and trademark white ten gallon cowboy hat. Note the big mule kick pinch in its crown. (Real photo postcard, ca. 1920-30)

An excellent charcoal grey Fedora with the small, neat appearance typical of the early twenties. This fine example was manufactured by Dobbs, Fifth Avenue, New York, and sold by Wells & Coverly, a prestigious men's store in Syracuse, New York. Note the similarity to *National's* fedora shown on the opposite page: the narrow brim, wide band, and central crease with "pinches" on each side. $50-$75.

The king of men's summer hats, the *Panama hat* was prized for its lightness and flexibility. Elegant and expensive, the prestigious Panama remains a favorite with the man of distinction to this day! The finest Panama hats are still woven in the Ecuadorian village of Montecristi. Each is unique, being painstakingly hand-woven from fibers of the Toquilla palm that grows along Ecuador's hilly coastline. Panamas come in three grades: standard, superior, and fine. While an ordinary Panama might be finished in a week, the finest can take several months to complete; some are so fine they resemble the texture of linen. Suggested care includes: lightly dust or vacuum using very low suction; wipe with a moist disposable facial cloth; NEVER use soap and water. They can be lightly steamed over boiling water; the brim may be pressed under a damp cloth.

The Panama boasts an august ancestry; it can trace its roots to the 1600s or even earlier, as some speculate that the Incas were the first to weave hats from Toquilla. It was adopted by the Spaniards, and by the eighteenth century Panamas were being exported to other countries (though made in Ecuador, they were often finished and exported from Panama).

During the Victorian era, the Panama hat was featured at the Paris Exhibition of 1855; one was presented to Emperor Napoleon III, and it soon became a favorite of kings, princes, and presidents. Bertie popularized the Panama in England; he reportedly paid his Bond St. hatter an exorbitant 90 pounds for one of the finest Panama hats. During the Spanish-American War of 1898, the US government requisitioned some 50,000 *sombrero de paja toquilla* from Ecuador for the troops, to be worn by Teddy Roosevelt and his Rough Riders! During the construction of the Panama Canal, workers wore the hat for protection against the blazing tropical sun. In 1906, Teddy Roosevelt was photographed while visiting the Canal's construction site, and his "Panama" hat quickly became the rage in America. By the twenties, when the dashing Prince of Wales was spotted wearing an elegant Panama, thousands of fashionable men followed suit.

Panamas were shaped into various styles, including the fedora and the Optimo, which features an outward ridge across the top of the hat. These ridged Panamas were said to be "foldable"; the ridge enabled the hat to be rolled or folded for travel. The popular black crown bands date to the date to the death of Queen Victoria in 1901.

During the twenties, period catalogs offered both "Genuine South American Panamas" and "Genuine Toyo Panamas" from Japan, a much less expensive alternative. The South American Panamas range from $4.25-$8.75, while the Japanese Toyo Panamas are "remarkable bargains" at $2.50-$3.65. Note that most Panamas are described as "bleached white." (*National Style Book*, 1920).

An elegant white Panama woven in the popular "Optimo" style, with an outward central ridge and black grosgrain crown band. $75-$125.

The snappy *sailor* or *boater* is also referred to in period catalogs as a "skimmer" or "sennet" (or "sennit") straw, sennet being the straw used in its manufacture. In the late eighteenth century, Admiral Horatio Nelson decreed that a round, braided straw hat be regulation for summer; the sailors varnished it to protect it from damp English weather and nicknamed it "The Boater." In the 1870s, after the development of a machine for sewing straw, the boater was quickly adopted by fashionable civilian men as a sporty summer hat. During the twenties, it was so popular with the smart young set that it was declared *the* summer hat of the decade. In 1924, *Men's Wear* noted that the favorite ensemble at Palm Beach was a "sports jacket worn with white flannel trousers—topped with a medium-brimmed Sailor of Sennit Straw."

This stylish young gent has just come from a flick starring Kitty Gordon. He's pizzazz personified in his snappy boater, striped shirt (with detachable collar) and striped tie! (Snapshot, ca. 1920-25)

Close-up of the inside satin lining of the boater below, with Dobb's label.

Summer's FAVORITE sporty straw…the sailor's heyday spans from the 1890s to the 1940s. Our sailor's satin lining is stamped: *Dobbs, Fifth Avenue*"; it was purchased from *The Safe Store Men's Shop, Dunkirk, N.Y.* $50-$100. It's shown beside Sarnoff-Irving's marvelous period hatbox, depicting a scene at a country club in Palm Beach. Note the straw boater on the seated gent in the blue suit! Hatbox, $75-125.

The peaked soft *cap* boasts a proud and ancient heritage. During the Renaissance, it was the mark of the working man, worn by "city workers," merchants, apprentices, and servants. Referred to as the "flat cap," it was remarkably similar to those still worn today.

By the 1920s, the humble cap had become a fashion statement—when the Prince of Wales adopted a dashing cap for golf, it quickly became the rage! Of course, the cap was not worn just for golf, but was a favorite accessory with all types of sportswear.

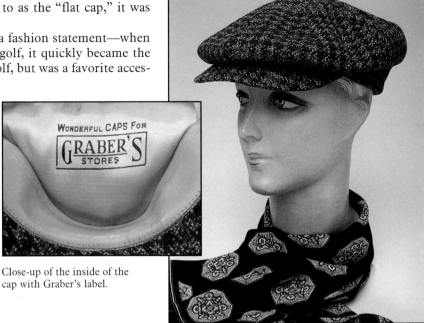

Close-up of the inside of the cap with Graber's label.

"Wonderful CAPS from Graber's Stores"! Graber's sporty twenties' wool tweed cap in hounds tooth checked maroon and grey. The interior is lined in satin, with a small bow to mark center back. $40-$55.

A dashing young man in sporty cap, vested Norfolk suit, and wide tie—he's as casually elegant as the Prince of Wales! (Snapshot, 1920-25)

"Our Leader for Men—New Plaited Golf Cap." *National's* announces their new "Overplaid Cassimere" cap for men and boys. (1923)

"Harry," the projectionist at the Happy Hour Theater in Lake Placid, New York, wears his cap backwards as he chomps on his cigar and revs his Harley! From an original glass negative plate by professional photographer J. Grover Cleveland, Lake Placid, New York. (ca. 1918-25)

155

Men's Coats and Outerwear

During the first half of the decade, coats mirrored the trim lines men favored in suit styles. Youthful coats, "of snappy style and jaunty swing to please the younger fellow" were worn. Many of the newest styles featured "swagger cut backs" with "snappy new raglan sleeves," though the majority of sleeves were cut-in. Other fashionable features included big patch pockets ("saddlebag pockets") and convertible collars that could be worn open or closed high, "doughboy" style; some had buttoned "chin straps." As the military influence lingered, belts often emphasized the trim, slightly high-waisted look; *National Style Book* advised, "Belts are preferred by younger men." Belts either encircled the waist, or extended across the back only. Unbelted coats were also worn, so catalogs offered versatile "detachable" belts; *National's* "three piece belt has detachable front and back sections; you can wear belted in back if you wish—or unbelted." (1922)

Among the most prestigious coat manufacturers of the decade was Burberrys, Ltd.; their coats were so famous the name "Burberry" was often substituted for the word "coat." As they advertised: "Overcoats designed and tailored in London by Burberrys invariably set the standard throughout the world for the correct attire of a gentleman…Dealers in every important city in the United States and Canada." Hart Schaffner & Marx and Kuppenheimer were among the leading American coat manufacturers.

The ulster and the chesterfield were the decade's two favorite coat styles. During the first half of the decade, the ulster was favored for every day wear. Historian Ruth Turner Wilcox describes this classic as: "a heavy overcoat originally worn by men and women in Ulster, Ireland; a long, loose fitting coat, usually double-breasted, with full or half-belt…very popular in the U.S. during the teens and twenties." Catalogs offered stylish "ulsterettes" for "You young men who welcome the latest touch of exclusive style!" (The ulsterette was less bulky than the ulster, with narrower lapels and collar). *National's* ad copy is en-

These two smartly dressed gents posed for a snapshot ca. 1920-25; the gent on the left wears an elegant velvet-collared chesterfield coat. Note their sporty caps and high lace shoes.

ticing: "…The Guard Model, a big double-breasted Ulsterette that smartly dressed men have adopted everywhere as this season's style leader, all wool plaid-back melton in THE NEWEST POWDER BLUE, with woven plaid inner surface; note smart lines of the back, with inverted plait and side pinch pleats and loose half belt (back only); convertible collar, set in sleeves with turn back cuffs, $28.50." (1924).

National Style Book offers five smart all-weather coats: "Stylish Double-Service Coats…For Wear—Rain or Shine." Pictured are: (top left) a single-breasted coat with belt in back only, of shower-proof grey checked cotton fabric resembling tweed; (center) a "snappy new double breasted sports model" featuring a "swagger cut back" with raglan sleeves, in a blend of wool and cotton cassimere, and shower-proofed by a "rubberized woven inner plaid surface"; (top right) a smart single-breasted coat with detachable belt, "suitable as a raincoat or general service coat," of rubberized cotton checked cloth; (lower left) a double breasted "raincoat for auto or general wear" with guaranteed rubberized inner surface, convertible collar, and storm tabs on sleeves; and (lower right) a belted, impregnated rubber fabric raincoat made in the double breasted sport style; the rubber outer surface is "guaranteed not to crack or peel." (1922)

This dynamic illustration by Herbert Paus pictures a dignified architect, clad in an elegant chesterfield, reviewing blueprints with his young associate. It's from the *Style Book for Young Men & Boys, Autumn & Winter 1921-22*, published by clothing manufacturers Hart Schaffner & Marx and available at J.M. Hutcheson's retail store in Eureka, California. The caption reads: "It's economy—good clothes save the price of new ones later on. Ours are good—stylish too!"

The conservative single-breasted chesterfield with its elegant velvet collar remained a favorite for dressy day wear. *National Style Book* described theirs: "For the man of distinction, the aristocratic velvet-collared Chesterfield is the coat of choice!…The man of quiet taste always prefers the well tailored Chesterfield. It is a dignified single-breasted model that never goes out of fashion and is suitable for men of all ages!" Their version featured "a black silk-faced velvet collar, fly front closing and two side flap pockets" for $19.98. In a 1923 survey held at Palm Beach, *Men's Wear* observed that the single-breasted chesterfield was the coat most worn. The chesterfield had a long, illustrious history; it was named for the Earl of Chesterfield, a fashion leader of the 1830s and 1840s.

For winter, nothing is warmer—and more luxurious—than FUR! The affluent might purchase a fur-lined ulsterette; *Men's Wear* describes a mink-lined ulsterette of oxford gray with an otter collar. More suited to the average man's budget, the 1924 *National Style Book* offered a double-breasted ulster of "Manchurian Wolf…the thick, dense and serviceable fur of the wolf dog!" at just $21.98. The raccoon coat remained a collegiate favorite—the coat of choice for a frosty fall football game or a ride in an open Model T!

This rakish young gent wears a huge fur ulster of "Manchurian Wolf." Note the large convertible collar. (Snapshot, ca. 1920-25)

For modest budgets, catalogs offered moderately priced winter coats lined with a variety of "cold-defying" materials, including sheepskin, blanket cloth, and "sheet rubber." Appealing to the "college man," *National's* extolled: "A big storm-defying sheep-lined coat; a handsome collegiate model of extra good quality heavy weight olive drab moleskin cloth, the body and sleeves interlined with sheet rubber, and fully lined with finest quality selected sheepskin; collar of Silver Wombatone Fur [described as "clipped sheepskin dyed silver grey" to simulate Australian wombat] for $19.98." Many inexpensive fabric coats add a touch of luxury with fur collars. *National's* offered "Beaverine" fur collars, described as "sheepskin dyed to resemble the real Beaver"; or Beaverette ("clipped Coney fur, resembling Hudson Seal"). These collars could also be purchased separately for around $4.98.

Sporty outer wear jackets were usually hip length or just above the knees. Favorites were lumberjack style "plaid mackinaws of extra heavy wool and cotton mackinaw cloth" ($9.95), and Hudson Bay blanket coats in traditional white with two to three bold stripes around the bottom. Warm sleeveless vests were also worn; *National's* advised men to "protect your health in severe winter weather and laugh at the cold with a warm, well made Government Quality Leather Jerkin (sleeveless vest) in 30 ounce wool olive drab Army melton cloth with all wool melton sleeves and lining" for $6.98. After WWI, the government was left with a large quantity of leather jerkins that had been worn by men in the trenches; these were also offered for sale at Army/Navy surplus stores.

Popular "all weather" coats for spring, summer, and fall were often rubberized; *National's* advertised: "cloth applied with a new rubberizing process to make it thoroughly waterproof and windproof." In 1823, Charles Macintosh had patented a method of molding rubber between two layers of fabric, and raincoats have been known as "Macintoshes" since.

Fabrics were often blends: "wool-mixed cassimere" (wool and cotton gabardine); worsted-filled "cassimere of worsted and cotton of very good quality"; cotton in grey check mixture resembling high-priced tweed; all-wool grey cheviot mix; wool and cotton tweed; and "Superfine cotton cashmere in indistinct herringbone stripe weave." Coats of "glove leather" were also popular; there were less expensive versions such as a "brown leatherette coat of brown moleskin cloth."

"Flaming Youth" favored the oilskin slicker, which not only protected in wet weather, but was a fashion statement as well! *National's* offered yellow slickers at $6.49, advising: "Yellow slicker coats are the latest word in rain coats! First seen on the college campus and now worn by smartly dressed young men everywhere…" (1924). *Men's Wear* also noted: "the college man chooses bright yellow and wears it with a sou'wester hat of the same color." Slickers were worn by both Sheiks and Shebas, sometimes with hand painted versions of John Held's "Hellions." Rain gear featured double stitched seams that were strapped and cemented.

The "trench coat" was developed for the doughboys of WWI to wear in the trenches; a light weight, water repellant coat, it allowed better ventilation than the rubber slicker. It was usually made of fine twill cotton gabardine, chemically treated to repel water. Later in the decade, the trench coat would overtake the oilskin slicker as a fashion statement.

The auto coat or duster remained a must for cruising dirt roads—and for repairing those frequent blowouts! It was cut longer (50") and roomier than other coats, and came in a variety of fabrics including gabardine, twill, duck, linen, silk, Palm Beach cloth, and "good weight Government Standard olive-drab bombazine." Many dusters featured "a guaranteed rubberized inner surface [that] makes it absolutely waterproof" and, as *National's* advised, "Storm tabs on sleeves are desirable for driving." Collars were "worn high, doughboy style, or open"; many featured a buttoned chin strap.

Men's Shoes

The shoe of the decade was the snappy low oxford! The classic "oxford" got its name from the durable leather shoes adopted by students at Oxford University in the seventeenth century. With the rage for cuffed trousers around 1900, low shoes began to be fashionable, and they were increasingly worn during the teens. By the twenties, the oxford had been jazzed up considerably; a favorite of the Prince of Wales, it had become the shoe of choice for both college students and returning doughboys...and it was considered the only correct shoe to wear with the knicker suit!

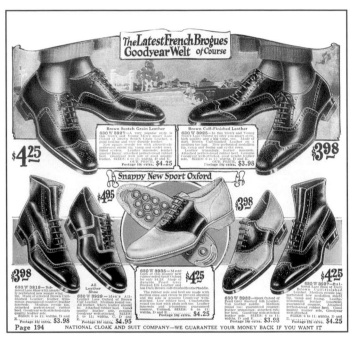

"The Latest French Brogues"—*National's* offers a fine variety of stylish shoes, including sporty low oxfords, and high "Balmoral Laces." At bottom center are the latest "Snappy New Sport Oxfords...Men! Look at this snappy new rubber soled Sport Oxford for only $4.25." It's "durable Pearl Grey Smoked Elk Leather...rubber sole and heel are made with suction cups and cleats to prevent slipping and the sole is genuine Goodyear welt stitched." (1923)

A stylish double-breasted duster; spots here and there attest that it's seen its share of auto repairs! This coat is a sturdy, buff colored cotton and fastens with a double row of wood buttons. It features adjustable storm tabs on the sleeves and a buttoned chin strap to fasten the collar high, doughboy style. Its huge circular patch pockets are big enough to hold the largest wrench! $75-$125.

Classic wing-tip oxfords from *Nettleton Shoes*—still popular to this day! They're elaborately perforated, punched, and pinked, with "perforated medallion" toes. They've come a long way from the original "oxfords" first worn by Oxford students in the seventeenth century! Nettleton's, based in Syracuse, New York, was world famous for fine shoes. $100-$200.

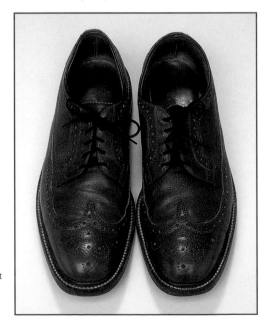

Oxfords lace "blucher" fashion, over the instep; the blucher style shoe had been invented by (and named for) Field Marshall Von Blucher, commander of England's Prussian Allies at the Battle of Waterloo in 1814. Early twenties' catalogs often described lace shoes as "bluchers"; low shoes were also described as "lace oxfords," while high shoes were "high lace shoes."

In the twenties, there was a plethora of "comfortable yet snappy" oxford styles to choose from; most were elaborately trimmed—both perforated and punched in smart designs, especially the toe, described as "perforated medallion" toes. Toes also came in different shapes. A fashionable gent could select "wing-tip," "shield tip," or "straight tip" style toes. For the businessman, oxfords were a bit more subdued; as *Men's Wear* advised: "Town shoes are rather modest; it is a bit newer to have the toe punctured in some inconspicuous pattern." Oxfords for sport were more flamboyant; oxford brogues, with their Scottish/Irish ancestry, were smartest for country wear and golf.

In addition to solid colors, two-tone oxfords were popular. An early version of the saddle shoe, catalogs referred to them as "sport oxfords" or "saddle oxfords." They came in a variety of color combinations, but "white buckskin oxfords trimmed with brown calf" were favored. These popular two-tone shoes had been introduced during the teens; in 1915, Brooks Brothers featured a buckskin shoe with a bright red "saddle" over the instep. By 1924, Palm Beach fashion scouts reported that the best dressed men were wearing white oxfords with tan wing tips with their flannel trousers, but "soft leather or buckskin are also seen" (*Men's Wear*, March 1924); in addition, "for golf, two tone brogue oxfords in brown and white or black and white are favored." During the twenties, with the tremendous popularity of golf, special "golf" shoes became available; *Men's Wear* noted two styles: a blucher tie with nonskid steel *studded* leather sole and heel; and an oxford with cleated rubber sole, designed "to grip and hold to the turf."

Fashionable shoes often combined two different materials as well as two separate colors; for instance, there was "gun metal finished leather combined with dull leather," and "calfskin vamp with pigskin top." A pair of dressy high shoes combined "black patent leather with imitation alligator leather uppers." Shoes and half boots with a center crease down the vamp, advertised as the "trouser crease," were also popular, *National's* calls them an "Officer's Blucher." The "congress shoe," a half boot with elastic side gores and pull-on loops at the back of the heel, was yet another choice; congress styles with elastic inserts had been worn since the mid-nineteenth century. Dressy patent leather shoes were affection-

ately known as "shiners." At the beginning of the decade, shoes had narrow toes for dress and more rounded toes for sport, but by 1924, shoes with squared toes were beginning to make fashion news.

The best-dressed men often wore shoe covers called "spats" (from "spatter-dashes") or "gaiters" over their shoes. Gaiters came in a variety of fabrics, usually in rather sedate colors.

The 1920 *Bellas Hess* catalog offers these "Extra Good Quality Soft Felt Gaiters for men in gray, black, fawn or dark brown." Gaiters, also called "spats," are very fashionable throughout the twenties; they're worn by such fashionable men as Paul Poiret, Jean Patou…and Al Capone! (1920)

These fine grey wool felt gaiters fasten with four buttons. A grey leather strap buckles under the instep. $45-$75.

As the decade progressed, ad copy became more flamboyant: "THUNDERING BIG SHOE BARGAINS—SWEEPING AWAY ALL COMPETITION...AND MEN, GET THIS STRAIGHT, THEY ARE QUALITY SHOES AT $2.98...Why do we do it? WE WANT YOUR TRADE!" and, "YOU COULDN'T FIND A MORE SNAPPY SHOE STYLE AT THIS LOW PRICE." Catalogs often gave shoes catchy names like "The Stadium," "The Broadway," "The Banker," and "The City." (*National's*, 1924)

Catalogs advertised shoes with "Goodyear welt" construction, described as a "method of attaching the upper to the sole without nail, giving hand-sewn strength and comfort at a fraction of the cost; easily repaired, flexible, comfortable. Beneath the inner sole is a cork cushion which makes the shoe 'Anti-Squeak.'"

Sneakers, "Tennis, Yachting or Outing Shoes" that were "suitable for general summer wear," were very popular; they were forerunners of the sneakers that would become the favorite footwear for people of all ages during the rest of the twentieth century...and into the twenty-first! In 1910, A.G. Spalding introduced rubber-soled shoes with "little suction cups," about 1/4" apart, on the soles. These early sneakers were available in leather as well as the traditional white canvas, in both low oxford and high laced styles.

$2.09 up

Canvas with Brown Leather

680 V 4282—Sport and Outing Shoes made of strong White Canvas with brown leather trimming as pictured. Comfortable round toe; full-length sole and spring heel of brown rubber with holes pierced for suction to give a firm grip. An excellent gym shoe.

Youths' Sizes: 11 to 2.
Postage 10¢ extra. $2.09
Boys' Sizes: 2½ to 5½.
Postage 10¢ extra. $2.29
Men's Sizes: 6 to 11.
Postage 10¢ extra. $2.55

A natty young gent in a striped shirt and tie, plus high top sneakers similar those offered in the *National's* ad shown next. (Snapshot, 1920-30)

The 1922 *National Style Book* offers high top "Sport and Outing Shoes." These early sneakers, in "White Canvas with brown leather trimming," feature a "spring heel of brown rubber with holes pierced for suction to give a firm grip."

Work boots offered by twenties' catalogs were similar to those worn today; they were "guaranteed for 6 months under any working condition" and were what "every working man—every farmer—every man who works outdoors has always wanted," with a waterproofing process "guaranteed to resist even barnyard ammonia and remain soft under the most difficult conditions," $6.45. (They were waterproofed with a mixture of paraffin, oil, and rosin). High over-the-calf boots were also available in "oiled tan storm proof leather with adjustable double buckles at the top. $8.50." Work shoes were also offered in brown duck, $3.45. (*National Style Book*, 1924)

During the early twenties, *galoshes* (aka "Artics") not only provided the ultimate shoe protection, but were one of Flaming Youth's favorite fads. They were worn by men, women, and children, and were often fleece-lined; many styles featured a "bellows" fold for extra protection. They fastened with one to four buckles, ending at either ankles or mid calf.

Men's Hosiery

Twenties' men wore two types of hosiery for day wear—dressy socks for the office and sporty socks for leisure. Wool was preferred for fall and winter; spring and summer socks were available in silk, artificial silk, lisle, combed cotton, and blends in various combinations. Though tops were rib-knitted or "elasticized," men often wore sock garters to prevent "the embarrassment of the slipping sock"!

Dressy Hose

Dress or "office" hose was rather conservative, and solid color or small figured pairs were favored. *National's* offered "dressy and serviceable hose" in black, white, navy or light blue, dark brown, dark oxford grey or pearl grey, cordovan (maroon), bottle green or dark green, and "Palm Beach" (a light tan). The "dressy thread silk with fashionable dropped stitch" (a ribbed effect) and "elastic ribbed tops of mercerized lisle" were priced at $.95, while their silk/rayon blend hose, "dressy lightweight socks knit from a durable mixture of thread silk and artificial silk in drop stitch," were just $.49. A blend of artificial silk "plated on lisle" hose was $.59; combed cotton socks were $.25. *National's* had a "big special" on mercerized lisle socks—3 pairs for $.69!

5 T 174—Men—don't miss this big value in Mercerized Lisle Socks. Three pairs of these splendid quality Mercerized Lisle Socks for only 69 cents! If the socks were serviceable only, they would still be very big value at the price. But they are very good looking too, for they are knit in fine gauge and have the lustrous finish that gives a dressy appearance to socks. They are of medium weight, knit seamless and have double soles, reinforced heels and toes. High-spliced heels. Elastic ribbed tops.
COLORS: white, grey, black or Cordovan. SIZES: 9½ to 11½.
OUR PRICE. **3** pairs for **69¢**
Postage for 3 pairs 2¢ extra.

National's "Big Special" on mercerized lisle socks—3 pairs for $.69! "If these socks were serviceable only, they would still be very big value at the price. But they are very good looking too..."; they come in white, grey, black, or cordovan (maroon). (1924)

Endwell Fine Hose, dressy hose in cordovan with elaborate white and red clocks. They're ribbed stitched in a blend of cotton and artificial silk (rayon). Old store stock hose with label, $20-$30.

The snappiest dress socks are "clocked"; that is, embroidered on the sides. *National's* offers these "Plated Artificial Silk Embroidered Clocks," described as: "Men's Clocked Socks of good quality Lustrous Fiber (artificial) Silk plated on lisle…double soles, high spliced heels reinforced with lisle…black, navy blue, white or Cordovan with fancy embroidered clocks in two-tone effects." (1923)

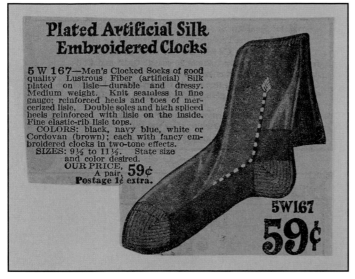

Casual, Sporty Hose

After WWI, with the popularity of low oxford shoes, hose for casual wear began to express more "personality" and to grow more flamboyant, with a rainbow of colors, stripes, checks, and plaids. Observing this new trend, a *Men's Wear* writer philosophizes:

"The somber garb of many a man today is a living lie. Man has not dropped the fancy for the effect of tartans, slashed doublet and hose and the brilliant trappings of the age of romance. That was only yesterday. Only a little further back of that man was the savage, decking himself out in the plumage of wild birds or with leopard skins. He is still a savage. The urge to wear brilliant trappings demonstrates a throw-back into the centuries. It is hereditary and natural. Man needs only the encouragement of hardier spirits undaunted by the insincere mirth of the envious to eventually follow suit and preen himself in all the glory of the artificial plumage now worn mostly by the female, the courageous sex. Who wears this vivid hose? They wear it who dare."

—*Men's Wear*, August 7, 1924 (quoted in *Esquire Encyclopedia of Men's Fashion*)

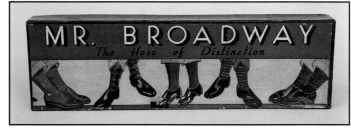

"MR. BROADWAY—The Hose of Distinction!" This marvelous twenties' hosiery box depicts a variety of popular styles. Left to right: solid color ribbed socks, smart Argyle plaids, elegant blue clocks, snazzy stripes, and conservative small figured socks. All are worn with low oxford shoes. Box, $75-$150.

Bold plaid socks of fine combed cotton, with "solid color reinforced heel and toe" by Endwell. Snappy plaid socks remain very popular throughout the decade; by mid-decade catalogs tout "The New Novelty Plaids," exclaiming: "The smartest dressers are wearing bright colored socks, and here are smart plaid lisle sport socks for only $.23 a pair!" (Rayon plaid sport socks with pure silk stripes are $.45.) (*National Style Book* 1927)

This wonderful studio portrait depicts a group of fashionably dressed fraternity brothers ca. 1924. Note that two of the brothers have donned very snappy hose; the guy at lower left sports snazzy stripes, while the gent at lower right has selected a bold plaid pair. You'll also note that nine of the brothers wear long ties in striped rep or plaids, while three have chosen natty bow ties. They've all slicked their hair; two wear round "Harold Lloyd" glasses and two are the epitome of sophomoric sophistication with long stemmed pipes! Note the fashionable Fair Isle v-neck sweater worn by the dashing guy at upper left. The small bag was perhaps a prize of some kind. By W.V. Hockett, Minn.

Men's Underwear

Like women's "unmentionables," men's undergarments were growing briefer and more comfortable to suit active twenties' lifestyles. "ATHLETIC!" was the keyword to describe these briefer undergarments—a favorite was the new one-piece "Athletic Union Suit," a combination of undershirt and shorts. As Sears advised, "these suits will fit you no matter how you are built…"

Union suit combinations featured either round or v-necks with button fronts. Deep sleeveless armholes provided ease of movement, and back closures featured either the famous "drop seat" (drops down from buttons on the waist) or the new "lapped seat" (a diagonal back flap placket with one button closure). The 1920 *National Style Book* praised the lapped seat as "a big improvement on the ordinary opening. It prevents chafing or binding at the crotch and gives a very wide convenient opening in the back. When closed it remains closed, owing to the special construction of the garment."

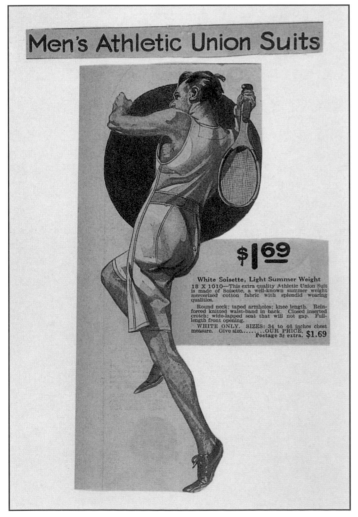

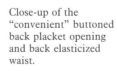

"Men's Athletic Union Suits" as offered by *National Style Book* for Spring/Summer 1920. Pictured is a mercerized cotton "Soisette" with "splendid wearing qualities" and a "wide lapped seat that will not gap."

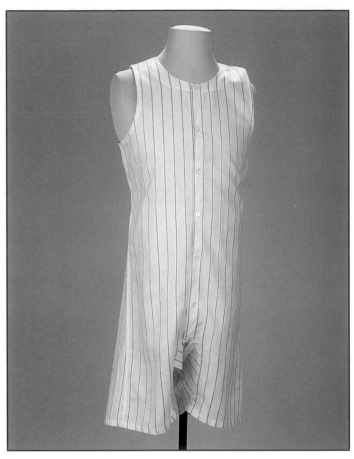

Cool and comfortable for those hot summer days is this blue pinstriped athletic union suit from Spick and Span Underwear in cotton nainsook. It's sleeveless, knee length, and closes down the front with eight pearl buttons. In back, an elastic waistband ensures a proper fit, and convenience is provided by the wide, lapped buttoned seat. Old store stock, never worn. $50-$75.

Label, *Athletic Spick and Span Underwear*.

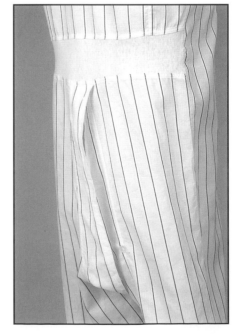

Close-up of the "convenient" buttoned back placket opening and back elasticized waist.

Ever alert to the desires of returning doughboys (and mindful of their purchasing power), advertising often referred to the recent war. *National's* offered: "Government regulation checked nainsook medium weight, strong weave, buttoned lapped seat." They advertised: "MEN'S ATHLETIC UNION SUITS guaranteed to give satisfaction or your money back…if we did not believe that this is the best athletic union suit on the market, we could not afford to make this guarantee." *National's* union suits featured "a shaped waist-band in back, of elastic knitted webbing reinforced at the center with an extra piece of webbing and finished flat seams. The band keeps the back from sagging and by providing expansion makes the suit give to every movement of the body without binding at the crotch." (1920)

Separate undershirts and knee length "drawers" were also worn. Athletic "coat style" undershirts buttoned down the front, while ribbed cotton sleeveless undershirts (similar to today's "Beater" shirts) slipped over the head ($.49). Matching "athletic" drawers (forerunners of today's boxers) featured buttoned yoke fronts above placket openings, and reinforced crotches ($.55).

Though both union suits and separates were generally knee length and sleeveless, short and long sleeved shirts were also worn, as were ankle-length drawers for both summer and winter.

Men's underwear was manufactured in a wide variety of fabrics. *National's* declared sturdy cotton nainsook "The Ideal Summer Underwear." (Nainsook is a durable, basketweave cotton.) Mercerized (shrink resistant) cottons, in madras or "Soisette," were also popular, as well as a summer weight balbriggan (described as a "light weight flat knit from good quality cotton yarn"). A woven cotton mesh that "allows for a circulation of air" was yet another option, as were the even more body-hugging ribbed cotton knits. Silk underwear was also popular; it had been worn during WWI, not for its luxury, but because it dried very quickly. During the twenties, underwear of less expensive "artificial silk" (rayon) tricot gained favor.

For winter, the traditional long sleeved, ankle-length union suits known as "Long Johns" predominated. *National's* offered "practical and convenient winter suits" of wool or "heavy winter weight cotton, well-fleeced inside"; also offered was a blend of heavy cotton and soft wool. Balbriggan, a perennial favorite for underwear, originally came from Balbriggan, Ireland. Winter weight balbriggan was "an unbleached cotton with a fleeced back," so popular that this type of underwear was often referred to as one's "balbriggans."

National's offers separate shirt and drawers described as "Athletic Underwear" in lightweight white checked nainsook that's "built to stand hard service…launders excellently." (1920)

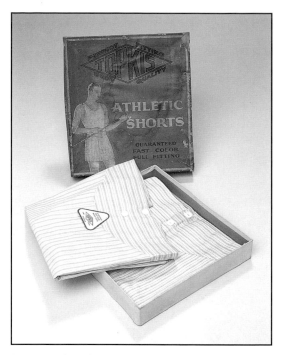

Two pairs of "Perfect Fitting – Topkis – Best Quality Athletic Shorts" in their original box, which depicts an avid golfer in his undershirt and Topkis shorts. The attached tags read: "Guaranteed fast color broad cloth." These early boxer type shorts feature elastic inserts at the sides of the waistbands and fly plackets with three pearl buttons. Box (worn), $50-$75; shorts with original tags, $45-$75 each.

A rare vintage photo of a young man in his "athletic underwear"—perhaps he's lost at strip poker! He's wearing boxer-type drawers that come to just above the knees, socks secured with garters, and a sleeveless ribbed cotton undershirt (these knit undershirts or "beaters" are still worn today). (Snapshot, ca. 1920-30)

55¢ Each Garment
White Checked Nainsook
Light Weight
Athletic Underwear
Made of good quality Checked Nainsook; built to stand hard service Launders excellently.
13 X 1119—Men's coat style Athletic Undershirt. SIZES: 34 to 46 inches chest measure. State size.
OUR PRICE, 55¢
Postage 2¢ extra.
13 X 1120—Men's knee-length Drawers. Reinforced crotch. SIZES: 30 to 44 inches waist measure. State size.
OUR PRICE, 55¢
Postage 2¢ extra.

DROP SEAT UNION SUIT
Natural Gray Only
Men's superior quality drop seat Union Suit. A practical and convenient Winter suit in medium heavy weight, made of soft Wool and non-shrinkable cotton mixed. This makes a comfortable, long-wearing garment. Suit has high neck; long sleeves and is ankle length. It has snug-fitting ribbed cuffs on wrists and ankles. Natural gray only. Last fall, this garment sold at $3.69.
14R738. Sizes: 34 to 46 chest....... $2.98
Postage 7¢ Extra

Bellas Hess offers this "Drop Seat Union Suit," described as "A practical and convenient Winter suit." Also known as "Long Johns," these full-length union suits were a necessity during frigid winters. Note that he's carrying his favorite Beacon blanket robe. (1921-22 Fall/Winter)

Men's Lounge Wear, Robes, and Smoking Jackets

The colorful, cozy blanket robe remained a favorite of twenties' men, and of women and children as well. The more flamboyant robes are highly prized by today's collectors, particularly those that have Art Deco or what catalogs describe as "Indian Designs." Though blanket robes were made by other companies, including the Lawrence Company, those manufactured by Beacon were so popular that their name is almost synonymous with the blanket robe. *Bellas Hess* lauded their "Genuine Beacon," described as "a handsome lounging robe of genuine bordered Beacon blanket; full cut, well proportioned and splendidly tailored throughout. Fancy silk cord finished collar, front closing, three pockets and deep cuffs; fancy rope girdle (belt), $8.48." Their "Genuine Lawrence" robe, "a bordered wool finished cotton blanket robe, with two pockets, rope girdle and cord neck tie," was much less expensive at only $4.98. Many catalogs offered matching blanket cloth slippers; just $.63 at *Bellas Hess*! (1921-22 Fall/Winter)

Beacon described their "Beacon Blanket Cloth" as "a wool-finished soft cotton fabric noted for its splendid wearing qualities." Single-breasted styles with rolled shawl collars were favored; some styles featured satin collars in "harmonizing color Skinner satin." Notched lapel "convertible" collars that could be buttoned high were also pictured. During the early twenties, lounging robes are shown about mid-calf to ankle length. (*National's* 1924)

From Beacon's advertising brochure, *Beacon Blankets Make Warm Friends*, a cozy boudoir scene: papa in his warm Beacon robe and slippers and mama in her mobcap and Beacon robe, while a Beacon blanket beckons from the DOUBLE BED!! Beacon exclaims: "Customers, when they feel the soft thickness of Beacon Blankets, are surprised to learn that they are **cotton**, often ask 'are they as warm as wool?'...Laboratory tests prove that weight for weight Beacon Blankets are much warmer than wool." They were washable too, so "choose a sunny day with the wind blowing; souse the blanket, never rub, with warm soap-suds never hot water; merely squeeze the water out, never wring; rinse twice and hang your blanket out over several lines, not over one." Beacon's mills were located at New Bedford, Massachusetts; their main office was in Providence, Rhode Island.

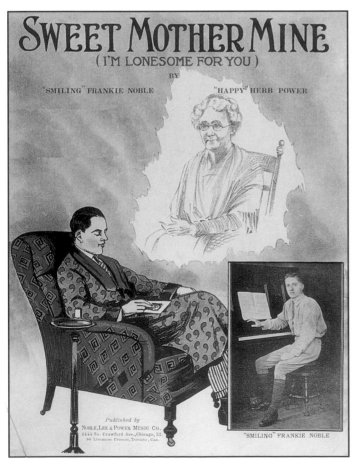

Relaxing in his favorite Beacon robe (worn over a shirt and tie), this handsome gent dreams of that "Dearest of gals, Truest of pals, Sweet Little Mother of Mine"! This 1924 sheet music, by "Smiling" Frankie Noble and "Happy" Herb Power, is to be sung "with feeling":
When your down hearted and blue – And the world frowns on you – And life don't seem worth while – When your friends are all gone – And all things go wrong – Just think of your mother and smile...
...And when you played hookey – From school with the bunch – And went fishing or swimming instead – Who was it that shielded you – And gave you a lunch – And saved you from going to bed – Who gave you her all – Your own dear old mother – Your best pal of all!

Label: *Beacon Genuine Ombre*.

What replaced childhood's beloved "blankie" in people's hearts? Why, the blanket robe, of course! Could anything be more relaxing than sitting by the fire and reading the paper in a robe as soft and comforting as your old blankie? This man's Beacon blanket robe, with its marvelous Art Deco blue "eyes" design, shades from brown to tan and cream. It features a shawl collar, two large patch pockets and a smaller chest pocket, all piped in brown/blue striped braid. The cord belt is a replacement, the original matched the brown/blue cord edging. $75-$150.

This loving young couple was photographed outside the door to their honeymoon cabin on their first morning as "Mr. and Mrs." He's wearing a splendid blanket robe in a great Art Deco pattern. (Snapshot, 1922)

For men in a more elegant (or seductive) frame of mind, luxurious silk brocade robes were favored!

The short "smoking jacket" paired with trousers was another favorite for lounge wear. The smoking jacket/trouser combination became popular in the 1850s as an at-home "leisure suit"; it eventually evolved into the "sack jacket" or suit coat of the modern business suit.

Both robes and smoking jackets often featured oriental frogs and tassels, for a lingering touch of the exotic East.

The silk frog ornaments on the jacket at right add an exotic touch!

The *Ladies' Home Journal Fashion Quarterly* for Winter 1922 offers these two patterns for men's lounge wear: an elegant smoking jacket with frog closures, and a fancy brocade robe (in sizes "for men and youths").

This handsome pinstriped smoking jacket bears a label from John Wanamaker, New York. It's a fine pinstripe in burgundy grey wool cheviot, with lapels (revers) patch pockets and cuffs in a contrasting stripe. Two flat grey covered buttons trim the striped cuffs. All edges are bound in matching striped silk braid. *National's* features a similar "Smoking Jacket or House Coat" for $5.89 (1924); today's collectors might expect to pay $75-$150.

Right:
Fit for any aspiring Valentino—a luxurious lounging robe of silk in a ribbed diagonal faille; its silver and gray herringbone pattern has an almost iridescent sheen. It's fully lined in vivid claret satin, which also forms the lapels and trims the cuffs and three slash pockets. The wide satin belt is tipped with oriental frogs with tassel fringe. $125-$200.

Far right:
Close-up of the robe's sash, tassels, and hounds tooth check pattern.

Men's Sleep Wear—Pajamas Versus Nightshirts!

Both nightshirts and pajamas were worn throughout the twenties, though the newer pajamas were beginning to relegate the venerable nightshirts to the ranks of old fogies. The nightshirt was considered an old-fashioned "early to bed, early to rise" garment, while exotic pajamas were a night owl's delight—they weren't just for sleeping, they were also worn for lounging and *indulging*! Even the name is exotic: the word "pajama" is derived from Hindi, meaning "leg clothing." Picture yourself in a pair of luxurious "Faultless" silk pajamas, relaxing and reading F. Scott Fitzgerald's new novel, *This Side of Paradise*!

Novelty Pajamas in Striking Manly Color Effects

"Novelty Pajamas in Striking Manly Color Effects" as advertised by "Faultless—the NightWear of a Nation."

167

Period catalogs described nightshirts as "full cut and roomy." The 1923 *National Style Book* promoted their slip-on nightshirt as a "Bachelors' Delight!" at just $.89. For winter, they offered "heavy weight Amoskeag Flannelette Nightshirts" in white or assorted color stripes, $1.45.

In addition to being trendier, pajamas were more expensive than nightshirts, being two pieces. Pajama tops came in both front button and pullover styles. Some styles were collarless; some had collars, including turnovers, shawl collars, and standup "military" collars. Multicolor stripes were favorites, along with fabric woven in striped patterns. Popular solid colors were white, tan, blue, and lavender. Many pajamas featured oriental "silky frog ornaments," and had a front chest pocket. Summer fabrics included silk; "fiber silk" (rayon); and cottons, including "silky mercerized Pongee," percale, and "durable soft cambric." For winter, flannelette was a wise choice. *National's* extolled: "Our best flannelette pajamas of genuine Amoskeag Flannelette, a heavy, warm, serviceable material that will last for a couple of winters. Made with Military style collar, with double braid frog fastenings on coat and patch pocket. Trousers have drawstring at waist; white and assorted color stripes, $2.25." (1924)

National Style Book pictures a choice of pajamas or nightshirt. The "very very durable" woven check pajamas feature "fiber silk (artificial silk) frog ornaments…draw-string at waist-band of pants." They're available in tan or blue as well as white. The woven check nightshirt, which features a pullover "middy style" collarless neckline, is described being made of "a light weight material that makes a cool and comfortable sleeping garment." It features "half sleeves, gusseted side seams, and patch pocket." (1923)

Close-up of the silk frog trim and pearl buttons.

Faultless pajamas in a woven striped silk that's thin as a whisper…guaranteed to make a man feel passionate as a pasha! The jacket features popular silk frog braid fastenings with pearl buttons; there's also a handy chest pocket. The pants fasten with a drawstring waistband and have a button fly. $75-$150.

Label: *Faultless – Since 1881.* Faultless advertises: "Everything desired in Men's Nightwear can be had with the Faultless label. At better shops everywhere."

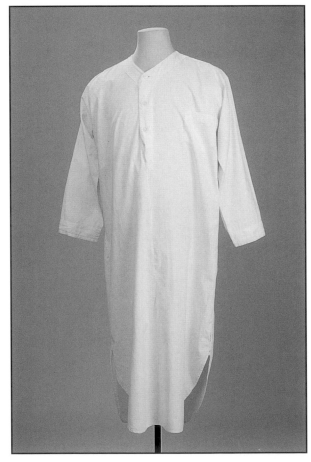

"Restwell" brand cotton percale nightshirt, featuring a collarless v-neck with a three-button front closure and a patch pocket; yoked back and flat seams. $25-50.

Children's Clothing

"Costumes For the Younger Generation Imitate Their Elders in Smartness!" proclaimed *Fashionable Dress* in their Spring 1922 issue, echoing the time-honored tradition that children should dress in fashions that resemble those of adults. Boys' clothes had "mannish" features, e.g., "Miniature Men Wear Clothes Like Dads" (1922 *Pictorial Review*); and for girls, "Frocks for both Mother and Daughter present the Same Youthful details." (*Butterick*, Spring 1922) However, though children's clothing may have had adult *features*, practical clothing geared towards children's special needs had become a necessity. This trend towards sensible children's clothing had begun with the nineteenth century's Aesthetic movement. By the twenties, some magazines recognized children's individuality with headlines like: "The Younger Generation Claims Their Place in the Sun," and "Fashions for a Girl's Active Life." (*Butterick*, 1920) Though children's clothing was often purchased ready made from shops and catalogs, clothes that mom ran up from patterns were also worn.

Boys' Clothing

For older boys, a dress suit with that "First Pair of Long Pants" remained a male rite of passage; it generally occurred on reaching the "double-digit years," though to turn from boy to man with a pair of long trousers marking the transition wasn't always easy! Many men remember awaiting this milestone as eagerly as they watched for their first whiskers, but most had mixed emotions—exhilaration warred with embarrassment when they made their first appearance in long pants. While some young Peter Pans vowed to "never grow up," being treated almost like a man was sure to be a heady feeling! Relatives assured them that girls would look at them differently when they wore long pants, and it was common knowledge that when a boy wore his first long pants, his "first kiss" would soon follow. It was customary for first long pants to debut at church on Sunday. Boys venturing out in their new long pants often banded together to bolster their courage; as one man recalled, "…like our hero Doug Fairbanks, we swaggered out, thinking that surely the earth would stand still on this momentous occasion…but the neighbors merely waved. Some smiled, and some shook their heads muttering, 'How time flies.'"

Popular catalogs called youths' suits "Students' Suits," "High School Suits," or "Prep Suits," advertising "Snappy Styles for Students' First Long Trouser Suits." Suits often came with two matching pairs of pants: "No need to tell you that extra pair means double wear!" *National's*, recognizing the tremendous popularity of the dark jacket/light flannel trousers combination, also offered "a versatile spring/summer three-piece 'High School Suit'…For summer evenings the coat can be worn with white flannel trousers in the fashion favored by well-dressed men."

Bellas Hess offers fine "Coat and First Long Trouser Suits" for youths. The wool serge suit on the left is double-breasted with two sets of buttons; it's "slightly shaped in at waist." The matching narrow, shortish trousers are shown cuffed, though they're offered uncuffed too. The double breasted ulster overcoat, center, is "smartly belted" with wide lapels, a "deep convertible collar," and warm plaid lining. The single-breasted, vested suit at right comes with two pairs of trousers, making it "doubly serviceable"; the jacket closes with one link button, "giving the long, slender lines," and a matching cap is just $1.25! (1921-22 Fall/Winter)

"Drugstore Cowboys or Valentines?!" Proudly showing off their First Long Trouser Suits, "The Blankenbiller Boys and Oscar Miller" pose in front of a Drugs and Cigars (and "Valentines") store in this snapshot taken ca. 1920-25. The boy at left wears a stylish ulster overcoat; the boy in the center, a slim single-breasted suit with "sack" coat. At right, Oscar Miller's suit has a snappy belted Norfolk jacket. All wear sporty caps.

169

Knickers

For boys age five and up, knickers were the overwhelming choice for casual wear. For dressier occasions, there were knicker suits with Norfolk jackets just like Dad's. *National Style Book* offered Norfolk knicker suits in boys' sizes 5 to 10 years; they also offered Norfolk suits with straight knee pants rather than knickers. Both were shown with shirts and ties.

"Best Show on Earth"! What young boy didn't dream of running off to join the circus...and boys who helped put up the tents were given a glimpse of the glamour with free tickets! This young dreamer wears knickers with a rolled-sleeve shirt, a jaunty cap, and long woolen stockings with high top sneakers. To his left, a stylish mom holds her young toddler's hand; he's wearing a practical "wash suit" and she's in a rather long dress with a dropped waist and tiered skirt, ca. 1922-24. Lining up to buy tickets are a small boy in bib overalls and a lady in a short plaid skirt.

For more rugged play, "boy-proof" knickers were worn with shirts (including button downs) and/or sweaters. For winter, warm woolen knickers were made of serge, worsted, cheviot, or cassimere (in all wool or wool and cotton blends); there was also serviceable cotton corduroy ("one of the most durable fabrics made—will stand harder wear than a woolen material"). Knickers were often lined in twill or flannel, with boy-proof reinforced seams; some advertised "Double Seat and Double Knees for Double Wear." Favorite fabrics for summer wear included Government Khaki twill, Palm Beach cloth, white drill, and sturdy cotton duck. Knickers were worn with knee socks, usually ribbed wool for winter and cotton for summer.

"These are the knickers you want for your boy if he is hard on his clothes! Here are knickerbockers built for lively, active boys...made with all seams reinforced and sewed so strongly that if your boy rips the seams, WE WILL SEND HIM A NEW PAIR FREE! (*National Style Book*, 1922)

From about age five on, the most popular boy's pants are...knickers! Our young "Joe" wears a sturdy pair of heavy wool serge knickers, a striped v-neck sweater, button-down shirt and boucle knit tie, along with his favorite "Jackie Kid" cap. These old store stock knickers are a very attractive pinstriped charcoal and light grey tweed from Cleveland Woolen Mills. They feature two-button adjustable cuffs, a four-button fly, and topstitched seams, and they're "boy-proofed" with inside seams that are reinforced with twill tape and double stitched. Boys need plenty of pockets, so there are two side slash pockets, a watch pocket, and one rear pocket. (Note: the button-down shirt and black oxfords pictured are similar to twenties' styles, but a bit later, ca. 1950). Store stock knickers, $50-$100; examples with some wear, $25-$50.

Right:
Great graphics! The label of Joe's tweed "Jackie Kid" cap.

Far right:
What boy wouldn't treasure this Jackie Coogan photo? Jackie Coogan, a vaudeville actor since age four, was "discovered" when he winked at Charlie Chaplin in a train station. Chaplin thought he'd be perfect for a role in *The Kid* (1920) and the movie rocketed the young boy to stardom. In 1921, Jackie starred in the popular *Peck's Bad Boy*; in 1922, he was billed as "The Greatest Boy Actor in the World" on a poster for *Oliver Twist*, and in 1923, he ran off to join the circus in *Circus Days*!

Little Boys

From about age two to five, little boys generally wore knee pants; that is, straight pants that weren't gathered and banded at the knee. *National's* also offered comfortable, practical, and tubbable "wash suits" for summer, in sizes 3 to 8. Wash suits were popular playsuits that featured straight short pants that either buttoned at the waist to a matching top or had an attached sleeveless top under a matching overblouse. The nautical "Middy Suit" remained a favorite; there were many variations with either short or long pants. Fabrics included sturdy cottons like jean, repp, drill, chambray, a "firmly woven cotton Crash" and "Peggy Cloth" (a strong, firmly woven, yarn-dyed cotton material). Linen and linen/cotton blends like "linene" and "Palmer Linen" were also shown. For winter, one-piece "overall suits" (coveralls) or bib overalls of blue denim or Khaki drill were favorites; they featured "riveted metal buttons, double stitched seams, all points of strain bar tacked." Little boys' pants had a small unbuttoned placket that served as a fly, and many pants advertised "drop seat" backs.

"Best for Your Boy – Best for Your Purse!" *National's* depicts the most popular styles for both older and younger boys, including two "mannish" knicker suits for older boys in sizes 8 to 16. At center, for boys size 3-8, *National's* spotlights "Our most popular sailor suit…2 pairs pants means double wear." A variety of practical wash suits for little boys are pictured, with shirts and matching "full cut straight pants." Some are overblouse style; some button to matching shirts. Those with a nautical theme are described as "wash suits in the favorite Middy Style." Note that sandals are worn by the young boys, while the older boys wear oxfords and ribbed black hose. (1923)

A snappy boy's sailor suit in white cotton duck, complete with Navy epaulets with brass anchor buttons, gold bar stripes, and a navy and gold piped belt with a brass buckle. Label, *R.H. Macy & Co., Inc., New York*. $75-$150. A wool serge sailor hat tops it all off; its black grosgrain band is embroidered "U.S. Navy" in gold, with an anchor emblem at each side. The inside lining is stamped "The Sailor," and its label reads: *Pekett Headwear Co., New York*. $35-$50.

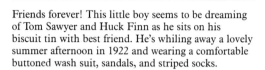

Friends forever! This little boy seems to be dreaming of Tom Sawyer and Huck Finn as he sits on his biscuit tin with best friend. He's whiling away a lovely summer afternoon in 1922 and wearing a comfortable buttoned wash suit, sandals, and striped socks.

Another extremely popular version of the sailor is the "Rah Rah" hat; *National's* version comes in a variety of color combinations for $.59. The Rah Rah could also be worn with its brim turned up (see boy at left center in the ad on page 172).

National Style Book offers this "Boys' popular Sailor Hat...for all around service and dressy wear," just $.95! (1922)

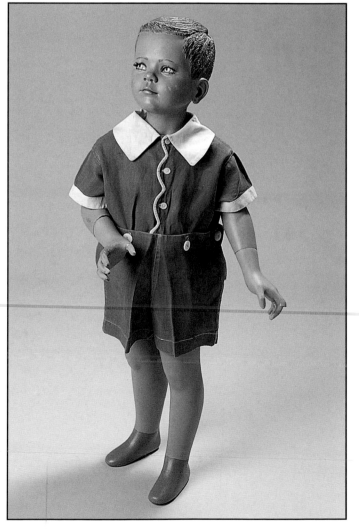

Dad and boys at the beach, ca. 1920-30! The little guy on the right, playing with his sand toy, wears a smart sailor suit with his pants rolled up; his younger brother wears a wash suit. Both boys wear sandals.

Mom may have run up this rough and tumble blue linen wash suit on her trusty Singer! It features a piped, scalloped closure, white collar and cuffs, and white top-stitched seams. The short, straight pants button to the shirt, and there's a small, buttonless fly placket. $45-$75.

National's offers popular bib overalls with adjustable suspender straps in a choice of "sturdy, durable Blue Denim" or "Hickory Stripe Cloth" (4 to 10 years). The blue denim long-sleeved "one-piece overalls, double seat and double knees" come in sizes 3 to 8.

This little tyke rides his scooter in a warm denim coverall. (Snapshot, ca. 1920-30)

Right:
"Warm 'Boy-Proof' Overcoats for the Little Fellows"! *National Style Book* pictures a selection of snappy ulster-style overcoats for boys sizes 3 to 10. Pictured at top is their "Extra Big Value" for $3.98: "this sturdy little model…will stand for all his rough pranks." *National's* advertising is right on the mark—the boy's German Shepherd could be a cousin of the famous Rin Tin Tin, who debuted as a Red Cross dog in Warner Bros. *Find Your Man* (1924). Note that even in winter, boys wear knickers with heavy ribbed wool socks.

Below:
Our little Jimmy is wearing a toasty brown wool ulsterette, double breasted and belted, just like Dad's! It's lined in a warm blue/grey/brown plaid flannel and has four handy pockets—two flap pockets below the waist and two "muff breast pockets" above. The back features a stitched-down box pleat, and the two-button belt is detachable. His herringbone tweed cap, the "Two in One Billy Boy & Tam," converts to a tam by tucking the visor inside. Store stock coat, $50-$100; cap/tam, $50-$75.

Label: *Two in One Billy Boy & Tam.*

Back view of coat and cap.

The hat worn as a Tam; note the nautical brass button with a red anchor.

Children's Shoes and Socks

Boys' shoes were "mannish" too! High "lace shoes" were favorites for boys of all ages (moms thought they prevented "weak ankles"), though the newer low oxfords were also popular. For summer, there were canvas shoes in a wide variety of styles, including high lace and low oxford styles. The classic leather sandal was another little boys' favorite; there was also a boys' version of the one-strap Mary Jane.

Two rough and ready guys! The boy on the left wears rugged high lace shoes; his best friend, high top "outing shoes" or sneakers. (Snapshot, ca. 1920-30)

National Style Book offers the most popular boys' shoes "For Service – For Dress." The rugged "Blucher-cut Lace Shoe" at left "will stand hard wear"; it features a round toe and outside pull strap. At center, the dressy "stylish and comfortable Balmoral-cut Lace Shoe" has a narrower toe, with "perforated medallion tip." The low oxfords pictured at right are "for play wear for the little fellows and for sports or general service for the older boys…one of the best low shoes you can buy." (1923)

National's "Specials for Infants and Children" pictures several of the most popular styles. Left to right are: patent leather Mary Janes ("instep strap pump"); classic leather "play sandals" for both girls and boys; two-tone high lace shoes; and two-tone "first step" button hightops with tassels. (1923)

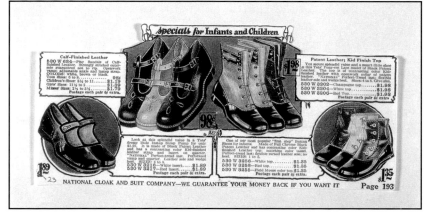

Three pairs of popular children's shoes. Left to right: 1) Toddler girls' high strap "Roman Sandals" in powder blue; they're side fastened with glass buttons, and satin bows with marquisite buckles adorn the centers. $150-$200. 2) Leather two-strap sandals with perforated toes; these classics have been favorites with both boys and girls for many generations! $25-$50. 3) Tasseled high lace boots, one of the most popular "first step" shoes for infants. This splendid tasseled pair is black patent and pink kid leather. $75-$125.

Perfect for bedtime—blue felt slippers with turnover cuffs decorated with hand-painted white rabbits! Leather soles. $25-$45.

White canvas Mary Jane pumps, with glass buttoned straps, spiffy grosgrain bows, and white rubber soles. Pictured with hand-painted "clown" shoe trees and pink silk socks with hand-crocheted tops. Mary Janes, $45-$75; Clown shoe trees, $25-$50; pink silk socks, $20-$40.

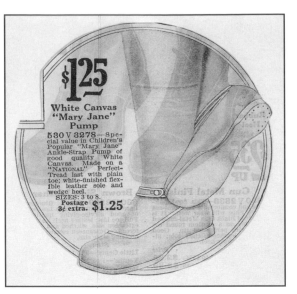

Classic one-strap Mary Janes, a perennial favorite with big girls, little girls…and their moms! Here *National's* offers them in white canvas for just $1.25. (Spring/Summer 1920)

Looking like the "Little Rascals" in Hal Roach's popular *Our Gang* films, these cute kids wear knee socks and Mary Jane shoes!

Though many children wore socks just over the ankle, knee socks were very popular for both boys and girls. For summer, silk or cotton lisle socks were worn; heavy wool socks were worn in cold weather.

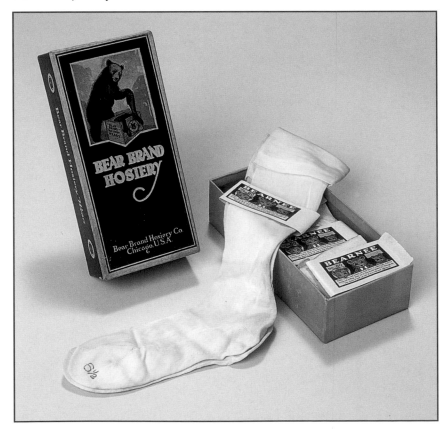

An old store stock box of Bear Brand Hosiery, containing "half dozen children's hose in white silk"; they're seamed up the back and feature turnover cuffs and reinforced heels and toes. Each has a label with the Bearnee Bears and this exciting offer: "Daddy, Mummy and Sammy are cloth bears 10 inches high, ready for sewing and stuffing. Send 10 cents to Bear Brand Hosiery Co, Chicago, for your choice or send 25 cents and all three will come right away!" Bear Brand box, $50-$75; store stock silk socks with labels, $20-$30 per pair.

"Playmate, Come Out and Play with Me, and Bring your Dollies Three…" Three young playmates on a slide; the one at the bottom wears the dreaded black wool knee socks that many mothers believed prevented "chillblains." My mother once said that her sweet, old-fashioned mom made her and her sister wear embarrassing black wool knee socks well into spring…and that they both took them off as soon as they were out of sight!

Girls' Clothing

Though older girls' fashions followed women's styles, most little girls wore simple, unwaisted dresses that either fell straight from the shoulders, or from a gathered yoke. Clothes had to be comfortable as well as attractive; as *Pictorial Review* proclaimed, "When One's Clothes are Right, Playtime is Even More Delightful." (1921) Period catalogs generally offered ready-made clothing for little girls in sizes 2-6, and for older girls in sizes 7-14. (Though sizes vary some according to the publication). For sports, it's clear that knicker pants weren't just for boys—knicker suits and knickers paired with middy blouses were very popular sportswear for girls.

Dolls were often dressed in exquisite, detailed fashions of their era, none more beautifully than the "Lencis"; they were perfectly clad down to their underwear! Looking like they just stepped out of the *Gazette* fashion plate, these two Lenci girls are no exception.

Kay, the little sister, has selected a charming dress of rose pink organdy, the full skirt trimmed with four rows of felt ruffles; a felt rose adorns the waist. The rounded neckline and short sleeves are piped, and she wears matching felt Mary Jane pumps with cotton socks. Felt roses and large bow loops adorn the pert "poke" bonnet that covers her bobbed curls. Her skirt has an attached organdy petticoat, and she wears matching bloomers beneath.

Older sister Teresa looks charming in a candy pink organdy dress, the full skirt with a windowpane effect formed by large pintucked squares. The fashionable scalloped hem is edged with tiny white accordion pleats with pink picot edging; these pleats also adorn the white Peter Pan collar and cuffs of the puffed sleeves. There's a petticoat attached to the skirt as well as a separate petticoat, both ruffled and edged with picot; she wears matching bloomers. She's chosen well; her curly auburn bob complements her ensemble!

DANSONS LA CAPUCINE
ROBE D'ÉTÉ ET ROBES D'ENFANTS, DE JEANNE LANVIN

5 de la Gazette du Bon Ton.   Année 1921. — Planche 57

Dansons La Capucine (Let's dance the Capucine). In this enchanting *Gazette du Bon Ton* pochoir, girls dance the Capucine, which seems similar to our "Ring Around the Rosie." They're dressed in Paris dresses from Jeanne Lanvin. Lanvin began her career as milliner; shortly after the turn of the century, she'd become famous for the dresses she created for her little daughter, Marie-Blanche, and soon she was designing for both mothers and daughters. Note that while the younger girls' lace trimmed dresses fall simply from a softly gathered neckline, the older girl's red dress (center) has a low waistline like that of the lady at center in the full robe de style. (1921)

Teresa shows off her ruffled petticoat and matching bloomers, while Kay's about to step into her bloomers; she wears a linen "step-in" or teddy that's very detailed with drawn work trim and picot finished edges.

Three sweet sisters in low-waisted frocks. The girl at right wears a big "Dolly Dingle" hair bow; mom's wearing a fashionable cloche! (Snapshot, ca. 1922)

Delineator illustrates patterns for an adorable array of popular styles for both older and younger girls. Note that the little girls' dresses have matching bloomers. They're high-waisted; some are gathered from a yoke while others simply fall straight from the shoulders. Smocking and embroidery are favorite trims. Older girls' dresses exhibit features like those of mom; most emphasize the low waistline. The blue dress at center right is very fashionable with its low belted waist, floating side panels, bell sleeves, and lattice trim. The lone little boy, by the blackboard, wears a crisp wash suit. Note the children's stylish shoes—Mary Janes, T-straps, and even saddle shoes! (September 1922)

Above:
Harriet is modeling a very pretty "bloomer dress" in pale green voile, with short ruffled lace sleeves and a scalloped, lace-trimmed hem. Both shoulders and hem are trimmed with pink floral embroidery that has been lovingly worked by mom. Her matching bloomers are edged with three rows of lace. She's wearing a very chic straw cloche, with mint green grosgrain ribbon trim. For moms who prefer ready made, B. Altman's "bloomer frocks" are priced from $2.95 to $5.25. Bloomer dress, $75-$150; girl's cloche, $75-$125.

Above center:
Close-up of lace and Mom's floral embroidery.

Enjoying ice cream cones with dad are three sisters in dresses much like Harriet's! Noted on the back: "Dad, 33 years; Alice 9 yrs., 7 months; Lovella 7 yrs., 7 months, and Tootsie 5 yrs, 1 month. August 1923, Thursday." Note that the two older girls' dresses have low waistlines, and that Tootsie's and Alice's hems are smartly scalloped.

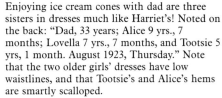

Above:
Many twenties' moms economized by making dresses from feed sacks, especially in rural areas. These treasures weren't often saved, but were passed down till they wore out—then often used for quilts or rag rugs so they're hard to find today. This adorable example, made from a sturdy cotton feedsack, has been painstakingly embroidered with a cute Dolly Dingle giving her puppy a bath…the pocket is cleverly disguised as a washtub! The soap has slipped away, and is embroidered near the hem at left. $125-$175.

Above center:
Close-up of mom's marvelous embroidery, which appears to be freehand rather than a pattern.

Dolly Dingle, who's also wearing an embroidered dress, looks on! A twenties' icon, Dolly was the creation of illustrator Grace G. Drayton. Dolly Dingle paper dolls appeared in *Pictorial Review* from 1913-1933, and when *Pictorial Review* arrived, little girls rushed to cut out Dolly and the fashions from her latest adventure. Her trademark Dolly Dingle hair bow was worn by girls everywhere.

179

"Party Frocks" for Older Girls

Period magazines often referred to a young teenage girl as a "Junior Miss," a "Prom Girl," or a "Sub-Deb," as the term "teenager" hadn't yet become common language. "Party frocks" were worn to events like graduations, birthdays, weddings, and holidays. They were either made up from home patterns, like these pictured in the *Ladies Home Journal*, or purchased ready made. They boasted many of the latest features; as *Vogue* advised: "Exposure to chic now will extend into fashionable adulthood!" *Vogue* cautioned, however, that the latest styles should be modestly modified for young ladies: "Chic should have the quality of simplicity, but with simple, youthful, unsophisticated lines…though this is apt to be the reason for the beginning of a long and active warfare between a young girl and her mother…" (June 1926)

"Dress up"—young girls' age-old rite of passage! These aspiring young vamps illustrate every girl's dream of becoming a *femme fatale*. On the back of this marvelous snapshot, mom has noted: "Florence and Pauline with my best evening gowns." Florence has the twenties' look of haughty ennui down pat, while Pauline, with her chic feather aigrette, coyly looks askance! (Snapshot, ca. 1920-22)

Though Florence and Pauline are decked out in mom's best evening gowns, "party frocks" suitable for young ladies are a bit more modest, as pictured in this charming array from *The Ladies' Home Journal Fashion Quarterly*. You'll note fashion features that echo the latest women's styles, including lowered waistlines, tiered or ruffled skirts, scalloped and handkerchief hemlines, and draped side bows. Pictured at upper right is a young lady's version of Marie Antoinette's eighteenth century open robe. These home patterns are offered in sizes 14-20 years. (Winter 1922)

The Discovery of Tut's Tomb

The year 1922 ended with the astounding discovery of one of the most famous children of all time—"The Boy King," Tutankhamun. "Tut" ruled as Pharaoh of Upper and Lower Egypt from about nine years of age until his death at eighteen, ca. 1336-1327 B.C., more than three thousand years ago.

On November 7, 1922, British archeologist Howard Carter and his backer, Lord Carnarvon, reached the entry to Tut's ancient tomb in the Valley of Kings. It was the only ancient Egyptian tomb that had not been pillaged by tomb robbers, and the discovery was hailed as one of the most important events of the twentieth century.

A water boy who'd stopped to take a break had found a step cut into a rock beside him; more steps were quickly uncovered that led to a door. Though this first door had been disturbed, a second had not; it bore seals with the name "Tutankhamun." When a small opening had been made, Carter peered in. Lord Carnarvon asked if he could see anything, and Carter replied, "Yes, wonderful things!" The tomb contained carved and painted chairs, chests, beds, gilded animals, statues of golden gods, a throne overlaid in gold, and two life size statues of Tut wearing the Pharaoh's scared cobra headdress. There were boats to take Tut on his journey into the next life, as well as food and drink so spirits of the dead could feast in the next world.

In a third room, beyond another sealed door, was a breathtaking wall of gold, picturing Tut arriving in the world of the gods, presented by Maat, Goddess of Truth, to Re-Harakhty, the sun god. A statue of Anubis, the jackal-headed God of the Dead, guarded the entrance to a third chamber—the burial chamber—where a faint smell of perfume still lingered. A tiny wreath of flowers, thought to have been a parting gift from Tut's Queen, Ankesenamun, had been placed around the sacred cobra and vulture of Tut's royal headdress. Jewels, amulets, and charms had been placed under the young king's bandages to protect him from the dangers of the underworld. Discovered later was an inscription on the central bandage of Tut's mummy: "Descend, my mother Nut, spread thyself over me and let me be the Imperishable Stars that are in thee." (Nut was one of the deities of the sky; the sky was represented by a falcon who spread his protective wings over Egypt, often in the form of Horus, the falcon god, Nut or Nekhbut.)

The Curse of the Mummy

Ancient Pharaohs took extreme measures to ensure their safe passage into the afterlife, measures that included a powerful curse on any who dared enter a Pharaoh's tomb—legend claimed that the hand of the mummy would reach out to strike anyone who disturbed it. As soon as Tut's tomb was discovered, there were rumors of Tut's Curse. Carter had a "lucky" golden canary; the day the entrance to the tomb was discovered, it was killed by a cobra—a symbol of Egyptian royalty. Carter's Egyptian aide told him that Pharaoh's serpent had eaten the golden bird because "it led us to the hidden tomb."

At a séance Lord Carnarvon attended just before leaving for Egypt, the spirits warned him that he'd be in danger if he entered the tomb. On April 5, 1923, five months after the discovery of the tomb, Lord Carnarvon died unexpectedly. His daughter, Lady Evelyn, wrote that her father had nicked a mosquito bite while shaving; he developed blood poisoning and subsequently contracted pneumonia. On the day Carnarvon died, all the lights went out in Cairo, and his favorite dog howled

In the tomb's first chamber, the first "wonderful thing" Carter saw was a brightly painted chest that held Tut's boyhood clothing: rush sandals, a gilded headrest, and royal robes to fit a young boy. The chest depicts this incredible scene, "Tutankhamun Slaying Syrian Foes," with Tut as a fearless archer in a gilded chariot, drawing his bow as he leads his forces into battle. Spreading their wings protectively over Tut's head are symbols of Nekhbut, the vulture goddess of Upper Egypt. Nekhbut, the guardian of mothers and children, was also the protector of ancient Egypt's Pharaohs.

Tutmania was assuaged with the introduction of a wide variety of Egyptian items, like this marvelous pigskin envelope purse, tooled and hand-painted with the same scene that decorates Tut's painted chest. The scene is bordered with red and blue lotus blossoms. The lotus was a symbol of creation and rebirth to the ancient Egyptians, as it sinks underwater at night only to rise and bloom again at dawn. Egypt's blue lotus, with its sky blue petals and golden center imitating the sky and sun, gave rise to ancient Egypt's legend of creation.

A note inside the bag reads: "Purse, Cairo, Egypt from Abdulla's The Son of Mohammed. Handkerchief [also inside bag] from shop in front of Shepheard's Hotel." (Shepheard's was Cairo's most prestigious hotel; famed British travel writer, Amelia B. Edwards, claimed it was *the* place to be and to be seen when in Cairo. The old Shepheard's Hotel burned down in 1952.)

and then dropped dead. When Tut's mummy was unwrapped in 1925, a small wound was discovered on its left cheek—exactly where Carnarvon had been bitten by the fatal mosquito! The Pharaoh's curse, of course, only added to the furor created by the discovery of Tut's tomb, and produced an unparalleled desire for any and all things Egyptian—known as *Tutmania!*

Those who could afford to, made pilgrimages to Egypt; those who could not, savored Tut's flavor with a plethora of "Egyptian" items including clothing, jewelry, perfume, and decorative items. Images of ancient Pharaohs peered from almost every portal, and exquisitely embroidered and beaded motifs lent clothing the look of the "Egyptienne" as haute couture saluted this miraculous discovery.

Chapter Five

1923 Women's Fashions

Timeline

A new dance, the Charleston, is featured in *Running Wild*, an all black off-Broadway production. It's named for its place of origin—Charleston, South Carolina—and will soon become so popular that its name will forever be linked with the twenties! Frigidaire introduces a new, greatly improved version of the electric "refrigerator" and soon the "Iceman" doesn't cometh any more! Pan American Airways now offers *passenger* air travel.

February 17: Bessie Smith records her first record for Columbia, "Downhearted Blues"; it sells a phenomenal two million copies, earning Bessie the title "Empress of the Blues."

March 2: *Time Magazine* debuts.

April 18: There's a sellout crowd on opening day of the new Yankee Stadium, dubbed "The House that Ruth Built," and The Sultan of Swat hits a triple homer!

August 2: President Warren G. Harding dies of apoplexy during a speaking tour, some say due to anxiety over the Teapot Dome Scandal. Vice president Calvin Coolidge is sworn in as the nation's thirtieth president.

October 17: From the *Syracuse Post Standard*: "The Syracuse City Police Department's Prohibition Squad raided the home of Mrs. Celia Gordon at 906 Orange Str., seizing two gallons of whiskey ad four gallons of wine. When police arrived, Gordon had a milk bottle full of whiskey in one hand and her attempt to bid it godspeed upon the floor was frustrated by the leader of the squad, Joe Kelley. A search of the house revealed a quart in the pantry, two gallons in the cellar and four gallons of wine in the front room."

On the Silent Screen

Clara Bow, a young Brooklyn girl, wins a beauty contest and is given a role in *Down to the Sea in Ships*. Avant garde author Elinor Glynn dubs Clara the "IT" girl ("IT" being sex appeal, naturally). Cecil B. DeMille directs his epic film *The Ten Commandments*. In Sweden, Greta Gustafsson appears in *The Saga of Gosta Borling*; in 1926, she comes to America to star in films as Greta Garbo. Colleen Moore stars in *Flaming Youth*. Lon Chaney thrills in *The Hunchback of Notre Dame*. Popular comedian Harold Lloyd stars in *Safety Last* and *Why Worry*.

Favorite New Recordings

Music hits include Bessie Smith's "Down Hearted Blues," King Oliver's "Dippermouth Blues," and "Yes We Have No Bananas," by Billy Murray.

In Literature

Kahlil Gibran's *The Prophet* is published to great acclaim. It's since been translated into thirteen languages; four decades later, in the 1960s, it becomes a favorite with the Peace and Love generation. Aldous Huxley's *Antic Hay* is published, as is P.G. Wodehouse's *The Inimitable Jeeves*. Popular new children's books include *The Voyages of Dr. Doolittle* by Hugh Lofting, A.A. Milne's *House at Pooh Corner*, and Felix Salten's children's classic, *Bambi* (in 1942, Walt Disney makes the film version—one of the best loved children's movies of all time!) Edna St. Vincent Millay wins the Pulitzer Prize for poetry, and Irish Poet W.B. Yeats wins the 1923 Nobel Prize for poetry.

In Fashion 1923—Tutmania!

It was the year of the Egyptian as *TUTMANIA* beat in the heart of haute couture. The ancient Egyptian influence proved irresistible (and profitable) following Howard Carter's discovery of King Tut's tomb in November 1922. In Paris, "Egyptiennes" were everywhere as many frocks featured the dramatic Egyptian Drape—"moulded" hips swathed like Cleopatra's. Dazzling Assuit shawls in hammered silver or gold motifs flashed in the night, mirroring the splendor of ancient Egypt. There were beaded Egyptian cinema capes, Cleopatra headdresses, even "Cleopatra" corsets! Women smoked Egyptian cigarettes in King Tut cigarette holders. *Vogue* recommended an embroidered "Tutankhamun Overblouse."

Callot introduced the "Indo-Chinese" or "Hindoo" (Hindu) look this year, with gowns girdled in a fashion similar to the Egyptian drape; Jenny, Drecoll and Premet and Madeleine et Madeleine were among the couturiers that follow suit, and many of 1923's frocks were spiced with a flavor of the mysterious East. The House of Leinef opened this year.

Couture Trends

The straight, vertical silhouette grew ever stronger; belts were either entirely omitted or emphasized a LOW waist. *Vogue* noted: "The waistline is placed in some instances exceptionally low, almost below the hipline." As both the new Egyptian and Indo-Chinese styles featured the modish new hip girdles, *Harper's* advised: "There has been an unusual development of the girdle, which in some houses has widened and flattened out, being very closely drawn about the hips with loops falling over it…" (April 1923). These tight "moulded hip" girdles were often beaded and/or embroidered. They were a style to be watched—they would be of utmost importance during the second half of the decade. Most couturiers continued to show very long skirts this year, though Chanel preferred hers about ten inches from the ground.

The eagerly awaited April *Spring Fashion Number* from *Harper's Bazar* provided fascinating insights into on the world of haute couture by famous fashion photographer Baron de Meyer. His descriptions painted a vivid picture of "Dresses Dreams are Made Of," with couture features that would soon be incorporated in fashions for all:

"The House of **Callot** *cast a spell on me I have never been able to shake off. Since over twenty years ago, the colorings and gorgeous embroideries in this house were of a kind seen as yet nowhere else… days when the Callot sisters entered China, Persia and Japan, in fact opened up the entire Orient for sartorial purposes…Callot's spring collection seems even more beautiful that last season's, though I dare say I shall feel inclined to repeat myself next year. Her unique Indo-Chinese gowns are probably the most fascinating—they cling to sinuous figures, are draped and have pointed panels hanging from strangely designed belts, giving the wearer a look of some rare idol…"* The Baron favors Callot's *"…gold brocaded sheath shimmering in greens and oranges with long panels embroidered in green metallic paillettes, emerald and pearl jewels placed on the bodice."*

*"***Jenny*** probably has the largest collection of models in any house—over 300 models; her collection favors Egyptian and Chinese influences."* She offers several splendid frocks *"of thinnest crepe…printed with color in an Egyptian design, embroidered with beads outlining the printed pattern…Her general line remains absolutely straight, with skirts of ankle length devoid of any drapery.* Jenny also features smart, straight little bolero tailored jackets this season. As the Baron notes, *"…she has, however, in every instance, succeeded in imparting the enchanting Parisian touch to her creations."*

*"***Chanel*** has consistently made, for several seasons, the straight-hanging chemise frock, eight or ten inches from the floor. It is very simple in line, in fabric and embroidery it is gorgeous…Chanel again shows many simple little pocketed tailleurs and skirts of wool under sweater-blouses of tricot.* For evening, the Baron praises Chanel's *"…night blue georgette crepe with Hindu embroidery in gold, red and green."* For day, he advocates *"Chanel's sports suit of knitted material in tiger-patterned gray and brown, with slipover sweater in plain grey jersey with collar and cuffs in the matching tiger pattern."*

*"***Lanvin's*** wonderful collection is again a matter of great joy from the artist's point of view. The periods between 1830 and 1880 have given her renewed inspiration for pictorial robes de style; she contrasts these with gowns of a long slender type, made on loose princesse lines and decorated by the marvelous embroideries and ornamentation for which this house is justly famed. Embroidered wheels of cut-out work, extraordinary cockades, metal*

laces combine with imaginative and exquisite details of hand-work are seen on many of the models. The Baron admires Lanvin's "…white crepe evening gown, very long and full; the skirt entirely covered by pearls and square bits of mother-of-pearl…"

*"***Patou*** is nowadays one of the dominating personalities in the dressmaking world; his opening is an event! He has personality, is modern and clever. His presence is felt, and he wears his popularity with becoming ease… He makes use of magnificent materials mostly reserved for his use exclusively. He is full of inventions, yet does not change his ever youthful line. This spring Patou has made skirts a feature, and has simplified bodices; he has returned to color, made lavish use of embroideries and used quantities of printed textiles. He's designed entirely new sport suits, with capes and coats made of tweeds or homespuns…"* The Baron recommends Patou's *"…evening gown of draped black crepe, having loops and ends bunched in front; a garland of blood-red roses starting from the shoulder and crossing the bare back…"*

Cheruit, *"The Aristrocrat"… "All Cheruit creations are marked by the strong individuality which seems to cling to this house build on its own traditions. Day gowns, be they crepe or printed materials lend an air of height and slimness to the wearer. In most cases they are beltless, and have an uninterrupted line from neck to skirt hem… Flounces at Cheruit's are very much to the fore—one model shown has a very short skirt in front and almost trailing at the back…"* (the famous "peacock" look that will be so popular by the end of the decade). The Baron raves over Cheruit's *"… black cire gauze cape lined with silver, with large hood edged with black lace to cover the head with rectangular patches of ermine incrusted all over the hood."*

*"***Molyneux's*** lines are still straight, with occasional flat drapery, the skirts narrow and not too long, especially for day and sports wear…in many cases the chemise frock is worn without any demarcation of waistline, with silk, metal or wool embroidery for day wear; bejeweled beyond belief for evening. Molyneux shows big, bold prints…everywhere printed crepe is used for the corsage (blouse), matching jacket and cape or coat linings.* At Molyneux, *"…a black afternoon gown made of a crepe scarf, which has strange flowers of mauve, blue, rose and green printed on a black ground"* catches the Baron's eye.

*"***Poiret*** proves to the world that he still retains the unchallenged mind for originality as well as genius for inventions…His circular skirts for day wear are a distinct innovation…though some measure 12-14 yards in circumference, yet they seem soft and clinging. His most original gowns are made of metal tissues with long, low-waisted draped bodices, devoid of sleeves or even straps, and having long trailing skirts of a different material, with a bog roll of twisted tissue almost like a glorified belt, placed low about the hips."*

*"***Worth*** can always be depended upon to show the very best in clothes…Worth shows a silhouette both straight and slender, the waistline a bit below normal; jackets are short and usually straight to the hips, some with capes either attached or removable. Many sports costumes of tricot are offered, trimmed with embroidery.* The Baron's favorite at Worth is *"…a black suit with a yellow blouse trimmed with white silk tassel fringe."*

Smart Shops and Catalogs Interpret the Mode for the "Average Woman"

The 1923 Spring/Summer *National Style Book* offered a variety of stylish frocks, adapting many couture features for the American woman. "Exact reproductions" were also shown: "An exquisite reproduction of a recent Paris Importation…in this smart model, note especially the Jenny neck, the wide flare cuffs, the basque effect with novelty girdle, the loose panels on the skirt and the irregular lower edge—all style features that have received Paris' highest approval." The girdle is "…composed of metallic ribbon and novelty rosettes adding a pleasing note of color. In all-silk Canton crepe, $14.98." *National's* offered the new sleeves with tantalizing cutouts, often edged with lace or beading. Skirts were shown between mid-calf and the ankle, and waistlines a bit lower than last year's. Overskirt side panels continued to be popular; many were narrowly pleated. Embroidery, beadwork, and soutache trims were used on street dresses as well on frocks for afternoon and evening.

The savvy *Chicago Mail Order* catalog cashed in on Hollywood with "Miss Marion Davies' Beauty Secrets—FREE for the exclusive benefit of our customers!" ("with merchandise order for $5 or more and this coupon," as noted in fine print!) Miss Davies (the paramour and protégé of publisher William Randolph Hurst) writes: "It is woman's right to be beautiful and all women can be beautiful—if they know how…Please tell your customers for me. I love them all and hope they will like my signed photograph which appears in 'Marion Davies Beauty Secrets.'"

Chicago offered a wonderful description of how Paris styles reach the American woman:

> *"Each season the Fashionables and Royalty of the world congregate at Biarritz and Deauville, the French Winter resorts. The world-renowned Parisian dressmakers maintain branch establishments right on the ground, and their mannikins intermingle with the guests at the fashionable hotels and at every social function, wearing the latest creations in gowns, wraps and hats. Any garment or hat which is greeted with marked admiration or enthusiasm is immediately rushed to the branch establishment, there to be copied. The copies are then sold to the representatives of Fashion Houses the world over—and thus another new style has come into being…*
>
> *"The moment the Parisian Couturiers deliver the samples to our Paris office, they are rushed to New York on the first steamship, and our staff of designers goes over each model, retaining all the style features, but modifying or adding to each garment, hat or shoe those American touches which the truly well groomed, conservative American woman demands in her clothes, with the result that our 'Style Queen' styles are often even more lovely than the high priced French imports themselves!"*

Chicago illustrated their catalog with pictures of both the "Original Paris Models" and "Our Reproductions," noting "From Paris to MAIN STREET, They all take off their hats to 'Style Queen Dresses'…AS FRENCHY AS THE MARSEILLAISE!"

1923 Fashions

By 1923, the name Tutankhamun was on everyone's lips. "Tut-Ankh-Amen has opened a new field for the imagination,"

This wonderful example of Egyptian Art Deco art, depicting a flapper Cleopatra in front of the Sphinx, is the cover for "Mystic Nile" sheet music. This twenties' Cleo flaunts her charms in an Egyptian headdress, shocking jeweled brassiere, girdle belt, and asp armband. (Cleopatra, Egypt's last Pharaoh, died ca. 27 B.C., dispatched by her infamous asp.) The tantalizing chorus to the song goes:

Oh, Mystic Nile, I'm longing all the while
To be near, and hear - Her love song
'Neath the palms - I'll hold her in my arms…

announced Henning Boot Shop in the April 1923 *Harper's Bazar*. "Henning, in advance of the modes, has already assembled shoes for Spring in keeping with the Egyptian treasure find. The tomb of the ancient Pharaoh has disclosed treasures of exquisite beauty. They reveal motifs so new and yet so old, so beautiful and yet so simple and exquisite in design." In "Paris Openings," *Harper's* praised the House of Jenny: "Frocks of thinnest crepe, printed with color in an Egyptian design, are embroidered with beads, the beads outlining the printed pattern which is arranged in crosswise stripes in Egyptian Fashion."

The ancient Sphinx, over twelve hundred years old when Tut ruled, is one of the most beloved symbols of ancient Egypt. With the head of a Pharaoh and body of a lion, the Sphinx measures 240 feet long and 66 feet high. It faces the rising sun, due east, and stands guard in front of the pyramid of the Pharaoh Khafre, who ruled ca. 2558-2532 B.C. Many Egyptologists believe the Sphinx was carved from a single block of limestone left in the quarry when Khafre's pyramid was built some 4,600 years ago. The Sphinx has retained his air of mystery with the passing of thousands of years; experts' opinions vary to this day. Some think the Sphinx's face was carved to resemble Khafre's. It's also believed that the Sphinx was originally beautifully painted, and although he's missing his ritual beard and part of the Uraeus cobra headdress, his majesty is awe-inspiring! After thousands of years, the astronauts discovered the Sphinx can be seen from the moon!

A splendid Art Deco sphinx! This colorful beaded bag shows his recumbent "lion" body as well as his Pharaoh's profile; the Great Pyramid is in the background. The celluloid faux tortoise frame is marked *Made in France*. $600-800.

There are three pyramids around the Sphinx. In addition to Khafre's, the Great Pyramid of his father, Khufu, rises to the right of the Sphinx. One of the Seven Wonders of the Ancient World, Khufu's Great Pyramid is 481 feet high; for over two thousand years it was the world's tallest structure (superceded only by the Eiffel Tower in 1889). British travel writer Amelia Blanford Edwards, in her nineteenth century classic, *A Thousand Miles up the Nile*, wrote of the Great Pyramid:

> *"When at last the edge of the desert is reached and the long sand-slope climbed, and the rocky platform gained, and the Great Pyramid in all its unexpected bulk and majesty towers close above one's head, the effect is as sudden as it is overwhelming. It shuts out the sky and the horizon. It shuts out all the other Pyramids. It shuts out everything but the sense of awe and wonder…"*

Khufu's Great Pyramid took more than twenty years to complete and was constructed by over 100,000 Egyptian workers; not slaves as was previously thought. To the left of the Sphinx stands the smallest pyramid, the Pyramid of Menakaure, another of Khufu's sons.

The pyramids at Giza were first noted by the historian Herodotus in 450 B.C., and when Napoleon first looked on them in 1798, he said to his men: "Forty centuries are looking at us." According to an ancient proverb, "Man Fears Time, and Time Fears the Pyramids."

The Sacred Cobra or *Uraeus*, worn on the crowns of royalty, was said to "rear up and spit fire at approaching enemies." This twenties' Egyptian tiara is hammered brass formed in the image of the Sacred Cobra. Encircling the head, it rears up in three loops, ready to "spit fire"; in the center are two tiny Egyptian bells. $200-$300.

James and Edith McKee and their daughter, Edith Louise McKee, from Johnstown, Pennsylvania, posed in front of the Sphinx for this magnificent photograph taken ca. 1923-24. To the right of the Sphinx towers the Great Pyramid of Khufu. As noted on the reverse, the McKees were visiting Egypt as part of an "Around-the-World Cruise" on the S.S. *Empress of France*. Edith Louise, called "Louise," is seated on the camel at left. Tragically, she died in Singapore on March 13, 1925, while they were still on their world tour…she was just twenty-two.

Egyptian Cosmetics

Men, women and children of ancient Egypt wore makeup that was applied in front of mirrors of polished silver; makeup was so important that Egyptians often carried makeup boxes with them when they went out. Their famous almond shaped eyes were painted with either green malachite or galena (powdered grey lead ore that was mixed with oil to make kohl, which was stored in small jars and applied with tiny wands). For "lipstick" and rouge, red ochre clay was ground and mixed with water and fat; rouge of red ochre that's survived for some four thousand years has been found in tombs. Nails were stained with henna. Egyptians used a mixture of lime, perfume, and oil as a cleansing cream, and applied perfumed oils daily.

The Cosmetics of Cleopatra

The Palmolive Company offers twenties' women the beauty secrets of Cleopatra: "How did Cleopatra wash her face? Did she enhance her beauty with cosmetics? Hieroglyphic records prove that while the finish of the royal toilet may have been rouging with carmine or vermilion, thorough, radiant cleanliness was always the foundation… Cleopatra used Palm and Olive oils, the same rare oils which produce Palmolive soap. Remember that rouge and powder are harmless enough when applied to a clean skin and profit by the beauty secret of Cleopatra!" (*Ladies Home Journal*, October 1920)

This fabulous Art Deco beaded belt or "girdle" would transform any frock into one worthy of an Egyptian queen. Exquisitely worked glass beads form the Wings of Horus; in the center is a thin bronze medallion of Cleopatra. $400-$500.

Egyptian Wings

Soaring wings are one of the most spectacular Egyptian symbols, symbolizing the sky offering its protection to the ancient Egyptians. Spread wings represented several deities, including Nekhbut and Horus. Horus the Falcon, or "Horus of the Horizon," was one of Egypt's earliest and most powerful gods. According to ancient legend, Horus was the son of Osiris and Isis, Ruler of the Day:

> *"His eyes are the sun and the moon, when he opens them it is day, when closed it is night; stars are attached to his body, the wind is his mouth and the water his perspiration."*

It was thought that a deceased's soul might take the form of a falcon with the head of the deceased and fly through eternity.

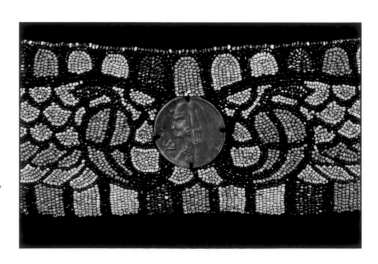

Close-up of the belt's "Cleo" medallion and beadwork.

Egyptian Revival Art Deco Items

If you couldn't go to Egypt, Egypt would come to you, as illustrated by these marvelous Egyptian revival items—a pleasing plethora from perfumes to parasols!

The essence of Ancient Egypt is captured in Cleopatra perfume from "Ahmed Souman—Cairo's Perfume King." This lovely perfume bottle depicts an Art Deco Cleopatra in classic Egyptian dress, with the headdress of Upper and Lower Egypt. It's hand-painted in colorful enamels and gold leaf, with a faceted amber and filigreed brass top and clear glass dauber. The small amount of perfume left in the bottle conjures up visions of ancient Egypt with its pungent, spicy aroma. $200-$300.

Even cigarettes pay homage to the Power of the Pharaoh—here, Tutankhamun's image graces Helmar's Turkish Cigarettes. This small box of cigarettes measures just 2" x 3"; the brilliant design is embossed and accented in gold leaf. $50-$75. Naturally, Egyptian cigarettes require a Pharaoh cigarette holder! This splendid holder is ivory, cleverly carved in the shape of the young Pharaoh. 6-1/2" long. $175-350.

Close-up of the ivory Pharaoh.

This magnificent Nile green to amber celluloid comb is hand-carved with Egyptian lotuses and buds. Very large, it measures 7-1/2" wide by 8-1/2" tall. $150-$200.

"No costume or outfit is complete these days unless Tut-Ankh-Amen figures in some way or other. Here is a decorative umbrella where one walks with King Tut and his pyramid wherever one goes," as the text from a twenties' fashion photo of a similar parasol advises. Our "Egyptian" parasol is decorated with hand-painted symbols of Tut driving his chariot, Horus the Falcon, and Anubis. (The jackal-headed god, Anubis, was the divine patron of embalming and mummified dead; he was the first to make a mummy.) $200-$400.

This fine beaded bag is a splendid example of Art Deco Egyptian Revival. Beneath the Wings of Horus are stylized papyrus flowers on long stalks; below are smaller lotus buds. The papyrus flower was a symbol of Lower Egypt, the lotus, a symbol of Upper Egypt; together they symbolize the union of Upper and Lower Egypt. Papyrus was extremely important to the ancient Egyptians; it was used not only for writing paper, but also for rafts and barges, clothing and sandals, even food and medicine. $500-$600.

Shopping for Tut's treasures? Carry them in this rare embossed leather "Pyramid Shopping Bag." Large leather shopping or tote bags were a twenties' necessity, and period catalogs offer plain "leatherette" shopping bags that are "convenient for shopping or school, adaptable for many purposes." A roomy 16" x 14" bag is just $.79! (*Bellas Hess*, 1920) $150-$250.

Inside Tut's tomb! This "Egyptian" vanity case has compartments inside for lipstick and rouge. It's both embossed and hand-painted. King Tut struts under the spread Wings of Nekhbut; there's a lamp to guide him on his journey into the underworld, a cartouche of hiero-glyphics, and in the background, scattered stars. Note that even the tomb's stones are delineated in the embossed leather. $150-$250.

Twenties' "Egyptian" Fashions

Of course, chic twenties' "Egyptiennes" wore fashions that
echoed the spelendors of ancient Egypt...

EGYPTIENNES

IMPRES
ART – GOUT
27, RUE DES
PAR

"Egyptiennes," a stunning pochoir from *Art Gout Beaute,* depicts two twenties' versions of
Cleopatra's clothes. The tubular silhouette's lines were well suited to these "ancient" styles. (1925)

This magnificent cinema cape is mocha silk crepe, with Egyptian scenes worked by hand in several sizes of marquisite beads. Depicted are lotus blossoms and buds, papyrus symbols, and Egyptian men and women holding lotus flowers and royal flails; kneeling camels border the hem. The high collar is hand-smocked, as is the hem. The vivid tie-died silk lining has an inside smocked pocket and fastens with long neck ties. $8,000-$10,000.

Close-up of the cape's spectacular marquisite beadwork.

Fanciful Pharaohs are embroidered all over this brown velveteen "knock-about" cloche. $150-$300.

The cape's dramatic tie-dyed lining!

Egypt's extreme version of the tight-across-the-hips-in-back silhouette

The mode on the Nile centuries ago was as narrow as the figure permitted

JENNY

DOUCET

DRECOLL

Reminiscent of Luxor and luxury is a gown of thin silver lamé, embroidered and beaded in soft colours and Egyptian patterns. The gown is so straight and narrow that it outlines the figure slightly; beaded shoulder-straps and red and green lacquer bracelets complete the effect

Cleopatra might have worn such a gown, had that exotic lady lived in modern times, for the girdle wrapped close round the hips, rising to the front, and the panels it secures, are as old as Egypt. The material is composed of jet squares on black chiffon. Coiffure from Agnes

In ancient friezes among the ruins of Egyptian temples, one frequently sees the silhouette which wraps the figure closely as far as the hips, and then descends in straight panels to the ankles. Drecoll has interpreted this ancient idea in lovely silver lamé with very interesting effect

The silhouette of ancient Egypt was wholly a matter of feminine grace

PARIS READS THE RIDDLE OF
THE EGYPTIAN SPHINX

They might swerve from the pencil silhouette, but not from the bateau neck-line

"Paris Reads the Riddle of the Egyptian Sphinx," headlines *Vogue* in their April 15, 1923 issue. Depicted are "Egyptian" creations from Jenny, Doucet, and Drecoll. Note the Egyptian Drape on the Doucet gown at center, with "…the girdle wrapped close round the hips…as old as Egypt." Illustration by A.E. Marty.

Close-up of the fascinating Egyptian beadwork.

Celebrate "Tutmania" in this exquisite panné velvet Egyptian Revival evening frock! Its breathtaking beadwork, executed in Egyptian motifs, includes prong-set rhinestones and glass bugle beads in silver, crystal, and white. The essential "Egyptian Drape" consists of a long beaded center panel, which descends from the center of the low waist to the beaded fringe hem. A wider beaded panel was included with the dress; perhaps meant for a headdress like the one fashioned here. A long rope of faceted crystal beads and a turquoise ostrich fan complete the ensemble. This sleeveless evening frock is a slip-on; it simply slips over the head. Note that pre-beaded fabric lengths were available during the twenties, and this fabulous beaded evening frock may have been made up in this manner. $500-$800 (price reflects an old repair to the velvet at the back of the shoulders).

The French fashion magazine *Mode Pratique* features two Egyptian headdresses in their March 29, 1924 issue. On the left is a lamé bandeau with dangling jewels; on the right is a lamé turban headdress. Note her magnificent fan!

Worthy of any twentieth century Cleopatra! This large "Egyptian" ostrich fan is composed of four full ostrich plumes mounted in a single faux tortoise handle. $150-$300.

Close-up of the Egyptian drape, and fringed hem.

Assuit (Asuite) Silver Shawls

One of the most dazzling (and desirable) examples of twenties' Egyptian revival items is the scintillating silver assuit shawl. Wildly popular in the twenties, these shawls were originally made in Egypt by natives of Assuit, who hammered low grade silver into sheets that were then cut into narrow strips and folded by hand into a coarse net of linen or cotton in fabulous designs. Some feature Art Deco geometric patterns, but the most desirable have stylized figures of Egyptians, camels, pyramids, palm trees, etc. White or cream colors are most common found today, then black; the Nile Green, lavender, brick red, and maroon shawls are rarer. Today, many will have a few holes in their net to repair, and there are often a few tarnished areas…though nothing can detract from their astounding beauty! Some assuits are gold tone or brass; some appear to be a silver wash over brass. Polishing and/or dyeing may be harmful. They're also known as "Coptic" or "Koptic" shawls. Some of this fabric was fashioned into capes and dresses. Buyers should be aware that new repros are available.

Far left:
To compliment our panné velvet Egyptian evening frock, a lady might have selected this assuit shawl with figures of trees, pyramids, and geometrics worked in strips of hammered silver. It's "Nile Green," a very fashionable shade of bluish-green. $350-$500.

Left:
Back view of the Nile Green shawl.

Right:
It's easy to see why black assuit shawls are so desirable! Here's a close-up photo of a splendid shawl's complement of camels, trees, houses, etc. $300-$450 (reflecting a few small old repairs to the mesh).

Far right:
Front view of the black assuit shawl in all its splendor!

The Robe de Style—Bustles and Bows

While the popular Egyptian and Indo-Chinese dresses enhanced fashion's tubular silhouette, couture's more feminine look was often expressed via history's perennially popular bustles and panniers. In these fanciful dresses, huge bows and/or ruffles often combine to form bountiful bustles, pert panniers, and even Elizabethan "bum rolls."

The twenties' fascination with Marie Antoinette's eighteenth century gowns is evident in George Plank's witty and wonderful *Vogue* cover! An enormous bow creates couture's favorite bustle effect, and the hips are emphasized by wide, draped side panniers. The wild Art Deco fan pays homage to ancient Greece, with a sexy satyr chasing a nymph! Her hair is styled in a towering do. (April 15, 1923)

Close-up of the bustle-pouf/bum roll, panniers, and gathered skirt.

Back view of a fanciful frock (perhaps worn to a masquerade) in pink silk taffeta. The back is gathered in two ruffled poufs reminiscent of an Elizabethan "bum roll"; they extend to dramatic eighteenth century side panniers lined in mint green (our panniers have been lightly padded with acid free paper to show them to best advantage).

Note couture's new deep v-neck, set off to the best advantage with a long rope of Tecla pearls! Pochoir ad for Tecla Pearls, *Gazette du Bon Ton*)

Front view of the gown, showing the v-neck with its tantalizing turnover collar of contrasting mint green. The skirt is gathered from a low piped waistline which comes to a center "v" in front, echoing the v-neckline. Note that the skirt, a bit lower in back, is also lined in mint green. Our lady has accessorized with an eighteenth century style wig, and long ropes of pearls. $250-$500 (price reflects some scattered small holes hidden in the gown's gathers).

Tantalizing Tubular Evening Gowns

For evening, fashion's long, tubular silhouette was often presented by a slim column of beaded splendor. As *Harper's Bazar* advised:

> *"The straight-hanging beaded frock is much favored by the French women just now…Chanel has consistently made, for several seasons, the straight-hanging chemise frock, eight or ten inches from the floor. It is very simple in line; in fabric and embroidery it is gorgeous. Gown above of white georgette crepe embroidered in crystal and rhinestones, is typical. Much of smart Paris wears it. (April 1923)*

Pola Negri, silent film vamp and paramour of Rudolph Valentino, poses in a magnificent "straight-hanging beaded frock." Slight gathers at the sides emphasize the low waist; the hem is fashionably scalloped. Before coming to Hollywood, "Madame" Negri had married (and divorced) a Polish count, giving her the title of "Countess Dombski" and starting a vogue for Hollywood "royalty." She wears a steamy look, a string of pearls (real, no doubt), and satin pumps with "Colonial" rhinestone buckles. Noted on the back of this studio portrait: "Pola Negri, European film star, who is at work on her third American picture for Paramount—*The Spanish Dancer!* (1923)

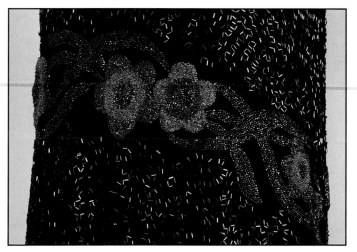

Art Deco at its finest! This crimson and black coq feather fan has three amber celluloid sticks and original silk tassel; it's 22" wide. $200-$300.

The long straight line of the tubular silhouette is exquisitely expressed in this lovely silk georgette evening frock. It's covered from neck to hem with thousands of jet bugle beads in a scrolly vermicular design. Slashing diagonally across the front is a beaded band of Art Deco flowers in pinks and reds with cobalt leaves and centers; these flowers are repeated at each side of the petal hemline. Crystal and red bugle beads border the bateau neck, hem, and armscyes. Completing the ensemble are a pair of kid evening pumps with jet trim (see page 218), a long strand of jet beads, and a period horsehair aigrette headdress (replaced sequin band). Beaded dress, $4,000-$5,000.

Close-up of the gown's floral beadwork—Poiret-like Deco flowers with cobalt centers and leaves.

Day Wear, 1923

Frocks for day wear also clung to a choice of fashion's two favorite silhouettes: the tailored tubular chemise or the fuller, more feminine frocks with ruffles and ruches. Fabulous Art Deco printed fabrics were increasingly popular.

Costumes That Vary Their Straight Lines with Plaits and Drapes

1727—Ladies' Overblouse. Designed for 34 to 46 bust. No. 1608—Ladies' Side-plaited Frock Skirt. Designed for 34 to 50 bust. Width at lower edge about 2½ yards. The costume in medium size requires 2 yards 40-inch mephisto (red) Canton crêpe—3½ yards 40-inch white Canton crêpe—2½ yards insertion—1¼ yard 36-inch lining for bodice. The combination of this overblouse and plaited skirt makes a smart-looking costume for sports wear. The skirt is attached to a long-waisted bodice which closes on the left shoulder and under the left arm. The Egyptian motif, design 12820, which adorns the front of the overblouse, may be worked in raised or flat satin stitch with silk floss.

1732—Ladies' Overblouse. Designed for 34 to 46 bust. No. 1616—Ladies' and Misses' Side-plaited Frock Skirt. Designed for 34 to 46 bust, and 16 to 20 years. Width at lower edge about 2½ yards. The costume in medium size requires 2 yards 40-inch printed crêpe—7¾ yards ribbon for tie-strings and to trim—3¼ yards 40-inch cinder (gray) flat crêpe—1 yard 36-inch lining. This attractive sports model combines an elaborate figured overblouse with a frock skirt of a soft gray crêpe which is attached to a bodice.

1737—Ladies' and Misses' Dress. Designed for 34 to 46 bust, and 16 to 20 years. Width at lower edge about 1⅝ yard. Size 36 requires 3½ yards 40-inch blue and white printed crêpe de Chine—¼ yard 40-inch white crêpe de Chine—1½ yard insertion—3⅞ yards satin ribbon for sash. The back of this frock extends over the shoulders and joins to the band of plain crêpe de Chine giving it a square neck-line. The sleeves are of the three-quarter type also finished with bands of the plain fabric. A bloused effect is given by elastic inserted through a casing which is stitched underneath the dress and concealed by a sash of satin ribbon with fringed ends.

DESCRIPTIONS CONTINUED ON PAGE 75

Dress 1742

Overblouse 1732
Frock Skirt 1616

Overblouse 1727
Frock Skirt 1608
Embroidery 12820

Dress 1737

Dress 1659
Embroidery 12820

Dress 1733

1727 1732
1608 1616 1742 1733

1737 1739 1740 1659

Dress 1739

Dress 1740

Patterns may be purchased from any Pictorial Review Agent in the United States and Canada or by mail, postage prepaid, if you address the Company, 222 West 39th Street, New York City.

Pictorial Review for July 1923 pictures the tubular silhouette for day, with "Costumes That Vary Their Straight Lines with Plaits and Drapes." The bold Art Deco print at center, #1737, has a slight bloused effect that *Pictorial Review* advises is "given by elastic inserted through a casing…and concealed by a sash of satin ribbon…" This is a popular method of emphasizing the ever lowering waist. Two smart frock skirt and overblouse combinations are pictured at upper left; the one at right, #1732, is an Egyptian-inspired "Caravan Print." A devastating "Egyptian Drape" print frock is pictured at bottom, second from right, #1739. Note that the length shown is just above the ankles. In 1923, *Vogue Shopping Service* offers similar ready made frocks for between $16.75 and $45.

This silk crepe de Chine print frock is similar to the one at center in *Pictorial Review*'s illustration. Its long, tubular lines perfectly display its "moderne" Art Deco geometric print. The wide bateau neckline is piped in white silk braid, as is the modish "cape" back. The waistline, virtually non-existent, is accented by a white grosgrain tie belt (replacement). The short sleeves are cut in one with the dress and seamed at shoulders only. It's "slip-on" style. $200-$300.

Clad in a similar short-sleeved tube, this fashionable flapper carefully buffs her nails in this whimsical pochoir from *Art Gout Beaute*. Note her stylish black Colonial pumps and favorite bangle bracelets!

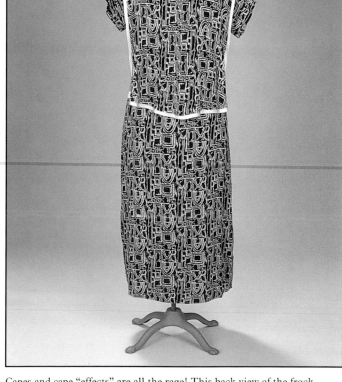

A pouch style beaded bag with an Egyptian scarab motif. The "French ivory" celluloid frame is both etched and hand-painted in an Art Deco design. The handle is knotted silk braid. These "pouch" bags were a fashionable alternative to the flat envelope "clutch" bags that were clutched in the hand or tucked under the arm. $200-$300 (noting a few missing beads).

Capes and cape "effects" are all the rage! This back view of the frock shows the chic cape back, which is attached at the shoulders and edged with white silk braid.

Frock Skirts and Overblouses...A Perfect Duo For Tennis And Golf!

By 1923, fashion's predominating tubular silhouette posed a dilemma for the popular skirt and blouse separates: how does one get a skirt to stay on when there's virtually no waistline?! The "frock skirt" was a practical solution—the skirt was simply attached to a camisole-slip top, thus no more slipping waistbands, no more unsightly indentations to mar that long lean look! These frock skirts, paired with overblouses or sweaters, had *style*, *versatility* and *comfort*; their freedom of movement made them perfect for active sports like tennis and golf. Though they were worn through the remainder of the decade, they're hard to find today.

Right:
The practical frock skirt! In this fine example, ca. 1922-25, the skirt portion is a checkerboard pattern, woven in silk faille and satin. Four large octagon pearl buttons trim each side. The camisole top is a very thin flat silk; it has a front snap closure. $125-$200.

Far right:
The May 1923 *Pictorial Review* pattern book offers this frock skirt pattern, which features a pleated skirt bottom and camisole top with vestee effect.

Frock Skirt 1608   Frock Skirt 1616

Patou was the first to use prestige couture monograms (as seen in the overblouse on the right in the fashion plate here), showing them in his Summer 1922 collection. One of the most modern of the decade's couturiers, Patou noted: "The fashions of today are indicative of a new and changed way of living..." He considered sportswear of utmost importance, as "the sportswear of one generation is the formal wear of the next." He designed sports clothes that "...are pleasant to the eye and allowing for absolute liberty of movement." Regarding their versatility, at the opening of his Deauville boutique in 1924, he observed: "If need be, a modern woman may wear a sports ensemble both in the morning and for lunch..."

In this charming pochoir from *Art Goute Beaute*, two ladies head for the courts clad in Jean Patou frock skirt and overblouse ensembles. Note the Patou monogram on the overblouse at right. Note the shoes; the lady at right wears sporty saddle oxfords, while her companion wears tennis shoes or "sneakers."

Above:
Presenting the frock skirt/overblouse ensemble! Here, our checkerboard frock skirt is paired with a chic beaded overblouse. The overblouse is one piece masquerading as two; the attached vestee snaps down the left side. The fabric is a very fine, wavy ribbed jersey in a rayon/cotton blend. The belted jacket portion is bordered with milk glass seed beads in a bold checkerboard pattern; the vestee is trimmed with parallel rows of milk glass beading. Checkerboard frock skirt, $150-$250; jersey overblouse, $300-$400 (reflecting a few tiny mends).
Above right:
Close-up of the top's superb beadwork, and the skirt's woven squares.

As charismatic tennis champ Suzanne Lenglen demonstrates, an active game demands freedom of movement! Suzanne wowed the crowds at Wimbledon in 1922—when she bounded onto the courts in Patou's short pleated skirt, v-necked top, and bright orange headband, everyone gasped! No confining girdles for Suzanne either; she wore white stockings with garters rolled to just above her knees. Suzanne was one of Patou's most famous clients; she wore his designs both off-court and on. Noted on the reverse of this photo sports card: "Mlle. Lenglen proved the greatest magnetic force in the game…A temperamental player [Suzanne was known to pout, cry and sip brandy during matches] who has never been beaten in a completed single…she has won nearly a score of Wimbledon Championships including 1919, 1920, 1921, 1922, 1923 and 1925." "Who's Who in Sport," photo sports card by Lambert & Butler, England, 1926.

Sport Shoes

Though classic canvas "tennis shoes" or sneakers are favorites for tennis, the saddle oxford or "saddle shoe" (now most associated with the 1940s and 1950s) was very popular for both tennis and golf in the twenties.

In 1923, as *National's* notes that the new "Saddle Oxfords" are "Gaining Favor Every Day," they offer "The Smartest Sport Oxford ever Designed." Perfect for sports, its soles are "scientifically molded with suction cups."

Naturally, every active woman needed a sport bandeau as jazzy as Suzanne Lenglen's! This bold striped rayon tricot "Sport Band" by Lorraine is old store stock. The celluloid buckle hides a snap closure. $50-$100.

The graphics on the reverse of the "Sport Band" card pictures women wearing it for tennis, riding, golf, and swimming.

Love all! Celebrating a smashing victory in her smart new saddle shoes, pleated skirt, knit cardigan, and Suzanne Lenglen bandeau, our champion is lifted aloft by her beau. (Snapshot, ca. 1923).

F. Scott Fitzgerald wrote of the decade's penchant for sports fashions; his Jordan Baker wears: "...her evening dress, all her dresses like sports clothes...there was a jauntiness about her movements as if she had first learned to walk upon golf courses on clean crisp mornings..." (*The Great Gatsby*, 1925)

WOW! Rare Suzanne Lenglen saddle shoes, just like those pictured in the photo of our lovely tennis champ! This pair is white suede, with brown simulated reptile "saddles." $200-$300.

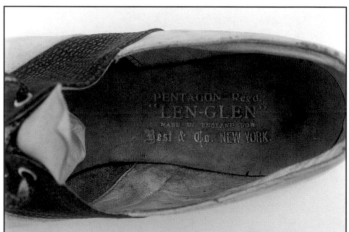

The insole of our *LEN-GLEN* saddle shoes: *Made in England for Best & Co., New York.*

"New, and very much in demand this year are colorful Fair Isle jumpers" (sweaters), as pictured on the golfer at left. Popularized by HRH, the Prince of Wales, the colorful Fair Isles were worn by both men and women. Descriptions for these two outfits: (left) "Another of the newest Fair Isle 'jumpers,' in gay color, is worn with checked tweed skirt and black velours hat"; (right) "It looks a bit like a rag rug, this wool suit of brown and white bound with white braid. The 'jumper' is yellow." (Illustration by L. Fellows, *Harper's Bazar* April 1923, noting "Fair Isle sweaters and knitted costumes from *MacDougall's*)

The Feminine Silhouette for Day Wear

The more feminine full silhouette remained a popular alternative to the slim chemise. It was a favorite with chic young women, especially during warm weather, as this romantic look lent itself well to the organdies and voiles of summer...they were adorned with feminine frills, tiers, ruffles, and even cutwork "slashes" reminiscent of the Renaissance!

Back view, showing the chic slashed sleeves and double-pleated center plackets.

This fabulous, flattering spring voile frock is something F. Scott Fitzgerald's Daisy Buchanan may have selected for a shopping excursion in Manhattan! Here, a twenty-first century "Daisy" models a dress similar in style to *National's*, but with exquisite couture detailing.

"Truly Parisian" styles as illustrated in the 1923 Spring/Summer *National Style Book*. "You will find none smarter, more distinctive or more becoming..." Headlined at center is a full-skirted frock with the latest cutout or slashed sleeves: "Note the daintiness of the new style short sleeves, open at the shoulder and trimmed with frills of self color silk ribbon..." Note that while *National's* offers this frock for $18.98, Stewart & Co. pictures similar "Paris-inspired" frocks in a 1923 *Harper's Bazar* for $49.50. (about $495 today!)

This pink and blue voile print has fashion's latest features, including cutout sleeves edged all around in tiny blue beads that also trim the bateau neck and border the three-tiered sash panels. It boasts the looser "new straight-line waist" emphasized by a low cummerbund "girdle" that fastens with two fantastic Art Deco flowers. It's mid-calf, the year's most popular length, safely between the very long and very short. $600-$800. Note her new "Colonial Tongue" pumps and stunning blue cloche hat!

Close-up of the dramatic celluloid buttons: carved, hand-painted Art Deco flowers with petals of blue lamé rick-rack.

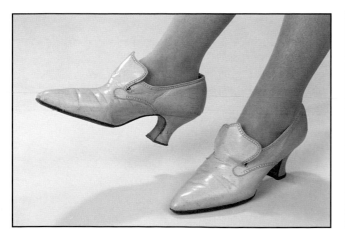

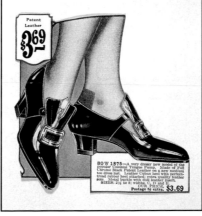

Left:
National Style Book offers chic "Colonial Tongue" pumps at $3.69. Versions of the ever popular "Colonial" style shoe have been revived many times since the days of the Pilgrims!

Far left:
Our Daisy's "Colonial Tongue" Pumps" in ivory kid, with perforated trim and French Louis heels. $75-$200.

The Reign of the Cloche

The cloche, a hat so popular it would become a symbol of the twenties, originated with a variety of cloche "prototypes" during the teens, and though the shallower-crowned bicornes, sailors, tams, and turbans that had been popular since WWI remained popular for the first two years of the decade, by 1922 the traditional deep-crowned cloche was beginning to create a stir! By 1923, it was well-established and its long reign had begun. In French, cloche means "bell," and this charismatic hat, with its deep, close-fitting crown pulled down to the eyebrows, does resemble a bell's silhouette.

In April 1923, *Harper's Bazar* announced:

> *"Paris cannot speak of hats without saying 'cloche' and 'capeline'. These two types of hats suit the two types of gowns now worn—the slim-silhouetted chemise or draped frock to accompany the little cloche; and the full-skirted picture frock [robe de style] to be worn with the large capeline."*

Harper's also noted: "The little cloche variety is sometimes referred to as the inverted pot hat," while they described the wide brimmed capeline as: "...one of those large capelines that the Parisienne wears when she isn't wearing a tiny cloche..."

One of the basic tenants of fashion is that as soon as a style has become the rage, it's time to replace it with a new look, so by fall 1923, milliners were already thinking of the cloche's successor. In September 1923, *The Illustrated Milliner*, noting the "anticipated demise of the chemise dress," observed: "One looks around for indications of the demise of the cloche, which has been with us for a long time, an incredibly long time compared with the usual duration of style crazes." It would be longer still, as the observation of *Harper's Bazar* proved true: "The cloche (like the chemise dress) is so youthful that women simply will not relinquish it."

Unsuccessful in attempts to banish the cloche, milliners resolved their dilemma by introducing every imaginable cloche variation, as *Illustrated Milliner* noted in 1923:

> *"What we find is a much chastened and modified cloche...Large hats, small hats, medium hats, hats with high crowns and flat, soft berettas, imposing turbans and demure pokes—here are just a few of the many, many styles submitted to their critical clienteles by New York's millinery houses!"*

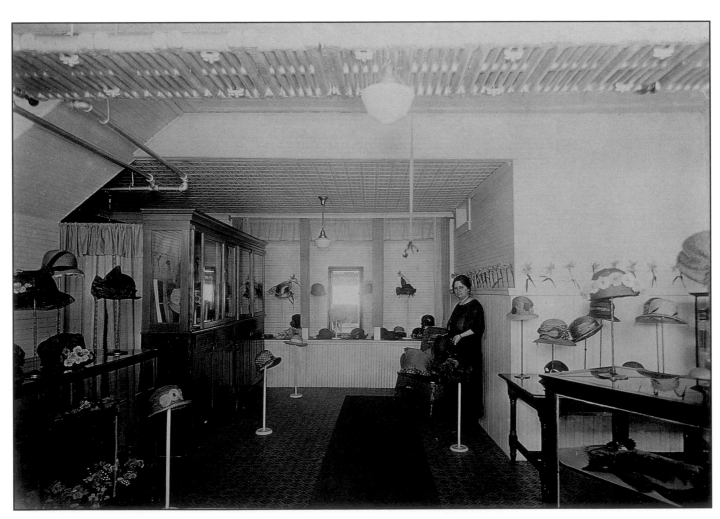

Cloches galore! A talented milliner awaits her customers in this photo taken ca. 1924; her tempting display ensures she'll have a lot of sales! Hats are arrayed on long, short, and medium stands, and the display cases hold a nice selection of trims...flowers at bottom left, feathers at bottom right.

A fine example of the tiny-brimmed, upcurving "poke" cloche. Similar to Maria Guy's cloche in the following pochoir plate (#4), this lovely brocade hat features a huge self bow bordered with straw; the front band has lattice braid trim with medallions of curly braided straw. Marcasite (marquisite) beads are scattered throughout. $300-$500.

This *Art Gout Beaute* pochoir plate depicts five haute couture hats from Marie Crozet and Maria Guy—two cloches and three capelines.

They also observed that:

> "*The introduction of many new shape ideas has not interfered so far with the prominence of the cloche and the capeline. Both are featured in tremendous variety, bearing the stamp of the new season in higher and more intricately composed crowns and more irregular brims.*"

The cloche would reign until the beginning of thirties, and it would enjoy revivals for many decades thereafter!

Many of the new variations introduced at this time became very popular in the second half of the decade, like Reboux's high, flat-topped "Directoire" cloche, "with the crown squared to resemble the stove pipe hat of Monsieur" (*Illustrated Milliner*, September 1923); by 1924, they were declaring this "high crowned Directoire hat smartest of season…" Joining the flat-crowned cloche was a parade of "ridged" crowns, "tucked" crowns, pleated crowns, "novel indented" crowns, draped-crown turban-cloches, and their kissing cousins, puffy crowned tam-cloches.

Not to be overshadowed by crowns, a wide variety of new "novelized" brims appeared, including tiny "slightly upturned" brims, medium-brims, wide-brimmed capelines, and NO brim helmets. There were *casquettes* brims (wide in front and very short in back), and brims that "turn up smartly only in back." There were even brims that sported pleats, and "flexible" brims that could be turned up or down to suit the mood of their wearer. The curved "poke" was one of the most popular brims; it paid homage to the demure bonnets of the late eighteenth century to mid-nineteenth century (which might

seem incongruous considering the spirit of the modern twenties' woman!). The poke was cherished throughout the decade, its "flattering curve" enhancing styles from capelines to helmets. Hats with brims that turned down, called "mushroom" or "drooping" brims, were also very modish, as were cloches with rolled or "off-the-face" brims. (Many examples of these new styles are shown in the companion volume to this book: *Roaring '20s Fashions: Deco*.)

To complement the cloches, trims were smart and sassy; cloches sprout flowers, feathers, and ribbons (including ribbon cockades and "rosettes"). Hats were adorned with embroidery, laces, rhinestone ornaments, buckles, and scarves. Of course, King Tut put in an appearance; the *Illustrated Milliner* saluted "Tut-ankh-amen," spotlighting a cloche from Louison's with "pompoms of Egyptian marabou on Baltic green velvet," noting that "round feather pompoms are especially chic!"

To ensure the cloche's essential "snug fit," as early as 1922 *Vogue* was advising readers: "When ordering hats, the head size should be given." By 1924, catalogs were offering: "Hats in Average Head Size or Smaller Head Size for Bobbed Hair!" During the second half of the decade, head sizes were specified in inches (22", 22-1/2", 23") and instructions were given for the proper method of measuring.

Catalogs enticed women to buy hats with irresistible ad copy; hats were: "Frenchy," "Rouguish," "Swagger," "Trig," "Jaunty," "Coquettish," and of course, "YOUTHFUL"! Parisian milliners' names were prominently mentioned—catalogs blatantly offered such delights as "an exact repro of Maria Guy." (*Chicago Mail Order*, 1922)

These are some of the new styles that would remain popular through the rest of the decade! Note that in *Vogue's Some Recent Arrivals in the Shops* section, similar cloches ranged from $18.50 to $19.50 (April 1923). In New York, the smartest hats could be found at such shops as Hattie Carnegie, Herman Patrick Tappe, Peggy Hoyt, Bruck-Weiss, and, of course, the millinery departments of the city's famous department stores.

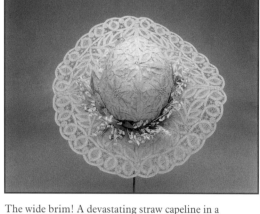

The wide brim! A devastating straw capeline in a Battenburg lace pattern with a spray of lilies-of-the-valley encircling the crown. The brim is 18" across. $500-$600.

The small brim! A tiny rolled brim of black horsehair accents this beautiful pale green ciré cloche; it's adorned with lush red velvet daisies with puffy padded centers, silvery "Old Man's Money," and orange chenille zig-zags. The crown is sectioned in pie shaped wedges piped in black. $300-$400.

A wonderful twenties' hatbox from HarrySon—at left, a clerk adjusts a lady's close-fitting cloche; at right, a lady in a large capeline admires herself in a mirror! At center, a large Spanish shawl has been draped over a scenic dressing screen. There's a brass handle on each side, as well as a more recent braid rope for carrying. $75-$100.

The *no* brim—a helmet! This chic velvet helmet is trimmed all around its curved "poke" front with large faille flowers formed of ruched ribbon cockades, accented by flocked velvet leaves. It's brimless edge is bordered with tiny lamé triangles. Label: *Evalina Hat, Utica, N.Y.* $300-$400.

Close-up of the medium-brimmed hat's exquisite silk flowers.

Two pretty flappers pose for a snapshot ca. 1922-24. The gal in front wears a "flower garden" cloche similar to ours at left.

The medium brim! This medium-brimmed cloche of lacy pink horsehair boasts a crown entirely covered with a flower garden of roses, rosebuds, and daisies! A band of pink silk tulle encircles the crown. $350-$450.

Chapter Six
1924 Women's Fashions

Timeline

Chicago, Illinois...truth is stranger than fiction! Maurine Dallas Watkins, a young reporter for the *Chicago Tribune*, covers the stories of two "celebrity" murderesses: Belva Gaertner and Beulah Annan, both jailed for "Murders Committed Under the Influence of DRINK AND JAZZ."

Belva Gaertner, age thirty-eight, a twice divorced cabaret singer, was arrested March 19, 1924, for the murder of her married boyfriend, Walter Law, a car salesman. Belva, extremely drunk on bootleg liquor, had shot Walter three times; his body, along with the gun and a bottle of gin, was found in her car. When police arrived at her apartment, Belva was still covered in Walter's blood; they found her blood-stained clothes on the floor. She told police that she was too drunk to remember what had happened. In her *Chicago Tribune* articles, Watkins quoted Belva as saying: "Why, it's silly to say I murdered Walter—I liked him and he loved me—but no woman can love a man enough to kill him. They aren't worth it because there are plenty more... Gin and guns, either one is bad enough, but together they get you in a dickens of a mess..." Belva was said to be the "Most Stylish Prisoner On Murderess Row." At trial, her defense argued that Law could have killed himself. On June 6, 1924, the all male jury quickly returned their verdict: "Not guilty!"

Beulah Annan was arrested on April 3, 1924, for the murder of her lover, Harry Kalstedt; they'd met at the laundry where they were both employed. Beulah shot Harry in bed when he told her he was leaving her. She reportedly was playing a fox trot recording of "Hula Lou" on her Victrola as she watched him die, then called her auto mechanic husband, Albert Annan, saying she'd just shot an intruder. She was very drunk when police arrived, and unable to keep her story straight, she was arrested for Harry's murder. In jail later than night, she met cabaret singer Belva Gaertner, and on April 6, the pair posed for press photos...a continuous stream of sensational articles followed. Beulah, "The Prettiest Woman on Murderess Row," received a flood of flowers, cards, and even marriage proposals! She was defended by W.W. O'Brien, a flamboyant attorney with a genius for manipulating the press. Though Beulah changed her story several times, at her trial she claimed that there was a gun on the bed, and "we both reached for it and it just went off!" After she learned another female prisoner had been sentenced to life, Beulah decided it would be a good idea to claim she was pregnant. On May 25, an all male jury deliberated two hours before returning a verdict of "Not guilty!"

Ms. Watkins subsequently returned to Yale and wrote a play, *Chicago!*, based on the two women's bizarre stories. Beulah Annan became "Roxie Hart" and Belva Gaertner, "Velma Kelly." W.W. O'Brien, Beulah's flashy lawyer, was "Billy Flynn." Though the names were changed, the crimes remained essentially the same. The play opened on December 30, 1926, at the Music Box Theatre in New York; it enjoyed 172 performances. In 1928, Cecil B. DeMille made Watkins's play into a movie, also entitled *Chicago!* There have been several subsequent plays and movies, including the spectacular 2002 Oscar winning musical, *Chicago!*

Also in 1924, Mohandas Gandhi begins a twenty-one day fast for unity in India, and IBM, (International Business Machines) is founded by Thomas Watson, who claimed: "Machines can do the routine work." In October, Andre Breton defines the growing Surrealist art movement in *Manifeste du Surrealisme*.

January 21: Lenin dies; Stalin begins eliminating his rivals.

February 12: George Gershwin's electrifying "Rhapsody in Blue" is performed at Aeolian Hall in New York City by the Paul Whiteman Orchestra, with Gershwin at the piano.

April 1: Adolph Hitler jailed regarding Beer Hall Putsch.

May 10: J. Edgar Hoover becomes Director of the Federal Bureau of Investigation, introducing training academy, fingerprint file, and science crime lab.

May 21: Wealthy teenagers Nathan Leopold and Richard Loeb murder fourteen-year-old Bobby Franks; the nation is riveted by reports of this "thrill" killing. Leopold and Loeb sent a ransom letter to the Franks demanding $10,000. Though Bobby's body was found in a culvert later that night, glasses belonging to Nathan Leopold were found near the body. The pair, claiming they'd killed Bobby for the fun of it, confessed. On July 21, the case opened in criminal court before Judge Caverly. The famed Clarence Darrow defended the pair, and in his August 22 summation, he gave the speech that saved them from the hangman, pleading: "You may hang these boys; you may hang them by the neck until they are dead, but in doing it you will turn your face toward the past." It must have been effective; on September 19, Judge Coverly sentenced them to ninety-nine years, life without parole, at Joliet. On January 28, 1936, Richard Loeb's cellmate attacked him with a razor; he died from his wounds at age thirty-two. In March 1958, after thirty-two years in prison, Nathan Leopold was paroled; he moved to Puerto Rico where he died in 1971 of a heart attack.

June 20: Diaghilev's *Ballet Russes* "Le Train Bleu" debuts; it is an avant garde "sports" ballet conceived by Jean Cocteau, with curtain by Picasso and fashions by Chanel. The opening scene is an exclusive beach, where passengers have just disembarked from the famous "Le Train Bleu." *Vogue's* reviewer comments: "To begin with, the Picasso curtain...terrific!...dresses by Chanel are perfect...girls with tennis racquets, men with golf clubs, bathing customs..."

September 15: Legendary Saks Fifth Ave. opens in New York. Sterling silver pocket flasks sell out immediately!

October 1: Philosopher, humourist, movie actor, and columnist Will Rodgers begins a nationwide tour. Rogers endeared himself to "plain folks" with down-home witticisms like: "I never met a man I didn't like." Part Cherokee Indian, Will once remarked: "My folks didn't come on the Mayflower, but they met the boat"!

November 4: Calvin Coolidge is elected President by a landslide. "Silent Cal" pronounces "The Business of America is Business"!

December 30: NEWS FLASH!!! Edwin Hubble announces the existence of other galaxies—we're no longer the only galaxy in the universe! Hubble, using the new 100 inch Mount Wilson telescope, discovers that Andromeda, our nearest neighboring galaxy, is some one million light years away from Earth.

On the Silent Screen

MGM Studio is founded as Goldwyn and Mayer merge with Loew's. *Greed*, Von Stroheim's classic realism film, is released. Douglas Fairbanks stars in *The Thief of Baghdad*, and Valentino in the eighteenth century theme *Monsieur Beaucaire*. (When a *Chicago Tribune* reviewer reported that Rudy, instead of being "the ideal lover" was more of a "Pink Powder Puff," an outraged Rudy challenged him to a duel.) John Barrymore stars in *Beau Brummel*. Pola Negri vamps in *Forbidden Paradise*, and Mae Murray in *Circe*. Lubitsch's classic comedy *The Marriage Circle* debuts, as does the risqué *Dante's Inferno*. German Shepherd star Rin-Tin-Tin is introduced in *Find Your Man*.

Favorite New Recordings

New tunes include Gershwin's "Rhapsody in Blue"; "Show Me the Way to Go Home," by Ted Lewis and his jazz band; and "What'll I Do," by the Paul Whiteman orchestra.

In Literature

Michael Arlen's *The Green Hat*, is published; some say his bad girl heroine, Iris Storm, is based on the life of Nancy Cunard, shipping heiress and Bad Girl of the decade. Arlen adapts it for a 1925 play, with Tallulah Bankhead as Iris. (Tallulah is scantily clad in luscious lingerie in many scenes!) In 1928, it's made into *A Woman of Affairs*, the classic silent film starring Greta Garbo and John Gilbert. Also published are Edwin Forster's *A Passage to India*, Mark Twain's autobiography, and Edna Ferber's *So Big*.

In Fashion 1924—The Tube Reigns Supreme!

As the long, tubular chemise reached its apex this year, *Harper's Bazar* exclaimed: "Though other silhouettes exist, none has the prestige enjoyed today by the tube!" Day dresses were long, straight and simple, and "devoid of fussy draperies"; many were completely beltless. Even the beloved tunic achieved an elongated look—it was very straight, usually about seven-eighths length, and on those that had a bit of flare, it was placed very low, as a bottom border. The versatile tailored suit remained a staple for day wear, and creative Chanel designed a culotte or "pantalet" suit that received a lot of attention. By fall, many couturiers were beginning to show the shorter dresses and natural waistline accents that are covered in *Roaring '20s Fashions: Deco*. Marcel Rochas opened in Paris this year.

Couture Trends

Vogue noted the "Soviet Season" as couture's "Penchant for the Peasant" continued. Chanel's affair with Russian Grand Duke Dimitri, ca. 1922-24, inspired her opulent tunics, Russian embroideries, and lavish fur trims. For evening, daring women flaunted couture's bared backs and low necklines. Chanel showed deep décolletage on *short* chiffon dance frocks, and Cheruit created a black satin frock that came to just below the knees. For working women, *Vogue* advocated Chanel-inspired "simple black frocks that can be accessorized with scarves, gloves and cloche hats." Scarves, both matching and contrasting, were ultra chic, and *Harper's* noted a new scarf trend: "The Scarf Lives On—one of its happiest applications is as the hip girdle of a frock of contrasting color..." *Harper's* advised that Chanel's "artificial pearls of superlative luster, color and weight, are among the smartest foibles of the moment!" (October 1924)

Buttons continued in the mode; they were used "in every conceivable way on dresses—even evening gowns." Patou received raves for his dashing day frock with vertical rows of buttons on either side of a wide girdle belt, and his crepe de Chine dresses with matching printed coats were extremely popular. Both Patou and Vionnet offered a more feminine silhouette by emphasizing the natural waistline. Vionnet presented a devastating Directoire coat with tucks at the natural waist, prompting Baron de Meyer to exclaim: "Madame Vionnet's coat has a waistline that is almost normal"! Molyneux continued to stress simplicity: "My new models will remain very simple in line...I shall keep the waistline low; yes, I've heard some houses mean to raise it, though my skirts will remain abbreviated as the type of suit I sponsor..." (*Harper's Bazar*, October 1924)

The daring lounging pajama had taken the world of haute couture by storm, and, as *Vogue* noted, they were beginning to venture out: "...the smartest negligee and simple versions are being worn for the beach and informal lunches at Deauville and Venice Lido." In an article for *Harper's Bazar*, Baron de Meyer interviewed Molyneux, noting: "It was Molyneux who started the modern craze for this attractive and exotic looking garment called 'Pajama'... he has made a special feature of his famous English tea gown and its modern development, the trousered lounge gown..." As Molyneux informed the Baron, "Pajamas are nowadays quite the thing for private dinner parties. They suit the modern women with bobbed hair, are boyish and young, and fit into the picture. There will be several in my next collection." Pajamas are also prominently featured in the collections of Lanvin, Callot, Lelong, Vionnet, and Patou and, of course, Poiret—who'd rocked the fashion world as early as 1911 with the famed "Harem Pantaloons" that his wife Denise introduced at their "1002 Night" soiree.

The latest trends, "First Noted" by *Harper's Bazar* included:" The 'costume complete' [ensemble concept] is now accepted and established...and the long tube silhouette...also the scarf; today almost every costume has a scarf. The shingle haircut, shorter, smoother and closer to the head than the bob, has now superceded the bob. Chanel pearls, very popular today, were first shown in *Harper's* February issue"; and, "ostrich as a trimming for evening gowns and feather boas—a strong fashion today." They foresaw plaids, "strong in the mode today and growing stronger." Herman Patrick Tappe exclaims: "There is nothing more refreshing, more buoyant, more youthful than PLAID!" (October 1924)

Smart Shops and Catalogs Interpret the Mode for the "Average Woman"

Butterick's 1924 Summer Fashion Quarterly pictured skirts that were the longest yet—just above the ankle. Long tubular chemises were prevalent; many were beltless, while others had a separate narrow buckle belt or narrow self-belt that tied in back. Side bows often fluttered from waistlines; some waistlines were accented at the sides with pintucks or shirring, giving a mere hint of feminine curves. Sleeves were either short—between elbow and shoulder—or long and tight, and some new sleeveless styles were shown for day wear. Many sleeves flared; one new "Antoinette" sleeve was open and flaring from the elbow to wrist. "Mannish" ties flew from collars, and narrow ribbon ties fluttered from v-necks.

"Capettes," frocks with cape-backs, were all the rage; capes were either attached to the frock or detachable. Long sleeveless jumpers, worn with mannish blouses were smart.

Knicker ensembles with long "sleeveless jackets" (vests) were shown; long vests were also worn with riding breeches. Coats were most often narrow and tubular; many had surplice fronts, though some were double breasted. They were generally either full or seven-eighths length. Many coats also had either attached or detachable capes.

For evening, *Butterick* advised: "Beaded dresses or lace gowns are distinctly the more elegant type of evening dress" and, "A moderate décolletage, sleeveless and beltless effects and a slightly longer skirt than in day clothes are correct." Bows, fan-shaped smocking and ribbon flowers often highlighted the left hip.

National Style Book for Fall 1924 offered styles with many of couture's latest features: "It is a real pleasure to offer you such handsome dresses at these money saving prices"! Of note is their robe de style afternoon dress in georgette and lace, which featured "the very latest style Cape Collar..." It extended over the shoulders and arms in front, "giving the effect of short sleeves." This cape collar or "Bertha" effect would last into the thirties! Beadwork and/or "peasant" embroidery decorated innumerable frocks; velveteen and satin were used even for day dresses.

Catalogs quickly adopted couture's favorite buttons, and rows marched down the sleeves and sides of both frocks and coats. Noting that "The scarf is an indispensable accessory this season," *National's* showed scarves draped around many models; they were either separate or attached to coordinating or matching frocks and coats.

1924 Fashions

"To drive one's own car is now a smart modern practice," as *Harper's Bazar* announced in their August 1924 issue! Driving one's own car had become the mark of a modern, independent woman and, as the adventurous woman who took to the road discovered:

"There are seven million pleasure seeking, mile-eating motor cars in the United States, and in the summer about half of them are seized with the wanderlust of sight-seeing fever and are off to somewhere over the best roads they can find..." (Vogue, 1920)

At the wheel of her sports car, "The Yellow Peril," socialite Peggy Otis speeds down Rome's ancient Appian Way, clad in a smart auto duster and cloche hat (properly pulled down to her eyebrows, of course). Peggy, who lived in Italy during the twenties, was the daughter of Harrison Grey Otis, a prominent diplomat from New England. Peggy noted "Myself" at the bottom of this marvelous snapshot taken ca. 1924.

This smart pair of nubby-textured silk/linen gauntlet driving gloves is trimmed with contrasting brown pigskin at the bracelet closure, between the fingers, and cuffs. $50-$75. Gauntlets were yet another twenties' favorite with a long fashion history; exquisitely embroidered gauntlet gloves had been worn by royalty during the Renaissance!

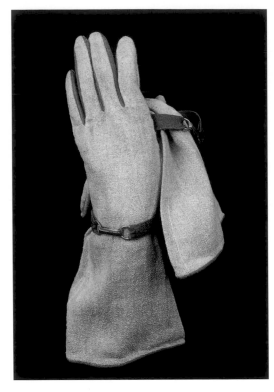

Mode Pratique

LE SAMEDI
29 MARS 1924
N° 13 :   o fr. 5o

This charming *Mode Pratique* cover depicts an independent flapper at the wheel of her sports car. She's clad in a chic duster, cloche hat, and gauntlet motoring gloves. (March 19, 1924)

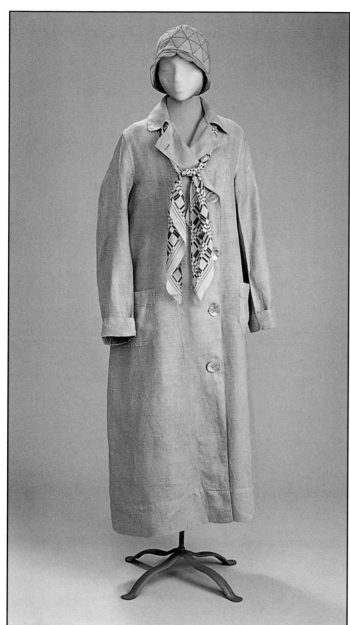

A necessity for motoring in one's own car! This coarsely woven natural linen duster features a left-of-center closure with large mother-of-pearl buttons, two roomy patch pockets, and cuffed sleeves. It's paired with a smart cloche hat, and geometric silk print scarf. Period catalogs offer dusters for about $10, while at Lord and Taylor a "motor coat with striped borders" is $75. Today's collectors may pay around $75-$150 for plain versions and $300 up for the more ornate.

On this Art Deco "Triangles" cloche, light and dark yellow triangles mix with triangles embroidered in a squiggly vermicular design; all are bordered with bright orange embroidery. A tiny scalloped brim frames the face. The long silk scarf boasts geometric patterns of yellow, white, brown, and green...scarves have become a very important accessory! Cloche, $200-$300; scarf, $40-$75.

Popular since the teens, the Auto Cap remained a favorite for motoring in the first half of the twenties. *National Style Book* offers this "becoming Auto Cap," reasonably priced at just $.59! An "Auto or Complexion Veil" was threaded across the visor through loops at either side and tied beneath the chin; it's offered separately for $.79. (1922)

This smart tweed linen auto cap is endorsed by none other than America's Sweetheart, Mary Pickford! A black silk georgette scarf is threaded through the side loops to fasten under the chin. $150-$250.

Close-up of the *Mary Pickford* label.

"Miami Fla. To Penn Yan NY or Bust"...and this looks like *BUST*! Demonstrating the practicality of the auto duster, these two flapper gals attempt to get their finicky Flivver back on the road again. The gent by the car window isn't wearing a duster, nor does he appear to be doing any of the dirty work!

Coats for Day Wear

Coats followed fashion's long, slender silhouette. Buttons were one of fashion's smartest accents in 1924—vertical rows of buttons emphasized the long, lean silhouette as they marched up and down the sides of coats and frocks. *Harper's Bazar* claimed they first predicted this penchant for buttons and "...now they are used in every conceivable way on dresses, even on evening gowns." (February 1924)

"If you were in New York this winter, you would see the most smartly dressed women wearing handsome coats of soft Bolivia cloth, for it is fashion's favorite coating for fall and winter...woven from a mixture of wool, artificial silk and cotton, and made on the newest straight UNBELTED lines, low closing held by a large fancy button..." The 1924 *National Style Book* entices women to buy their "Beautiful Fur Trimmed Coat For 'Dress and General Wear'"! It's "smartly trimmed with decorative heavy stitching and a close row of buttons...An especially desirable and fashionable feature of this handsome model is the modish convertible 'stand-up' collar and cuffs of Mandel fur, a dense, soft, warm fur." *National's* price is $35, while at New York's prestigious Stewart & Co., a similar coat "inspired by Paris, approved by Fifth Avenue and reproduced by Stewart & Co. for the woman of discerning taste" is $69.50.

A splendid chocolate brown coat of "Bolivia," a diagonally woven plush pile with a silky, lustrous sheen. Each side is accented with six parallel rows of chain-stitched embroidery from the front slash pockets to the hem; adjacent, a row of ten decorative button loops adorns the side seams. Two covered buttons trim the sides of the pockets; the cuffs are trimmed with a triple row of embroidered chain-stitching and a single covered button. Center front closure with a large pleated-effect celluloid button; a smaller matching button fastens the "modish convertible stand-up collar" of shearling lamb. Brown and cream plaid lining; no label present. $350-$500.

The long, lean silhouette, fur trimmed and embroidered, as depicted in *Art Gote Beaute's* delightful pochoir, ca. 1924. Note the chic ensemble look at left—a dress with matching seven-eighths length coat.

"Mary and Doug arrive in New York, Dog, Baggage and All!" On the back of this news photo dated February 15, 1924, is noted: *"Photo shows Mr. and Mrs. Douglas Fairbanks, or as they are better known to the movie world, 'Mary and Doug,' as they arrived in New York straight from the Pacific Coast, dog, baggage and all. They received a hearty reception in the metropolis...Photo supplied by International Newsreel, 226 William St., New York City."* Mary's wearing a fashionable tubular coat with a big convertible fur collar, cuffs, and hem.

Frocks for Day Wear

STRIPES, both woven and printed, accent fashion's vertical lines while providing that important Art Deco geometrical look.

This chic brown straw cloche features a "flexible" brim, which may be worn turned up as shown or "drooping" down. It's trimmed with brown grosgrain ribbon in a floral pattern, and worn with a brown rayon jersey striped scarf. Cloche, $200-$350; scarf, $35-$45. Note that scarves are very fashionable. As *Harper's* proclaims: "The scarf lives on...Today almost every costume has a scarf...one of its happiest applications is as the hip girdle of a frock of contrasting color..." (August 1924)

This witty plate from *Art Gout Beaute* depicts *"Madame Librarian"* in a chic tubular day dress that combines a horizontally striped bodice with a vertically striped skirt. The bodice crosses surplice style to button at left; the skirt features a scalloped hem.

Right:
A very stylish Art Deco day dress in rayon jersey knit, woven in both satin and bouclé finishes to produce the chic horizontal and vertical stripes. It's the fashionable tunic style, with a vertically striped bodice and underskirt; the tunic skirt and sleeves are horizontally striped. Each side of the tunic is adorned with a row of twenty-two Bakelite buttons placed on mocha braid trim, and two matching buttons accent the low waistline. The bodice portion features a mocha crepe de Chine vestee trimmed with appliquéd strips of brown soutache; it has a snap closure at left. The slightly belled cuffs of the long, tight sleeves are accented with three Bakelite buttons. $350-$500 (shown with a brown Bakelite "arrow" necklace).

Far right:
A close-up photo of the jersey frock's row of decorative buttons!

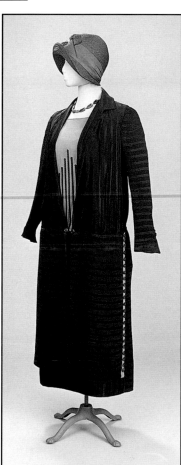

Though evening wear had long been both sleeveless and décolleté, sleeveless day wear had long been thought "indecent." This ban on sleeveless day wear was yet another convention to be abolished in the twenties, and though outraged old fogies screamed "SCANDALOUS!", as early as 1922 *Delineator* was advising: "...the very short sleeve just covering the top of the arm is used a great deal."

Vogue, however, in an article featuring advice to the "Working Woman," cautioned that for the office "...sleeveless street dresses and tight dresses are vulgar"!

SHORT SLEEVES UNDER A CAPE, STRIPES AND DRAWN-WORK ARE EXCEEDINGLY SMART

Dress 5199

Dress 5192

Dress with Cape 5197
Hat 4973
Transfer 10138

Other views and descriptions are shown on page 76

KEY TO THE MATERIAL QUESTION ON PAGE 42   9   BUTTERICK QUARTERLY *&* SUMMER 1924

Three long, tubular frocks from *Butterick's Summer 1924 Quarterly*...and the red frock at left is scandalously *sleeveless*! Though short sleeves are most common, sleeveless styles are beginning to be shown for day wear by 1924. Many frocks, like the three shown here, are "slip-overs"; no closures are necessary as wide bateau or deep v-necklines permit them to simply slip over the head. In this issue, *Butterick's* advises on fashion's newest features, noting: "The vogue of very short sleeves and sleeveless blouses and dresses...an excessively slender, straight silhouette...the growing importance of tailored or 'boyish' styles for day clothes in dresses as well as suits," and "many beltless styles." In 1924, just before skirts begin their historic ascent, hemlines are at their longest. Though *Butterick's* shows hemlines just above the ankles, they advise readers there's a change coming, with: "Skirts shorter, several of the French couturiers making them twelve inches from the ground for day clothes, the average being eight to ten inches for day and sport clothes and six to eight for evening." Note the enchanting Japanese parasols, and the variety of shoe styles: strapped pumps, including T-straps and cutout straps. A capeline "poke" is worn with the sleeveless red dress, while a smart new helmet is shown with the caped ensemble at right.

Far left:
A lovely SLEEVELESS day dress with graduated white satin stripes bordered with emerald green satin on a sheer silk background; these stripes are woven into the fabric, not applied. Wide openings that extend barely over the shoulders provide the bold new "sleeveless" look. The low waist is accented with triangular faux pockets; a bit of fullness is provided by unpressed pleats which fall from these pocket flaps. Loose, flirty ties float down the back. Note the popular v-neck with wide turnover collar; this slip-over dress needs no fastenings. $250-$350. Her straw Battenburg capeline is pictured on page 206.

Left:
Back view, showing flirty self tie belt, and armholes.

Looking like they just stepped from the *Butterick's* fashion plate shown opposite, these two fashionable gals enjoy a ride on the carousel! Note the very long skirts, smart neck ties, chic cloche hats, and bags. The gal on the left has selected snappy strappy pumps, while her companion wears the ever popular Mary Janes. (Snapshot, taken 1924)

Shoes

"High society" in the twenties, of course, selected haute couture shoes for their haute couture gowns! They patronized such legendary shoemakers as Andre Perugia and Salvatore Ferragamo, whose shoes are considered works of art today.

Andre Perugia claims the distinction of being the first of the "haute couture" shoe designers. An eccentric artist who opened his first shop at age sixteen, Perugia was so enthralled by his shoes that he even *talked* to them (and, it would seem, they listened!) He rose to prominence during the teens, when he designed a series of jeweled slippers to complement Paul Poiret's opulent oriental gowns. From 11 Faubourg Saint Honoré in Paris, Perugia created some of the most imaginative shoes of the twenties—shoes with innovative new heels and vamps, and sensuous straps! Straps were often the focal point of twenties shoes, and one of Perugia's most imitated designs featured straps that crossed in the shape of a figure eight. Another of his most famous creations was the 1928 "Turban Sandal," designed to complement Josephine Baker's trademark turban; these shoes featured a draped heel that tied handkerchief style around the ankle and had scandalous open toes!

These stunning gold and silver lamé pumps look like they stepped straight out of Van Gogh's *Starry Night*— they undoubtedly danced many starry nights away! The decorative gold leather cutwork and sensational interlocking circle straps shout "Art Deco"; they've been a feature on "society" shoes since the early twenties. Note the new "modish plain medium round toe" and gold leather heels in the less curved Louis style fashionable at this time. Straps fasten with two pearl buttons. Stamped on insole: *"John Wanamaker, Philadelphia, New York, Paris, London."* $250-$350 (noting some small splits in the lamé).

Salvatore Ferragamo, a "Cinderella" shoemaker, came from a poor family of Italian farmers; at age nine, he made his first pair of shoes for his sister's confirmation, using tools and materials borrowed from a local cobbler. He studied in Naples, and at age fourteen, opened a shop in his parents' home. At sixteen, he left for Hollywood, soon to become "Shoemaker to the Stars." Ferragamo's Roman sandals and cowboy boots can still be seen in silent classics by D.W. Griffith and Cecil B.

DeMille. Stars like Gloria Swanson, Mary Pickford, and Greta Garbo were among those who flocked to his shop on Hollywood Boulevard. He was noted for creating shoes from unusual materials, including Spanish shawls, tree bark, and even hummingbird feathers! In homage to King Tut, he crafted "Pyramid" shoes, with heels in the shape of an inverted pyramid. In 1927, Ferragamo returned to Italy and set up shop in Florence.

Other famous "bottiers" of the decade include the Parisian firm of Hellstern & Sons. Famed for their extravagantly beaded vamps, they also produced some of the era's most fabulous fetish footwear. The prestigious House of Pinet was known for ornately beaded, embroidered pumps. A sign in front of Yantorny's Paris salon declared them to be "The Most Expensive Custom Shoemaker in the World"; they were especially noted for their exquisite alligator and reptile shoes. The Swiss Bally Shoe Company created some of the decade's most sought after shoes. Bob, Inc., an American company, was noted for spectacular Art Deco dance pumps with parallel rows of rhinestone buckles over the vamps. Delman was famous for their exquisite shoes; a marvelous publicist, Herman Delman enticed film stars to endorse his shoes. He was the first to insist the "Delman" name appear in his shoes as well as the store name. The prestigious I. Miller stores (in New York, at 562 Fifth Avenue) carried couture footwear, including some Perugia creations. They enticed women to buy with poetic ad copy: "Beautiful creations with the youthful charm of spring and lines as deftly modeled as the peeping petals of a flower." (*Harper's Bazar*, April 1923).

Other fine New York shoe shops or "booteries" include: Cammeyer, 677 Fifth Avenue (lists no prices but "illustrated brochure will be mailed on request"); Frank Brothers Fifth Avenue Boot Shop (near 48th Street); Andrew Alexander (548 Fifth Ave.) with "Shoes designed for those who appreciate fine workmanship and well-bred restraint in the style," $12-$16, and K.M. Stone Importers (12-24-16 E. 22nd St.). Henning Custom Made Boot Shop (579 Madison Ave), offered shoes that "spell sophistication, demureness, languour or tailleur—whatever the custom or the moment demands..." The French Bootery, 36 West 50th Street, met "smart about town needs...perfectly adapted to the requirements of sportswear," $15-$16.50, and The Peacock Shop boasted "The Smartest Fifth Avenue Shoe Styles" at around $9.85-$14.

PERUGIA
BOTTIER
▼
11, FAUBOURG SAINT HONORÉ PARIS

"Perugia Bottier" advertising card (*Harper's Bazar*, August 1924).

CHEZ PERUGIA
OU
LE BOTTIER A LA MODE

N° 7 de la Gazette.   Année 1924. — Planche 54

Chez Perugia, Pierre Mourgue's delightful pochoir, depicts an elegant couple at the famed House of Perugia. The imperious lady inspecting a shoe through a lorgnette wears a chic tubular fur-trimmed coat and very pointed two-strap pumps. Her dapper companion is clad in a slim topcoat, voluminous scarf, and spats; he carries a walking stick and snappy fedora. Another lady, seated by the window, considers a high-heeled shoe. Note the saleslady's selection of shoes—all with extremely pointed toes! (*Gazette du Bon Ton*, 1924)

Note that these extremely pointed shoes are the exception rather than the rule; they're not shoes the average woman would have worn. More moderately pointed toes and curved "Louis" heels were very much in vogue in the teens, and they remained fashionable until the second half of the twenties, when couturiers decreed that the new, shorter frocks cried for shoes with rounded toes and straighter, higher heels. High heels were yet another ancient feature; they were worn during the Renaissance. In documents dating to 1595, shoes made for Queen Elizabeth I are described as having "high heels and arches"! The curved "Louis" or "French" heel was named for France's illustrious seventeenth century "Sun King," Louis XIV.

The curved "Cupid's Bow" strap, though rare, was a feature that had been seen since around the turn of the century. By the early twenties, both decorative straps and Art Deco cutouts were growing ever more "modish."

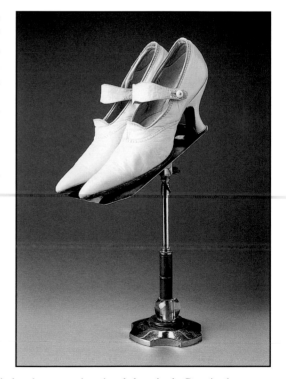

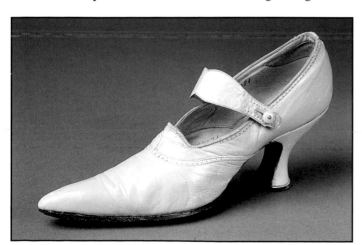

Close-up view of the dramatic pointed toes on the shoes at right!

One might think that the extremely pointed shoes in the Perugia plate were simply an artist's stylization, but these exceptional shoes show they really did exist...perhaps inspired by the outrageously long, pointed poulaines of the Middle Ages. Understated elegance is evident in their long, sweeping lines, graceful cupid's bow straps, discreet perforated trim, and graceful, sculpted Louis heels. This pair is well-loved and well-worn; barely visible, the word "STONE" (perhaps K.M. Stone, noted on page 216) is stamped on the inner soles. Ca. 1918-24. $75-$150 (reflecting worn condition).

217

Shoes for the "Average Woman"

While Perugia patrons purchased the crème da la crème of footwear, the average woman wore more practical, comfortable, and economical shoes. Since straps scream *chic*, marching to fashion's tune were Mary Jane one-straps, two-straps, three-straps (or more), and, of course, T-straps! Cutouts were the rage with their Art Deco drama. Though the toes of the dress shoes remained rather pointed, you'll note they were not as extreme as those at Perugia. By 1924, heels as well as toes were changing; the curved French or Louis heel was giving way to a straighter heel some catalogs dubbed the "Half-Spanish" heel.

The "Modish Medium Round Toe"! These dressy afternoon/evening pumps are black kid leather with exquisite jet vamps beaded in a Renaissance-style motif. The graceful Louis heels are almost 3" high. The maker's name on the insole is illegible, but stamped on the left side is: *"370 5164 1401; Sep. 17, 1921."* $200-300.

With "Footnotes from the World of Style," the 1924 *National Style Book* offers a nice selection of shoes for all occasions. The "Style Sensation" at top center is the shoe of the future—it features the dramatic Art Deco cutwork so popular in the second half of the decade. Note its "Half Spanish Heel" and less pointed "modish plain medium round toe," though still quite narrow. *National's* "New and Smart Lace Oxford" (top right) sports a more comfortable rounded toe. The chunky "Military" heels on the dress boots (bottom right) were also very popular, though note that while the dress boot or "High-cut Lace Shoe" is still worn, by 1924 it's beginning to fall from favor. The trendy "low" flat heel is pictured on dress shoes as well as sporty styles.

National's also pictures four chic one-strap Mary Janes, a practical style that had been worn by both men and women as early as the Renaissance. By the twentieth century, they'd become known as "Mary Janes," after a cartoon character in "Buster Brown" (introduced by the *New York Herald* in 1902).

The removable ornaments at lower left are offered separately. The large "Chic Butterfly" is a "silver-effect metal ornament set with rhinestones" that "can be worn on vamp of any pump." To its right, the "smart fan-shaped rhinestone ornament slips over any one-button strap pump."

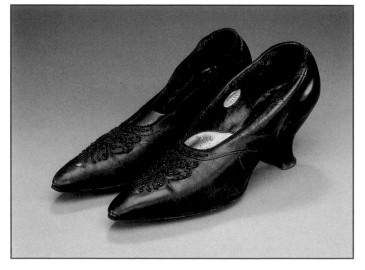

Full view of the beaded pumps, showing the Louis heel.

Opulent Orientalism!

*"In Xanadu did Kubla Khan
a stately pleasure-dome decree..."*
—Samuel Taylor Coleridge, 1816

UNE ROBE DU SOIR, DE MADELEINE VIONNET

Gazette. *Année 1923.*

Modèle déposé. Reproduction interdite.

An exquisitely designed pair of flat heeled sports or "walking" shoes; these flat heels were also called "college heels." These chic two-tone, two finish Mary Janes combine cordovan leather and camel suede. The cordovan toes are "straight tips"—finely stitched with parallel rows of camel-colored thread. Giving these shoes an Art Deco air, double rows of lattice cutwork trim the camel suede on each side; this cutwork is backed with cordovan leather. The Mary Jane straps fasten with two smoky pearl buttons. Leather soles, rubber "Grip" heels. Never worn, they're old store stock. Stamped on inner quarters is: *"Peters, St. Louis."* $250-$350.

A twentieth century Xanadu! Bringing visions of Kubla Khan's famed "pleasure-dome" to life, Thayaht's Cubist pochoir of Madeleine Vionnet's oriental *"Robe du Soir"* appeared in *Gazette du Bon Ton* in 1923. This dress beautifully expresses Vionnet's belief in fluid movement. "You must dress a body in a fabric, not construct a dress into which the body is expected to fit." You'll note that Vionnet's waistline, even as early as this, is somewhat defined.

The trendy *Chicago Mail Order* catalog takes things one step further, offering foot fetish fanciers "Fashion's Fairest Daughter," a rather risqué "Persian Anklet" that's described as: "A Classy Patent Leather Persian Ankle Bracelet from which hang Black Finish Bangles, and which fastens with a tiny black finish buckle." The anklet is shown with "beautiful 2-strap buckle cut out pumps...with military rubber heels." (1922)

219

Since the thirteenth-century journeys of Marco Polo, westerners have been enchanted by visions of the exotic East as recounted in his medieval bestseller, *The Travels of Marco Polo*. The Polos set out for the fabled court of Kublai Khan (near what is now Beijing), traveling through Armenia, Persia, and Afghanistan, over the Parmirs and along the Silk Road to Cathay (China). In *Travels*, Polo describes the palace of Kublai Khan as... "A fine marble palace, the rooms of which are all gilt and painted with figures of men and beasts...all executed with such exquisite art that you regard them with delight and astonishment...the Hall was so large that it could easily dine 6,000." Dreaming of these wonders some five hundred years later, British poet Coleridge was inspired to write his famous poem about Xanadu (Shang-du). To silence those who doubted his stories could be true, Polo avowed on his deathbed: "I have only told the half of what I saw."

By the mid-nineteenth century, even the long-isolated island of Japan revealed its splendors, following the sailing of Admiral Perry's ships into Yokohama in 1854. The West's fantasies of Japan finally became reality, causing a fervor for flavors of the Land of the Rising Sun.

"Orientalism," the West's *Dream Visions* of the East, remained a tremendously important source of inspiration to haute couture in the twentieth century—from Paul Poiret's fashion revolution of 1908 through the Roaring Twenties. The long, tubular dresses, at their extreme in 1924, lent themselves well to exotic Eastern themes, and magazines like *Vogue* and *Harper's Bazar* conjured up visions of the East with whispers of lands whose names were synonymous with sensuality, mystery, and eroticism:. "Cathay," "Indo-China," "Japan," "Hindustan," and "Persia." Western Salomes and Scheherazades dressed accordingly in saris, kimonos, burnouses!

Mah jongg, an ancient Mandarin gambling game, was introduced to America by a Standard Oil Co. executive returning from Soochow, China. It quickly became the rage; mah jongg clubs formed and soon some ten million women were meeting regularly to play, often dressing for the occasion in kimonos, paper fans, and hair ornaments!

All decked out in Japanese kimonos and lacquered hair ornaments, these three "Japanese" flappers at tea bring to mind "Peep-Bo, Yum-Yum, and Pitti-Sing" who sang "Three Little Maids from School are We" in Gilbert & Sullivan's operetta, *The Mikado*. Perfectly expressing the mood of the twenties, Pitti-Sing chants, "Life is a Joke That's Just Begun," while Yum-Yum counters, "Everything is a Source of Fun"! (Snapshot, ca. 1920-24)

Right:
Lacquered ebony jeweled hair ornaments paid homage to "Orientalism"; they were all the rage as illustrated here. The lacquered sticks are inlaid with abalone. Left, a single freshwater "pearl" with brass filigree and seed pearls. $45-$75. Right, faceted crystal beads and pearls dangle from the top and sides of this mesmerizing hair ornament. $75-$125.
Far right:
Adding a touch of oriental spice, this beautiful hand-painted paper fan pictures a lovely geisha surrounded by wisteria. $100-$200.

Close-up of the "Bird of Happiness."

Luxurious silk pongee, light as a feather! This "Coolie Coat" kimono is screen printed in a vibrant oriental design of flowering trees and exotic birds, with a vibrant front border and hemline—perfect for a mah jongg party! Coolie Coats were popular throughout the twenties and thirties; they were also called "Happy" or "Happi" coats and often came in sets with matching pajamas. Label: *"Made in Japan."* $75-$150.

Back view of Coolie Coat.

Afternoon Orientalism

For afternoon, an elegant embroidered coat and a batik printed tunic dress to enchant any audience.

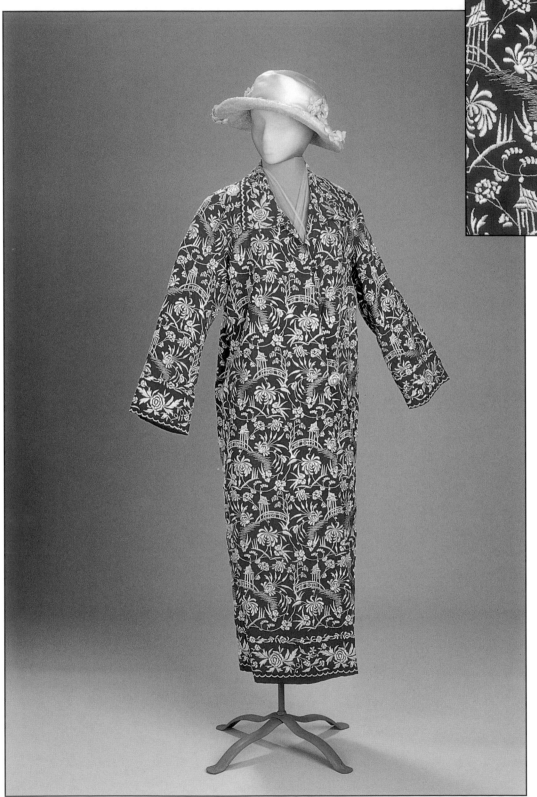

Close-up of an embroidered scene, with bridge, pagoda, and trees.

From the mysterious East, a royal blue silk crepe coat fit for any twenties' "Empress of the East." Enchanting Japanese motifs—pagodas, bridges, wisteria, and mums—are finely embroidered in white silk floss, covering the entire surface. Collar, cuffs, and hem have a border of roses. Left front surplice closure with a single rose-embroidered button. The silhouette, of course, is long and tubular. Made for export. $2,000-$4,000. (It's shown with a silk tulle vestee and white satin cloche.)

Poiret can achieve a
definite picturesque feeling in even the smartest
frock. This tube frock
he makes of white wool,
with a vivid black and
red border, woven into
the fabric, as trimming.

Far left:
By 1924, perhaps anticipating the shorter mode to
come, long two-piece tunic dresses are very chic, as
Paul Poiret's design from *Harper's Bazar's* August
1924 issue illustrates. *Harper's* notes: "Poiret can
achieve a definite picturesque feeling in even the
smartest frock. This tube frock he makes of white
wool, with a vivid black and red border woven into
the fabric as trimming." Note the slight cap sleeves,
her bangle bracelets, and the elegant matching
shawl!

Left:
Perhaps inspired by the splendor of India's Taj
Mahal, this dramatic afternoon dress, batik-printed
on navy silk velvet, is perfect for the cinema or
dining out. In two pieces, the tubular tunic top is
worn over a navy silk frock skirt with matching
printed velvet hem. A matching turban wrap and
rope of jet beads completes this magnificent
ensemble. $500-$800.

Close-up of the printed velvet "Persian" motif.

The exclusive French pochoir publication *Art Gote Beaute*
presented a very similar printed velvet in 1924. Their
version boasts bell sleeves with fur trim, which also
borders the hem.

223

Haute Couture Orientalism

Jean Patou

By 1924, Jean Patou was one of the top five couturiers in Paris, dressing such luminaries as Mary Pickford, Gloria Swanson, Louise Brooks, Lady Diana Cooper, and Josephine Baker, as well as the incomparable Dolly Sisters—who created a sensation when they modeled for Patou during his spring 1924 trip to America! In the fall of 1924, Patou, a supreme publicist, put the following ad in the New York papers:

"Mannequins Wanted for Paris: Jean Patou desires to secure three ideal types of beautiful young American women who seriously desire careers as mannequins in his Paris atelier…selection to be made at the offices of Vogue, *14th floor, 10 West 44th St. Apply Friday morning 10:00 to 12:30."*

As Patou had hoped, this ad created a furor; some five hundred hopefuls lined up outside *Vogue's* offices that Friday morning…so lovely that Patou expanded his choices to six! One of the six was Lillian Farley, known as "Dinarzade," who described modeling for Patou in her memoirs: "The salons were brightly lighted with spotlights and flowers were everywhere. Tables, seating from two to six people were placed in a single line around the walls, leaving space in the middle for the mannequins to show. At each table, in an ice-bucket, was either a bottle or magnum of champagne. The names of guests were on cards at each plate." She said she stepped into an electrified atmosphere with "…men in their correct black tailcoats, with sleek pomaded hair, the women in gorgeous evening dresses plastered with jewels. It was so hot and the air was stifling with the mixed odours of perfumes and cigarettes…"

Sports and day wear fashions were shown first, and after an intermission with a buffet supper, the evening gowns were presented: "These were the big numbers in the collection, to be photographed and sketched by every fashion periodical in the world and ordered as many as a hundred times by foreign buyers and clients." (From Lillian Farley's memoirs as quoted in *Patou*, by Meredith Etherington-Smith)

By the fall of 1924, it was rumored Patou was planning to introduce a new look—a departure from the extremely straight lines of the tubular chemise. In *Harper's* August 1924 issue, fashion commentator and photographer Baron de Mayer broke the story. After much coaxing, Patou commented: "The chemise gown is quite passé de mode. In fact, most of my really elegant clients, including important foreign buyers are very tired of it…I am, therefore, planning new developments…" Patou planned to introduce styles that highlighted the NATURAL WAIST! When de Meyer asked "Will you persuade women to forego slimness and line?" Patou replied: "Certainly not, but there a thousand ways of producing line, for line does not necessarily spell 'chemise.'" Patou didn't intend a tight waistline, but rather one *accented* by various means. Both Patou and Vionnet were emphasizing the natural waistline before mid-decade; *Harper's* also showed a Vionnet "Directoire Coat" with "a waist-line that is almost normal."

Patou was often quoted regarding his thoughts on fashion:

"Fashion is not a subject of deduction like a system of logic. It is made up of a thousand different influences. Fashion is a living thing and in consequence evolves from day to day, hour to hour and minute to minute…"

"A modern style is not a style which forgets all tradition of the past and from day to day pretends to impose a new rule. To be modern is to have the thought, the tastes and the instincts of the epoch in which one lives."

There was an intense rivalry between Patou and Chanel. Though both were famous for their revolutionary modern designs, each had a different attitude towards the women they designed for. Patou felt women should dominate their clothes rather than being "couture clotheshorses," claiming: "Women are not dolls to be dressed by designers." Chanel, in contrast, professed to "dictate" styles to her clientele. De Meyer quotes Chanel, a strong advocate of simplicity, as stating: "Having a following, I shall dictate to them, and decree 'good taste.' Good taste is to become the latest fashion, and we shall see if I am strong enough to put a stop to the ever increasing vulgarity in dress, so much a la mode just now." (*Harper's Bazar*, August 1924)

The masterpiece of haute couture shown here is a signed and numbered Jean Patou *original*—a resplendent Coromandel evening dress, the elaborate beadwork designed to resemble Japan's famed Coromandel screens. The length and vertical silhouette suggest a date ca. 1924, as does Patou's clever suggestion of a natural waistline.

SOME OF THE NEWEST INTERPRETATIONS OF THE TUBE SILHOUETTE

"Some of the Newest Interpretations of the Tube Silhouette…Though other silhouettes exist, none has the prestige enjoyed today by the tube…it was only the discerning eyes of the few which saw in it the dominating mode of the future." (*Harper's Bazar*, August 1924) *Harper's* pronouncements accompany this oriental evening tube by Lenief, that's quite similar to our original Patou gown, shown next.

Though "making an entrance" is very chic, making an *unforgettable exit* is just as desirable! Patou places the emphasis on the back with this oriental scene; its incredible beadwork defies description, and its subtle gold metallic embroidery lends an almost three-dimensional effect. Beads used include: seed beads in shades of light pink to hot pink; gold and silver seed beads; both large and small faceted marquisites; and red cabochon coral beads, both round and oval. In back only, the beading ends at a flirty bias hem flounce. The fabric is the softest of black silk velvets. In the de Meyer interview, when asked if his new collection would include velvets, Patou replied: "I consider silk velvet the king of winter materials...vive le velours!" This dress is fully lined in sheer silk crepe. $10,000-$15,000.

Close-up of the back's beadwork; the oriental motif, including a capricious bull, is worked in vivid coral, hot pink, silver mercury glass beads, and silver bugle beads.

Close-up of Patou's label: *7 Rue Saint-Florentine, Paris*. A small tag, basted to the reverse side of the label, reads what appears to be *"J570Patou"* in script.

On the front of the gown, Patou, while emphasizing the tubular silhouette with vertical beaded and embroidered bands, ingeniously accents the *natural* waistline with a scenic design that is bordered at the natural waist with a double row of light coral seed beads edged in gold. From this beaded border, the dress falls straight to its hem in front. The top portion is comprised of fine silk tulle with beaded "cloud scrolls" over black velvet; the sheer tulle alone extends from the top of the bust to the wide bateau neckline.

225

Mariano Fortuny of Venise (1871-1949)

Today the legendary Mariano Fortuny is considered more an artist than a couturier. His classic creations never followed the current mode's silhouette, but rather stood alone—timeless as the Grecian columns and Renaissance motifs that inspired them. His pleated gowns and printed silk and velvet robes are now exhibited in the world's most prestigious museums.

MARIANO FORTUNY

Grecian Plaited Dresses
Gold Printed Venetian Garments
Evening Mantles
Tea Gowns   Negligées

67, Rue Pierre-Charron
Cor. Champs-Elysées
PARIS

Fortuny advertising card. (*Harper's Bazar*, 1924)

Fortuny Fabrics, a pamphlet by Elsie McNeill, Inc. (Fortuny's American agent). Stamped on the inside is: "*Mariano Fortuny Venise*, Elsie McNeill, Inc., 509 Madison Avenue, New York." Inside, the text includes this paean to Fortuny:

"In the Palazzo Orfei, Venice, lives and works a man whose almost incredibly versatile artistry awakens again the spirit which was De Vinci...Mariano Fortuny...artist, sculptor, artisan, scientist...

"Mariano Fortuny's gifts and tireless efforts have won success in many avocations, but the creation of the Fortuny Fabrics *is one of his greatest triumphs. Velvets stamped in gold and silver... exquisite in color and texture...at once the glory and despair of the textile world, for no one can catch and duplicate the softness and everlasting durability of this artist-scientist's metal stamping. Silk tea gowns in rich, glowing, hand-dyed shades...the magnificent colors which once animated the paintings of the Venetian school... tones never repeated and never found elsewhere."*

Fortuny was born in 1871 in Granada, Spain, into a family of prominent artists. When he was only three years old, his father died of malaria, and his mother decided to move her young family to Paris. When Mariano was eighteen, they moved again, this time to the ancient city of Venice. Venice had been a portal between East and West long before Fortuny's birth, and the lands to the East proved as fascinating to him as they had centuries before to a young Marco Polo. Venice was famed not only for its works of art, but also for its luxurious textiles—incomparable brocades and velvets. As a young man, Fortuny was inspired by this city steeped in centuries of splendor.

Though Fortuny was *inspired* by this heritage, his designs came from his own fertile imagination; they were not exact copies from any specific place or time. Each one was unique, a one-of-a-kind design, which, like Aladdin's magic carpet, could transport its wearer to the magical, mythical places of her dreams as they whispered of places long ago and far away…ancient Greece, Egypt, India, Persia, Africa, China, and Japan. Fortuny recreated such classic garments as the Greek chiton, Indian sari, Turkish dolman, North African burnous, Moroccan djellabah, and Japanese kimono in his own inimitable manner.

In 1899, Fortuny moved to the Palazzo Orfei, a magnificent Venetian palace built in the thirteenth century; there he began to experiment with textiles. He preferred silks and silk velvets for his creations, and imported only the finest fabrics from China, Japan, and France; he also purchased exquisite glass beads from Murano's famous glassworks. After the materials arrived at his Palazzo Orfei, each step in a garment's creation was done by hand, including dyeing the fabric, pleating, and printing or stenciling. Fortuny used natural dyes rather than synthetics, mixing them himself to reproduce every hue in nature's rainbow, and he dipped the fabrics several times to enrich their tones. With his background in chemistry, Fortuny spent many hours in his lab, investigating and refining old dyeing and printing techniques for the stenciled silk gauze or velvet capes and coats he created to be worn over his dresses.

His first textile creation was designed for the theater—in 1906, he introduced a sheer silk scarf called the "Knossos." Similar in shape and size to the sensuous saris of India, these scarves were woodblock printed in ancient motifs. Fortuny's most famous creation soon followed—a classic column of tiny pleats called the "Delphos Robe" after *The Charioteer of Delphos*, an ancient Greek statue. Though the shape of his Delphos was inspired by the Greek chiton, the inspiration for its famous pleats is said to have come from the pleated gowns of the ancient Egyptians. Fortuny used pre-pleated silk; the pleating was done by hand on wet or damp fabric and "…held in place with stitches and set with heat." His first Delphos dates to 1907-08; it was patented in Paris on November 4, 1909. Though Fortuny's famous pleats have been imitated by many, they've never been exactly duplicated.

In his patent application, Fortuny explained that though his Delphos derived from the ancient Greek chiton, its design was "so shaped and arranged that it can be worn and adjusted with ease and comfort…consisting of a sheath open at the top and bottom…side ribbons are threaded obliquely so that one can adjust or modify the distance which determines the bottom of the sleeve according to the height and measurements of the wearer. These laces are placed for preference inside the garment so as to be invisible."

The Delphos proved an answer to dress reformers' prayers. Worn as a tea gown, it provided an elegant alternative to the tightly corseted Edwardian gowns. Dancer Isadora Duncan, the "Salome" of the early twentieth century, wore Fortuny gowns both onstage and off. Long a crusader against the era's tortuous corsets, Duncan felt a style that "…liberated the body and freed it from the restraints of conventional dress" was essential. As Fortuny's flowing gowns fulfilled these requirements with grace and beauty, Duncan and other dress reformers became ardent advocates. By the twenties, Delphos gowns had become society's darlings. Lady Bonham-Carter remarked in her memoirs: "Everybody went to Fortuny then…I think everyone I knew had a Fortuny dress…"

The Delphos was often belted, either with a length of narrow, stenciled silk, or with knotted silk cord. The early Delphos had "batwing" sleeves that laced up the shoulders, held in place with hand-blown Murano beads; most had wide bateau necklines. Belts are shown either slightly above or at the natural waistline; though some are belted Grecian fashion, wound criss-cross between the breasts and around the waist. Some belts snap fasten; others are pictured simply tied (with short ends). Until his death in 1949, Fortuny made many variations of the Delphos: some with short sleeves, some with long wide sleeves sometimes tied at wrist, and some sleeveless. A tunic version, the "Peplos," appeared in the twenties, and Fortuny even created some rare pleated trousers. His creations are difficult to date as they were purchased for so many decades…and they never went out of style!

"Is it their historical character, is it rather the fact that each one of them is unique that gives them so special a significance that the pose of the woman who is wearing one while she waits for you to appear or while she talks to you assumes an exceptional importance?"

—Marcel Proust

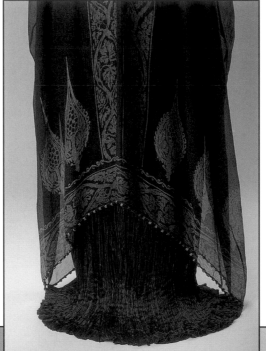

Close-up of bottom, showing Murano beaded hem and gown's pleated hem. Fortuny designed his gowns to fall in a graceful line, pooled around the feet, as shown in these photographs.

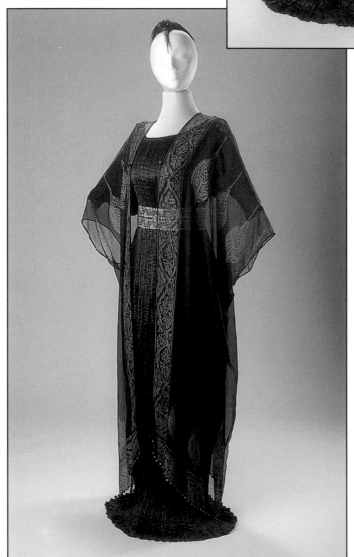

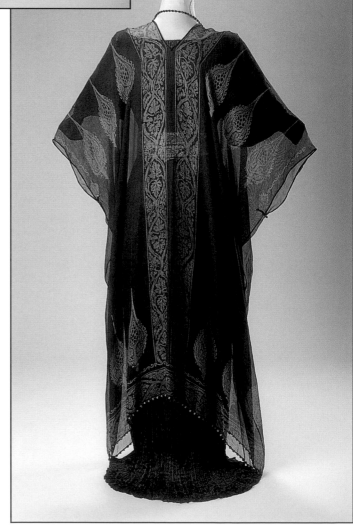

Classic Fortuny Delphos gown worn with its stenciled belt and sheer silk kimono-style robe, which is stenciled in gold in an ancient Persian motif and edged at the hem with Murano beads.

Back view of ensemble showing the cape's stenciled center border and beaded hem, which curves up in the center and dips down at each side.

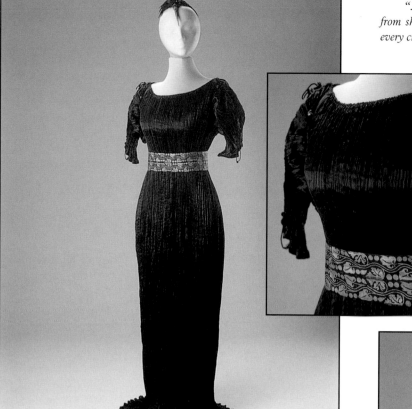

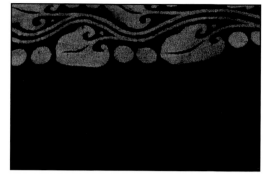

"...timeless dresses of pure thin silk cut severely straight from shoulder to toe, and kept wrung like a skein of wool. In every crude and subtle color, they clung like a mermaid's scales."
—Lady Diana Cooper

Detail of the stenciling on the belt, with Fortuny's signature on reverse.

Close-up of batwing sleeve, lacings, and stenciled belt.

This rippling column of exquisite tiny pleats clings to the body to the body in undulating waves! Here's the batwing Delphos worn with its stenciled belt. The headpiece is an Art Deco "Raven," with a marquisite studded gold beak.

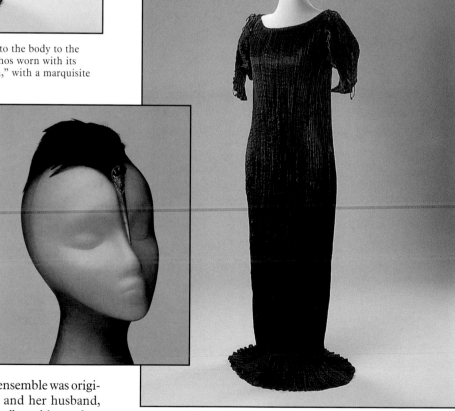

Close-up of Fortuny's patented "undulating" pleats and silk laces with Murano beads. The signature here is on the gown's inner tape.

A close-up of the Raven headpiece!

A view of the Delphos robe worn without the stenciled belt.

Provenance: This magnificent Fortuny ensemble was originally owned by Louise Thompson. Louise and her husband, J.J. Thompson, were known as "adventurers," world travelers who often sailed to Europe and Africa during the twenties. Their main residence was in Grand Rapids, Michigan; they kept summer homes in Baldwinsville, New York, and Maine. Mr. Thompson, a graduate of Brown University, was an executive with the American Seed Co. This ensemble was found in their Baldwinsville summer "farm," and, according to rumor, was perhaps worn to the debut of Gershwin's "Rhapsody in Blue" on February 12, 1924 at the Aeolian Hall in New York City.

Value: Delphos gown and belt: $7,000-$12,000; stenciled silk gauze cape, $7,000-$12,000 (in excellent condition); Raven headpiece, $200-$300.

Shoes

What shoes could possibly be magnificent enough to wear with a Fortuny ensemble? We've chosen these breathtaking satin evening slippers—the heels adorned with a Fortuny-ish motif in gold and rhinestones!

Close-up of the black lacquered heels. The design is intaglio, pressed into the heel, and hand-painted in gold leaf. Rows of inset rhinestones alternate with trailing vines in the center of these 3" Louis heels.

A front view, showing their original "colonial" style rhinestone buckles. Note the less pointed, slightly rounded toe fashionable at this time.

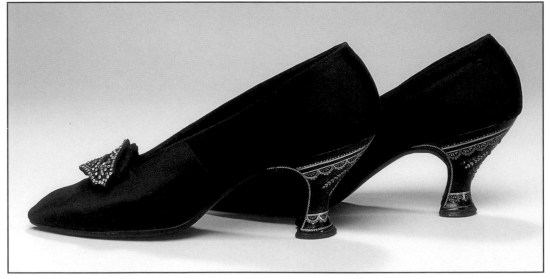

Side view, showing the shoes' graceful lines. $400-$600.

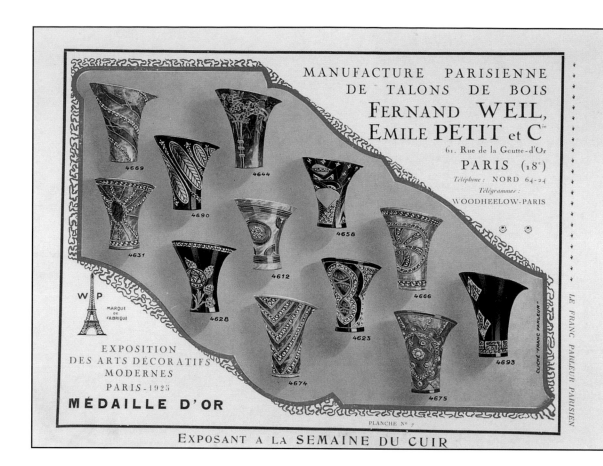

By 1924, preparations were underway for the 1925 Expo that gave Art Deco its name. Incredible Art Deco items like these stellar heels were now being created of celluloid by firms like Fernand Weil, Emile Petit et C.

The famous Art Deco Exposition (*Exposition des Arts Decoratifs*) was held in Paris; it set the stage for the second half of the twenties, as The Party of the Century heats up! During this time, you'll see women's skirts begin their legendary climb to the knees—only to come crashing down by the end of this magical decade—as our fun loving flapper dances off into the mists of time, to be replaced by a more mature, feminine woman capable of facing The Great Depression. See these legendary fashions in the companion volume to this book, *Roaring '20s Fashions: Deco*!

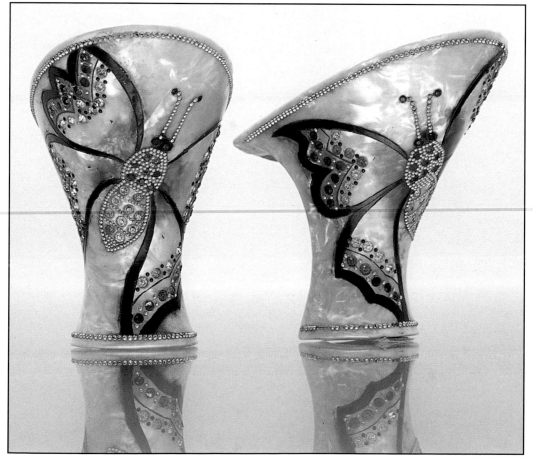

True works of art! This superb pair of "marblelized" celluloid heels is adorned with Art Deco butterflies and features inset rhinestones, both clear and amber, and delicate gold beading. $200-$300.

Care and Storage of Antique Clothing

Included here are conservators' recommendations for antique clothing. Since the following may seem complex to novice collectors, the most important things to remember are:

1) Get antique clothing out of cellars (damp conditions cause mildew) and attics (extremes of heat and cold make fabrics stiff and brittle, leading to eventual disintegration).
2) NO plastic bags or unprotected cardboard boxes for storage.
3) NO unprotected wire hangers.
4) NO fabric glue or fusable iron-on patches for repairs.

To Wear or Display?

If you're the lucky owner of antique clothing, the choice of wearing or displaying is up to you. You should be aware though, that museum conservators as well as many experienced collectors advise not wearing antique clothing. Every year the number of existing antique garments dwindles; wearing items, poor storage, and careless cleaning have all taken a toll. Wearing antique clothing puts tremendous strain on old fibers and seams, and body oils and perspiration also contribute to fiber breakdown. Replicas are suggested for re-enactments, mystery theaters, costume parties, etc. Many collectors think of their pieces as works of art, or as important remainders of their era's history, rather than as something to wear.

Pristine and/or very rare pieces, including couture labels, are best displayed on a mannequin only. If you feel you need to wear an antique or vintage piece to a special event, consider wearing something that's not in pristine/excellent original condition, but rather something that's already seen some repairs. Consider wearing the piece for a short time only—for a studio photo or portrait, for example—rather than subjecting it to strenuous activities like dining or dancing.

When displaying your treasures, rotate displays and change them often—around every one to four months. Don't display items in strong light, directly in front of a window; use indirect lighting. Display items only in areas away from cooking odors or cigarette smoke, and keep them away from food and/or drinks. Conservators also recommend wearing clean cotton gloves or washing hands often when handling antique clothing, and be sure to remove all jewelry that could catch or snag fabrics.

Storage

Flat Storage

Ideally, items should be stored in controlled temperatures and as flat as possible to avoid stress, folded as little as possible. To prevent fiber breakdown, lightly pad any folds with a small rolled piece of acid free paper or polyester batting. Lay items flat in large acid free boxes, using acid free tissue. (Non-buffered tissue is recommended for many fabrics, including silks and woolens, while buffered is suggested for cottons, linens, and metallics.) Store metallic lamés separately. Unbleached, undyed cotton muslin is also recommended as a wrapping material in lieu of acid free tissue for storage. Bias cuts, beaded dresses, and other heavy pieces are among the items that are most important to store flat.

Hangers

If you have a large collection, and it's necessary to hang some of the lighter items, you may want to hang them from the waist rather than the shoulders to more evenly distribute the weight and avoid undue shoulder stress. Some collectors cut a cardboard roll down the center and place it over the bottom of a sturdy hanger, taping it securely; then the roll is thoroughly covered with acid free paper, the open ends stuffed with tissue to prevent slippage. The item can then be hung from the waist, if necessary padding any folds. If the garment has long sleeves, place the cuffs over the top. If a garment is hung from the shoulders, even a padded hanger should be wrapped with acid free tissue or covered with polyester batting to provide maximum support. CHECK ITEMS YEARLY, replace acid free tissue, and look for any insect/rodent damage. Moth balls are not recommended for storage due to harsh chemicals. Some recommend placing materials such as eucalyptus leaves or a few slivers of soap in the storage box (not touching the fabric) to discourage pests.

Cleaning and Repair

Washing

Washing is not recommended by clothing conservators as it may damage old fibers, and the results are chancy at best. (Keep in mind that stains that have set for decades are not likely to come out without resorting to stain removers containing harsh chemicals, and the result may be a hole rather than a stain.) Washing can damage old gelatin/cellulose sequins or bugle beads that have coated centers. Metallic fabrics, lamés, and brocades should not be washed, and woolens can both shrink and shred. Vacuuming on LOW power, with the item placed under a length of nylon tulle is suggested by conservators. To freshen garments that are sturdy enough, air them in a gentle breeze (on a covered porch or breezeway if possible).

If you do feel the need to wash, cottons, some silks, and linens are the safest fabrics; first try a test in an inconspicuous spot to check for color bleeding, shrinking, shredding, etc. Before washing, remove any delicate trim that may be damaged and any celluloid buttons or covered buttons that may rust; mark the exact placement by basting with contrasting color thread. Wash items in room temperature distilled water, soaking for around ten minutes in a small amount of Orvis paste (available at archival supply stores). Strong stain removers are not recommended; better a small stain than a hole. Rinse in distilled water until there is no soapy residue in the rinse water (about ten times). Don't wring or twist, but gently blot and smooth flat to dry (not in direct sunlight). Keep steaming/ironing to a minimum as heat leads to fiber breakdown.

Dry cleaning is NOT recommended for antique clothing, as the harsh chemicals used in the process can cause permanent damage.

Mending

Use the same fabric for mends whenever possible; look for additional fabric and/or beads in hems, seam allowances, and waist tucks. If not enough original fabric is available, use period fabrics that are as alike as possible, or transparent crepeline, with period thread, buttons, snaps, and hook & eyes (search estate sales, flea markets, and Internet auctions). HAND STITCH patches from the underside, using a larger patch than the weakened area/hole; if the surrounding fabric is weak, you'll need to take a bit larger stitches as tiny ones will pull through. NEVER GLUE OR IRON ON fusable iron on tape or patches. These will not only stiffen the fabric, they will lead to the fabric eventually tearing around the bond.

Recordkeeping

Many choose to keep records of garments with a numbering system, basting a numbered fabric tag to each item in an inconspicuous place. The number is then stored with a description of the item, including a photo, any provenance (history), date and price of purchase, and approximate date the item was originally worn. Information may be stored on disk or in a file box. Some collectors simply note information in pencil on a cloth tag or piece of acid free tissue and baste it to a hem or inner seam. (Don't use pins, iron-on labels, or write directly on fabrics.)

Informative Websites

Kent State University Museum (dept.kent.edu/museum/staff/care.html), an excellent clothing website, includes a section on care of antique clothing.

Costume Society of America (costumesocietyamerica.com), an informative group that offers symposiums on antique clothing.

Vintagefashionguild.org, is an interesting and informative website for vintage clothing fanciers.

The Ladies Treasury of Costume and Fashion (tudorlinks.com/treasury)

The Textile Museum, Washington, D.C. (textilemuseum.org/care/brochures/guidelines.htm), provides guidelines for the care of textiles.

Archival Supplies

Talas
talasonline.com
(212) 219-0770

Light Impressions
lightimpressionsdirect.com
(800) 828-6216

Gaylord
gaylord.com
(800) 448-6160

Archivart
archivart.com
(800)804-8428

University Products Inc.
archivalsuppliers.com
(800) 628-1912

Appendix

Listed here are some of New York's fine department stores and exclusive specialty shops that were regularly seen in period magazines like *Vogue* and *Harper's Bazar* (shown as "V" and "HB" in the following descriptions). Also included are samples of the stores' original ad copy.

Arnold Constable (Fifth Ave., 39th - 40th St.) – One of New York's finest department stores. *Harper's* October 1926 article features a Patou original evening gown with ostrich bands, imported to Arnold Constable, priced at $85.

B. Altman (Fifth Ave. at 34th) – 1927 *Vogue* article features Altman imports from Chanel, Patou, Lelong, Molyneux. In Altman's Men's Shop, a four piece "Golf and sport suit" is $55.

Henri Bendel (Fifth Ave. and 57th) – Exclusive shop offering exact copies of Paris couture as well as his own designs; Bendel also wrote for *Harper's Bazar*.

Bergdorf Goodman (Fifth Ave. at 58th) – "On the Fourth Floor, our made to order department reveals its selections from the Paris openings and its own exclusive designs for 'les chic Americaines'... on the Third Floor, a ready to wear collection... the new clever ensembles...chiffon evening gowns of infinite grace...and the Salle Moderne with the latest sports clothes... On the street floor, the most successful and magnetic hats of the season...matching bags and scarfs; smart stockings and jewelry. In each of these salons, with their spring vivacity, you will discover that inexplicable something which distinguishes art from routine." (V3/29) In 1923, Bergdorf's offered dresses from their ready to wear department, priced from $85.

Best & Co. (Fifth Ave. at 35th, 1928) – Best featured imported couture as well as their own designs; they sold sports clothes under their own "Nada" label and a line of hats under their "Fortmason" label. "Our representatives hold fashion exhibits in most of the larger cities east of the Mississippi. Write for date of showing in your town or nearby. Charge accounts solicited. Mail orders filled." Branches in Paris, London, and Palm Beach.

Bloomingdales (59th and Lexington) – Bloomingdales's enormous emporium was founded by Lyman and Joseph Bloomingdale in the 1860s on New York's lower east side as a notions shop; hoop skirts were one of their best selling items! In 1886, they moved to 59th and Lexington; by the twenties, "Bloomies" covered an entire city block.

Bonwit Teller (Fifth Ave. at 38th, 1928) – "As one would know...the most distinctive of the new fashions are found in the Bonwit-Teller collections"! (V4/28). In addition to imported Paris originals, Bonwit's touts: "Paris **inspirations** and our own 'originations'—the latest word in fashion..." (HB10/26)

The Brick Shop (18 East 56th St) – Importers, "French apparel exclusively...sports wear a specialty."

Bruck-Weiss (6-8 West 57th) – "The World's Show Place of Fashion," an exclusive shop, offered "The Total Ensemble" look: "Hats, bags, hosiery, jewelry and accessories that are perfect complements to the ensemble effect...It is our aim to interpret and express in terms of dress the personality and style of each individual customer." (HB23)

Hattie Carnegie (42 East 49th St, 1925) – "Gowns and Millinery...Clothes to Suit Your Individuality...The greatest success of Hattie Carnegie has been achieved in making clothes to suit each individual type—designed in their every detail to enhance the smart woman's own style." (HB5/23) Enterprising Hattie Carnegie sold her own house designs as well as Paris originals she bought on her seven annual trips to France; by the late twenties, she was also offering stylish ready to wear.

Deja (550 Seventh Ave) – Specialized in couture "inspired by" replicas. Also available "at your favorite shop or write to Deja...for Lanvin, Martial et Armand, Patou, Lelong, Molyneux... copies in the newest colors and fabrics will be on sale at well known shops at the uniform price of $39.50." (V9/26)

Dobbs (681 & 620 Fifth Ave) – "Sports clothes whose dash and certain becomingness are an expression of careful taste, smart Dobbs hats—costumes for street, sports and afternoon are created with Dobbs' bright, particular genius..." (HB10/26)

Eldridge Manning – Exclusive import shop often featured in *Vogue*.

Frances Clyne (Fifth & 50th) – Imported Chanel, Lanvin, and other prestigious couturiers.

Franklin Simon (Fifth Ave. 37th & 38th Sts.) – "A Store of Individual Shops!" The "New Trousseau Room, first floor" featured "Paris handmade lingeries with real laces—chemises $4.95-$59.50; step-in drawers, $4.95-$59.50." (HB5/23). In "Mademoiselle's Suit Shop, Second Floor," ensembles were priced at $155-$195; in the "French Blouse Salon, Third Floor," an "Indo-Chinese tapestry blouse" was $55. (V4/28) In addition to Paris imports, Franklin Simon offered their own patented in-house "Bramley" designs.

Gervais (16 East 48th St.) – Exclusive shop often featured in *Vogue*.

J.M. Gidding (Fifth at 56th & 57th) – Import/design house. "The latest French Spring Fashions, personally selected by

Gidding Representatives abroad, are coming each day through The New York Entrance to Paris to delight the American Woman!" (HB23) Gidding's featured imported couture and creations of their in-house designer, Evelyn McHorter.

Gimbel Bros. – New York store was located near Macy's, in Herald Square; founder Adam Gimbel opened the New York store in 1910.

Grande Maison de Blanc (538-540 Fifth Ave) – An exclusive specialty-import shop.

Hickson, Inc. (Fifth at 52nd) – "Gowns created for the most superb collection of advance winter modes ever shown in our Salons…characterizing the individuality and chic associated only with Hickson apparel." (HB10/26) Hickson also wrote articles for *Harper's Bazar*.

Peggy Hoyt (16 E. 55th St.) – "Hats, Dresses, Suits, Wraps of unsurpassing beauty and originality designed and executed for America's most distinguished gentlewomen." (V28) Her exclusive shop featured her own designs as well as imports.

Jay-Thorpe (57th & 56th Sts. W) – Importers, and by 1929: "We are now couturiers—announcing the opening of a new dressmaking salon, a superior custom order department…staffed to design in the French manner and make to order dresses, coats, ensembles, evening costumes and bridal gowns of great chic and superlative hand workmanship. The Spring collection of new French imports and original models is ready now… in the Louis XVI Salon, Third Floor." (V 3/29) Resort branches at Palm Beach and Miami Beach.

Joseph (2 West 57th St.) – A prestigious import house.

Kurzman (Fifth, 52nd & 53rd) – Prestigious importer; also featured their own original in-house designs.

L.P. Hollander (552 Fifth Ave) – An exclusive custom/import shop with a branch in Boston. "For seventy-five years, couturiers to the Gentlewomen of America." (HB23)

Lord & Taylor (Fifth at 38th) – "We have in readiness a new collection from France…"; French imports included Mary Nowitsky, Redfern, Louiseboulanger, Cheruit, (priced around $200-$700). "Mail and telephone orders promptly filled." (V28)

MacVeady Inc. (10 East 56th) – Importer, advertising hats, gowns, sports clothes; branches in Palm Beach and Southampton (V29)

McCutcheons (Fifth at 49th) – "The Ensemble Vogue, smart for town or country, $69.50." Also known for fine imported fabrics. "Write for samples of these exclusive materials." (V2/22)

R.H. Macy (Herald Square) – Famous for moderately-priced fashions, including ready made knitted sports apparel in the $16-$25 range; afternoon and dinner gowns, between $25-$50; and "Whitby Frocks, exclusive with R.H. Macy & Co.," priced at $14.74-$24. (V23, V26)

Maxon Model Gowns (11 East 36th St.) – "Exclusive frocks and coats, half-priced! We specialize exclusively in the choicest, no two alike Original Models of the pre-eminent modistes; samples, we get them for much less and sell them at about half the usual cost." (V9/26)

Milgrim (6 W. 57th, 1925) – Milgrim's exclusive shop offered both custom made and ready to wear; they featured creations of "America's Foremost Fashion Creator," their famous in-house designer Sally Milgrim. Realizing the selling potential of the silver screen, Milgrim photographed stars like Louise Brooks in creations named for them. As the store notes: "Milgrim creations may also be obtained at the foremost shops in leading cities."

Russeks (Fifth at 36th) – "America's Most Beautiful Store," advertised "a vast assemblage of the winsome modes of youth…" (V10/27)

Saks Fifth Avenue (49th to 50th) – Saks Fifth Avenue opened in September 1924, heralding "Our collection of exquisite originals from the PARIS couturiers—and our faithful replicas—have the sure distinction characteristic of fashion by Saks-Fifth Avenue." "The personal shopping service will gladly answer inquiries or fill orders promptly." (V10/27)

Stein & Blaine (13 & 15 W. 57th) – Exclusive specialty shop. "A Creative House… Furriers Dressmakers Tailors," who promoted the in-house creations of the talented E.M.A. Steinmetz (which she also illustrated). (4/28V)

Stewart & Co. (Fifth at 37th) –"Correct Apparel for Women and Misses!" Stewart's offered "Paris Reproductions, inspired by Paris, approved by Fifth Avenue and reproduced by Stewart & Co. For the woman of discerning taste…," such as a cape for $124.50, day coat for $69.50. (HB 23).) In the September 1, 1925 *Vogue*, Stewart's announced: "College Club Fashions, exclusive with Stewart & Co. will be exhibited by us at the leading colleges," moderately priced between $15-$40. Stewart's noted, "Paris and Fifth Avenue Fashion Book sent on request." (HB8/24)

The Sports Shop for Women – An exclusive shop that imported early Schiaparelli. A English hand-woven grey tweed Schiap ensemble was featured by *Vogue* in October, 1928.

Tailored Woman (632 Fifth Ave) – An exclusive import/design shop. "The shop that puts LINE, WORKMANSHIP and GOOD TASTE above everything is naturally the port of call for copies—exact in very detail—of the more subtle Paris models most shops necessarily ignore." "Patou-inspired" day dress, $78.50; "Chanel" print ensemble, $118. (V4/28)

Tappe (Herman Patrick Tappe - 57th St.) – This famous importer/designer was often featured in *Vogue*. A fashion commentator and illustrator, Tappe was noted for hats as well as gowns.

Thurn (15E. 52nd St) – "Exclusive Fashions for Women." A prominent import/design shop. Noted in a 1928 *Vogue*: "Announcing a new collection of ORIGINAL models!"

Wanamaker's (Broadway & 9th) – Philadelphia based John Wanamaker opened a New York store in 1896; they offered fine Parisian couture as well as their own creations. Wanamaker fashions for misses' were labeled "Mimi": "Mimi was designed with a keen appreciation for the many and varied activities in the day of a modern young woman…chosen from the best of Paris designers after a careful study of smart young women's tastes." (V10/28)

For sportswear, both men and women shopped at **Abercrombie and Fitch** (Madison Ave. & 45th), "The Greatest Sporting Goods Store in the World"; their famous clients included Amelia Earhart, Ernest Hemingway, and the Prince of Wales! **Fairyland, Inc.** (10 West 50th) and **The Children's Shop** (425 Madison Ave) specialized in exclusive clothing for children. **Nardi** and **Berkowitz** offered fine riding habits. And for mourning, one visited **Mullen Mourning for Aristocrats** or **Thurn's.**

Glossary

Adrian, Gilbert (1903-1959). Designed costumes for Broadway shows until 1925, when he went to Hollywood. From 1926-1928, he worked for DeMille, then MGM; he designed some of Rudolph Valentino's wardrobes.

Agnes. Famous French milliner, located at 6 rue St. Florentin, Paris.

Antoine (Hairdresser). Antoine, one of several self-proclaimed "inventors" of the famous "bob," claimed he cut the hair of French actress Eve Lavalliere in 1910 in this short, sassy style. He worked in both Paris and New York (at Saks). He also claims credit for the even shorter twenties' "Shingle" hairdo.

Argyle (Argyll): Sporty, diamond patterned originally worn by Scottish clan Argyle.

Armscye: sleeve opening, armhole.

Art Gout Beaute: Exclusive French pochoir magazine published between 1920-1933.

Augustabernard. Parisian couturiere who opened in 1919 at 3 rue du Faubourg St. Honore. She was noted for tasteful yet cutting edge fashions in pale pastels. She retired in 1934.

Baker, Josephine (1906-1975). Queen of Parisian nightclub entertainers, Josephine left home as a young teenager to join a touring group, "TOBA." In 1925, she joined the "Revue Negre" and sailed for Paris, where she became a star at such glittering clubs as the Casino de Paris and the famous Folies-Bergere.

Barbier, George (1882-1932). Famous French illustrator for such magazines as *Gazette du Bon Ton, Vogue*, etc.

Batik. Method of wax printing where wax is applied to areas of fabric to prevent those areas from taking dye. Popular in the twenties, it enjoyed a huge revival in the sixties and seventies.

Beer. Prominent couture house established by Gustave Beer, a German designer who was the first to open on Place Vendome in 1905. Beer was known for "conservative elegance." The house merged with Drecoll in 1929.

Benito, Edouard. Famous Spanish illustrator for *Gazette du Bon Ton, Vogue, Harper's Bazar* and others.

Bertha. A large cape collar that had been a nineteenth century favorite; it was revived to become very popular during the second half of the twenties through the mid-thirties.

Boa. Fluffy neck scarf of feathers, fur, or fabric; often with tassel ends.

Boue Soeurs. Established in 1899 by two sisters, Sylvie Boue Montegut and Baronne Jeanne (Boue) d'Etreillis, the House of Boue Soeurs at 9 rue de la Paix advertised "Robes [gowns], Manteaux [coats] and Lingerie bearing the cachet of exclusiveness and originality and of unsurpassing beauty…" They were noted for their signature ribbon roses, for lavish use of embroidery and lace, and for their gold and silver lamés and metallic laces. In the twenties, Boue Soeurs had a New York branch at 13 West 56th Street in New York.

Boutet de Monvel, Barnard. Talented fashion illustrator. A fellow Zouave officer of Patou, he often illustrated Patou fashions.

Boutiques. Became very trendy in the twenties as couturiers opened small branches in popular resorts, selling accessories, sportswear, jewelry, and ready to wear.

Braque, Georges. Cubist artist, he met Picasso in 1907; both helped develop the art form known as Cubism.

Callot Soeurs. A top couture house established in 1895 by the daughters of a Paris antique dealer: Marie Callot Gerber, Marthe Callot Bertrand, and Regina Callot Chantrelle. (Marie, the eldest, was the designer.) Around 1919, they moved to 9-11 avenue Matignon where they remained until 1928, when Mme. Gerber's son took over and moved to 41 avenue Montaigne. Callot Soeurs is famed for their work with antique fabrics, laces, and ribbons; for their exceptional robes de style and oriental gowns; as well as for gowns with moderne Cubist themes. Vionnet, who trained at Callot, noted that "…without the example of Callot Soeurs, I would have continued to make Fords…because of them I have been able to make Rolls Royces." The House closed in 1937.

Cardigan. Originally, a long sleeved braid-trimmed military jacket that buttoned up the front. It was named for James Thomas Brudenell, the 7th Earl of Cardigan, who led the famous Charge of the Light Brigade in the 1850s during the Crimean War. In the twenties, the classic cardigan gained couture cachet as a sweater that was extremely popular for sportswear.

Carnegie, Hattie. As a young girl, Henrietta Kanengeiser left Vienna with her family and moved to America; they "Americanized" their name to "Carnegie" after the steel magnate. At fifteen, Hattie got a job in Macy's Millinery Department; by 1909, she and a friend had opened their own millinery shop. In 1918, she presented her first collection; during the twenties, she imported French couture as well as her own designs. She employed Claire McCardell, Pauline Trigere, James Galanos, and Travis Banton.

Cascade. A rippling ruffle or frill, vertically placed.

Castle, Irene (1893-1969). Irene and her husband Vernon became a world famous dance team in the teens—the toast of Paris, as well as America. During the teens, Irene helped popularize shorter skirts when she took up her own for dancing. She was one of the first women to bob her hair, and to adapt menswear for women's sports clothes.

Chanel, Gabrielle ("Coco") (1883-1971). Considered by many to be the most influential couturier of the twenties, Chanel's clothes "fit" the decade—simple yet elegant, comfortable and easy-to-wear. She was the epitome of the boyish, independent *la Garconne* and was an avid advocate of the era's straight "chemise" dress. (She created her version ca. 1914.) Chanel was born August 19, 1883; she was twelve when her mother died and her father placed her in a convent, then disappeared from her life. At eighteen, she left the convent and got a job as a tailor's assistant in Auvernois. Nights she sang at a local night club; her favorite song, a sultry "Ko-Ko-Ri-Ko" earned her her famous nickname, "Coco." In the nightclub, she met Etienne Balsan, a dashing cavalry officer. His friends admired the hats she'd designed for herself, and by 1908, she was selling hats from Balsan's Paris apartment. In 1910, Balsan's friend, polo player Arthur "Boy" Capel, became her new amour and set her up in a shop on the rue Cambon. With a goal of "liberating" the female body, she started designing clothing with simpler, straight lines and shorter hemlines. Since her lease didn't permit her to sell couture dresses, she started making dresses of jersey—a clinging knit fabric then commonly used for undergarments. Around 1913, following the beau monde, she opened a boutique in Deauville, followed by another in Biarritz in 1915. During the war, she also moved to a larger establishment, still on the rue Cambon, but across from the Ritz Hotel. By the mid-teens, her "simple" jersey fashions were creating quite a stir. She also introduced her famous "little black dress"—a "uniform" for afternoon into evening. She was devastated when Capel was killed in a car accident in 1919.

During the twenties, the flamboyant Chanel typified the new garconne. Her lifestyle was bold and unconventional, and everything she did made news! In the early twenties, her affair with Russian Grand Duke Dimetri inspired her lavishly embroidered "Russian" styles. As early as 1920, anticipating the pants-for-women trend, she was borrowing from men's wear to show wide-leg "yachting pants" ensembles for women. She was famous for her evening gowns, lavish but with much more simple lines; her beaded dresses were often constructed in the round (with one seam rather than two). She was also noted for unusual combinations of fabrics, and for matching coat linings to dresses. By mid-decade she was embroiled in a torrid affair with the Duke of Westminster, and producing chic tailored tweeds with "mannish" English lines. Chanel also claimed as her own "bobbed hair" and the "suntan"! She closed at the start of WWII in 1939; and in 1954, at age seventy-one, made a remarkable comeback, showing her beloved classic suits. (See additional information in *Roaring '20s Fashions: Deco*)

Chemise. A straight, slip like undergarment worn next to the body, beneath a corset, since medieval times. During the twenties, this term referred to a dress with a straight silhouette, as "simple" in line as its ancient ancestor.

Cheruit, Madeleine. Opened ca. 1906; by 1914, Cheruit was famed for walking suits, cinema capes, and full-skirted robe de style or "fantasy dresses." In 1925, she was lauded for her spectacular hand-painted Cubist dresses. Cheruit closed in 1935.

Cocktail Dress. When prohibition made the "cocktail" a popular drink, a short, informal dress worn for cocktails was born. The "little black dress," which could be dressed up or down with various accessories, became a favorite cocktail dress.

Co-Respondent Shoe (Spectator Shoe). A sporty oxford trimmed with perforations, generally in white and black or brown; often pointed "wingtip" style on the toe.

Crepe. A fabric with a slightly crinkly or puckery texture, in silk, rayon, or wool. In the twenties, both "Georgette" crepe and "satin-backed crepe" were favored. *Also see "Georgette."*

Crepe de Chine. Originally silk from China, a luxurious, light-weight silk.

Cuban Heels. A practical, short, thick heel popularly worn with twenties' sportswear; named for the boots worn by gauchos.

Cubism. Ultra "modern" abstract art movement beginning at the turn of the twentieth century, championed by such artists as Georges Braque and Pablo Picasso. Its streamlined, geometric lines inspired many couturiers of the twenties.

Dache, Lilly (1904-1989). Famous milliner, trained with Reboux. In 1924, she was briefly employed by Macy's; that same year she bought out The Bonnet Shop, launching her career.

Dali, Salvador (1904-1989). A noted Cubist artist. In the second half of the twenties, Dali was spearheading the Surrealist movement, painting bold, fantastic scenes. During the thirties, he designed surrealist fabrics for Schiaparelli.

Delaunay, Sonia. Famous Cubist artist; her paintings are noted for geometric designs in vivid primary colors. She produced bold, Cubist designs for textiles, and received acclaim for patchwork coats she produced with Jacques Heim. (See additional information in *Roaring '20s Fashions: Deco*)

Delman Shoes (Herman B. Delman). Shoe manufacturer noted for very stylish, high quality shoes; after WWI, Delman opened shops in New York on Madison Ave, and in Hollywood.

Doeuillet. Couture house established in 1900 by Georges Doeuillet after he trained at Callot Soeurs. Doeuillet introduced the famous "barrel" silhouette in 1917 that endured into the early twenties. In the twenties, Doeuillet was located at 24 Place Vendome. In 1929, after Jacques Doucet's death, Doeuillet merged with Maison Doucet and closed in the late thirties.

Dolman Sleeve. Sleeve cut as part of bodice with no armscyes, often wide at the top and tapering to a tight wrist.

Doucet, Jacques (1853-1929). Doucet was founded in 1824 as a lace and lingerie shop owned by Jacques Doucet's grandmother. A couturier considered to be as important as Worth, Jacques Doucet opened Maison Doucet ca. 1875. The house was known for its sumptuous, elegant designs, and clients included the world's rich and famous—royalty, actresses, and socialites. During the twenties, Doucet was considered a venerable, traditional house, located at 21 rue de la Paix. On Doucet's death in 1929, the house merged with Doueillet.

Drecoll. A popular couture house noted for luxurious though conservative fashions. Originally founded in 1902 in Vienna by Baron Christoff von Drecoll, the Paris branch was opened in 1905 under the direction of designer Besancon de Wagner. In 1929, Drecoll merged with Beer, then in 1931 with Agnes, which continued until 1963.

Dryden, Helen. One of the twenties' best illustrators, noted for her exquisite *Vogue* covers.

Dufy, Raoul. Artist who designed stunning Art Deco fabrics for Paul Poiret; he also designed for Bianchini-Ferier, the French textile manufacturer.

Duncan, Isadora. Famous dancer who scandalized society around the turn of the century by performing in scanty, flowing Grecian style robes, uncorseted and barefoot. Associated with the dress reform movement, she favored Fortuny gowns!

Duvetyn. A smooth, soft, velvety fabric.

Eric (Carl Erickson)(1891-1958). Famous illustrator who worked for *Gazette du Bon Ton*, and was one of *Vogue's* chief artists until the 1950s.

Erte (1892-1990). Russian artist and designer Romain de Tirtoff. Worked with Daighilev on designs for the Ballet Russes; from 1916-1926 illustrated for *Harper's Bazar*. Erte designed many of Josephine Baker's exotic costumes, and also sets for the Folies-Bergere and Ziegfeld Follies. From 1925, he also worked on several Hollywood films.

Eton Crop. Very short straight hairdo named for prestigious British public school, Eton College.

Fagoting. (Faggoting). A vertical or criss-crossed decorative embroidery or filling placed between an open seam; *see* hemstitching.

Faille. Lightweight silk or rayon fabric with a fine ribbed effect.

Fair Isle. Sweater originating from the Scottish island of Fair Isle, with geometric or jacquard type designs. Especially popular for golf, it was a sportswear favorite, popularized by the Prince of Wales. It was worn by both men and women.

Fedora. Originally a man's sporty hat from Tyrol; it has a tapering, center-creased crown with two "pinches" on either side. Very popular in the twenties, the classic "snap-brim" fedora's brim tipped smartly down in the front. Named after the 1882 Sardou play, *Fedora*, this sporty hat was soon adopted by women.

Flapper. Term used around the turn of the twentieth century referring to a young pre-teen or teenage girl. During the twenties, it described the "New Woman," who bobbed her hair, wore short skirts and makeup, rolled her hose, and danced the Charleston till the wee hours.

Flounces (Ruffles). Pieces of fabric of various widths, bias, circular cut or straight, often pleated or shirred at the top, used to add flare to garments.

Fortuny, Mariano (1871-1949). Renaissance man, artist, and textile magician, Fortuny was the originator of the famed pleated Delphos and Peplos dresses and stenciled silk and velvet capes. In the twenties, Fortuny's Paris establishment was located at 67 Rue Pierre-Charron cor. Champs-Elysees. (See pages 226-229)

Gabardine. Sturdy fabric with a fine diagonal ribbed weave, in wool, silk, cotton, or synthetics; used in suits, coats, dresses, slacks.

Garbo, Greta (1905-1990). Swedish actress who began her career in Sweden in the early twenties; in 1925, she came to Hollywood to work for MGM. Her beauty—and independent attitude—influenced women, helping to turn the boyish flapper into the sophisticated woman of the thirties.

Garconne. French version of "flapper"; taken from the 1922 novel, *La Garconne*, by Victor Margueritte, about a liberated woman. Coco Chanel typified the garconne, both in her designs and her personal life.

Gazette du Bon Ton. Lucien Vogel's superb French fashion magazine, published from 1912-1925, famous for its hand-stenciled pochoir plates of couture designs. Pochoir prints, especially from the *Gazette*, are avidly sought after by today's collectors.

Georgette. Very lightweight, translucent fabric in silk or rayon with a slight puckery texture. A favorite fabric of the twenties, it was often beaded in Deco designs, or printed in floral or geometric designs. *Also see* "crepe"

Girdle. A briefer version of the corset, waist to hip length, with elastic panels and attached "supporters" (garters) to secure stockings. Or, a tight swathed or draped belt, extremely popular during the second half of the decade.

Godet, Gore. Tapering, triangular-shaped inserts, narrow at the top and wide at the bottom, employed to provide ease of motion…and flare!

Grosgrain. Silk or rayon ribbon with a pronounced rib, often used in millinery and skirts' waistbands. *Also see* "petersham"

Haberdashery. A retail menswear/accessories shop.

Handkerchief Hem. A full skirt hem ending in triangular points; especially popular for afternoon and evening dresses of the late teens through the twenties.

Harper's Bazar (Bazaar after 1929). A prestigious American fashion magazine originally published by the Harper Bros. in 1867; it was taken over by Hearst in 1913.

Hartnell, Norman. English designer who had his first showing in 1927; Hartnell became the royal family's official dressmaker.

Hemstitching. Decorative vertical embroidery or stitches to fill an open seam. *See* fagoting.

Homburg (English, Trilby). A man's felt hat with a center crease and narrow, rolled brim.

Iribe, Paul. Artist best known for his fabulous Art Deco pochoir illustrations in *Les Robes de Paul Poiret*, published in 1908.

Jabot. Originally a lace or fabric frill at the neckline of a dress; during the twenties, it referred to a large vertical ruffle or flounce.

James, Charles (1906-1978). Famous designer who began as a Chicago milliner in 1926, under the name "Charles Bucheron." Ca. 1928, he moved to New York and began designing clothing, showing his first collection ca. 1928.

Jane Regny. A popular couture house in the twenties, especially noted for sportswear—very modern, futuristic sweater ensembles and beachwear. Located at 11 rue de la Boetie.

Jenny. Couture house opened in 1909 by Jenny Sacerdote; Jenny moved to the Champs Elysees in 1915. The house was known for elaborate beaded evening gowns as well as very chic "simple" sportswear. Jenny closed in 1938.

Jersey. A very flexible knit fabric in a tricot stitch, in silk, wool, cotton, or rayon. It was named for the Isle of Jersey in the English Channel, where it was knitted by women for fishermen and sailors. A comfortable fabric, it was popularly used for undergarments. It became a fashionable favorite in the mid-teens when Coco Chanel began creating "simpler" fashions of jersey.

Jodhpurs (Breeches). Popular pants used for horseback riding and by aviators. Tight at the waist, they ballooned at the hips, narrowed at the knees, and were tightly "step" buttoned. Named for a state in northern India, they were originally worn by British troops in the nineteenth century.

Knife Pleats. Sharp, narrow vertical pleats especially popular during the twenties.

Lady Duff Gordon. *See* Lucile

Lalique, Rene (1860-1945). Famous artist noted for fabulous designs in jewelry and glass sculptures. He opened in 1885, and designed for Cartier and Bucheron; he also created jewelry for Sarah Bernhardt's plays.

Lamé. Heavy, shiny cloth woven with metallic gold or silver threads, very popular for twenties' evening fashions.

Lanvin, Jeanne (1867-1946). One of the most famous of the haute couture designers, Lanvin opened a millinery shop at 11 rue du Faubourg Saint-Honore in 1890. She began creating clothes for her younger sister and daughter so lovely that clients began requesting dresses for their daughters; by 1909, she was designing her famous mother/daughter fashions. Just before WWI, ca. 1914, she introduced the full-skirted eighteenth century-inspired "robe de style," which would remain a "youthful" favorite for afternoon and evening throughout the twenties and thirties. Also ca. 1914, she created her version of the straight chemise dress, later to become *the* silhouette of the twenties. In the twenties, Lanvin Couture was located at 22 Faubourg St. Honore, and Lanvin Sport at 15 Faubourg St. Honore; she also opened branches in Biarritz, Cannes, and Nice. Lanvin introduced My Sin perfume in 1925, followed by Arpege in 1927. In 1926, she became the first to open a men's section. Her house was noted for its up-to-date yet romantic creations, for its lavish use of exquisite embroideries, and for the robin's egg blue color known as "Lanvin Blue." On Lanvin's death in 1946, Castillo became premier couturier; followed in 1963 by Jules Francois Crahay. In 1997, Claude Montana began designing for the House of Lanvin.

Lawn. Sheer, translucent cotton fabric, named for the French town of Laon.

Legroux Soeurs. Couture house founded in 1917 by sisters (soeurs) Heloise and Germaine Legroux. In business until the 1950s.

Lelong, Lucien (1889-1958). Prominent couturier who opened his couture house after WWI in 1919, at 374 rue St. Honore. Lelong was among the first to open resort branches in Monte Carlo in Biarritz. The house was noted for modern, "youthful" creations, impeccable workmanship and luxurious fabrics. (See additional information in *Roaring '20s Fashions: Deco*)

Lenglen, Suzanne (1899-1938). Champion French tennis player, who won at Wimbledon from 1919-26. A champion also of briefer, easier to wear sports clothing, she created a sensation when she abandoned her garter belt and rolled her stockings over elastic garters. Patou designed her chic pleated skirts and sweaters. Millions of women also adopted the famous bandeau headband she wore to accent her ensemble. (See page 201)

Lenief. Couture house opened in 1923; often featured in *Vogue* and *Harper's Bazar*. Lenief was located at 374 rue St. Honore, Paris.

Lepape, Georges (1877-1971). One of the most talented and prolific of all the pochoir artists. In 1911, he illustrated Paul Poiret's famous second pochoir book, *Les Choses de Paul Poiret*. He worked for *Gazette du Bon Ton*, *Vogue* and *Harper's Bazar*, illustrating creations for many prominent couturiers.

Liberty of London. World famous London department store from the mid-nineteenth century on, especially known for silks imported from the Orient, flowing Grecian "aesthetic" dresses, luxurious lingerie, and many other unique items.

Linen. Fabric made from fibers of the flax plant. Linen was a favorite of the ancient Egyptians; remnants have been found in tombs that are over five thousand years old. Linen is finished in many textures, from tightly woven to a fine gauze or mesh.

Lisle. Knitted cotton fiber used for stockings. It took its name from the French town of Lille, where it originated.

Little Black Dress. A versatile classic dress introduced during the twenties. Designed to go from day into evening, it could be dressed up or down and was beloved by the new "cocktail" set. Though the "little black dress" is synonymous with Chanel, many other couturiers had versions as well.

Louis Heel. One of the twenties' favorite heels for shoes, the graceful Louis heel narrows in the middle, flares out at the bottom. Originally named for the France's Sun King, Louis XIV (1643-1715), it was very popular during the eighteenth century.

Louiseboulanger (1878-1950). Noted couturiere who opened her house at Champs Elysees, 3 rue de Berri ca. 1926, after working at Cheruit and Callot. She was noted for "pouf" frocks (fitted around the torso and draped to bustle effects), bias cuts, and "peacock" tails.

Lucile (also Lucille) (Lady Duff Gordon) (1863-1935). English couturiere, known as Lady Duff Gordon after her 1900 marriage to Sir Cosmo Duff Gordon. Lucile had branches in Paris, London, New York, and Chicago, and was noted for her luxurious evening gowns, tea gowns, and lingerie. Such notables as actress Sarah Bernhardt and dancer/fashion icon Irene Castle patronized Lucile. Her sister, author Elinor Glyn, coined the famous twenties' term "IT," meaning sex appeal! Lady Duff Gordon and her husband Cosmo were survivors of the 1912 *Titanic* disaster; they were in Lifeboat 1, which carried only twelve people despite having a capacity for forty. Their lifeboat did not return to attempt to rescue any of those still in the water. Questioned later by the Wreck Commissioner's Inquiry★, Lady Duff Gordon testified: "It [the *Titanic*] is such an enormous boat; none of us know what the suction may be if she is a goner." In an interview in the *New York Sunday American*, she'd been quoted as saying: "An awful silence seemed to hang over everything, and then from the water all about where the *Titanic* had been arose a bedlam of shrieks and cries…And it was at least an hour before the awful chorus of shrieks ceased, gradually dying into a moan of despair." (She denied saying this at the inquiry.) The Duff Gordons were the only passengers questioned. During the twenties, Lucile's Paris house was located at 11 rue de Penthievre, Paris, advertising "exclusive designs now under the personal direction of Monsieur Decio Rossi." ★See details at titanicinquiry.org

Madeleine et Madeleine. A prominent couture house founded in 1919; very popular in the twenties. In 1926, the house merged with Anna, the creator of the avant garde "le smoking" women's tuxedo suit.

Maillot. Extremely form-fitting knit fabric, similar to tricot, sometimes used for bathing suits in the twenties.

Mainbocher (1891-1976). American designer Main Rousseau Bocher, originally from Chicago, in 1922 illustrated for *Harper's Bazar*; from 1923-1929 was the editor of French *Vogue*. Combining his name to "Mainbocher," he opened his couture house in Paris in 1930 and became the first successful American couturier, famous for dressing the Duchess of Windsor.

Marcasite (Marquisite). Silvery grey steel beads.

Marcel Wave. A twenties' favorite hairstyle with Art Deco lines, it consisted of a series of waves rather than curls, produced with multi-layered curved curling tongs. It was originally designed in 1872 by French hairdresser Marcel Grateau.

Martial et Armand. Popular twenties' couture house located at 10 Place Vendome, 13 rue de la Paix, with a branch in London.

Martin, Charles (1848-1934). Famous artist who illustrated for the prestigious pochoir *Gazette du Bon Ton, Vogue* and *Harper's Bazar.*

Marty, Andre (1882-1974). Very well known artist, illustrating for the *Gazette, Vogue* and *Harpers Bazar.*

Mary Janes. A favorite shoe style for women and girls, generally with a low or small heel and fastened with a strap over the instep. Popularly worn for day or sportswear in leather, patent, or canvas, but also used on dress shoes.

Mary Nowitzky. A couture house located at 832 rue des Petits Champs (Place Vendome); very popular in the twenties for sportswear, particularly swim wear and accessories.

Moiré. A rather stiff, heavy fabric, usually silk, with a wavy pattern in shades of the same color (also known as "watered silk").

Molyneux, Captain Edward (1891-1974). Famed Irish couturier, who began his career by winning a contest sponsored by Lucile, where he trained. He was a Captain during WWI, when he was blinded in one eye; he opened canteens in London and Paris and established a camp for war wounded. After the war, in 1919, he opened his own couture house at 14 rue Royale and was noted for exquisitely "simple" creations, including beaded chemise dresses and "unequaled" lounging pajamas. He soon established branches in Cannes, Biarritz, London, and Monte Carlo. The house closed in 1950, taken over by Jacques Griffe.

Mondrian, Piet (1872-1944). Holland born artist Piet Mondrian took up Cubism in 1917; he was to become one of the world's foremost Cubist painters.

Mousseline. Slightly stiff, lightweight fabric in silk, wool, or cotton.

Muslin. A plainly woven cotton fabric originally named for the middle eastern city of Mosul, and fashionable since the late eighteenth century's "empire" gowns. Popular in different weights for dresses, blouses, undergarments, linens.

Negligee. A loose, flowing informal robe, worn at home in the boudoir between clothing changes. *Also see* "tea gown."

Norfolk Jacket. A sporty tweed jacket originating in the nineteenth century, named for the English Duke of Norfolk. Originally men's wear, it was soon adapted for women and children. It was either self-belted only in back, or the belt encircled the waist; it featured roomy patch pockets and box pleats. During the twenties, it was a favorite paired with knickers for all types of sporting activities.

Nylon. A synthetic fabric developed by DuPont scientist Dr. Wallace H. Carothers, who began research in 1927; it was not introduced by DuPont until 1938, when it was first used for nylon hosiery.

Organdy (Organdie). A very sheer but stiff translucent cotton fabric, similar to voile, and very popular for summer day and afternoon dresses in the twenties.

Oxford Bags. Wide legged trousers immortalized by John Held Jr.'s illustrations of the "Sheiks" of the twenties. They were introduced by students at Oxford University who began to wear them over the knickers that were banned. "Bags" often measured 20-24 inches around the cuff.

Paillettes (Sequins, Spangles). Shiny, usually circular disks pierced to stitch on evening/afternoon garments. Twenties' paillettes or sequins were often gelatin based, and can be irreparably damaged by washing, dry cleaning, and extremes of heat or cold.

Pajamas (English, Pyjamas). Pants and top sets worn by men, women, and children for sleep wear. During the twenties, women's pajamas for "lounging" and "beach" also became the rage; beach pajamas were the first commonly worn pants for women to venture out with in public.

Panniers. Horizontal, hooped "cages" very popular during the eighteenth century, worn under the "robes" or gowns of that era; they were revived in the twenties to emphasize some of the more dramatic "robe de style" gowns.

Patou, Jean (1880-1936). "We are witnessing a renaissance..." (Jean Patou). Jean Patou, considered one of the twenties' top five couturiers, was a man of the twenties—tall, dark and handsome, he was a lover of fast cars, fast women...and fabulous fashions! Unlike his rival Chanel, who'd claimed to "dictate" fashions to her clients, Patou believed that "women should dominate their clothes rather than being couture clotheshorses," i.e., that clothing should reflect the wearer's personality. Patou opened his first house, "Maison Parry" in 1912, but closed during WWI, when he was a Captain in the Zouaves. After the war, in 1919, he reopened as "Jean Patou" on the rue St. Florentin, an eighteenth century home originally built by Tallyrand for his mistress. He was extremely successful, creating the simple, classic clothing that became synonymous with the modern woman of the twenties. He promoted a return to the natural waistline as early as 1925, and is credited with establishing the longer hemline that would lead to the look of the thirties. He was famous for his elegant evening gowns, chic day frocks, and especially sports clothes. He and was the first to introduce departments solely for sports, and was especially noted for his Cubist sweaters, inspired by such artists as Braque and Picasso, and for knit bathing suits adapted for sea water. He also introduced the couture monogram. Patou had branches at Monte Carlo, Biarritz, Deauville and Venice. (See pages 224-225)

Peplum. A short ruffle or flounce at the bottom of a bodice used to emphasize the hips and make the waist look smaller.

Permanent (Permanent Wave). Developed in 1904 by Karl Nessler (later changed to Charles Nestle), permanents became very popular during the twenties after a steam process was developed.

Perugia, Andre (1893-1977). Premier shoemaker whose famed creations spanned many decades; Perugia created shoes for such famous couturiers as Poiret, Fath, and Givenchy.

Petersham. A sturdy grosgrain type waistband used inside a gown to support the waist. *Also see* "grosgrain"

Picot Edging. A narrow band with tiny loops on one or both sides; a twenties' favorite used to finish edges.

Plus-four Knickers. A sports craze during the second half of the twenties introduced by the fashionable Prince of Wales; plus-fours were very baggy knickers worn for sports such as golf and cycling; they were cut so full they extended about four inches below the cuffed knees. (There were also "plus-eights.")

Poiret, Paul (1879-1944). "I am merely the first to perceive women's secret desires and fulfill them in advance…" (Paul Poiret, self proclaimed "King of Fashion") Today, if not the "King," Poiret might be considered the "Father" of modern fashion, as the revolutionary fashions he initiated paved the way for the styles of the future. He demolished the Edwardian hourglass silhouette by promoting slimmer yet opulent styles that presaged the chemise dresses of the twenties. His creations were often modeled by his striking, though then unfashionably slender wife, Denise. Orientalism, a favorite theme, was reflected in his coats and gowns as well as his famous turbans. Entering the world of fashion at the age of eighteen, Poiret sold a dozen sketches to Cheruit, then approached Doucet, where he worked from around 1897 to 1900; he later declared that at Doucet, "I learned everything." He briefly worked at Worth before opening his own couture house in September 1904 at 5 Rue Auber. He was so successful that in 1906 he moved to a three story mansion at 37 rue Pasquier; and from 1909-1926 to an eighteenth century mansion at avenue d'Antin & Faubourg St. Honore (where he briefly opened a nightclub, the Oasis, in 1919). From 1926 until 1929, with its popularity waning, Maison Poiret was located at 43 Avenue victor-Emmanuel III (1 rond-Point des Champs-Elysees).
Shortly after the turn of the century, Poiret set out to abolish the cruel corsets demanded by the Edwardian "S" silhouette, a shape that he felt was contrary to the laws of nature: "…on one side the bust, and on the other the whole of the rear end, so that women were divided in two…" In October 1908, Poiret presented his revolutionary "Empire" or "Grecian" gowns in a pochoir booklet, *Les robes de Paul Poiret*, illustrated by Paul Iribe, which was followed in February 1911 by *Les Choses de Paul Poiret*, illustrated by Georges Lepape. In May 1908, *Vogue's* Paris correspondent announced: "The fashionable figure is growing straighter and straighter, less bust, less hips, waist and a wonderful long, slender suppleness about the limbs…the petticoat is obsolete, prehistoric. How slim, how graceful, how elegant women look!" Poiret claimed the modern brassiere or "cache-corset," the famous "hobble skirt" (1910), and promoted pants for women. At his famous Persian "Thousand and Second Night" party held on June 24, 1911, Denise created a sensation when she stepped from a gilded cage in a harem costume of filmy chiffon pantaloons under a wired lampshade tunic and turban with tall aigrette. In his 1911 *Les Choses*, Poiret showed four stunning pantaloon outfits, including a pants dress for gardening and one for tennis, as "Fashions of Tomorrow." And, though his "jupe culotte" pantdresses that followed were considered scandalous, they paved the way to Pants for Women. Poiret collaborated with many artists— Raoul Dufy designed incredible Art Deco "fantasy" prints for him and Andre Perugia designed shoes to complement his fashions. Poiret established two enterprises named for his daughters: his perfume establishment "Rosine," after his eldest daughter; and his design house "Martine," after his youngest. Though one of the top designers of all time, he's considered a casualty of WWI. By 1924, his fame was waning as women increasingly demanded the even "simpler" styles of couturiers like Chanel, Patou, and Vionnet. In 1929, he reluctantly closed the doors of his couture house.

Pongee. A favorite fabric of the twenties, with slightly irregular texture, available in different weights. Silk pongee was used for women's dresses, blouses and lingerie; pongee was also advertised in both silk and cotton for men's shirts. The word "pongee" originates from the Chinese "pen-chi," meaning "hand-loomed."

Premet. Successful French couture house, established by Mme. Premet in 1911 and popular with twenties' new woman or "garconne." Madame Gres, later known as "Alix," trained at Premet. During the twenties, Premet was located at 8 Place Vendome; the house closed ca. 1930.

Pret-a-porter. French term for ready to wear or off the rack clothing.

Prince of Wales (1894-1972). The male fashion icon of the twenties, he popularized such fashions as baggy "plus-four" knickers, golf caps, tweed suits and Glen Urquhart plaids. Prince of Wales in 1910-36, he was to become King Edward VII, but abdicated in November 1936 to marry "The woman I love…," Wallis Warfield Simpson, an American divorcee.

Pringle of Scotland. Established in 1815, Pringle was noted in the twenties and thirties for their cashmere sweaters in Scottish argyle patterns and cardigan twin sets.

Raglan. Type of sleeve named for the British Lord Raglan, who commanded the famous Charge of the Light Brigade during Crimean War in the 1850s. The raglan sleeve is cut in one with the bodice, so there is no armscye seam connecting the shoulders and arms.

Rayon. The first widely used synthetic fabric made of cellulose in several different finishes. Named in 1924 by Kenneth Lord Sr., it was formerly known as "artificial silk." During the second half of the twenties, it became popular for dresses, skirts, and blouses as well as stockings and lingerie. Couturiers such as Lanvin and Poiret touted rayon in period magazine advertisements.

Reboux, Caroline (1837-1927). Easily one of the world's top milliners from the mid-nineteenth century until her death. In the early twenties, Reboux was one of the chief promoters of the famous cloche hat.

Redfern (1853-1929). English couture house famed for fine tailoring and traditional designs. Redfern was originally established in 1841 at Cowes on the Isle of Wight, making yachting clothes. During the Victorian era, The House of Redfern was noted for smart sports clothes; in the 1880s, John Redfern created the famous clingy wool jersey dress designed for Lily ("The Jersey Lily") Langtry. In the 1880s, Redfern opened a Paris branch; others were located in London and New York. In the twenties, Redfern was still a noted, though conservative house located at 242 rue de Rivoli, Paris, with branches in Deauville and Nice. The house closed in the late twenties.

Robe de style. A popular alternative to the twenties tubular silhouette, the robe de style was a romantic, full-skirted favorite for afternoon and evening inspired by the eighteenth century robes favored by Marie Antoinette. Couturiere Jeanne Lanvin was its chief promoter, having first showed the style in the mid-teens; many other couturiers followed with their own versions.

Rochas, Marcel (1902-1955). Well known couturier who opened his establishment in 1924; Rochas was an innovative couturier who remained popular up to the 1950s.

Rouff, Maggy (1896-1971). A popular designer whose parents directed Maison Drecoll; she opened her own establishment in 1928.

Sautoir. A long necklace or rope of pearls, very popular during the twenties for afternoon and evening wear.

Schiaparelli, Elsa (1890-1973). One of the most famous designers of all time, "Schiap" opened "Pour le Sport" in 1927. Her success was assured with the introduction of her trompe l'oeil bow sweater, ca. 1928. Her clothes were witty but wild, elegant and eccentric, often influenced by Cubist and surrealist art. (See additional information in *Roaring '20s Fashions: Deco*)

Shirring. Parallel rows of gathered stitching, employed both to provide ease of motion and accent feminine curves. Similar to "smocking," which has a more honeycomb-effect stitch.

Snow, Carmel (1887-1961). Fashion editor of *Vogue* from 1923 to 1932, when she became editor of *Vogue's* arch rival, *Harper's Bazar*, until her retirement in 1958.

Surplice. Diagonal wrap or cross-over closure very popular in the teens and twenties.

Surrealism. An abstract, fantasy art form that gained popularity during the second half of the twenties, promoted by artists like Salvador Dali, Picasso, and John Miro.

Tailleur. A feminine tailored suit, or "tailor-made."

Tango Dress. Originally described a teens dress either draped for fullness or slit up the side to facilitate easy movement when dancing the then daring "tango." The term was used through the early twenties.

Tea Gown. A frothy, flowing at-home lounging gown popular since the Victorian era, traditionally worn during tea time, before dressing formally for the evening. During the second half of the twenties, tea gowns began to be replaced by the racier "lounging pajamas." (See pages 61-62)

Tea Dress or Frock. A dress worn to an afternoon event, an afternoon "tea" party, or tea dance.

Trompe l'oeil ("fool the eye"). A design created to resemble an object. In 1928, Schiaparelli's trompe l'oeil sweater created a sensation, with a large trompe l'oeil bow knitted into the sweater, rather than having an added on separate bow. (See additional information in *Roaring '20s Fashions: Deco*)

Tulle. A very fine and fragile net, usually silk or cotton. It was first made during the second half of the eighteenth century in Nottingham, England on a stocking machine, and became popular on headdresses, veils and tunics, and gown accents. Made of sturdier nylon since ca. 1950.

Vionnet, Madeleine (1876-1975). "You must dress a body in a fabric, not construct a dress into which the body is expected to fit." (Madeleine Vionnet). Vionnet is hailed as one of the most talented and innovative designers in the history of haute couture. Though not as flamboyant as Poiret or Chanel, she was one of the first to design simpler, more natural clothing for women; she developed the bias cut, and, like Poiret, fought to abolish the corset (at age seventy-nine, she told an interviewer: "…it was I who got rid of corsets; in 1907, while I was at Doucet, I discarded corsets.". Vionnet married in 1894 at age eighteen; she had a daughter who died very young and was divorced in 1898. She worked briefly in London before returning to Paris in 1900 to become design assistant to Mme. Gerber at Callot Soeurs; while at Callot Soeurs, she was par-

ticularly known for her lovely lingerie. Ca. 1907, she left Callot, and worked at Doucet for five years before opening her own couture house at 222 de Rivoli in 1912. Shortly after WWI, Vionnet began experimenting with her revolutionary "bias cut," creating clothes that caressed the body rather than forced it into an artificial silhouette. In 1922-23, she moved to 50 avenue Montaigne, Paris. Vionnet retired in 1939. (See additional information in *Roaring '20s Fashions: Deco*)

Vicose Rayon. Most common type of rayon, patented in 1892 by Beadle, Bevan, and Cross, three English chemists.

Voile. A sheer, soft, translucent fabric, similar to organdy, but without organdy's stiffness. Most often made in cotton fibers, but also in silk, wool, or synthetics.

Volants. Ruffles or flounces often used on twenties' dresses, particularly evening gowns.

Weighted Silk (Shredded Silk). Weighted silk is silk fabric that has had metallic particles added in the finishing process, to lend more body to the fabric; silks were "weighted" with metallic salts, usually tin or iron. This was a process that was used from the mid eighteenth century up to the mid twentieth century; its heyday was ca. 1890-1930. These metallic salts eventually broke down fibers, creating long, shredded tears (think "ripped to shreds"). Though it was most often used in linings, it was also used for the outer part of garments. Needless to say, it's impossible to repair, and if it touches other non-weighted parts of the garment, it may damage them as well.

Worth. Couture house founded in 1858 by the "Father of Haute Couture," Charles Frederick Worth. His sons took over the House of Worth on his death in 1895—Jean-Philippe becoming the premier designer, and Gaston the business manager. In the early twenties, Jean-Philippe retired and Gaston's son Jean-Charles became the new couturier. During the twenties, Worth was considered one of the more traditional, conservative houses. It was located at 7 rue de la Paix in Paris, with branches in London, Biarritz, and Cannes. Worth merged with Paquin in 1954.

Zipper (Zip). A fastener for clothing and accessories. In 1851, Elias Howe patented his "Automatic Continuous Clothing Closure," which was followed in 1893 by Whitcomb L. Judson's "Clasp Locker" that used an intricate hook and eye system. In 1913, Gordon Sundback, an employee of Judson's Universal Fastener Co., developed a version using interlocking metal teeth; known as a "hookless fastener," it was used by the military during WWI. In the early 1920s, B.F. Goodrich ordered Sundback's hookless fasteners for their rubber galoshes or "Mystic Boots," and noting the sound made when the fastener was opened and closed, Goodrich christened it the "zipper." By the second half of the twenties, zippers were used mainly on items like boots, luggage, and purses. In 1935, Schiaparelli shocked the world of haute couture with her "fashion zippers," and in 1934, Lord Mountbaten coaxed the Prince of Wales to try trousers with zipper flies. However, it wasn't until the late 1930s that zippers came into common use as fastenings for clothing.

Bibliography

Books

1920s Fashions from B. Altman & Company. Mineola, NY: Dover Publications, 1999.

A Singular Elegance: The Photographs of Baron Adolph DeMeyer. Exhibit sponsored by *Harper's Bazaar.* San Francisco: Chronicle Books, 1994.

American Heritage. *American Heritage History of the 20s & 30s.* New York: American Heritage Publishing Co., Inc., 1970.

Armstrong, Nancy. *The Book of Fans.* New York: Mayflower Books.

Baker, Jean-Claude, and Chris Chase. *Josephine, The Hungry Heart.* New York: Cooper Square Press ed., 2001.

Baron, Stanley, with Jacques Damase. *Sonia Delaunay, The Life of an Artist.* London: Thames and Hudson Ltd., 1995.

Bata Shoe Museum. *All About Shoes: Footwear Through the Ages.* Toronto: Bata Limited, 1994.

Batterberry, Michael and Ariane. *Fashion, The Mirror of History.* New York: Greenwich House, 1997.

Battersby, Martin. *Art Deco Fashion, French Designers 1908-1925.* London: Academy Editions, 1974.

Battersby, Martin. *The Decorative Twenties.* New York: Collier Books, 1975.

Blum, Daniel. *Pictorial History of the Silent Screen.* New York: Grosset & Dunlap, 1953.

Blum, Dilys E. *Ahead of Fashion: Hats of the 20th Century.* Philadelphia Museum of Art Bulletin, 1993.

Blum, Stella, ed. *Eighteenth Century French Fashion Plates.* New York, Dover Publications, 1982.

Bowman, Sara. *A Fashion for Extravagance, Art Deco Fabrics and Fashions.* New York: E.P. Dutton, 1985.

Bradfield, Nancy. *Costume in Detail: 1730-1930.* New York: Costume & Fashion Press, 1997.

Brough, James. *The Prince & The Lily.* New York: Coward, McCann & Geoghegan Inc., 1975.

Davenport, Millia. *Book of Costume, Volume II.* New York: Crown Publishers, 1948.

de Buzzaccarini, Vittoria. *Elegance and Style, Two Hundred Years Of Men's Fashions.* Milan: Lupetti & Co., 1992.

de Osma, Guillermo. *Fortuny, The Life and Work of Mariano Fortuny.* New York: Rizzoli, 1985.

DePauw, Linda Grant, and Conover Hunt. *Remember the Ladies, Women in America 1750-1815.* New York: Viking Press, 1976.

Deslandres, Yvonne. *Poiret, Paul Poiret 1879-1944.* New York: Rizzoli, 1987.

Druesedow, Jean L. *In Style, Celebrating Fifty Years of the Costume Institute.* New York: Metropolitan Museum of Art, 1987.

Etherington-Smith, Meredith. *Patou.* New York: St. Martin's/ Marek, 1983.

Fitzgerald, F. Scott. *Novels and Stories 1920-1922* (Library of America): *This Side of Paradise* (1920); *Flappers and Philosophers* (1920); short stories including "Dalyrimple Goes Wrong," "Bernice Bobs Her Hair," and "The Ice Palace"; *The Beautiful and the Damned* (1922); Tales of the Jazz Age short stories including "May Day" and "A Diamond as Big as the Ritz."

Fitzgerald, F. Scott. *The Great Gatsby.* New York: Charles Scribner's Sons, 1925.

Gernsheim, Alison. *Fashion and Reality, 1840-1914.* London: Faber and Faber, 1963.

Ginsburg, Madeleine. *Paris Fashions: The Art Deco Style of the 1920s.* London: Bracken Books, 1989.

Glennon, Lorraine, Editor in Chief. *The 20th Century.* North Deighton, MA.: JG Press, 2000.

Goldthorpe, Caroline. *From Queen to Empress.* New York: Metropolitan Museum of Art, 1988.

Griffith, Richard, and Arthur Mayer. *The Movies.* New York: Simon and Schuster, 1957.

Howell, Georgina. *In Vogue.* New York: Schocken Books, 1976.

Kamitsis, Lydia. *Vionnet.* Paris: Editions Assouline, 1996.

Kyoto Museum. *Fashion (A History from the 18th to the 20th Century).* Taschen Press.

Kyoto Museum. *Revolution in Fashion 1715-1815.* New York: Abbeville Press, 1989.

Laver, James. *Costume & Fashion, A Concise History.* New York: Oxford University Press, 1982.

le Bourhis, Katell, ed. *The Age of Napoleon.* New York: Metropolitan Museum of Art, 1989.

Lencek, Lena, and Gedeon Bosker. *Making Waves, Swimsuits and the Undressing of America.* San Francisco: Chronicle Books, 1989.

Lynam, Ruth, Ed. *Couture, An Illustrated History of the Great Paris Designers and Their Creations.* New York: Doubleday & Company, Inc., 1972.

Martin, Richard, and Harold Koda. *Bare Witness.* New York: Metropolitan Museum of Art, 1996.

Martin, Richard, and Harold Koda. *Bloom.* New York: Metropolitan Museum of Art, 1995.

Martin, Richard, and Harold Koda. *Haute Couture.* New York: Metropolitan Museum of Art, 1995.

Martin, Richard, and Harold Koda. *Orientalism.* New York: Metropolitan Museum of Art, 1994.

Martin, Richard, and Harold Koda. *Splash! A History of Swimwear.* New York: Rizzoli, 1990.

Martin, Richard. *Cubism and Fashion*. New York: Metropolitan Museum of Art, 1998.

Martin, Richard. *Fashion and Surrealism*. New York: Rizzoli, 1987.

Milbank, Caroline Rennolds. *Couture, The Great Designers*. New York: Stewart, Tabori & Chang, Inc., 1985.

Moore, Doris Langley. *Fashion Through Fashion Plates 1771-1970*. New York: Clarkson N. Potter, Inc., 1971.

Morgan, Sarah. *Art Deco, The European Style*. New York: Gallery Books, 1990.

Mulvagh, Jane. *Vogue History of 20th Century Fashion*. London: Viking, 1988.

O'Keeffe, Linda. *Shoes, A Celebration of Pumps, Sandals, Slippers & More*. New York: Workman Publishing, 1996.

Olian, JoAnne, ed. *Authentic French Fashions of the Twenties*. New York: Dover Publications, 1990.

Parrot, Nicole. *Mannequins*. New York: St. Martin's Press, 1982.

Payne, Blanche. *History of Costume*. New York: Harper & Row, 1965.

Piña, Leslie, and Donald-Brian Johnson. *Whiting & Davis Purses*. Atglen, PA: Schiffer Publishing, Ltd., 2002.

Pratt, Lucy, and Linda Woolley. *Shoes*. London: Victoria and Albert Museum Fashion Accessories, 1999.

Robinson, Julian. *The Fine Art of Fashion, an Illustrated History*. New York/London: Bartley & Jensen.

Robinson, Julian. *The Golden Age of Style, Art Deco Fashion Illustration*. New York: Gallery Books, 1976.

Robinson, Julian. *The Brilliance of Art Deco*. New York/London: Bartley & Jensen.

Rothstein, Natalie, Ed. *Four Hundred Years of Fashion*. London: Victoria and Albert Museum, 1984.

Schoeffler, O.E. *Esquire's Encyclopedia of 20th Century Men's Fashions*. New York: McGraw-Hill, 1973.

Time-Life Books. *This Fabulous Century, 1920-1930*. Time-Life, Inc., 1969.

Tozer, Jane, and Sarah Levitt. *Fabric of Society, A Century of People and Their Clothes 1770-1970*. Carno, Powys, Wales: Laura Ashley, Ltd., 1983.

White, Palmer. *Poiret*. New York: Clarkson N. Potter, Inc., 1973.

Wilcox, R. Turner. *The Dictionary of Costume*. New York: Charles Scribner's Sons, 1958.

Wilcox, R. Turner. *The Mode in Costume*. New York: Charles Scribner's Sons, 1958.

Wood, Barry James. *Show Windows, 75 Years of the Art of Display*. New York: Congdon & Weed, 1982.

Periodicals (These refer to complete magazines, not fashion plates):

Art Gout Beaute: June 1922; October 1927; May 1928.

Butterick Quarterly: Spring 1920; Spring 1922; Summer 1924; Autumn 1925; Spring 1926.

Delineator, The: May 1921; March 1922.

Fashion Quarterly, Ladies' Home Journal: Winter 1922.

Fashionable Dress: October 1922; June 1926.

Flapper, The (magazine): May to December 1922.

Harper's Bazar: April 1923; May 1923; September 1923; August 1924; January 1925; October 1926; October 1927.

Illustrated Milliner: September 1923.

L'Illustration, Exposition des Arts Decoratifs: Aout (April) 1925.

Ladies' Home Journal: July 1920; October 1920; November 1920.

Milliner, The: May 1925; August 1925.

Mode Pratique: March 1924.

Pictorial Review Fashion Book: Spring 1921; Winter 1922-23; Summer 1925.

Vogue Fashion Bi-Monthly: June/July 1927.

Vogue Pattern Book: August/September 1927; October/November 1927; December 1927/January 1928; August/September 1929.

Vogue: July 15, 1921; February 1, 1922; June 1, 1922; April 15, 1923; February 15, 1925; September 1, 1925; April 1, 1926; June 15, 1926; September 15, 1926; October 1, 1926; January 15, 1927; July 1, 1927; September 1, 1927; October 1, 1927; April 1, 1928; March 2, 1929; June 1, 1928; October 13, 1928; January 5, 1929.

Catalogs:

Bellas Hess: Fall/Winter 1920-21; Fall/Winter 1921-22; Spring/Summer 1925; Fall/Winter 1925-26; Spring/Summer 1926.

Chicago Mail Order: Spring/Summer 1922; Spring/Summer 1923; Fall/Winter 1927/28; Fall/Winter 1928-29; Fall/Winter 1929-30.

National Bellas Hess: Spring/Summer 1928; Fall/winter 1929-30.

National Style Book: Spring/Summer 1920; Spring/Summer 1922; Spring/Summer 1923; Spring/Summer 1925; Fall/Winter 1924-25; Spring/Summer 1927; Fall/Winter 1926-27.

Pierre Imans: Catalogue of Mannequins, 1927.

Index